# Sons of Saviors

JEWISH CULTURE AND CONTEXTS

Published in association with the Herbert D. Katz Center
for Advanced Judaic Studies of the University
of Pennsylvania

Series Editors: Shaul Magid, Francesca Trivellato,
Steven Weitzman

A complete list of books in the series is available from
the publisher.

# SONS OF SAVIORS

The Red Jews in Yiddish Culture

Rebekka Voß

**PENN**

UNIVERSITY OF PENNSYLVANIA PRESS

PHILADELPHIA

Copyright © 2023 University of Pennsylvania Press

All rights reserved. Except for brief quotations used for purposes of review or scholarly citation, none of this book may be reproduced in any form by any means without written permission from the publisher.

Published by
University of Pennsylvania Press
Philadelphia, Pennsylvania 19104-4112
www.upenn.edu/pennpress

Printed in the United States of America on acid-free paper
10 9 8 7 6 5 4 3 2 1
Hardcover ISBN: 978-1-5128-2432-2
eBook ISBN: 978-1-5128-2433-9

A Cataloging-in-Publication record is available from the Library of Congress

*For Robert*

# Contents

| | |
|---|---|
| List of Illustrations | ix |
| Note on Translations and Transliteration | xii |
| List of Abbreviations | xiii |
| Introduction. Visual Thinking in Yiddish | 1 |
| Chapter 1. Red Jews: A Medieval Christian Label | 21 |
| Chapter 2. Reclaiming Red: The Red Jews in Early Modern Yiddish | 52 |
| Chapter 3. The Little Red Jew: A Vernacular Icon of Ashkenazic Identity | 84 |
| Chapter 4. From West to East and Beyond Yiddish: The Transmission History of *Ma'aseh Akdamut* | 121 |
| Chapter 5. Into Modernity: The Wandering Jew in Bright Red | 138 |
| Epilogue. An Old Yiddish Legend in a Brooklyn Fridge | 167 |
| Appendix. *Ma'aseh Akdamut* | 173 |
| Notes | 183 |
| Bibliography | 227 |

| | | |
|---|---|---|
| Index | | 273 |
| Acknowledgments | | 279 |
| *Color plates follow page* | | 162 |

# Illustrations

Figure 1. Redheaded Jews, Russian matryoshka dolls, 2016

Figure 2. The Red Jews beyond the Sambatyon River, panel in the Antichrist window at St. Mary's Church, Frankfurt an der Oder, ca. 1370

Figure 3. Alexander imprisons Gog and Magog behind the Caspian Mountains, colored woodcut in Pseudo-Methodius, *Revelations* (Basel, 1498)

Figure 4. The Red Jews beyond the mountains of darkness, in a medieval book of heraldry, Strasbourg, ca. 1401–1425

Figure 5. Alexander encloses the Red Jews, in a historiated Bible, fifteenth century

Figure 6. "Today's Costume of the Jews of Worms," in Marcus zum Lamm, *Thesaurus picturarum*, late sixteenth century

Figure 7. *The Jews' Entrance with Their Messiah*, undated colored reproduction from Dietrich Schwab, *The Jewish Disguise* (Mainz, 1619)

Figure 8. *The Last Supper*, detail of an altarpiece by Bertram of Minden, 1391–1400

Figure 9. Gog and Magog break free from the Caspian Mountains, colored woodcut in Pseudo-Methodius, *Revelations* (Basel, 1498)

Figure 10. The rulers of the world submitting to the Antichrist, including the Red Jews and the Amazon queen, in *Antichrist and the Fifteen Signs of the Final Judgment*, Franconia/Nuremberg[?], ca. 1450 (no later than 1467)

Figure 11. The Antichrist with the Red Jews beside the Sambatyon, panel in the Antichrist window of St. Mary's Church, Frankfurt an der Oder, ca. 1370

Figure 12. The Antichrist resurrects the dead, panel in the Antichrist window of St. Mary's Church, Frankfurt an der Oder, ca. 1370

Figure 13. A Red Jew accepts the Antichrist, panel in the Antichrist window of St. Mary's Church, Frankfurt an der Oder, ca. 1370

Figure 14. The Holy Roman Emperor accepting the Antichrist, panel in the Antichrist window of St. Mary's Church, Frankfurt an der Oder, ca. 1370

Figure 15. The Red Jews being identified with the Turkish threat, in Justus Jonas, *The Seventh Chapter of Daniel* (Wittenberg, 1529)

Figure 16. The Red Jews emerging from beyond the mountains, frontispiece of a German pamphlet, *Concerning a Great Multitude and Host of Jews* (Augsburg, 1523)

Figure 17. The land of the Red Jews, enclosed in the Caspian Mountains and proximate to nations of cannibals, on Andreas Walsperger, *Mappa mundi* (Konstanz, 1448)

Figure 18. *The Last Supper*, detail of Hans Holbein the Elder, predella of the Frankfurt Dominican altarpiece, 1501

Figure 19. The Antichrist causes fire to rain down, panel in the Antichrist window of St. Mary's Church, Frankfurt an der Oder, ca. 1370

Figure 20. The Red Jews in league with the Amazons, in an illuminated German manuscript on the Antichrist, Bavaria, fifteenth century

Figure 21. The Red Jews in the Red Sea, Gog and Magog behind the Caspian Mountains, on Hans Rüst, *Mappa mundi* (Augsburg, ca. 1480)

Figure 22. A Jew from beyond the Sambatyon bends a tree to the ground during the magical prelude to the disputation, in a Hebrew-Yiddish booklet for children, *Beyond the Sambatyon* (Jerusalem, n.d.)

Figure 23. Marc Chagall, *The Jew in Bright Red*, 1915

Figure 24. Marc Chagall, *The Jew in Red*, 1914

Figure 25. Marc Chagall, *The Jew in Green*, 1914

Figure 26. Jewish garb in Worms, second half of the sixteenth century, in Friedrich Hottenroth, *German National Costumes* (first edition, 1898–1902)

Figure 27. Isidor Kaufmann, *Man with Fur Hat*, ca. 1910

Figure 28. Reuven Rubin (1893–1974), *Red-Bearded Jew*, 1923, oil on canvas

Figure 29. Edward Okuń, *Red Judas*, 1901

Figure 30. S. C. Dumont, *The Wandering Jew*, 1852, colored wood-engraving based on Gustave Doré

Figure 31. Reuven Rubin (1893–1974), *The Poet Uri Zvi Greenberg*, 1925, oil on canvas

Figure 32. Michael Levin, *Shrine to the Red Jews*, 2012

# Note on Translations and Transliteration

All translations are my own unless otherwise noted. Biblical quotations from the Hebrew Bible follow the *JPS Hebrew-English Tanakh* and from the New Testament follow the King James Version. Those from the Babylonian Talmud are according to the Hebrew-English edition of the Soncino Talmud by Isidore Epstein. The transcription of Yiddish and Hebrew follows the YIVO standard and the principles in the *Encyclopaedia Judaica* (2nd ed., 2007), respectively. Terms and names in Hebrew are rendered in the current English form.

# Abbreviations

ATU      Aarne-Thompson-Uther Index
BT       Babylonian Talmud
IFA      Israel Folktale Archives
IMHM     Institute of Microfilmed Hebrew Manuscripts
JT       Jerusalem Talmud
JTS      Jewish Theological Seminary of America
NLI      National Library of Israel
VD 16    Verzeichnis der im deutschen Sprachbereich erschienenen Drucke des 16. Jahrhunderts (Bibliography of books printed in the German speaking countries of the sixteenth century; http://www.vd16.de)

# Introduction

## Visual Thinking in Yiddish

> The blind man cannot imagine color,
> as the deaf person cannot experience sounds.
> —Maimonides, *Commentary on the Mishnah:*
> *Sanhedrin*, chap. 10

The Red Jews are a mythical people who populated a shared Jewish-Christian imagination. They are envisioned as a tribe of ruddy-faced, redheaded, red-bearded Jewish warriors, bedecked in red attire who reside in isolation at the fringes of the known world. They are generally identified with the Ten Lost Tribes of Israel who, according to a well-known Jewish legend, have been living in an uncharted place since being exiled in the eighth century BCE, when the Assyrians destroyed their ancient kingdom. The red variant of these lost tribes is a singular invention of late medieval vernacular culture in Germany and is unattested anywhere else in Europe. This idiosyncratic figure, together with the peculiar term "Red Jews," existed solely in German and Yiddish, the German-Jewish vernacular. These two language communities assessed the Red Jews differently and contested their significance, which is to say, they viewed them in different shades of red.

Christians saw the Red Jews' physical coloration as a telltale sign of their bloodthirst. German vernacular texts of the Red Jews spurred fear of this barbaric horde, not only for their future service as the Antichrist's shock troops but for their potential to inflict harm in the present. Jews could appreciate this scenario: as the Messiah's army at the end of times, the Red Jews would bring a vengeful close to centuries of Christian oppression. In the interim, emissaries of the Red Jews would occasionally emerge from seclusion to ease the burden of exile when their fellows in the Diaspora were in desperate straits. The imagology of the Red Jews highlights the interconnectedness of Jewish and Christian notions of identity and the Other in bright hues. The "Yiddish eye"[1] reappropriated the Red Jews for its own purposes: it subverted the Christian color symbolism by adjusting the focus on redness from a negative stereotype into a proud badge of self-assertion. Whereas the Christian lens followed the Red Jews with an oppressive gaze, the early modern Yiddish eye reappropriated this personage in an effort to negotiate a sense of place vis-à-vis its neighboring Christian society. Once adapted by Yiddish culture, portrayals of the Red Jews became ever more versatile. Time and again, the Red Jews were recast as messianic heroes, resourceful underdogs, strong women and handsome men, and—in modern times—wandering Jews.

The journey of the Red Jews from their medieval Christian nascence, through early modern Old Yiddish literature, to modern Yiddish culture in Eastern Europe, Palestine, and America is the story of this book. On this voyage through the Christian and Jewish imagination, I present an argument on the visuality of the Red Jews. This study does not narrowly examine pictorial illustrations, though the extant renderings from mostly German contexts are featured here; rather, I primarily analyze textual representations of the Red Jews, since this visual motif was depicted verbally in Yiddish. Indeed, language can be used to create textual images that operate much like iconography. Therefore, my use of the word "image" signifies graphic, verbal, and mental phenomena.[2] I contend that the distinctive coloring of this fictive people is not merely a descriptive flourish. Building on research on the significance of sight in premodern cultures, I offer a new visual approach to early modern Yiddish literature by showing how the Red Jews enlist human fascination with visual stimuli and accommodate the sensual attraction of color. As we shall see, they render ideas visible; vision functions in these tales as a medium for reinventing identity.

This book explores the visual dimensions of the Jewish-Christian encounter by analyzing the myth of the Red Jews. Color is a key element in crafting this potent figure and its intended message, bridging not only religious and linguistic communities but also social cohorts. As a purely vernacular Germanic phenomenon, the Red Jews were exclusive to German and Yiddish, and absent from the formal *linguae francae* of religion and learning, Latin and Hebrew, respectively.[3] How the Red Jews were seen therefore reflects the cultural perceptions and beliefs of a Yiddish audience of "ordinary"

Jewish men and women who often remain invisible in history. Moreover, meaning as conveyed through color is accessible across educational strata since its message is independent of literacy. The next five chapters trace how the image of the Red Jews, which was fiercely disputed between Jews and Christians, became continuously transformed from the Middle Ages through modernity to shape religious, social, and political identities in changing environments.

## The Red Jew

The perception of each color is intrinsically bound to its symbolic meaning. Color symbolism in Western imagination is primarily rooted in biblical exegesis, but various other references contribute to the interpretation of colors, including the classical elements, nature, and human experience.[4] The color red, for instance, has denoted fire and blood since the earliest recorded times, and most allegorical connotations are based on these references; it signifies love, martyrdom, and war (among other experiences), at one and the same time.[5] The fluidity of meaning ascribed to a given color depends on context and is informed by numerous factors, such as time, place, purpose, creator and audience, and its relationship to other colors.[6] Indeed, among the five most prevalent colors and color spectra—red, green, blue, yellow-gold, and black-white—red was by far the most versatile in medieval and early modern European languages. In Latin, for example, in addition to the primary terms for "red" (*ruber/rubeus*) over thirty lexemes denote this color. In the Middle High and Early New High German corpora, red and its variants (such as crimson, scarlet, roseate) account for 350 records, one-quarter of all color-related vocabulary. Much like other languages, the symbolic use of *rôt* (red) in Middle High German includes both positive and negative connotations, with joy, beauty, and love on one end of the spectrum and sickness, grief, anger, shame, and sin on the other. At its most extreme, amid the ambiguous logic of moral significance attributed to this color, red implied falsehood, deceit, danger, violence, and bloodshed.[7]

The symbolic value of colors addressed all aspects of life. Thus, for example, the colors (and fabrics) of an individual's wardrobe were influential signifiers of economic and social status, gender, and age. To illustrate this multivalent color symbolism, the red cap worn by a Christian man in fifteenth-century Naples could signify wisdom and his wife's red gloves could indicate her charitable involvement, while the same red color identified Jewish men through the head covering they were required to don in seventeenth-century Venice.[8] In the later Middle Ages, directives (especially sumptuary laws) were devised to regulate clothing and, thereby, to visibly preserve social hierarchy. Certain hues distinguished nobility from the bourgeoisie, lepers and prostitutes from the rest of society, Jews and Muslims from Christians. With the prescription by the Fourth Lateran Council (1215) for Jews to wear clothing that would differentiate them from the Christian majority, yellow and red became prominent colors for Jewish badges and garments across Europe.[9] Since these two colors had strong negative connotations, they were among the hues that most commonly underscored anti-Jewish stereotypes and, thus, were used to stigmatize the "enemies of Christ," eventually entering works of art as visual motifs.[10]

Color symbolism also informed perceptions of the human body. Physiognomy along with hair and skin color have long been taken as windows on temperament and personality. Given that moral dimensions were attributed to these visually discernable indices, they were laden with social implications: external features were trusted as reflections of character traits and behaviors, and facial coloring was considered an indicator of emotions. In medieval and early modern medicine, the coloring of the body signified physical and character traits that, following humoral theory as described in the late antique medical teachings of Galen, were determined by an individual's distinct mixture of the four cardinal body fluids, known as humors: black bile, yellow bile, phlegm, and blood. Each humor was thought to correspond to one of four traditional temperaments: melancholic, choleric, phlegmatic, and sanguine. These *complexiones* (i.e., body constitutions) were measured by two pairs of opposing qualities (hot and cold; dry and moist) and three body tones (white, black, and red).[11] In this system, extreme skin tones were considered indicative of disparaging attributes: pale northern Europeans were denigrated as barbaric, while dark skin was tantamount to ugliness and considered terrifying. By comparison, an ideal *complexio* was defined as a blend. Thus, rosy facial coloring signified physical beauty across medieval and early modern European cultures and attested to a well-balanced character.[12] In short, the simplistic correlation between external form and moral character translated beauty as goodness and ugliness as evil.

The preferred complementarity of white and red can be traced to biblical exegesis. Song of Songs 5:10, for example, describes the beloved as "clear-skinned and ruddy." The great medieval Jewish commentator Rashi

(1040–1105) interprets this verse as praise for the beauty of a young man whose skin is white as milk with a ruddy complexion.[13] King David embodied this perfect ruddy appearance.[14] The divergent perception of the redness of another biblical character, Esau, who is equally described as ruddy exemplifies the polyvalence of color symbolism: often read in relation to red hair, Jewish and Christian traditions agree on Esau's negative character.[15] As we shall see, the dissonance between these biblical figures epitomizes the contrasting interpretations of the Red Jews by Jews and Christians.

Attitudes toward the mythical tribe of Red Jews in the Christian and Jewish *imaginaire* primarily relied on the value assigned to persons with red coloring by each community. Red hair (often paired with ruddy, freckled skin) was almost uniformly assigned negative meaning. The suspicion toward red hair can already be traced to the Greco-Roman world as well as rabbinic Judaism.[16] In popular physiognomy throughout medieval and early modern Europe, red hair was considered an outward sign of a demonic and duplicitous character and, therefore, redheads were deemed menacing. Congruent with the strong negative associations that red hair could provoke, red hair and beards had currency as a stereotypical trait of the Jewish Other from England to Spain and France to Russia.[17] Although the redheaded Jew assumed significance as a social construction across Europe in the Middle Ages, it was especially pronounced in premodern Germany; fourteenth- to sixteenth-century German art provides the most abundant evidence of the traditional Christian assertion that Judas Iscariot, the notorious disciple who betrayed Jesus, had red hair.[18] This cultural setting fostered the shared Jewish-Christian myth of a tribe of Red Jews in the late Middle Ages.

While ascriptions of red hair and ruddy skin to Jews, a cliché that endures into modern European belles lettres, and even through the present (fig. 1),[19] have a centuries-long history and were no less present or significant than better-known stereotypes about Jews, this symbol of difference has rarely been addressed in studies of the embodied history of Jews. This is at variance with the disparaging representations of the Jewish body that are more familiar today, such as the hooked nose or distinctive Jewish odor, and, by contrast, the beautiful Jewess. A noteworthy exception is Ruth Mellinkoff's work on portrayals of Judas with red hair in medieval Christian art.[20] The present book, for the first time, brings Jewish perspectives on the Jewish redhead and the ruddy Jewish face to scholarly discourse: not as a study of the body but as a history of cultural reappropriation qua an investigation of the power of sight and color symbolism in Yiddish literature. Jewish and Christian assumptions of what the eye should see upon encountering a Red Jew exemplify the ambiguity of color and its potential for promoting divergent views of the same image.

The sole in-depth study of the Red Jews is a monograph by Andrew Gow, whose detailed analysis is devoted to the German myth. The Yiddish variant, on the other hand, is only briefly mentioned, citing a late, eighteenth-century source.[21] Gow is not aware of the much earlier literary origins of the Yiddish Red Jews nor their unparalleled significance in premodern Jewish culture. Curiously, studies dedicated to Old Yiddish literature similarly overlook Yiddish tales of the Red Jews, with the noteworthy exceptions of Chone Shmeruk's brief reference to the tale's major iteration, *Ma'aseh Akdamut* (The Story of Akdamut; translated into English in the appendix), and Sara Zfatman's edition of a different Red Jews story.[22] Shmeruk, however, does not mention the term "Red Jews." Like most other scholars who have encountered the Red Jews in Yiddish literature, he simply equates them with the Ten Tribes.[23] Moreover, the "little Red Jews" (*royte yidelekh*) in modern Yiddish are commonly mistaken for a relatively recent, humorous Eastern European Jewish tradition.[24] Few studies have attempted to untangle the etymology of this peculiar idiom. At most, there has been conjecture that their redness was derived from ethnic groups that have been identified with the Lost Tribes: an Arab tribe known as the *Ḥimir* (from the word root for "red" in Arabic); groups in China or Native Americans who have been described as "red-skinned"; the Mongols who invaded Europe in the thirteenth century wearing red garments and headdresses; or the Chazars, with their purportedly "slight Mongolian pigmentation."[25] In contrast with such ethnographic explanations, Zfatman has tentatively—albeit accurately—postulated the Yiddish Red Jews' connection with the German term *Rote Juden* (Red Jews).[26]

## Reappropriating Redness

As intercultural encounters often involve modifying concepts that are translated between societies, the perception of Jewish physiognomy as red is particularly telling; indeed, we witness multidirectional semantic transfers between German and Yiddish. Picking up earlier Jewish themes, this stigma was essentially instigated by non-Jews then productively reappropriated in Yiddish folklore. Since many of the Yiddish sources are difficult to date with precision, given their presumed origins in oral transmission, reconstruction of the term's evolution is complicated. There is no conclusive way of telling where it appeared first, in German or Yiddish, and which language subsequently absorbed the Red Jews trope from the other. However, we can say with certainty that after its initial appearance, presumably during the thirteenth century, the term "Red Jews" soon became a common expression in German- and Yiddish-speaking communities. In both Christian and Jewish culture, the Red Jews were introduced in historicized literature. In Middle High German, they are first mentioned in several heroic romances dated to the 1270s to 1290s. Over time, the figure of the Red Jew entered a broad span of German genres: works of history, exegesis and other theological treatises, travelogues, *mappae mundi*, ethnographic writings, polemics, and broadsides, as well as pictorial renderings that appear in illuminated manuscripts, early printed block-books, and monumental religious art. The evolution of the myth in Yiddish began in a liturgical context, possibly around the same time. The oldest and most popular version of this Yiddish legend explains why Rabbi Meir Shatz of Worms allegedly composed *Akdamut Milin*, his most famous religious poem, and the Red Jews' role in the emergence of that work. Known among scholars as *Ma'aseh Akdamut*, this tale was guaranteed exceptionally broad reception when, around the sixteenth century, some Ashkenazic communities began to recite it from a special scroll (*Megiles Reb Meyer*) on the festival of Shavuot. In contrast to the generic diversification in German, the Yiddish term *rote yudn* (Red Jews) and its corollary image of mythical Jewish red men and women were chiefly transmitted, created, and re-created through *Ma'aseh Akdamut* and other captivating stories that circulated widely among the literate and unlettered alike, in oral and written forms.

Scholars have shown that minority cultures often reappropriate or reclaim derogatory terms and tropes used against them as a subversive tactic.[27] Similar mechanisms for the adaptation and reversal of symbols of marginalization into marks of dignity are at play with regard to the Red Jews. For the purposes of this book, the notion of cultural reappropriation is applied to studying how Yiddish-speaking Jews adapted "red," a descriptor that was known among Christians as a pejorative epithet, in reference to their heroic kinsmen of the Ten Tribes. The (re)appropriation paradigm helps trace the many uses and meanings of the vernacular motif of Red Jews in various historical and cultural contexts, including transformations that stemmed from the move from German into Yiddish, as well as the term's evolution in German culture. Peter Burke's description of cultural translation emphasizes the decisive role of "the actor" (or "the reader") in the "double process of decontextualization and recontextualization, first reaching out to appropriate something alien and then domesticating it."[28] This process is available to members of both dominant and minority cultures who, as in the case of the Red Jews, adopt a concept from the other and integrate it into their own system of ideas.

When exercised by the majority, cultural appropriation typically seeks to silence a vulnerable minority. Thus, in cultural studies, this phenomenon was initially conflated with deleterious ramifications, as articulated in Edward Said's classic description of a binary relationship between unequals in *Orientalism*, where a dominant majority wields power over the subaltern Other. Said considers Western depictions of Eastern societies as an intellectual conquest, where European academics appropriated cultural representations from these societies during the late nineteenth and early twentieth centuries. Similarly, late medieval Christian interpretations of the Ten Lost Tribes as Red Jews contrasted strongly with the original Jewish legends of those tribes, a positive image that the German myth of the Red Jews appropriated and sought to counter. Subsequent theorists, however, have pointed out how reappropriation can also strengthen the subaltern voice. In her famous essay, the leading postcolonial theorist Gayatri Spivak critiques the construction of the non-European Other as mute; rather, cultural (re)appropriation should be seen as a complex model of potential two-way adaptation.[29] The form of reappropriation observed with regard to the Red Jews in Yiddish is typical of agents who hold lesser degrees of conventional social and political power within hegemonic structures. These groups often use reappropriation to counter that imbalance by cultivating spaces of resistance to the dominant majority: they articulate a self-affirming identity through a means that had been devised with oppressive intent. Once adapted in Yiddish, the fictional Red Jews were granted power in the hands of the actual Jews who embraced them, for this legendary people offered a subversive mode of spiritual rebellion, as this volume demonstrates.

The model of cultural reappropriation has been introduced to various fields of Jewish studies: Ivan Marcus has termed it "inward acculturation," by which premodern Jews "expressed elements of their Jewish religious cultural identity by internalizing and transforming various genres, motifs, terms, institutions, or rituals of the majority culture in a polemical, parodic or neutralized manner."[30] Another pioneering study on Jewish reactions to and reclamation of Christian portrayals of Jews and Judaism (and its inverse, on

Christian responses to Judaism and Jewish depictions of Christians and Christianity) that bears mention is Israel Yuval's *Two Nations in Your Womb*. Similarly, Marc Michael Epstein addresses the intentional reappropriation of negative iconography from the dominant culture in his study of Jewish subversion of medieval Christian imagery.[31] Much like my approach and other more recent studies on cultural entanglement, these scholars affirm that Jews and Christians drew from a set of shared symbols, but each group ascribed different meanings to them.[32]

Whereas material (re)appropriation of the term "Red Jews" occurred without linguistic modification between German and Yiddish, its defining attributes were transformed when redness was imbued with new meaning in the different cultural setting. In conjunction with their distinctive coloring, the Red Jews assumed unique significance in Yiddish that reflects readers' distinct strategies to make sense of their world. My analysis shows that this trope is not simply a vernacular synonym for the Ten Tribes. Diasporic Jews often discussed existential questions through the prism of the Ten Tribes and projected both their travails and aspirations on this legendary populace whom they envisioned dwelling in isolation beyond the impassable Sambatyon River. The modes of presenting this Yiddish variation of redheaded, red-bearded, red-faced, and red-dressed Jews serve as a magnifying glass for the sensitivities and cultural perceptions of its authors, editors, and readers, which distinguish the Red Jews from the generic myth of the Ten Tribes. For historians, the Red Jews open a portal onto vernacular cultural spaces.[33]

I use "vernacular" in this book as a means of historical analysis to emphasize the manifold interactions between various cultural currents. First of all, cultural interpretations that were expressed in either the vernacular or in *loshn koydesh* ("the holy tongue" of the traditional Jewish canon, namely Hebrew-Aramaic) form a continuous spectrum of Jewish culture that was tailored to particular segments of the populace and their specific needs, changing linguistic codes accordingly. As Chava Turniansky has remarked, "popularization is the name of the game."[34] Based on similar observations regarding early modern French print culture and the blurred distinctions between its audiences, Roger Chartier has argued that, rather than defining an object, or a set of texts, ideas, or attitudes, as "popular" from their inception, we should consider how cultural goods that were often shared by multiple societal strata have been adopted, understood, and redefined by individuals and groups for their own purposes.[35] In addition, Chartier highlights local features of what is generally termed "popular religion."[36] When applied to

Yiddish culture, this means that, on the one hand, the delineation of Yiddish and *loshn koydesh* underscores the cultural and sociological roles that these languages fulfilled within internal Ashkenazic diglossia. On the other hand, Yiddish represents a regional Jewish identity, as articulated by Michael Stanislawski in his articles on Jewish popular religion, in an argument that strongly resembles Chartier's approach. In several case studies on Yiddish adaptations of various genres of Hebrew texts, Stanislawski refers to this factor as "Ashkenization," stressing its geographic locus.[37] Similarly, the Red Jews must be understood as a Germanic regional variant of the Ten Tribes, adapted for a Yiddish readership.

As the mother tongue and daily spoken language of Ashkenazic Jews, Yiddish was never the exclusive domain of a single social stratum. In contrast, religious and educational conventions rendered Hebrew (and Aramaic) as exclusive to Jewish men who had achieved the formal training required for full comprehension of the language of synagogue services, religious ritual, and textual learning. The readership of Yiddish encompassed Ashkenazic Jewry irrespective of whether they had mastered Hebrew well enough to read and understand Hebrew texts, that is to say, women and children, adolescents of both genders, and a considerable percentage of adult men (as determined by social and economic status, and personal capacity). Simply put, the vast majority of Ashkenazic society would read and listen to Yiddish with greater ease than Hebrew.[38] The entertaining style that characterized Yiddish works also appealed to those who could readily understand Hebrew, even distinguished scholars.[39]

The Ashkenazic audience thus possessed wide-ranging levels of comprehension and interpretative approaches, depending on their capacities for deciphering a given text. Jeremy Dauber has demonstrated this heterogeneity in his investigation of these readers' knowledge base, as well as their intellectual and literary skills, within his analysis of early modern narratives on the supernatural. Dauber's theoretical approach is undergirded by the assumption of a close writer-reader bond. Given such a relationship, based on an analysis of the literature, it should be possible to reconstruct the early modern author's (compiler's or editor's) expectations of his readership and, thus, the background and levels of comprehension among his anticipated audience.[40]

Due to its linguistic accessibility throughout the Ashkenazic diaspora and its wide availability, often in cheap print editions, Yiddish literature has been linked to popular empowerment and the democratization of knowledge.⁴¹ This pattern was reinforced by diverse approaches to reading, in contrast to our modern definition, which is based on silent, solitary reading. In the premodern context, "reading" also encompassed reading aloud and listening, in other words, both active reading and the passive consumption of a text; thus, the reading public included various levels of literacy and illiteracy.⁴² Those who engaged with Yiddish literature typically included those who lacked the skills needed to directly encounter the written word. Thus, Yiddish texts were shared aloud in informal settings, whether at home or in public. Such presentations were augmented by oral commentaries that provided elaboration, explication, and complementary information that expanded the scope of the original sources.⁴³

The use of illustrations further broadened the definition of reading beyond actively decoding words in a text or independently following a text read aloud. The renowned historian of Yiddish Chone Shmeruk has shown that Yiddish translations of Hebrew books often appeared with illustrations, whereas the original Hebrew versions continued to be reprinted without those visual supplements. These images lent tangible form to the literary content and provided aids that could even serve as an alternative method of reading.⁴⁴ Visualization as a component of Yiddish language and literature has not been substantively discussed beyond illustrations in Yiddish books. As this study argues, visual characterizations of the Red Jews and the emphasis on their coloration contributed significantly to the potency and immense popularity of this figure in both German and Yiddish. The Red Jews' tales belong to a literature that can be "seen."

## Seeing Vernacular Color Symbolism

Images offer a powerful medium for communication, for they are usually apprehended and internalized more effectively than words alone. Rudolf Arnheim has famously spoken of "visual thinking," that is visual perception as a productive cognitive activity, a process that defines mental images as perceptual containers that are essential for thought and verbal operations.⁴⁵ In her groundbreaking work on memory, Mary Carruthers argues that, due to the "intermediary relationship between sensory information and intellectual abstraction," "words and images *together* are two 'ways' of the same mental activity—invention."⁴⁶ Medieval and early modern rhetoric and poetics strove to weave narratives of such visual intensity that readers would picture them mentally.[47] The color red played a prominent role; decisive passages were literally highlighted in red to engage the reader's memory.[48]

Analogously, the Red Jews are described and defined by the allegorical attributes of this color to achieve what the renowned sixteenth-century kabbalist Moses Cordovero of Safed defines as the main purpose for incorporating color into mysticism: "to make things as intelligible as possible to the material ear (of the body)."[49] In our Yiddish myth, vision is invoked by words, per the term "Red Jews," which verbalizes an image. In the following chapters, I demonstrate that the Red Jews are similar to pictorial representations, since they are seen with the mind's eye. Like other verbal imagery, the Red Jews affect memory by appealing to the sense of sight. Moreover, written depictions of the Red Jews are configured as visual narratives that guide the reader to look closely with his inner eye. My approach to discursive visualization is informed by Rachel Rafael Neis's and Marc Bregman's analyses of rabbinic literature that relies on the mind's eye: "The graphic artist portrays the scene to the viewer's physical eye; while the midrashic artist portrays the scene to and through the imaginative faculty of the reader's mind's eye."[50] This midrashic technique utilizes literary markers that mention sight or the eyes, or feature aesthetic descriptions that engage vision or other senses.

Jewish and Christian cultures have always been permeated by visual experiences, as has been convincingly demonstrated by Kalman Bland, Katrin Kogman-Appel, Marc Michael Epstein, and Richard Cohen for Jews from the medieval and early modern periods into modernity.[51] This tendency reflects the general notion in Western culture of sight as the superior sense.[52] On the basis of the apparent rationality of ancient visual theory, which claimed that direct contact between the eyes and a perceived object was requisite, the eyes were regarded as receptors for objective knowledge of the world. Ancient optical theories had ongoing influence and provided the foundation of medieval and early modern views of cognition through the Keplerian turn in the seventeenth century.[53] This philosophical-scientific emphasis on sight merged with theological teachings that elevate the eyes to the pinnacle of the hierarchy of senses. The physiological mechanism for vision was deemed an instrument of spiritual elevation since the eyes of the soul would metaphorically "see" the divine in the world perceived by the corporeal sense of sight. In premodern religious thought, all physical reality pointed to something beyond its tangible presence, that is, the invisible, divine realm.[54]

Medieval and early modern cultures were attentive to the power of sight, literally and with the mind's metaphorical eye. The faculty of sight was consciously employed by premodern authors and artists for various ends. Whether illustrated or textual, real or envisioned, images were typically appreciated for their distinct religious, social, and pedagogical functions. It was commonly believed that shapes and images influenced emotions and could modify behavior. The capacity to elicit emotional responses equipped images with an important didactic function, essentially enabling viewers to experience these pictures. Infusing content with emotional visuality as a prerequisite for cognition was typical for medieval and early modern communication at large.[55] Imagery was often justified as an instructional guide for the illiterate in particular (notwithstanding the oral explication and sociocultural imprints required for "reading" it).[56] Contemporaneous works of art strategically harnessed emotionalization, much as religious and secular dramas and literature did, as a means to deliver their message in an era when full literacy (in its modern sense) was restricted to an elite few.

Anthony Bale understands visual images and textual descriptions of Jews "as affective memory-images, designed to bring the edifying and pleasurable experience of fear, violence and contrast into the medieval reader/viewer's aesthetic world." He observes that medieval scenes of Jews inflicting violence effectively instilled dread of potential persecution by the implied Jewish perpetrators into the Christian viewer's present.[57] These Jews were often depicted as physically unappealing, a code for their wickedness; this indictment was compounded by their portrayal with red hair. Beyond triggering intellectual knowledge that such unseemly physical characteristics signaled danger, grimy and distorted corporeal features in visual and verbal polemics were consciously employed to arouse negative emotional reactions, such as contempt and fear, as a strategy for erecting social boundaries.[58] The imagined Red Jews in German literature occupy the realm that David Nirenberg has termed "aesthetic theology" as an exemplary corporeal artifact that renders Christianity's spiritual teachings vivid to its adherents.[59]

The Yiddish reappropriation of the image of the Red Jews utilizes many of these same techniques: with their red attributes, color was harnessed to invite a certain kind of "seeing." The language of color was often employed in premodern speech and literature for its emotional effect, much as medieval art intentionally employed chromatic color schemes that could easily be apprehended.[60] The affective force of color activates the audience's experiential repertoire and, via its symbolic function, mediates sensual perception and conceptual thought. Modern psychological studies have affirmed that color affects consciousness and the psyche through its ability to evoke emotions, trigger memories, and spark fantasies.⁶¹ Indeed, the act of envisioning color stimulates the same area of the visual cortex that is engaged when the eye encounters external stimuli.⁶² Distinctive coloring is the pivotal cultural marker that situated the Red Jews in a framework that was familiar to the average Ashkenazic Jew as color represents the lowest common denominator for comprehension. Color could express a world that was exempt from the confines of language, formal definitions, and cogitation.⁶³ The basic elements of color semantics were neither formally studied nor explicitly taught—they were part of common cultural experience. Encountering red as the color of blood and fire, for example, was an inevitable part of life; moreover, this color's link to royalty and power was anchored in cultural knowledge, outside the bounds of rational comprehension.⁶⁴

Based on the pioneering work on color discourses by Michel Pastoureau, John Gage, Christel Meier-Staubach, and others, newer research extends into the practical effects of color in various historical contexts, from arts and architecture, religion and politics, to language and literature.⁶⁵ The fluid and multivalent use of color codes in medieval and early modern Christian Europe has been studied extensively; considerably less has been written on color symbolism in Jewish culture. At the conference "The Realm of Color" in 1972, Gershom Scholem presented a paper on select colors in the Bible, rabbinic literature, and Kabbalah which, echoing the scholarly consensus of that era on the pervasiveness of Jewish iconoclasm, claimed that color was less important in Judaism due to the biblical ban on representational images.⁶⁶ Prior scholarship even alleged that Jews had a deficient sense of color, coupled with higher occurrence of color-blindness than the general population.⁶⁷ Since then, however, several studies on the significance of color in Jewish culture have begun to rectify this assessment, most notably Moshe Idel's work on the visualization of color in kabbalistic prayer and Gadi Sagiv's studies on the meanings and uses of blue in Jewish mysticism, magic, and ritual.⁶⁸ The present analysis of color in the Yiddish myth of the Red Jews broadens this emerging scholarly perspective on colors in Jewish culture.

This book explores the red color symbolism that saturated cultural usage and everyday oral communications (language and proverbs), authoritative texts (biblical commentary, rabbinic literature, mysticism, and liturgy), and humoral theory and considers how it bestowed meaning upon the Red Jews in Jewish and Christian culture. The following chapters document how vernacular authors, editors, storytellers, poets, preachers, artists, and their audiences in medieval, early modern, and modern times creatively engaged these color codes. Notwithstanding common ground, colors evoke culturally, religiously, socially, and historically defined associations and, therefore, are seen differently across communities.[69] I argue that Jews were often aware of the cultural conventions of seeing in their societal surroundings, which they simultaneously shared and disputed through their own view of the Red Jews.

Jews and Christians fervently pursued a proper intellectual understanding of seeing correctly what the eye encounters, and this was no less intensely debated. While Judaism and Christianity agreed that the world as perceived by the senses had transcendental meaning, both religions claimed a singular way of perceiving God's creation, and neither wearied of accusing the other of blindness and distorted vision. This charge had grave implications since both groups held that the blind could never be truly religious.[70] Jewish and Christian theologians asserted that the eye was vulnerable to deception and was thus a source of unwitting seduction and moral corruption. Color was central to this discussion. While, due to its sensory nature, color was praised as a universal language, at the same time it was criticized as a distraction to the unversed because its sensual lure could distort proper spiritual apprehension. Bernard of Clairvaux (1091–1153), founder of the Cistercian order, famously cautioned against believing "more holy, what is more colorful."[71] Similar Jewish opposition to the seductive capacity of art is exemplified by Rabbis Isaac b. Moses of Vienna (ca. 1180–ca. 1250) and Meir of Rothenburg (ca. 1215–1293), who voiced concerns that aesthetically pleasing imagery in prayer books and synagogue decor might distract worshippers from study and prayer.[72]

The question of whether vision with the eyes could be trustworthy remained a preoccupation, particularly among European thinkers in the early modern period. Stuart Clark has shown that a profound crisis of vision shook the foundations of the certainty of sight. Notwithstanding the importance of empirical observation in the sciences and the emergent "optical naturalism" in Renaissance painting, intellectuals—in disciplines such as philosophy, theology, magic, demonology, and art—systematically explored the extent to which sight was subjective rather than veridical. During the fifteenth to seventeenth century, rationalist concepts of sight were being dismantled with growing intensity. Confidence in the reliability of the eye diminished as the realization that sight could err was furthered, with the recognition that vison was often mistaken and, at times, could be manipulated. Vision became mediated, an "interpretative skill acquired socially and learned through experience."[73]

The awareness of the subjectivity of sight and related concerns about sensory deception left their mark on the visuality of the Red Jews. Both their German and Yiddish presentations responded to these epistemological notions of sight. When analyzing how the distinct coloring of the Red Jews was treated on different exegetical levels in Yiddish, we see cautions against the unreliability of the untrained eye. By contrast, imagining the Red Jews directed the Yiddish eye to see them correctly. The Yiddish reappropriation of the Red Jews is in fact a story about power: sovereign sight was regained by subverting a Christian image. This act of countering a Christian hegemonic vision that was associated with political and social oppression emphasized Jewish agency and social control. This book shows how the Yiddish Red Jews created what Clark, in his study on vision in early modern Europe, has called a "visual field" that "was tantamount to a visual kingdom."[74] The power of figurative language contributed to the landscape of "Yiddishland," the imagined sovereign territory of Yiddish speakers.[75]

## Variations on the Red Jew

The five chronologically arranged chapters that follow trace distinct phases of the cultural reappropriation of the Red Jews among Jews and Christians from the Middle Ages through the twentieth century. In each historical stage and every cultural space, new ways of seeing are inscribed onto this figure, in response to shifting social, religious, and political concerns. The opening two chapters uncover how the symbolically laden image of the Red Jews became a visual emblem among Christians and Jews in the German- and Yiddish-speaking areas in the late Middle Ages and the early modern period. By analyzing the usage of the expression "Red Jews," with special attention to its etymology and the associated legend about this fictitious people, I demonstrate that their entangled history draws on a shared Germanic color symbolism that links the color red (specifically, red hair) to deceit, despite their divergent interpretations.

The story of the Red Jews, as recounted in Chapter 1, begins with a Christian reconfiguration of the messianic Jewish legend of the Ten Lost Tribes of Israel. Medieval Christianity appropriated the Ten Tribes of Jewish imaginings, envisioned as mighty warriors who would liberate Israel from Christian dominion with the coming of the Messiah. It wove them into its own view of the apocalypse by predicting that the Ten Tribes would assist the Antichrist in his attempt to devastate Christendom at the end of days. During the late thirteenth century, this fearsome horde was dubbed "Red Jews" in Middle High German, with their purportedly abhorrent nature cast in visual terms, just as Christian art was unifying its portrayal of Jewish bodily features into a malformed caricature that allegedly reflected Jews' moral depravity. The Red Jews enjoyed great popularity through the Reformation era, reflecting Christian fear of a revolt by the oppressed Jewish minority. After over three centuries, however, they lost currency in German around 1600. Their gradual disappearance resulted from a complex process of recoding that was influenced by geopolitical transformations, a new ethnographic discourse, and the crisis of vision.

As the Red Jews faded from Christian awareness, their image began to gain currency and ever more versatility in Yiddish culture, where it persisted as a visual icon. By the sixteenth century, at the latest, "Red Jews" had become an accepted term for the Ten Tribes in Yiddish. Chapter 2 discusses the Yiddish Red Jews' relationship to their German counterparts in connection with their roots in medieval Hebrew tradition, focusing on the Rabbi Meir story. The Yiddish narrative of the Red Jews competed with the German variant via the construction of a polemical counterstory that transmitted its visual opposition.[76] When the image of the Red Jews was recast within a distinctly Jewish frame, the Christian apocalyptic vision was retransformed into a reassuring Jewish legend of salvation that expressed an anti-Christian posture.

Much like the legend of the Ten Tribes, the myth of the Red Jews conveys multidimensional meanings that originated in messianic thought, but color symbolism augmented this tale with features that responded to essential questions of Jewish life in the Diaspora that went beyond eschatological concerns. Treating other material on the Red Jews besides *Ma'aseh Akdamut*, Chapter 3 studies the intrareligious functions of this myth, showing that redness shifted from representing stigma to embodying a confident Jewish self-awareness. Red as a color of shame was translated into a color of pride and resistance in early modern Yiddish lore. Most importantly, by contrast to the eschatological escapism that was often employed as a strategy for coping with the harsh realities of quotidian life, this rebellious Jewish identity was not limited by messianic promise. The Red Jews were extricated from a distant eschatological future and positioned in the immediate present as a signifier of Jewish agency. This transformation was not restricted to a metaphorical level, for I argue that sensory perception of the Red Jews was crafted to influence the Yiddish reader's thoughts and actions. These protagonists became role models to be emulated through sight.

Chapters 4 and 5 trace the incorporation of the Yiddish image of Red Jews into new cultural and linguistic settings, beyond the German-Jewish vernacular and into modernity. Chapter 4 explores how the unprecedented encounters between Jews from different cultural backgrounds during the early modern period, concomitant with the invention of the printing press, affected transmission of Yiddish tales about the Red Jews, particularly *Ma'aseh Akdamut*. In contrast to its unbroken popularity in Yiddish throughout west-central and eastern Europe, the number of Hebrew, Judeo-Arabic, and Ladino adaptations of stories about these saviors from beyond the Sambatyon among Italian, Sephardic, and Mizrahi Jews from the seventeenth century onward is remarkably small. I contend that the failure of this tale to gain currency in Hebrew and other Jewish vernaculars may be ascribed to the absence of a visual code for the Red Jews, alongside this idiosyncratic phrase, which defied ready translation into other sociocultural milieux.

Chapter 5 then examines the transformations of the myth of the Red Jews in modern times. Even as the Red Jews' long-lasting popularity came to a close in late eighteenth-century central and western Europe, where Yiddish ceased to be a medium of cultural creativity, their presence intensified in eastern European Yiddish culture. The image of red-haired, red-bearded, and ruddy-faced Jews continued to thrive in various literary and artistic forms, being further appropriated to suit novel intellectual and political contexts. I present well-known eastern European Yiddish writers and artists as agents who engaged the personage of the Red Jew in new ways from the late nineteenth to early twentieth century. Each utilized the Red Jew as a vehicle for expressing their generation's experience of exile in response to intensified rejection of Jews by Europe's emergent nation states. At the forefront were the founders of modern Yiddish fiction, Mendele Moykher Sforim, Sholem Aleichem, and Y. L. Peretz, who penned short stories about Red Jews living in the Pale of Settlement. The painter Marc Chagall drew on these literary models when he famously immortalized the association of eastern European Jewry with this mythical red people in his *Jew in Bright Red* (1915). Mendele, Sholem Aleichem, Peretz, and Chagall fused the previously proud image of the Red Jews with the originally anti-Jewish figure of the Wandering Jew, who was cursed to roam the earth until the end of time. I conclude this analysis by juxtaposing that cultural use of the redheaded Jew with its translation into modern Zionist politics. In contrast to the aforementioned weavings of the Wandering Jew's destiny into new narratives and illustrations of the Red Jews, Uri Zvi Greenberg and Naphtali Herz Imber, two leading poets of the Zionist movement in eastern Europe, tapped this ever-triumphant figure as a source to inform the new Jew, who shed the meek mind-set of the ghetto in his quest for a Jewish homeland in Palestine.

The evolution of the Red Jews brings the oft-occluded realm of vernacular perspectives into discussions of major developments in Jewish and European history. Studying these modes of seeing with the role of color contributes to our understanding of the formation of minority awareness and the construction of Ashkenazic Jewish identity through visual cultural encounters. It also spotlights the vitality of folklore by demonstrating how the premodern motif of the Red Jews informed modern Yiddish literature, and how the stereotype of the Jewish redhead found its way into Jewish social critiques, political thought, and arts through the present day.

Chapter 1

# Red Jews
## A Medieval Christian Label

> Colour could not simply be ignored or dismissed; it was always there. It had to be contained and subordinated—like a woman. Colour was a permanent internal threat, an ever-present inner other which, if unleashed, would be the ruin of everything, the fall of culture.
>
> —David Batchelor, *Chromophobia*

Upon entering St. Mary's Church in Frankfurt an der Oder, the visitor's gaze is drawn to the magnificent stained-glass windows at the far end of the ambulatory. As rays of sunlight pass through this late fourteenth-century glasswork, they are transformed into rich colors that illuminate the scenes depicted in those windows and enliven its imagery before the spectator's eyes. When traversing the nave toward the choir, the details of these three nearly twelve-meter-high windows come into focus: the center window retells the life of Jesus, framed by the creation to the left and the drama of the end times to the right. Among these three representations, the apocalyptic scenes that focus on the Antichrist, who will establish his reign of terror before the second coming and the last judgment, are unique.[1] Thirty-nine panels form a pictorial narrative that presents the biography of this infamous figure. Among this vivid imagery, a single Jew, clad in a bright red garment, catches the eye (fig. 2). He is one in a band of glowering, red-faced Jews (identified by their pointed Jewish hats), some with teeth bared. This formidable corps, known as the Red Jews, is destined to spearhead the army that will wage the Antichrist's apocalyptic campaign against Christendom. Their redness, a quality otherwise reserved for the devil, who appears as the Antichrist's loyal escort, symbolizes their diabolical nature and emphasizes their hostility.[2] The deep red glow of their angry faces is designed to awaken fear at the very thought of the bloody horrors of those final days.

## Red Jews and the Apocalypse

The fearsome specter of the Red Jews who would be unleashed at the end times was widespread in late medieval and early modern German lands. Familiarity with this mythic Jewish people extended across social strata, from scholars to laity, among men and women alike. The tale of the Red Jews permeated vernacular texts of various genres, from theology, history, and literature to the imagery of illuminated manuscripts, block-books, and monumental religious art. In essence, the Christian construct of the Red Jews was a distortion of the Jewish legend about the Ten Lost Tribes of Israel, as Andrew Gow's seminal study demonstrates.[3] The Ten Lost Tribes are the heroes of one of the most vibrant and enduring myths in Jewish culture. During the eighth century BCE, the Northern Kingdom of Israel was destroyed by the Assyrians. Despite its inhabitants' historical dispersion, myths about their survival as an independent kingdom of Ten Tribes in a remote land enticed the Jewish and non-Jewish imagination for centuries. Their isolated realm was said to exist in an uncharted location beyond the mysterious Sambatyon River, whose waters were reputed to be nearly impassable. The Ten Tribes would therefore remain stranded on its far banks until the Messiah's arrival, when Israel would be restored and where the descendants of the Northern Kingdom would rejoin their fellow Jews from the Diaspora. In Jewish apocalyptic thought, the Ten Tribes were envisioned as mighty warriors who would free the people of Israel from Christian dominion. Most notably, in Ashkenazic messianism, especially among Jews in German-speaking areas, salvation was defined in part by revenge for Jewish suffering and the Tribes from beyond the Sambatyon would have an instrumental role in that divine plan.[4] Thus, it is no coincidence that their Christian contemporaries also held a vindictive image of the Ten Tribes, whose ferocious guise as Red Jews would become a resilient motif in German literature.

Christians were often familiar with internal teachings that had been culled from Jewish and convert sources, both written and oral. Martin Przybilski has shown that Christian authors adopted fragments of Jewish motifs and that instances of exegetical, talmudic, and midrashic material were incorporated into the German literature of the Middle Ages, albeit often altered during the process of reception.[5] The association between the Lost Tribes and the color red in fact appears in the Hebrew textual corpus, among other places in midrashim, and it has been suggested that this is the source of the Yiddish expression "Red Jews."[6] Annette Weber has proposed Eldad ha-Dani, the ninth-century traveler who identified himself as a member of the lost tribe of Dan, as the origin for the attribution of redness to the Ten Tribes. According to Eldad, the Sons of Moses, who used cochineal to dye their robes scarlet, resided near his own tribe of Dan.[7] It is thus a plausible possibility that Christians adopted the Red Jews trope from Jewish stories.

Regardless of whether this particular notion of color was picked up by German sources from Hebrew or Yiddish, Christians were aware of the anti-Christian dimensions of Jewish messianism and responded accordingly when they adopted and integrated the Ten Tribes of Jewish imagination into their own system of thought.[8] It seemed logical from a Christian perspective that the menacing Ten Tribes would play a central and active part as the Antichrist's servants. It was reasoned that as the Jews continued to reject Jesus as Messiah, they would become the Antichrist's first and most faithful allies. The Christian mind even equated the Antichrist with the Messiah for whom Jews had long awaited to avenge their oppressors, and thus inextricably linked Jewish messianism with a desire to obliterate Christendom.[9] The fears that originated in anticipation of the Antichrist and his apocalyptic reign were thus projected onto the Jewish Messiah and his hidden Jewish legion.

This Christian version conflates the Jewish myth of the Ten Tribes with two unrelated traditions, one from classical antiquity and one from the Bible. According to the Alexander Romance, in an effort to protect the self-professed civilized world, Alexander the Great banished the supposed barbarians behind a barrier in Asia. This episode was merged with the Jewish-Christian tradition of Gog and Magog, apocalyptical foes that were rooted in various prophetic references and, by the early Middle Ages, had become known as the peoples whom Alexander had confined. This equation first appears in the eighth-century Latin translation of the *Revelations*, an influential apocalyptic work by Pseudo-Methodius.[10] The 1498 Basel edition illustrates the account of Alexander confining the fiendish hordes, picturing two demons atop their mountain prison (fig. 3). By the second half of the twelfth century, Christians in Europe identified this imaginary nation as the Ten Lost Tribes of Israel.[11] Gow concludes that the gradual fusion of these three tales yielded a potent myth about the Ten Tribes as "unclean apocalyptic Jewish destroyers of Christianity."[12] While their ruthless future role was known throughout Christian Europe, only in late thirteenth-century Germany, where this legend would gain incomparable sway, were the Ten Tribes given the vernacular appellation: the Red Jews (*rote Juden* or *Rotjuden*).

The Red Jews made their initial appearance in German literature during the final third of the thirteenth century. The earliest extant text that mentions the Red Jews is the courtly epic *Der Jüngere Titurel* (The Younger Titurel), dated to the 1270s. Its protagonist claims to have encountered the Red Jews in Asia, where they are enclosed on one side by a pair of high mountains, Gog and Magog, eponymously named for the two ominous end-time peoples mentioned that reside there; on the other side, their territory is bounded by a river of stones that flows so furiously that any attempt to forge it would be futile. The narrator characterizes the Red Jews as savage beings and argues that if they are not safely contained, "swift and wild is their host over the whole world," threatening "Christians and heathens" with their military power.[13] A little later, *Der Göttweiger Trojaner Krieg* (The Göttweig Trojan war), a Middle High German verse romance that originated in northern Switzerland (ca. 1270–1300), likewise speaks of a terrifying legion of Red Jews. The narrative draws on the Trojan War of Greek antiquity, entwined with motifs from the Arthurian romance. Here, during their battles against Troy, the Greeks come face-to-face with the "foul" Red Jews, "a poisonous lot," "virtue and modesty / they all lacked."[14] Over the ensuing centuries, the Red Jews' popularity would gradually increase, reaching its apex during the Reformation.[15]

This apprehensive Christian fantasy in German-speaking lands conjured redness as the defining attribute of this fictitious Jewish people. The extant pictorial sources show that the Red Jews were envisioned in red garments and with red faces, as in the Antichrist window at the Church of St. Mary. In a book of heraldry from the early fifteenth century, the Red Jews are similarly presented with ruddy complexions (fig. 4). They were often visualized with red hair and red beards as well, a uniformly negative symbol in premodern Europe. A fifteenth-century historiated Bible depicts a variant on this redheaded theme by portraying Alexander banishing the Red Jews to Asia. Their red hair and beards are contrasted with the fair-haired, and thus positively cast, Alexander (fig. 5).

## The Thirteenth-Century Backdrop

Several catalysts may have contributed to the genesis of the German term and the image of the Red Jews in the late thirteenth century. Anti-Jewish sentiment was on the rise in Europe during the late twelfth and thirteenth centuries. The fantasies that cast Jews as perpetrators of ritual murder and host desecration had parallels in eschatological demonization.[16] The Ten Tribes complemented the Jewish Antichrist as a core actor in an anti-Jewish apocalypticism that spliced horrific visions of the end time with scorn for the Jewish people in this world. With the Mongol invasion of Europe in the 1240s, the potential danger represented by the Ten Tribes as the Antichrist's henchmen, who had previously been securely restrained by Alexander, came to be seen as an imminent threat. Both Jews and Christians identified the Mongols with the Lost Tribes, so these religious communities eagerly anticipated or dreaded their arrival, respectively.[17] Consequently, the heightened profile of this legend may have provided fertile ground for the German myth of the Red Jews, which would hone pan-European fears of the Ten Tribes roughly three decades later.

At the same time, medieval Europe saw a growth in investigations of the human body and classifications of its various forms, as evidenced by the inclusion of physiognomy within the fields of science and philosophy. In the context of these intellectual trends, Christian stereotypes of the Jewish physique developed. Interest in the Jewish body was accompanied by the appearance of anti-Jewish figures in Christian imagery aimed for the general public, which became ever more commonplace. Sara Lipton has shown that the alleged defining characteristics of Jewish faces, like a distinctive beard or nose, as well as the pointed Jewish cap, gained currency in the twelfth century and gradually grew in moral import. She concludes that the physical features assigned to Jews in European art were unified into a hook-nosed, pointy-bearded Jewish caricature by the mid-thirteenth century.[18] Depictions of Jews with physical deformities and as associated with disease were intended to reflect the eternal state of sin that resulted from their refusal to accept Jesus as the Messiah.[19] Two persistent canards that claimed physical evidence of the Jews' fall from grace appeared in European thought at this same historical juncture. The thirteenth century witnessed the rise of Christian polemical traditions of Jewish male menstruation[20] and of the Wandering Jew, who was cursed to roam the earth undying until the end times, as retribution for having taunted Jesus while he struggled toward the crucifixion. This figure of eternal repudiation symbolizes the Jewish exile.[21]

The introduction of the red-haired, red-bearded, and ruddy-faced Red Jews as a vernacular epithet and literary motif in Germany, which coincides with these developments, was part of this trend to define Jews as outsiders on the basis of their physiognomy. The Hebrew polemical work *Sefer Nizzahon Yashan* (An old book of victory), which was compiled in Germany during the late thirteenth or early fourteenth century, reflects a common Christian notion from that era: "Gentiles [are] fair-skinned and handsome," but Jews are "dark and ugly."[22] Dark hair and skin were standard elements in Christian depictions of "the hideous Jew" that abound in medieval and early modern visual and textual sources. This palette was dominated by black and red hues, as we will discuss, colors that were deemed signs of a sick and corrupt body in Western thought.[23]

## Red Hair, Bad Hair

Andrew Gow accurately observes that the Red Jews manifest the negative qualities associated with the color red across Europe.[24] In accordance with color symbolism, humoralism, and physiognomic typologies, the terrifying army of the Ten Tribes was dubbed "the Red Jews" and painted from that palette. As an extension of the sharp increase in the study of physiognomy, personality was inscribed onto the body, particularly the face. Character was thought to be evidenced by humoral complexion (in the Latin sense of *complexio*, i.e., physical constitution, rather than formal skin color) and derived from somatic qualities that pertained to the shape, size, and color of certain body parts, such as the eyes, hair, and skin. Compilations of medical compositions translated from original Latin sources were intended to communicate physiognomic knowledge more broadly by making it available to a vernacular readership for practical use. From the fifteenth century onward, hundreds of printed treatises, whose extensive lists catalogued physical features and their typological meanings, proliferated throughout Europe.[25]

In this literature, red coloration was often linked to a range of undesirable traits (much as black was). In the spirit of humoralism, the health manual *Regimen sanitatis Salernitanum* (The Salernitan rule of health) states that yellow bile is dominant in ruddy bodies. This tremendously popular didactic poem was written in Latin in the twelfth or thirteenth century and translated into almost every European vernacular, including German, Hebrew, and Yiddish.[26] Each complexion was associated with specific characteristics; the abovementioned choleric type was classified as hot tempered and vengeful (among other traits). Similarly, the classic volume by the Italian doctor Giambattista della Porta (Latin 1586, German 1601) describes an irate person as having an overall red cast, whereas red skin color could also signify one who is dangerous and conniving.[27] In addition to providing a guide to temperament, facial coloring has long been thought to reveal temporal emotions. In this context, blushing could be interpreted as a sign of agitation that results from momentary anger.[28]

Red hair was considered particularly indicative of a malevolent character, as exemplified by della Porta and others.[29] During the first half of the sixteenth century, two works, both based on *Liber physionomiae* by Michael Scotus (after 1227), inundated the German book market in numerous editions: the popular *Book of Complexions* (first printed in 1510) and the physiognomic compendium that has been ascribed to Bartolomeo della Rocca Cocles from Bologna. Both list red hair as a mark of ignorance and anger. Redheads are defined as unhappy, jealous, haughty, venomous, and deceitful.[30] The vilification of red hair was often charged with theological connotations that linked red hair to hellfire.[31] In Latin, it was a common insult to call someone *rufus* (redhead).[32]

Such typologies entered the cultural imagination: theological discourse and religious life were major catalysts; horoscopes regularly coalesced physiognomy, character, and fate; literature and oral lore conveyed folk wisdom.[33] Countless sayings in European vernaculars attest to the deep wariness toward red hair and red beards that was embedded in daily linguistic usage, as represented by the German sayings: *Rother Bart, Teufels Art* ([A] red beard [is] devilishness) and *Rotes Haar, bös Haar* (Red hair, bad hair), which imply that redheads cannot be trusted.[34] Accordingly, someone with red hair would commonly be referred to as a "redheaded rogue" (*rothaariger Spitzbub*) or "redheaded devil" (*rothaariger Teufel*) in German.[35] In his popular collection of stories and anecdotes *Wendunmuth* (1563), Hans Wilhelm Kirchhof portrays a conversation between a messenger and an innkeeper who are both redheads.

The messenger asks the innkeeper to keep his twenty gold coins safe overnight but then changes his mind, doubting the proprietor's character due to his red beard. The innkeeper responds: "You are red yourself, even redder than I am! Do you mean to defame yourself?" "Exactly!" says the visitor. He is far too familiar with redheaded behavior to consider entrusting his property to one of them.³⁶

Given the negative view of red hair that pervaded European culture, it is hardly surprising that red hair was also thought to indicate Jewish identity in the medieval and early modern periods, thereby echoing the standard accusation that Jews were duplicitous, violent, and aligned with the devil.³⁷ In several medieval German cities, select houses were nicknamed *Haus zum roten Juden* (house of the red Jew). While it is unclear whether this designation was given because Jews had previously resided there, this moniker underscores the conflation of Jews and red hair.³⁸ A similar understanding of redheadedness as a prototypically Jewish quality is displayed in a diatribe that was spearheaded in the sixteenth century by the German Humanist Ulrich von Hutten, targeting the convert Johannes Pfefferkorn. He spread the calumny that Pfefferkorn had kidnapped two Christian children with the intent of murdering them for ritual purposes. He allegedly sold one of the children to Jews, who tortured and stabbed the boy to draw his blood; but the other child was lucky for, having red hair, Pfefferkorn purportedly released him unharmed.³⁹ At the same time in Spain, redheaded Christians were thought to have converso lineage, and this seems to have informed Inquisition trials.⁴⁰ Profiles in police records from eighteenth-century Germany include descriptions of redheaded and red-bearded Jewish criminals, who occasionally wore white or brown wigs to camouflage as non-Jews during their criminal activities.⁴¹ Since red hair was reputedly "Jewish," the 1690 French *Histoire des perruques* (History of wigs) generally advises redheads to wear wigs to disguise their real hair, whose color horrifies all who behold it.⁴²

As a common stigma, red hair lent itself to signaling "Jews" in the arts. Thus, historians of Elizabethan England have shown that onstage the costume for Shylock in Shakespeare's *The Merchant of Venice* often featured a red wig.⁴³ Similarly, in medieval English bestiaries illustrations of cannibalistic manticores with a blood-red pelt and stereotypical grotesque facial features, replete with a red beard and a pointed hat, display a discursive proximity to images of Jews.⁴⁴ In early modern German visual arts, redheaded Jews were ubiquitous. For instance, the sixteenth-century *Thesaurus picturarum* by Marcus zum Lamm shows a red-bearded man in the garb traditionally worn by the Jews of Worms during the second half of the sixteenth century (fig. 6). *Der Juden Einritt mit jhrem Messia* (The Jews' entrance with their Messiah; fig. 7), a color etching that reproduces a copperplate engraving from Dietrich Schwab's ethnographic work *Jüdischer Deckmantel* (The Jewish disguise; Mainz, 1619), contrasts Jewish and Christian hair color. This polemical depiction of a Jewish messianic procession, led by a so-called *Judensau* (Jews' sow) and Elijah the prophet, who is followed by the Messiah in the form of a horned Moses, concludes with several Jews and Christians riding the Messiah's donkey. The Jews all have reddish beards whereas the Christians, who sit on the donkey's tail, are blond.[45]

The prototype of the notorious redheaded Jew was the biblical traitor Judas Iscariot, preserved in Christian thought as the archenemy of Christianity and the visual model of the Jew. This image was so prevalent in German culture that, in a 1543 sermon delivered in Halle, the provost of the Castle Church at Wittenberg, Justus Jonas, deployed the phrase "red-bearded riff-raff in a yellow cloak with a money pouch" as code for the pernicious traits embodied by Judas.[46] Visual art was often referenced in sermons and religious instruction, and Jonas's words may indeed have reminded his congregation of traditional artistic depictions of Judas. Most explicit in late medieval and early modern Germany, these images tangibly evoked his betrayal via fiery tresses and a red beard, and occasionally a red complexion. The altarpiece by Bertram of Minden (1391–1400) demonstrates this use of color in scenes of the Last Supper and the betrayal of Jesus to the Romans. In the *Last Supper* (fig. 8), red features distinguish Judas from the other disciples, marking his status as a derided outsider (furthered by being positioned at a distance from the group).[47]

Ruth Mellinkoff has observed that colors have been exploited very differently for Jewish villains in Christian art. While red and yellow dramatized Judas's treachery, the redness of the biblical murderer Cain supplied the association with the color of blood.[48] Bloodshed in the medieval Christian mind-set often denoted Jews as the purported murderers of Jesus and the alleged persecutors of Christians. Indeed, most anti-Jewish accusations involve blood, among them ritual murder and host desecration.[49] Similarly, the Red Jews were not simply anticipated as traitors who would turn Christianity over to the Antichrist, but their redness was frequently connected to blood. In the end-time battles, the Christian blood that the Red Jews were destined to shed would be on their murderous hands. The Red Jews' envisioned brutality led to their nickname "bloodhounds" (*Bluthunde*).⁵⁰ A German pamphlet from 1562 on the army of Red Jews reports that one of their regiments has a black and gray banner with a dog chasing a deer, "and on it is written in their language 'Dead or alive.'"⁵¹ Indeed, Jewish culture read hunting scenes as symbolic of a desire for messianic vengeance.⁵² The aforementioned Basel edition of *Revelations* features a similar image of Gog and Magog bearing a banner of a dog as they break free from the Caspian Mountains (fig. 9). In his commentary on the Book of Daniel (1529), Jonas builds a different animalistic metaphor. He states that, at the end time, the Red Jews will successfully escape from their mountain prison when one of their cunning hunters tracks an equally sly fox to a tunnel leading to the world beyond their domain.⁵³ The Red Jews' redness thus symbolized their perfidious as well as their violent potential.

## The Etymology of the Red Jews

Despite the ubiquity of negative associations with the color red and its links to Jews in European culture, the Red Jews were exclusive to the German-speaking realm and this phrase remained without an equivalent in any other European language, except Yiddish. The sixteenth-century French scholar Guillaume Postel was puzzled when he encountered the term *Judaei rubri* in a Latin translation of a German work. He pondered whether this people was a *figmentum* of the author's imagination. Postel made a note in the margins of his copy of the book, asking: *Ubi est regestum*? (Where is this written?).⁵⁴ Obviously, Postel was unfamiliar with this uniquely German vernacular name. As a rule, scholars did not introduce the Red Jews into Latinate vocabulary; however, it appears in their vernacular writings, where they utilized language that would be comprehensible to a less-learned readership. The works of Justus Jonas offer such an example: his German interpretation of the Book of Daniel incorporates the legend of the Red Jews, whereas I have found no evidence of their mention in his Latin writings. An earlier example, cited by Gow, is the Middle High German version of the *Passau Anonymous* (ca. 1330), whose editor translated "Gog and Magog" in the Latin original into "the Red Jews," which he deemed more familiar to his German audience.⁵⁵

If we turn our attention to language, we are able to recover the valence of redness in German culture with greater accuracy. The ominous qualities of the color red became ingrained in speech: "red" acquired the secondary meaning of "false" and "cunning" in Middle High German; therefore, every German speaker was inculcated in the sinister dimension of this color.[56] "Red" came to serve as an intensifier for pejorative expressions. The most outstanding example in Middle and Early New High German is the term *rote Juden*, which encompassed the deceptive qualities that purportedly characterized Jews who, in the popular imagination, sought to harm Christians in every possible way.[57] While feigning loyalty to Christian law and order, Jews were thought to threaten their Christian neighbors' spiritual and physical well-being through blasphemy, usury, and physical violence. For medieval and early modern Christians, the apocalyptic Red Jews epitomized the ultimate Jewish evildoers, Christianity's final and most daunting antagonists.

Similar linguistic use of the adjective "red" is further exemplified by the word *Rothure* (or *rote Hure*; red harlot), an Early New High German expletive that referred to a prostitute's red makeup, a means for masquerading in red lips and cheeks, the ideals of natural beauty. Like the Red Jews, the red harlot also appeared as an apocalyptic figure, whose red clothing recalls the mother of harlots (Rev. 17:3–5), who is "arrayed in purple and scarlet color."[58] In each case, red is understood as a facade that signifies a disingenuous nature. David Batchelor describes the ambiguity of makeup as colors that are applied to the body and "can often confuse, cast doubt, mask or manipulate; they can produce illusions or deceptions."[59] Indeed, in Latin, *colorare*, "to color," is derived from *celare*, "to conceal." Accordingly, in premodern German culture, makeup symbolized pretense and deception.[60] Another parallel linguistic construction that emerged during the same era as the phrase *rote Juden* is *Rotwelsch*, meaning "deceitful speech" (perhaps as early as 1250). This epithet referred to late medieval sociolects that were spoken among vagrants, beggars, and criminals but were incomprehensible to outsiders. While the origins of this term are contested—that is, it is unclear whether *rot* refers to "red" in the sense of "false" or is derived from the word for "beggar" in that dialect—speakers of Middle and Early New High German surely understood this term to imply "dishonest or sinister doings."[61] A pamphlet from the sixteenth century refers to the Red Jews' language as *Rostart Hebräisch*, that is, a Rotwelsch style of Hebrew.[62]

Additional linguistic traditions must be considered to explain the etymology and later interpretations of the name "Red Jews." The sources suggest that this expression was read in accordance with the traditional Christian identification of Jews with Edom, whose name has the same triliteral root as "red" in Hebrew (*adom*). This personage is introduced in Genesis 25:23: "Two nations are in your womb, two separate peoples shall issue from your body; one people shall be mightier than the other, and the elder shall serve the younger." The older son is Esau (typological twin and progenitor of the nation of Edom), who is described as "ruddy" (*admoni*) at birth, usually understood as red hair covering his body.[63] Esau's association with redness is twofold: his appetite for red lentil stew is reflected in his name Edom.[64] The younger son in the Genesis narrative is Jacob (later given the name Israel, patriarch of the Jewish people), who takes possession of his brother's birthright as the firstborn.

Christian typological exegesis of the competition between Esau/Edom and his twin Jacob/Israel inverts the Jewish self-understanding by equating Israel with the younger religion, Christianity, and thereby relegating Judaism to the position of the elder brother and servant, Edom. This verse served as a scriptural reference for the Christian claim that the Church had superseded the people of Israel, the latter having been rejected as God's chosen one, thus becoming the new, true Israel (*verus Israel*). In contrast, the Jewish interpretation of this typology deferred the fall of that elder to the messianic future. When the Temple was destroyed in 70 CE and the Israelite kingdom lost its last vestige of political independence to Rome, Edom became synonymous with the Roman Empire. With the Christianization of Rome in the fourth century, Edom was henceforth identified with the Church, not only as a political entity. Israel's redemption became contingent upon the fall of Edom/Rome, that is, Christianity.[65]

Christians and Jews were each keenly aware of the other's designation of their own group as Edom and vigorously denied that identification while vindicating their own interpretation. In their ideological struggle over the elevated identity of Israel, both religions have frequently drawn on the biblical etymology of Edom as the red one when marking the despised Other as Israel's counterpart, underscoring his association with the color of blood, that is, persecution. Melito of Sardis, Maurus Hrabanus, Rupert of Deutz, and other medieval Christian exegetes agree that Jews were called Edom because they were red, with the blood of Christ clinging to their hands.[66] Conversely, the piyyut *Ma'oz Ẓur* (Fortress of rock) refers to Christianity as "the red one in the shadow of the cross."[67] *Midrash ha-Gadol* explicitly describes Esau's ruddiness as "bloody" because "he hates the blood of circumcision"; and Rashi reads this feature as a sign that Esau, that is, the Christians, will commit bloodshed.⁶⁸ We also know that Ashkenazic Jews in the thirteenth century related the fall of Edom to Esau's florid coloration. *Sefer Nizzaḥon* explains that Esau is described as reddish in Genesis 25:25: "because of the evil that would befall him, as it is written, 'Who is this that comes from Edom with dyed garments?' [Isa. 63:1]. This implies that God will kill Edom."⁶⁹

It is unclear whether this tie to Edom reveals the intellectual grounding of the German Red Jews' myth or whether that connection was retroactively claimed by the learned to explain the origins of this folk legend. Sixteenth-century Reformation theologians at least linked the color of the Red Jews to this long-established Christian formula that equated Jews with Edom via the color of blood, as Jonas remarked in 1529: "It seems to me [. . .] that this term Red Jews indicates that they are Edom, since Edom means red."⁷⁰ This connection is compelling to Jonas because he sees redness as proof of the Red Jews' destined participation in savage wars and the oppression of Christians, compounded by their alleged aspirations to rule the world. Several decades later, Georg Nigrinus (Schwarz), a pastor in Giessen, supported this interpretation of the phrase *rote Juden* by speculating that they "are called the Red Jews, perhaps from Edom or their bloodthirst. Therefore, the European Jews secretly favor them and hope they will free them to return to their land. . . . they hope the scepter shall then be taken from Christians because their scribes all say that they cannot regain their kingship while the Edomites hold the scepter. By such name they call us, the Christians."⁷¹ Nigrinus affirms the evidence that we have seen thus far: in an effort to reinterpret the Ten Lost Tribes of the Jewish apocalyptic imagination, Christian narratives transfer the role of Edom, who is condemned to perish, from Christians to the Red Jews. Whereas the rival Jewish view envisions them as Edom's ultimate nemesis, in the Christian version of this dramatic history, the Red Jews who ally themselves with the Antichrist will suffer defeat with him. As his notorious henchmen, they will only briefly triumph before being vanquished when Jesus returns to earth.⁷²

## The Visual Text

With appearances in vernacular sources that range from literary and theological to historical, the Red Jews reached a broad, socially and educationally heterogeneous readership.⁷³ The proliferation of vernacular printed materials from the 1450s onward brought texts to an ever-growing audience.⁷⁴

Block-books and pamphlets especially reached quite a large market, with the Red Jews being regularly showcased in these popular media. Widespread knowledge of the Red Jews may primarily be attributed to their place in the Antichrist legend, German vernacular versions of which were accessible through written, oral, performative, and pictorial media. Visualization was essential for expanding the reach of the Antichrist narrative and the legend of the Red Jews in particular. The modalities that portrayed the Antichrist story through imaginative description typified premodern religious instruction for the lay public. Church windows, as in Frankfurt an der Oder, were an architectural means for augmenting religious education during mass. If positioned in the choir loft, a window would be visible to all congregants, even from afar, and serve as an iconographic representation of liturgical content for illiterate parishioners. Much as sermons and artwork invited contemplation in church settings, strategic didactic functions were fulfilled by Antichrist and last judgment plays as well as vivid biographical depictions of Christ's final enemy conveyed in German picture books.[75] *Antichrist and the Fifteen Signs of the Final Judgment*, for example, appeared in manuscript and also in several xylographic and typographic print editions from the mid-fifteenth century onward, some in color: this volume mentions the Red Jews in two captions, as the Antichrist preaches to them and when they enlist in his legions.[76] A few editions of this work render a Red Jew draped, like the Antichrist himself, in a red robe (fig. 10).

The artist who designed the aforementioned stained-glass portrayal in Frankfurt an der Oder had numerous sources to consider when arranging its scenes of the life of the Antichrist. Drawing on the major works of the Antichrist narrative, including popular plays of that period, the window lends an intriguing plot variant to the legend.[77] Upon the Antichrist's arrival at the Sambatyon River to assemble his apocalyptic army, the Red Jews do not greet him with the expected enthusiasm (fig. 11). On the contrary, a Red Jew in the front row looks confounded and scratches his beard when the Antichrist grabs his hand. Apparently, the Red Jews are skeptical as to whether this figure is truly their long-anticipated Messiah. Unlike his followers in other scenes, the Red Jews are not yet marked with the tau cross ("T," shaped like the Greek letter tau), the sign of the Antichrist. Even while watching the Antichrist resurrect the dead in another scene, one Red Jew (identifiable by his ruddy complexion) seems unconvinced as he tugs on his beard with uncertainty (fig. 12).[78] Only when the Antichrist's supporters renounce Christianity, symbolized by the Antichrist holding an inverted cross and placing one foot on it, do the Red Jews accept him as their Messiah. One of these Red Jews rejects the cross with a downward-pointing *schwurhand* (the typical gesture in Germanic culture when swearing an oath). From this moment onward, he and two other individuals bear a "T" on their foreheads (fig. 13).

In the current arrangement of the Antichrist window, this episode precedes the Antichrist crossing the Sambatyon and raising the dead. I would suggest, however, that this was not the original sequence, given that changes were introduced during a restoration of this window in the nineteenth century.[79] The tableau where the Red Jews ally themselves with the Antichrist in our window could plausibly reflect a narrative that corresponded with the well-known storyline of the Tegernsee Antichrist play (ca. 1160), among the most impressive of the last judgment plays in German lands and one of the artist's sources. In that theatrical interpretation, the Antichrist's ability to revive the dead convinces the Holy Roman Emperor to submit to him and be branded with his mark, as seen in the window (fig. 14).[80] It would thus be more logical for resurrection of the dead to analogously precede the Red Jews' acceptance of the Antichrist, contrary to the window's current design.

In an effort to maintain the close connection between word and image that characterized the transmission of the myth about the Red Jews from its earliest stages, Jonas's booklet on Daniel features a woodcut that warned his readers that the raging Turkish wars were an unmistakable sign of the fast-approaching end of time (fig. 15). That image integrates the Red Jews, whom Jonas equates with the threatening Turks, as natural members in Daniel's cast of eschatological characters, beside the four sea creatures that symbolize the four successive kingdoms whose rise will precede the world's demise, with Rome as the fourth and final empire.[81] This telling woodcut incorporates several standard elements from earlier depictions of the Red Jews. First, wearing pointed hats signals that they are Jews. Second, they are drawn as a powerful army, fortified with armor, lances, swords, and shields, bearing flags, and led by cavalry. Third, the Red Jews are depicted as the horde whom Alexander confined behind a chain of mountains and, in Latin, are referred to by their cartographic name, *iudei clausi* (or *iudei inclusi*, the "enclosed Jews").[82]

In some pictures, the Red Jews are about to break out of their stone prison, as in a pamphlet from 1523. During that year, apocalyptic expectations were heightened and "news of the saviors from beyond the Sambatyon River spread throughout all lands," reaching both Jews and Christians.[83]

Accordingly, in 1523, several German pamphlets circulated widely, all claiming that the Red Jews had breached their barriers and were heading to the land of Israel; one is titled *Concerning a Great Multitude and Host of Jews*. Its frontispiece depicts a heavily armed band of Red Jews, unmistakable with their Jewish hats, the emblem that also adorns their flag. In this illustration, the Red Jews have emerged from beyond a mountain range and are about to ford the Sambatyon River, which flows calmly before them (fig. 16).[84]

This pamphlet demonstrates that the Red Jews were not merely relegated to the realm of legend; they were considered a political-military force like any other and their existence across a vast, unknown territory was virtually undisputed. On the basis of their connection with Alexander, the Red Jews are on numerous medieval and early printed world maps, which combined geographic knowledge with historical, theological, and legendary material, typically in the mountains near the Caspian Sea or the uncharted reaches of northeastern Asia.[85] On the 1448 *mappa mundi* by Andreas Walsperger (fig. 17), a Benedictine from Salzburg, for instance, an inscription marks the dwelling of Gog and Magog in the land of the Red Jews behind the Caucasus Mountains. Their menacing image is underscored by their proximity to monstrous races, illustrated by a cannibalistic creature, busily gnawing on a human leg. Via their identification with Gog and Magog, who had been depicted as cannibals in Latin sources and the Alexander legend, the Red Jews were also placed in this category. The Ebstorf World Map (ca. 1300) thus depicts Gog and Magog as man-eaters who were imprisoned by Alexander, while the *Nova Cosmigraphia* (ca. 1440) in the lost Vienna-Klosterneuburg map corpus groups the Red Jews with Gog and Magog (as single entities), dog-headed men, and cannibals.[86]

Such gruesome illustrations and verbal descriptions of Red Jews attacking en masse were exploited to instill fear in the audience. Multiple strategies for appealing to the senses and triggering emotions are evident in these works. As the pictorial feature that first attracts attention and is best retained, color was critical for the launch and perpetuation of this myth. Gow points out that the phrase "Red Jews" was not simply a German synonym for "Ten Tribes"; it connoted a more complex anti-Jewish characterization, that is, a wicked, repulsive, and dangerous nature. Although he acknowledges that this specific term helped sustain this legend, he does not address sight as a vehicle for its resilience. I would contend, however, that naming its protagonists the "Red Jews" brings to the fore their cultural roles, stimulating the affect rather than the intellect.[87] The name "Red Jews" was as catchy as it was graphic and, therefore, accessible to a diverse audience. While the legend's plot and complex theological messages, such as its exegetical link with Edom, likely required a degree of formal schooling to be grasped fully, everyday color symbolism had no such prerequisites. The tangible quality of the term "Red Jews" conveys the myth's unique character. Its message and emotional impact are encapsulated in a single phrase: for all who were literate in the symbolism of red outlined above, the Red Jews' signature red hair, ruddy complexions, and red garments embodied deceit and danger, corresponding to their scripted function.

The visual quality of the Red Jews engaged a general principle in medieval art, where select characteristics were deliberately presented in symbolic colors for emphasis. In contrast to the realistic replication of a nuanced palette, artists chose simple color schemes that were easily remembered and could thus be readily activated.[88] Moreover, the quality of coloration used to depict the Red Jews reflects the late medieval trend that sought to intensify the affective experience of viewing images, a technique that was most commonly articulated in relation to the Christian passion: blood was rendered using red paints with high-gloss finishes in illuminations in books and manuscripts; red stones decorated religious artifacts and furnishings, such as crucifixes, bookcases, altarpieces, and reliquaries; and red ink or purple vellum was used in text. These techniques all cultivated the illusion of having personally seen (and even touched) the blood of Christ and his martyrs.[89]

Many of the medieval and early modern church altarpieces in European towns, cities, and monasteries that were designed to generate emotional responses to their anti-Jewish content enlist color to amplify their messages. The retable by Hans Holbein the Elder, for example, crafted circa 1500 for the Dominican order in Frankfurt am Main shows Judas with the traditional red coloring (fig. 18).[90] The visual message of this altarpiece, which spans 6.5 meters in height and width when open, corresponds with the anti-Jewish content of the Passion play that was performed in Frankfurt in 1498, shortly before Holbein created his work. As a massive, pictorial Dominican sermon in dazzling color, one can imagine the provocative effect of Holbein's painting on those who beheld it. Viewers' emotional responses may have been comparable to their plot-driven reactions at the conclusion of the Passion play, when the actors playing "the Jews" led the character of "Jesus" through the neighborhoods of the city amid raucous shouts.[91] Passion and morality dramas also harnessed the power of color symbolism. In these performances, the character of Judas often dons a yellow robe and appears with red hair.[92] In the topsy-turvy world of the late fifteenth-century Donaueschingen Passion play, Jews blaspheme Jesus by claiming that he had a red beard.[93] Regina Toepfer has argued that the stage directions in this play are intended to supplement even private reading, so the reader might envision its staging, including the colors of its set.[94]

These visual signals—whether explicitly drawn or supported by the imaginings of the inner eye—represent an illiterate audience's craving for clear messages communicated through the senses. Like the image of the Red Jews, the figure of Judas distills the entire drama of his betrayal into his iconographic form. The Red Jews' ominous appearance is not limited to the use of color, however. Similarly, Holbein's altar blends medieval symbolism with early modern realism, augmenting Judas's red portrayal with his unkempt and unseemly attributes in the rendering of the Last Supper: disheveled red hair, a scraggly red beard, and an unsightly red face.[95] His mien contrasts sharply with Jesus's beatific countenance as rendered in this altar piece, reflecting the notion that the divide between these religions and their adherents' natures cannot be bridged.[96] In the abovementioned book of heraldry, as Debra Strickland has noted, the threat posed by the Red Jews is conveyed not only by their choice of color but by menacing facial expressions, as they glare from their mountainous prison with clenched teeth (similar to the Antichrist window). In addition, this volume portrays Red Jews with grotesque faces as outward signs of immorality—bulbous noses, distorted eyes, and oversized teeth behind bulging lips.[97]

The eyes are not the only sensory organs that were stimulated to prompt repulsion and horror in reaction to the Red Jews; the ears were also engaged for a heightened emotional response. The *Göttweig Trojan War* is such an audiovisual text. It explains that even the most skillful and experienced knights, who had successfully waged campaigns against formidable enemies, were distressed as never before when they saw the "huge and horrible" Red Jews.[98] Through the eyes of fearful Ulysses and his men, the reader views "an innumerable horde" of Red Jews and surely shares the Greek heroes' horror at the graphic description of "these hateful hell-hounds" who were eager and equipped for battle, their armor unscathed from prior campaigns: "They all wore / Terrible body armor made from horn / With whole steel rings underneath, / Their helmets were very shiny; / Well-fashioned and skillfully forged, / Their shields remained unscarred but from great effort / From a hand-held a sword." These accounts were inflated by reports of a horrific slaughter that lasted for twelve days and took the lives of innumerable Greeks and Red Jews, whose heads were viciously cleaved by the sword. The author comments that "no one can accurately describe the prowess of these creatures." The readers' imaginations are sparked to envision and expand on these verbal sketches. A soundscape of this battle is suggested as well: "The clamor of men and striking swords / was extremely loud." Through these auditory prompts and scenes of violence, this text seeks to stir the emotions of its audience and to trigger physical manifestations of terror at the implication that none who encountered the Red Jews could fare better. The mere thought of the Red Jews would evoke these sights and sounds that, by extension, induced shudders of fear.[99] This phenomenon is comparable to a scene in the Frankfurt Passion play: After the foot washing at the Last Supper, the devil arrives onstage and whispers in Judas's ear. Without hearing his words, the audience, assembled in a wooden gallery that framed the stage on all sides, was invited to imagine what Judas heard before he approached the Jews to betray Jesus.[100]

Such lurid descriptions of the Red Jews transformed reading into a multisensory experience, thereby enabling participation beyond actual readers to an audience of "viewers" and "listeners." Rather than building on intellectual access alone, the German myth of the Red Jews offers bold imaginings of malice and violence, accompanied by the sounds of threat and aggression. By harnessing the affective qualities associated with red in medieval color coding, the propagation of its message was uniquely bolstered. When the horrors of battle resounded with shrieks and the clang of arms, their landscape was soon to be blood-red.

## Timeless Fears

Through this red-tinted lens, the Red Jews' sinister attributes appeared timeless, immutable from the past to the present and future. They were seen as a constant threat, not only at the dawn of an apocalyptic future, as demonstrated by the assertion that the Red Jews were culpable for the Black Death (1347–51). The plague, which claimed the lives of an estimated one-third of the European population, was often blamed on Jews who were rumored to have poisoned the wells throughout Europe. A yearbook from Zurich specifically ascribes the plague to the Red Jews, contending that the wells and streams were infected with poison that European Jews produced from snake venom supplied by the Red Jews. This toxin was allegedly "so foul and devilish, that any person touched by this poison could live no longer than three days." Its exceptional potency bolstered suspicions that Jews could contaminate anything that they touched, explaining the plague's unprecedented virulence and rapid transmission: "The sickness was so poisonous that when a healthy person came close enough to a sick one to be touched by the breath or miasma of that sick person, or touched his garment, he was sure to die. And it went from one [person] to the next."[101] Later sources perpetuate the Red Jews' purported arsenal of lethal potions. In his polemical tract *Jüden Feind* (Enemy of the Jews, 1570), Nigrinus enumerates the towns and cities where the plague erupted, among them Strasbourg and Basel, tracing its origins to Jews who had purportedly been abetted by the Red Jews.[102] Notably, the aforementioned frontispiece of *Concerning a Great Multitude* shows two snakes slithering along the banks of the Sambatyon River, representing the noxious creatures that populated the otherwise uninhabitable deserts where the Red Jews reportedly dwelled.

The Red Jews' rumored adeptness with deadly tonics was inevitably correlated with their alleged expertise in magic. Their number was said to include brilliant sorcerers, "skilled in unknown fireworks, who can make fires burn in the sky as though the fire came from heaven."[103] These magicians were reputed to cause fire to rain from the heavens as a sign of the end, as the Antichrist is depicted in Jacobus de Voragine's *Legenda Aurea* (ca. 1265) and accordingly in the Antichrist window (fig. 19), in reference to Revelation 13:13.[104] Premodern views of magic often conflated black and white arts. For example, a seventeenth-century Yiddish source claims to document a belief among Christians that the sacred waters of the Sambatyon River could heal skin ailments, such as scabies and shingles. These waters were thought to be imbued with such holiness that neither humans nor animals were worthy of drinking it, but those with physical afflictions were permitted to bathe in that river or wash with its curative waters.[105]

The myth of the Red Jews reflects Christian fears that Jews could unleash their attack at any time. This trepidation was rooted in the anxiety of a majority society that its oppressed minority would revolt against their mistreatment sooner or later. From a Christian perspective, Jewish attainment of social or political control would be tantamount to undermining the dominion that Christians had merited since becoming God's chosen people, instead of the rejected Israelites. In fact, an unchecked surge in Jewish power was as objectionable in a male-dominated Christian world as unbridled expressions of female authority. Discomfort with women exercising power rose in the early modern period: women's legal and economic rights and social freedoms were curtailed throughout Europe in the Renaissance, as their activities were ever more regimented and portrayed in negative terms.[106] Significantly, the myth of the Red Jews paired the concern of the anomalies of Jewish and female authority, tapping into a tradition that Amazons, a mythic nation of female warriors, guarded the iron gates that restrained the Jewish hordes under their watch. A popular travelogue by John Mandeville (ca. 1356, originally written in French), for instance, states that Amazons served as gatekeepers for Gog and Magog or the Ten Tribes (or the Red Jews, in German translations).[107] Accordingly, fifteenth-century pictorial tales of the Antichrist depict the Red Jews (dressed in red robes and shoes, wearing Jewish hats) as the Amazons' comrades-in-arms (fig. 20; cf. fig. 10). Under the leadership of their queen (also dressed in red), these women, together with their vassal army of Red Jews, would ultimately lead the Antichrist's campaign of destruction. This narrative conveys the fear that two subordinate groups would band together against their oppressors. Both female and Jewish agency were castigated as undesirable since their ascendance could presage the overthrow of established hierarchies—a gendered warning that, as we will see, would be picked up in early modern Jewish sources to great effect.[108]

The Red Jews were intensely feared by German speakers through the Reformation. However, this dread slowly dissipated over the early modern period until this mythic people vanished from German discourse. This transition is evidenced by Johann Fischart's *Affentheuerlich Naupengeheurliche Geschichtklitterung* (1575), a free and expanded German translation of Francois Rabelais's *Gargantua*. Rather than speaking of the Red Jews with foreboding, he simply mentions them among the array of peculiar beings and peoples—including Turks, demons, beaked men, and Blue or Red Jews—that would emerge from behind the Caucasus if the iron gates that Alexander had erected were unlocked.[109] While, in an earlier context, the anticipation of these nations being unleashed would have stirred long-held fears, in Fischart's writing, this arbitrary assemblage is merely odd. In one respect, the humor in this text confirms broad knowledge of Red Jews among early modern German speakers in the late sixteenth century; indeed, picturing Blue Jews—with color-coordinated blue faces, hair, and beards—would only be funny to an audience that was familiar with the original coloration. However, the parodical approach to the Red Jews in Fischart's volume suggests a shift in their significance: the clear-cut message of this myth was fading as its cultural context changed.[110]

What prompted the decline of the Red Jews? I would suggest that, in the course of the sixteenth century, the Red Jews began to wane in German language and imagery because these mythic redheaded and ruddy-faced enemies, held captive in the distant reaches of the East in anticipation of their entrance on the apocalyptic stage, could not endure the historical and cultural developments that gained momentum throughout the early modern period: a changing political climate that resulted from the rise of Ottoman Turkey, the naturalizing tendencies of early modern ethnographic discourse, and a crisis of vision that manifested in Reformation iconoclasm. The Red Jews lost their original position due to a complex process of recoding that undermined the visual potency that had been their defining trait and anchor in folklore.

## A New Enemy: The Turkish Threat

During the fifteenth century, a new enemy appeared on the horizon to challenge Christian dominance in Europe. In 1453, the Ottoman Turks conquered Constantinople, the capital of Eastern Christendom, and started their unrelenting advance toward the European heartland, reaching Vienna twice (in 1529 and 1683). As was typical in this age of geopolitical turbulence, Europeans appropriated newly encountered peoples and places by situating them in familiar cultural frameworks. Their own territorial expansions prompted mythic peoples to be ushered into the widening boundaries of the charted world as geographical finds became associated with these legends and various populations were identified with the Red Jews, the Ten Tribes, or Gog and Magog. Their vaguely marked homelands were consequently located in the recently engaged regions of Asia, Africa, and the Americas, whose indigenous populations were often labeled as "lost Jews."[111]

Correspondingly, several early Reformation thinkers in Germany conflated the Turks with the Red Jews. This ascription resonated with the fearsome specter of a Jewish-Turkish entente in circulation at that time. After the fall of Constantinople, European Jewry was increasingly suspected of supporting the Ottomans; this accusation was motivated by the assumption that Jews hoped a European defeat by the Turks would augur the coming of the Messiah.[112] In 1529, when the Turks first reached Vienna, Martin

Luther was revising his German translation of the New Testament, in which he equates that contemporaneous threat with an aggregated force of Gog and Magog and the Red Jews.[113] Elsewhere, Luther adds nuances to this exposition: he differentiates between these three groups, contending that the Red Jews no longer existed per se; however, he identified the Turks, who are synonymous with Gog and Magog, as their descendants.[114] Jonas also considers the Red Jews to be a historical people, namely the Scythians, whom Alexander the Great defeated in the Caucasus. According to Jonas, their progeny, known as the Turks, were referred to metaphorically as "Red Jews."[115]

Paradoxically, while some regarded the Red Jews as Turks throughout the sixteenth century, others embraced them as prospective comrades in arms against the Muslim threat from the East. This reversal of the Red Jews' position seems to have been fueled by the appearance of David Reuveni, who introduced himself as an emissary from the Ten Lost Tribes during the 1520s and 1530s. This Jewish visitor claimed that his brother was the monarch who ruled over two and a half of the Ten Tribes. Reuveni allegedly sailed from his kingdom, located east of the Red Sea in the fabled desert of Chabor, to Nubia, then Egypt, and the land of Israel, before crossing the Mediterranean Sea and disembarking in Venice in 1523, a year that was imbued with apocalyptic significance, as we have seen. His stated purpose was to liberate the Holy Land from Ottoman rule and leading Diaspora Jewry to their homeland. Not only did Reuveni's mission ignite Jewish messianic hopes for a speedy return to Jerusalem, but his plan was encouraged by a number of Europe's most powerful rulers: Pope Clement VII, King John III of Portugal, and Charles V, King of Spain and Holy Roman Emperor. When Reuveni offered an introduction, European sovereigns reacted by reaching out in an unprecedented direction to form an anti-Turkish pact: the Ten Tribes.[116]

Within this dynamic political landscape, variable concepts of the Red Jews' participation in the drama of the Last Days were articulated and the Red Jews were rendered as an ever more welcome presence. The German pamphlet *Concerning a Great Multitude* details the ramifications of Reuveni's activities for the legend of the Red Jews, as it became synchronized with contemporary events. According to this leaflet, in summer 1523, an army of Red Jews, numbering 500,000–600,000, began to move against sultan Suleiman the Magnificent, demanding that he surrender the land of Israel to the Jews as its legitimate inheritors. The report states that the Red Jews, encamped in Egypt, thirty days' distance from Jerusalem, were preparing to seize the city. Having appeared against the backdrop of Reuveni's mission, this pamphlet was the first to depict the Red Jews in a role other than apocalyptical enemies of Christians.[117] However, the prevailing image of Turks and their Jewish allies, which became the subject of a high-profile case at the imperial court in the early 1530s, was compounded by centuries-old fear of the Red Jews and tainted Reuveni's mission in Germany. Right after his audience with the emperor in 1532, Reuveni and his companion Solomon Molkho were arrested and subsequently burned at the stake.[118] Thus, the portrayal of the Red Jews as apocalyptic enemies ultimately overshadowed their newly propagated cooperative potential.

And yet, even after Reuveni's failed attempts, the theoretical possibility of joining forces with the Red Jews against the Turks remained an option in sixteenth-century German consciousness. For nearly a century, this fresh perspective coexisted with suspicion of the Red Jews. For example, in 1560, an anonymously authored list of purported Jewish blasphemies included the classic allegation that European Jews would eagerly help the Red Jews, who are located next to Turkey, to break out of their mountainous prison in order to wipe out Christianity.[119] During the summer of 1561, the cleric Johann Oldecop notes the Red Jews' aggressive posture, as recorded in the *Hildesheim Chronicle*, had been victorious in the East: news from Constantinople had purportedly reached Venice that the Red Jews, en route to the Holy Land, had captured Babylonia.[120] One year later, a pamphlet, titled *Neüwe Zeittung* (New newspaper), likewise reports on the Red Jews as a serious threat against the Turks.[121] Two revised editions of this pamphlet stress the reversal of the Red Jews' role in the context of the Turkish threat by replacing the phrase *rote Juden* with "new Jews" (*newe Juden*) throughout.[122] Similarly, a pamphlet from 1574, which strongly resembles the 1562 edition, speaks of alarm among Turks for "new Jews" had reached the Ottoman border.[123] The printers apparently deemed the sinister symbolism of the term "Red Jews" inappropriate for a nation that had become military allies.

Even though the Red Jews were still associated with the Turks as late as 1595,[124] two pamphlets from the following year, which also draw from the 1562 pamphlet as a common source, explicitly refer to the Red Jews as allies of Christendom, considering them an instrument of divine retribution against the Ottoman Turks.[125] One of these publications even claims that the sultan initially attempted to persuade the Red Jews to join his struggle against the Christians. However, after his envoys reached the Caucasus Mountains and delivered their appeal, the Red Jews killed them and set out to conquer the

Holy Land for themselves.[126] As Gow has argued, the imminent menace by Ottoman Turks, which cast the Red Jews as a potential ally, contributed to the dissolution of the vision of the Jewish tribes as ominous end-time antagonists.[127] As fear of Ottoman incursions into Europe escalated, the Turks eclipsed the legendary Red Jews in Christian thought, leading this mythic nation to be gradually relieved of its relevance as a looming threat.[128]

## Empirical Ethnography

Some of the same pamphlets that linked the Red Jews with the Turkish threat highlight another concurrent shift in the interpretation of the myth: an environmental-ethnographic approach to anthropology led to a connection between the Red Jews and the Red Sea, while their skin "darkened." Alongside humoral theory, from classical antiquity through medieval and Renaissance scholarship, physical appearance was also related to external natural factors, such as geography, climate, and astrological constellations. For example, a dark complexion was often associated with exposure to the southern sun or with cultural norms, such as hygiene or diet. European expansionism and the influx of information about previously unknown lands and peoples, paralleled by an emergent scientific empiricism, intensified this trend to view coloration (along with other markers, such as social conduct, culture, and religion) as a signal of circumstantial and ethnic diversity.[129]

Notwithstanding the European tendency toward naturalistic views on ethnicity in the early modern period, this remained a deeply moral subject: human appearance continued to be inextricably bound to theological and moral implications that were based in part on semantic fields that had long been associated with specific colors. By way of illustration, this ethnographic approach to skin color seems to have influenced biblical translation in early modern Germany. In his German translation of the Bible, Martin Luther translates King David's ruddiness as *braunlicht* (brownish).[130] It is plausible that Luther attempted to associate David with ethnographic traits that typify the Middle East, the historical setting of the Bible. Given the negative valence of the color red in German, perhaps Luther was attempting to avert the moral dissonance that could have arisen if ruddiness were applied to David, the famous ancestor of Jesus. In reference to wicked Esau, in contrast,

Luther renders the ambiguous biblical lexeme *admoni* as *rodlicht* (ruddy), following the traditional translations of the Vulgate and Septuagint.[131]

The aforementioned pamphlet from 1523 underscores the implications of this changing discourse for the Red Jews. In his account of their apocalyptic advance toward Jerusalem, the publisher interchangeably describes these Jews as "red" or "black." Their new designation as "black" explicitly refers to the darker complexion that typified the inhabitants of the African deserts, whence the Red Jews ostensibly originated. They are described as "black Moors," of whom this author claimed to have learned from historical writings by erudite geographers.[132] The relocation of the Red Jews to Africa thus "darkened" their skin tone in accordance with the burgeoning ethnographic emphasis. At the same time, their well-established "redness," which reinforced the pejorative connotations of black skin, was apparently associated with another natural cause: the Red Sea. A related pamphlet from the same year identifies the Red Jews not with the Ten Lost Tribes but a half tribe that did not leave Egypt with the majority of Israelites (here, eleven and a half tribes) that departed for Canaan during the Exodus.[133] This unusual, and allegedly Jewish, variant on the Exodus account explicitly denotes its traditional typology in Judaism as a prefiguration of the messianic return to the land of Israel: the Ten Tribes' crossing of the Sambatyon River is read in parallel to the Israelites crossing the Red Sea—and the Sambatyon, referred to as the *wüten meer*, "the angry sea," is conflated with this body of water.[134]

The association of the Red Jews with the Red Sea, which was brought to the fore by Reuveni's appearance, in fact reflects another "original" location of the Ten Tribes apart from certain areas in Asia. It was common knowledge among Christian and Jewish audiences in late medieval and early modern Europe that the Lost Tribes were found in Abyssinia on the southwestern coast of the Red Sea. This site was home to a mythical realm in Christian lore: the kingdom of Prester John, whose reign was intertwined with the Ten Tribes. Soon after news of a Christian kingdom in Ethiopia reached Europe in the twelfth century, the territory of Prester John became regarded as that East African realm.[135] Analogously, certain medieval Jewish authors, like Benjamin of Tudela, during that same century, write of the Ten Tribes at the shores of the Red Sea.[136]

The Red Jews' placement by the Red Sea was crucial in the process of anchoring their characteristics to topographical features: rather than associating their name with physical features, this descriptor became linked to their purported dwelling place by the Red Sea. This alternative etymology for the epithet "Red Jews" gained currency in the late fifteenth century. In 1477, Peter Schwarz (Petrus Nigri), a Dominican preacher and faculty member at the University of Ingolstadt, wrote of Jews "beyond the Red Sea" to invalidate the spurious Jewish belief in a remote yet sovereign Jewish kingdom.[137] A century later, in his aforementioned satire, Fischart too locates this tribe on the Red Sea.[138] Accordingly, the war pamphlets of 1596 claim that the Red Jews would arrive from beyond or via the Red Sea.[139] The Red Jews' updated residence by the Red Sea as a naturalistic derivation of this Jewish tribe's peculiar appellation and coloring is reflected in the vernacular *mappa mundi* by Hans Rüst of Augsburg (published as a broadsheet in three different editions around 1480; fig. 21): it labels an island in the—red-tinted—Red Sea as the home of the Red Jews. On maps, its waters often have an unmistakable red hue, representing ancient legends that attribute the alleged red cast of this sea to the actual color of its waters or its sands, or the reflection of the sun on its surface, among others.[140] The curious decision to situate the Red Jews on an island has precedents in earlier cartography. On some maps, the Red Jews' antecedents, Gog and Magog, too were consigned to an island, though in the Caspian Sea rather than the Red Sea.[141] The *Nova Cosmigraphia* even labels a peninsula in the Caspian Sea as "The Land of the Red Jews" (*Der Roten Iuden Lant*), detailing that the Red Jews are confined by its northeastern waters.[142]

Rüst's *mappa mundi* is exemplary of the *longue durée* shift to naturalistic conceptions of ethnicity that pertained to the Red Jews myth consistent with their geographical relocation from Asia to Africa. In the typical encyclopedic style of premodern cartographic presentation, this Jewish tribe is envisioned in more than one site, indicating a coexistence of different interpretations of this legendary people: in addition to their new placement in the Red Sea, their traditional position in the Caucasus Mountains is identified as the empire of Gog and Magog by a figure wearing a Jewish hat. While efforts to harmonize the Red Jews with the changing ethnographic discourse fostered additional schema for interpreting their name and appearance, these novel readings naturally did not replace older conceptions of physiognomy and color symbolism at once. In the long run, however, akin to the endeavors to recast the Red Jews' role vis-à-vis the Turkish threat, these adaptive perspectives seem to have contributed to the destabilization of the myth. This argument is strengthened by Surekha Davies's findings that in the seventeenth century, maps began to become impractical as an epistemological format to understand human diversity. In the face of the giddy explosion of new information on faraway places, peoples, and cultures, the straightforward representation of ethnographic and geographical knowledge at a glance, which had made this genre so attractive, became almost impossible.[143] As cartography was reshaped by Renaissance scholarship and the exploration of the world, certain legendary peoples ultimately disappeared from maps in the course of the early modern period. While Gog and Magog continued to appear on maps throughout the seventeenth century, the Red Jews made their last cartographic appearance as *iudei clausi* in the 1530s.[144]

For centuries, the Red Jews, as an idiom and an image, had served as a medium for synthesizing their menacing meaning, offering a simplified way for German Christians to codify the place of Jews in their society. As their role and physical depiction changed amid early modern dynamics, however, the term "Red Jews" lost its relevance. When the Red Jews could be both friend and foe, a red-haired people from beyond the Sambatyon River and black-skinned Jews living in the Red Sea, this multiplicity of functions and colors coexisted and competed. The characteristics of this nation became so flexible and, at times, contradictory that they were too fuzzy and arbitrary to be unambiguously expressed by their imagined redness. Folk narratives are told as long as they remain meaningful.[145] The adjustments of the Red Jews that modified their image to changing historical and cultural tides obviously effectuated quite the contrary, and consequently the myth eventually fell out of favor.

## Reformation Iconoclasm

This phenomenon of redefinition and eventual disappearance of the myth of the Red Jews may have been furthered by changes in narrative tastes in the age of the Reformation. Gow has suggested that the biblicism of the Reformation was a catalyst for the waning interest in the Red Jews in German culture. He argues that this fresh commitment to studying the Bible affected popular beliefs and thus contributed to the disappearance of the Red Jews, who are not mentioned in Scripture (in contrast to apocalyptic figures that originate in the Bible, such as Gog and Magog, whose presence persisted).[146] We have seen that reformers—from Luther and Jonas, through Philipp Melanchthon to Johannes Brenz of Württemberg—regularly linked the Red Jews to their biblical parallel, Gog and Magog, and the contemporary

Turks, as the encroaching apocalyptic enemy. My understanding of the role of the Reformation differs somewhat from Gow's biblical focus: I posit that Reformation iconoclasm, more specifically, impacted the Red Jews' legend.

Iconoclasm was central to Reformation thought. It was related to a broad transformation in visual experience during the early modern period, albeit reviving an earlier Christian skepticism toward visual symbols in religious life.[147] In late medieval piety, the sense of sight had become a vital means for direct engagement with the divine, as exemplified by viewing the sacramental host in mass as the body of Christ; veneration of sacred images, icons, and relics; and the didactic use of imagery to educate and spiritually elevate the laity. Such visual forms and rites were dismissed as mere illusion by the Reformation's leading thinkers. Reformers such as Luther and Melanchthon directed the religious emphasis away from sight and stressed the centrality of hearing the word of God as a means to awaken faith—*fides ex auditu*. Although confessional positions in the debate over the power of sight varied, certain shared approaches were evident. While Swiss Calvinism dismissed sight as superstitious "eye-service" in the old Church, German Lutheranism was less strictly iconophobic despite its similar emphasis on the literal word of the Bible, especially through homilies. Luther famously called for "put[ting] your eyes in your ears."[148]

Even as Protestant intellectuals devalued the place of the senses for religious belief, Reformation-era religious practice often maintained forms of piety that stimulated the sensorium.[149] And yet, the trend toward demystifying the visual elements of religious experience during the Reformation had a sweeping impact on religious life and the praxis of piety. It affected not only iconography, worship, and devotion but also literature, from the simplest to the most sophisticated texts. Thus, in liturgical dramas, the didactic emphasis went from *compassio* to *moralisatio*, from a sacramental show to preaching the salutary word. The biblical plays of the Reformation schooled their audiences in theological doctrine through rational perception and memorization. By contrast, pre-Reformation drama sought to enhance the viewers' affective participation through emotionalization. For example, to evoke compassion, the Frankfurt Passion play intensified the visual display of Jesus's agony and the detailed articulation of fierce violence in a monologue, both intended to activate the imagination. Post-Reformation plays abandoned this visual emphasis and placed trust in auditory engagement, comparable to sermons in church.[150]

I suggest that this revaluation of sight may similarly have lessened the popularity of the myth of the Red Jews, at least as a medium of religious instruction. Protestant voices would have advocated the power of the word over the use of visual stimuli to convey a message; depicting the Ten Tribes in provocative coloring may have been deemed passé as a communicative tool.[151] Indeed the reformers' use of the Red Jews suggests an effort to downplay sight: Luther, Jonas, and Melanchthon stress that the Red Jews did not exist in their day anymore. However, since these theologians were keenly aware of their potent symbolism that remained entrenched in German folklore, they transferred the term "Red Jews" to a metaphor for the Turkish menace that would be readily received. Jonas asserts that the Turks were symbolically referred to as "Red Jews" solely due to their purportedly common character traits and the alleged similarities in their religious rites, including circumcision.[152] In this interpretative framework, the red hair, red skin, and red clothing that had been the Red Jews' signature feature were no longer pivotal.

The cultural developments that I have reviewed here eventually reduced the Red Jews to a figure of speech. "Red Jews" became a phrase that symbolically referred to the Turks or to their home by the Red Sea. After three centuries as a mythical people whose potency had been inextricably bound to their palpable visual impact, their physical redness faded into the realm of allegory. These changes in the perception and use of the fabled Red Jews' coloration thereby effectively eroded their popularity. In other words, by the early seventeenth century, Christians no longer had a clear view of the Red Jews.

The new political, scientific, and theological considerations would have spread among readers top-down and gradually led to the decline of what had been a ubiquitous Red Jews trope across many different genres. The textual record indicates that this legend ceased to be compelling for the majority of Christian authors in Germany around 1600. The use in convert sources is indicative: texts written by converted Jews in the sixteenth century do not explain the term, since they wrote in German for a Christian audience and were obviously aware of the idiom's currency among Christians. Later convert authors, by contrast, felt the need to clarify that this peculiar term denoted the Ten Tribes beyond the Sambatyon.[153] German references to the Red Jews in the seventeenth and eighteenth centuries are in fact found exclusively in convert sources. While these texts point to a continued, albeit limited, interest in the topic among Christians, above all they reflect a shift in the Red Jews' popularity from the Christian into the Jewish sphere.

As both a linguistic expression and a literary motif, the Red Jews took root in late medieval German vernacular culture as well as in Yiddish terminology in a distinct Jewish variant. Familiarity with this fictitious Jewish people permeated religious and cultural boundaries to such an extent that versions of this vernacular legend were shared among Jews and Christians in the German- and Yiddish-speaking lands of central and eastern Europe, even as its message was fiercely contested. As the Red Jews were receding from Christian awareness, their tale was flourishing in the early modern Yiddish world. The synchronous decline of the Red Jews in German society and the ascendant value of this reappropriated phrase and its affiliated myth in Yiddish during the sixteenth century may be related: as German speakers gradually gave up strict control over the significance of this source image, the persona of the Red Jew became freely available for Yiddish speakers to recycle and redesign. Perhaps Christian awareness of the enlivened successful Jewish reappropriation of the Red Jews accelerated their evanescence from that sphere.[154] The image of this people was indeed gaining valence, visibility, and ever more versatility in Yiddish culture. In the next chapter, we will consider how Jewish writers and readers translated the myth of the Red Jews into their own visual language and upended its German counterpart amid the European visual crisis.

# Chapter 2

# Reclaiming Red
## The Red Jews in Early Modern Yiddish

> How many nations are there in the world who think that the features of the Jew are disfigured and unlike those of other men, and ask whether a Jew has a mouth or an eye!
> —Abraham ibn Ezra, *Commentary on Isaiah*

> There are some obvious characteristics of the bodies we see, which are not visible to all, but only to those who have sharp-sighted eyes in their mind.
> —Philo, *De Josepho*

Centuries after the magnificent stained-glass windows in St. Mary's Church in Frankfurt an der Oder had been crafted, perhaps by dint of historical fortune, a native of that city who was born a Jew but is better remembered as Friedrich Albrecht Augusti, the name he adopted upon conversion to Christianity, published a German booklet on the mysteries of the Red Jews beyond the Sambatyon River. Augusti's modest tract, published in 1748, offers a glimpse into the image of this apocalyptic people among contemporaneous German Jews. In stark contrast to the scenario prominently displayed in the windows of the main church of his birthplace, which depicts the Red Jews forming an alliance with the Antichrist, Augusti revealed the Jewish view that they would play a crucial role in paving the way for the Messiah.[1] The prospect that a force of red-faced Jewish warriors in red robes was waiting, somewhere in the distant reaches of the earth, to usher in redemption from Christian dominion was as reassuring for Jews as it was frightening for St. Mary's congregation.

Much like other Jewish converts to Christianity, Augusti disclosed aspects of Jewish teachings to his new religious community as erroneous beliefs, while conveying the dissonance between these two entangled interpretations of a shared myth. Another convert, Victor von Carben, attests in 1508 that his former coreligionists, young and old alike, awaited "the mighty Red Jews" (*die rodten Juden vnnd starcken*).[2] After his own conversion, Antonius Margaritha, son of the chief rabbi of Regensburg, reports in his ethnographic writing on contemporaneous Jewish belief and practice from 1530 that Ashkenazic Jews firmly believed that "the Red Jews" would someday deliver them.[3] Later compositions by converts and compilations of Christian polemics confirm that "the Red Jews" as a term and a myth continued to have currency among Ashkenazic Jews throughout the early modern period.[4] These sources even mention a peculiar variant anticipating that the Messiah will originate from the realm of the Red Jews. According to one such account, which parallels the talmudic dictum noting that the Messiah sits before the gates of Rome, the Red Jews were holding the redeemer captive, bound in iron chains, until the divinely appointed time when he would cross the Sambatyon River to liberate the people of Israel.[5]

It is no coincidence that Augusti's critique of the Jews' persistent belief in the Red Jews is replete with visual language. Not only did he reject this tale as a fabrication that kept his former coreligionists under a spell of blindness, but he dedicated himself to unmasking this deception before the eyes of Christians. He found fraudulent evidence in the form of flasks purportedly containing waters from the Sambatyon that swirled with red sand. Augusti claimed that he beheld these precious vessels during his childhood, where they were mounted beside the Torah ark, the place of greatest honor, in the synagogues of Prague and Lviv, among others. He described the cantor unveiling the flask each Friday evening to the awestruck community, which witnessed its waters calm as the hymn *Lekhah dodi* (Come my beloved) was sung to welcome the Sabbath, just as the current of the Sambatyon River itself was said to be quieted at sunset, like a clock that marked the arrival of the day of rest. Augusti accused rabbis and cantors of conspiring against common folk by staging this ridiculous illusion. He further claimed that a fellow convert, Christoph Wallich (formerly Anshel Moses) of Worms, told him how, as a cantor in the eminent Jewish community of Frankfurt am Main, he controlled the actions of those waters with a wire from the lectern.[6]

In this composition, Augusti, at the time a Lutheran pastor in Eschenbergen (near Gotha), might have drawn from Protestant discussions of visual deception to bolster the classic topos of the blind Jew in Christian polemic. As discussed in the previous chapter, reformers attributed pre-Reformation failures of religiosity to a visually "idolatrous" Catholic culture that transferred divine qualities onto objects and decried "the false miracles of the old Church" as spurious claims of authenticity.[7] Perhaps Augusti applied this anti-Catholic critique to his own condemnation of the myth of the Red Jews, which, in its Yiddish version, centers on visual illusions that ostensibly lead Christians to err.

Indeed, the deceptive nature of sight is the principal motif that saturates the Yiddish fable of the Red Jews. Against the backdrop of the European crisis of vision, we will see that early modern Jews were also responding to notions of visual intelligibility that were "unsettling the relation between what was seen and what was known."[8] This chapter explores the unique ways that Ashkenazic Jews approached the religious, cultural, scientific, social, and political contexts of visual experience when sensory veracity was threatened by heightened attention to the nature of miracles and dreams, the prevalence of illusions in magic, and the workings of demons and spirits. Through the figure of the Red Jews, Yiddish authors and readers productively harnessed the constructed nature of visual perception for their own purposes, affirming the well-established symbolism of the color red that had informed the Christian myth, while negating its significance and unmasking it as an optical falsehood.

The Yiddish reappropriation of the Red Jews represents a visual intervention by an oppressed minority. Rather than accepting the anti-Jewish value of this image in German culture, early modern Yiddish speakers reinterpreted the term "Red Jews." With their proliferation in the Jewish vernacular, the traits of the Red Jews were dramatically transformed and instilled with distinctive Jewish meaning upon emerging from visual competition with their Christian parallel. While the red symbolism of the Christian myth signified subjugation, I argue that the Yiddish interpretation of the color reclaimed visual autonomy. Vision has often been critiqued for being "bound up with coercion, power, and oppression," because one who possesses sovereign sight retains power.[9] Michel Foucault's concept of "panopticism" incisively describes the power structures inherent in vision, evoking the architectural structure of the panopticon (a circular prison whose inmates may be watched at all times by guards stationed in its rotunda, yet they cannot tell when they are actually being surveilled) as a metaphor for the system of control and the associated mechanisms of social discipline that became manifest in the societies of the eighteenth century.[10] Early modern political systems in fact capitalized on iconographic representations that visually reinforced their claims to absolute authority.[11] Controlling the significance of shared language and imagery has equally broad social and cultural implications for Jewish-Christian relations.

## The Emergence of the Red Jews in Yiddish

As in German, "Red Jews" in Old Yiddish (רוטי יודן, *rote yudn*) referred to the familiar Ten Lost Tribes of Israel who dwelled beyond the Sambatyon River. A sixteenth-century Yiddish text confirms the claim of the converts mentioned above: Ashkenazic Jews were confident that "when the exile will come to an end, they will also come to our aid."[12] This mighty army of the Lost Tribes would be instrumental in preparing for the Messiah and freeing Israel from the yoke of life under Christendom.[13] Unlike the surviving illustrations of Red Jews from Christian culture, we have no equivalent Jewish illuminations.[14] Several textual sources, however, suggest that Jews envisioned the Red Jews with some of the same ruddy features that characterized the Christian version. For instance, in his booklet on the Red Jews, Augusti describes "the red and lively color of their faces and their exquisite purple clothes."[15] It is hardly coincidental that the Red Jews, as presented in St. Mary's Church, in the city of his youth, are portrayed with red complexions and red garb. Although Jews may not have been familiar with their depiction in Christian literary traditions, they surely witnessed the pictorial renderings of the narratives in local church windows.[16]

By the early modern period, the Red Jews had become a pervasive element of a shared Jewish-Christian culture in Germany. Despite the absence of firsthand evidence that Yiddish speakers adopted the phrase "Red Jews" in the late Middle Ages, it seems to have been incorporated into Yiddish around the time it was coined in the majority vernacular during the late thirteenth century. While Yiddish had become the universally spoken language of Ashkenazic Jewry by that period (and probably much earlier), a significant volume of Yiddish texts has only been transmitted from the fifteenth century, and especially the sixteenth century, onward. The first Yiddish writings about the Red Jews discussed here are dated to the late sixteenth century. However, the earliest documentation for Jewish use of this phrase is in the above-cited sources by converts, authored early in that century, which indicates that Red Jews had already become a common expression for the Ten Lost Tribes in Yiddish.[17] By the sixteenth century, the association of the Ten Tribes with the Red Jews was in fact so firmly anchored in Yiddish that, for speakers of the Ashkenazic vernacular, these two terms had become interchangeable: for example, Margaritha uses them as synonyms. His account signals that the expression "Red Jews" had been part and parcel of Jewish parlance long enough that knowledge of its provenance had been lost; Margaritha muses why Ashkenazic Jews refer to the Ten Tribes with this particular phrase.[18] Typically, original Yiddish material ascribes the signature features of their red counterparts to the Ten Tribes, even in the absence of the phrase "Red Jews."[19]

The textual transmission of the oldest known Jewish tale about the Red Jews, which ultimately became its most widespread and enduring version, corroborates the surmised medieval Yiddish adoption of the Red Jews: namely, the legend referred to by scholars as *Ma'aseh Akdamut* (The Story of *Akdamut*), which describes the composition of the Aramaic piyyut *Akdamut Milin* (An introduction of words).[20] The dating of the Yiddish *Akdamut* story, the main text analyzed in this chapter, is tricky. The earliest surviving version, which also documents the earliest Yiddish use of the term "Red Jews," is preserved in a Yiddish manuscript collection of edifying narratives that was written in the late sixteenth century (after 1579).[21] Approximately two decades earlier, the story had appeared in print in Cremona (ca. 1560) under the title *Megiles Reb Meyer* (The scroll of Rabbi Meir)—this title honors its hero and author of the piyyut, Meir b. Isaac Shatz of Worms, a famous eleventh-century composer of liturgical poetry.[22] Although no copy of this edition has survived, its popularity is attested by the censor's list of all books owned by the Jews of Mantua in 1595, which details eight copies of *Megiles Reb Meyer* that were owned by five families.[23]

Typically, such folkloric material could have been transmitted orally for centuries before finding its way into writing, often first in Hebrew, included in commentary literature. When these tales entered written circulation independently, they were sometimes retranslated into Yiddish.[24] Indeed, the first known separate print of the *Akdamut* story that appeared in Cremona was a translation from Hebrew into Yiddish. The earliest written records of our tale were apparently composed in Hebrew and included in far older Ashkenazic prayer books, stemming from the Middle Ages.[25] Margaritha was probably referring to such prayer books ("gepet vnd gesang büchlin"), which purportedly recorded information about the Sambatyon.[26] Notwithstanding the previous Hebrew transmission of *Ma'aseh Akdamut*, according to extant sources, the idiosyncratic term "Red Jews" seems to have had no presence in Hebrew.[27] As in the Christian context, where this phrase was familiar to German speakers without having entered Latin or other European vernaculars, it was apparently unknown in Jewish languages other than Yiddish.

Due to their appearance in *Ma'aseh Akdamut* the Red Jews became the heroes of one of the most popular folktales in the early modern Yiddish world. During the seventeenth and eighteenth centuries, we know of up to six printed editions of *Ma'aseh Akdamut* that appeared under various titles.[28] The Red Jews became a frequent motif in Old Yiddish literature, appearing also in other narratives, as discussed in Chapter 3. By comparison, Yiddish iterations of Hebrew lore about the Ten Tribes do not usually transform them into Red Jews, whether literally or indirectly. Yiddish translations from earlier Hebrew sources generally follow the vocabulary of the Hebrew original. This pattern is evidenced in Yiddish renderings of biblical prophecies and prayers for their return,[29] as well as in accounts by medieval travelers who would routinely journey to the Sambatyon, bringing back extraordinary reports of the tribes on its far shore. These travelogues regularly appeared in print from the fifteenth century onward (in Hebrew and translated into Yiddish and other European languages) and enjoyed great popularity among European readers, Jewish and Christian alike. Two eighteenth-century Yiddish adaptions of the account of Eldad ha-Dani retain the phrase "Ten Tribes."[30] The Yiddish printing of the travelogue by Benjamin of Tudela (Amsterdam, 1691) includes "sons of [the] tribes" (בני שבטים).[31]

## The Eye in the Text

The Yiddish reappropriation of the Red Jews draws on a shared physiognomic color symbolism that linked a red body to negative attributes, especially red hair to duplicity. Parallel to the wave of interest in physiognomy throughout late medieval Europe, physiognomic discourse among Jews also ascribed pejorative significance to red coloration.[32] The Polish Jewish physician Tuvia ha-Kohen correlates a number of negative traits with those who have yellow bile and yellow or reddish skin in his medical-scientific compendium *Ma'aseh Toviyyah* (The work of Tuvia; first printed in Venice, 1708). He lists various manifestations of this *complexio*, such as the tendency to be irritable and short-tempered, bellicose and vengeful, and hold grudges like a snake. Moreover, this coloration signifies people who do not keep their word, love lies, and are impostors and troublemakers.[33] These medical assessments also influenced exegesis: the renowned Isaac Abravanel cited humoral theory to explain the difference between Esau and Jacob in his commentary on the Pentateuch (Venice, 1579): Esau's redness showed his hot blood and angry temperament. Jacob's nature was opposite in disposition because he was not red complexioned but rather white, the sign of a perfect character.[34]

Analogous to German (and other European) folk cultures, Jewish lore reckoned redheads to be malicious and devious. A rare example from Jewish art that depicts Esau with a red beard is presented in the fourteenth-century Sephardic Sarajevo Haggadah.[35] In his fifteenth-century *Sefer Toldot Adam* (A book on the history of man), also known as *Sefer Ḥokhmat ha-Parẓuf* (A book on the wisdom of the face), which was widespread in Hebrew and Yiddish during the early modern period, Moses b. Elijah Galina writes that redheads are jealous, irascible, and deceptive.[36] Jacob b. Mordecai of Fulda, in *Shoshanat Ya'acov* (Rose of Jacob; Amsterdam, 1706), a guide to palmistry and the so-called wisdom of the face, states: "Red hair [signifies]: a jealous person, a fraud, an irritable person, one whose speech and tongue are no good."[37] These stereotypes persisted in Yiddish daily language usage, as documented in anthologies of sayings that were collected from speakers of the Ashkenazic vernacular in eastern Europe during the nineteenth and twentieth centuries: "A redhead (*a royter*, lit. "a red one") is an impostor" (אַ רױטער איז אַ רמאי) and "Beware of redheads" (פֿאַר אַ רױטען זאָל מען זיך היטען).[38] In light of corresponding early modern evidence cited above, Yiddish proverbs such as these may very well be much older.[39]

Much as Christian and Jewish sayings warn that redheads should not be trusted, so too the Yiddish myth of the Red Jews affirms that red can be misleading. This color could disguise its bearer's true qualities to the beholder's physical eye. Yiddish stories of the Red Jews strategically guide readers to picture the redness of their heroes from a particular vantage point, positioning them to grasp the intended significance of red as a color and symbol. Among these Jewish narratives, *Ma'aseh Akdamut* is particularly saturated with "eye-play" and verbal stimuli that relate to sight. With frequent occurrences of the verb "to see" (זעהן in Yiddish), its language relies heavily on metaphors that involve eyes and eyesight, and its plot centers on vision and illusion, what is easily seen and what is not. The story provides instructions to accompany its audience's imaginary journey that resemble the directions in a film script, offering an animated narrative for the mind's eye that is painted with words.⁴⁰

*Ma'aseh Akdamut* depicts a vicious Christian sorcerer—a monk who is a master of the dark arts (in the manuscript version, he is called a "black monk") and a notorious hater of Jews—who exercises his powers to murder his declared enemies by the thousands. We discover that the monk murders every Jew that he encounters; after just a blow or light flick in passing, or when he simply touches him, a Jew would die upon returning home that same day. When the Jews appeal to the authorities for protection, the monk proposes a deal: he will never harm a Jew again if, within one year, the Jews bring a representative whose skills can best his in a magical contest. Should the Jews fail, the sorcerer will destroy them all.⁴¹

The Jews desperately begin to pray for help. One day, a prophetic dream simultaneously appears to several pious Jews throughout the land. In this dream, a deep darkness enfolds the world. Suddenly, a bright star pierces that darkness, revealing a huge bear and a young goat embattled with one other. Their struggle concludes with the kid slaying the bear. This nocturnal sequence is paradigmatic of the emphasis on sight in *Ma'aseh Akdamut*, reflecting "the tendency of the visionary tradition to posit a higher sight of the seer, who is able to discern a truth denied to normal vision. Here the so-called third eye of the soul is invoked to compensate for the imperfections of the two physical eyes."⁴² When the dreamers are concerned that their dream may be discredited as a mere fantasy, a dream interpreter (*ba'al ḥalomot*, lit. master of dreams) comes to them again during the day to encourage them to search for a miracle worker who might compete with the dreaded magician. Their quest extends far and wide but is unsuccessful. With advice from the dream interpreter, the imperiled Jews eventually recognize that only a Red Jew beyond the Sambatyon could successfully confront the monk: "The darkness is the monk who brings darkness upon the people of Israel. And the star means that it will once again become light, help will be found. The kid is a small Jew who will help you and the bear is the mighty monk, who will be killed."⁴³ This little Jew would be found among the Red Jews, who were famed as *ba'alei shemot* (masters of the [divine] names), wonder workers who could access the hidden powers of God.⁴⁴

Finally, the Jews choose Meir Shatz of Worms as an envoy to the Red Jews. Accompanied by three messengers, Rabbi Meir departs from his home in the Rhineland to enlist aid from the Red Jews, who agree to dispatch one from their ranks to compete in the contest. To commemorate this event, Meir Shatz composes his best-known hymn, *Akdamut Milin*, that concludes by depicting the splendor of Israel's salvation in messianic times. He requests that his Rhenish congregation recite this auspicious poem in synagogue on the first day of Shavuot as an annual celebration of the anticipated victory over their nefarious adversary, which was scheduled to take place on the eve of that festival.[45] Meir's companions, however, are overcome with fear when they first behold the Red Jew who has been selected, for they are dubious that he could withstand the monk. Contrary to everyone's expectations, the Red Jew in *Ma'aseh Akdamut* is described as an outwardly weak character from the first mention: This *rot yudlan* (רוט יודלן, little Red Jew), as he is called in the story, is "old and lame."[46] In his mind's eye, the reader/listener would picture a short, elderly man with an uneven gait. Given his limp, the messengers assume that he would even need help on the way back to their country, especially since the fateful contest was fast approaching. Unexpectedly, the Red Jew assumes the lead and, using his supernatural powers, he takes them on a shortcut (*kefizat ha-derekh*, path jumping) that brings their party home in two days.[47]

At the climax of the story, the Red Jew duels with the Christian sorcerer. In yet another visual play, readers are subtly invited to view this scene, which accounts for a third of the story, through the eyes of the spectators who convened for the magical contest: when the Jewish champion from beyond the Sambatyon steps forward, the audience, like the messengers before, doubts his potential as a worthy opponent for the mighty Christian sorcerer who is allied with the devil and is unable to envision him as triumphant.[48] The magician too skeptically asks if the Jews are mocking him by presenting this contender: "Look how the Jews are making a mockery of me! With what have they presented me? A small shaking little man with whom to do magic?"[49]

At first, the odds thus look promising for the self-assured favorite: the monk hurls a heavy steel post, which, upon landing, penetrates deep into the ground before the sovereign's throne, then he bids his adversary to extract it. Sardonically, the little Red Jew retorts: "You should not have thrown it so deep in the earth. How can I possibly take it out again?" But the tide turns quickly. After calling out to the spectators, "See, beloved brothers, Jews and non-Jews, excuse the comparison, and pagans, watch carefully," the little Red Jew effortlessly raises the embedded pole with his pinky. He then tosses it into the sky—so high that it is barely visible—and goads the monk to retrieve it. Otherwise, "everyone will see that your head will be stuck on the pole today and I will drive it into the desert where no one may set foot." The monk ignores this challenge and conjures two millstones, which he then crumbles with his hands "just as one grinds flour or stones to bits of lime and chalk" in an attempt to lure the Red Jew's attention from the steel pole floating high above them.[50] For a brief moment, the sorcerer seems to have succeeded when the Red Jew feigns awe. But the little Red Jew then creates a wind that blows with such force that it reconstitutes the crumbled pieces and, adding more material, he forms two bigger millstones, which he too grinds to dust in his bare hands. He also performs this feat effortlessly. Another gust of wind then reassembles the millstones and whisks them up to the steel post, which the little Red Jew has not forgotten. The monk is clearly incapable of reaching it, making him a laughingstock for all to behold.[51]

The next round involves fire. The little Red Jew sarcastically asks how much longer he must engage with a defenseless opponent, but he amicably agrees to continue a while longer. He offers the monk a choice between conjuring something or spiriting it off. The monk opts for the latter. The little Red Jew then causes fire to rain from the heavens, which quickly covers the ground but, miraculously, does not burn any foliage. The monk produces a spring of water to extinguish the fire but finds that, rather than quenching the flames, the water fuels them with such force that they rise to the heavens to incinerate the demons that had been the force behind his magic. Knowing that he is a mere mortal without these unseen partners, the monk begins to plead for his life and swears to the Red Jew that he will be his servant forevermore. "I will not take your life," the Red Jew declares, "although you killed so many of my brothers." He then shifts his attention from the monk to the audience: "See what people use to make fire—with that I will extinguish it while the monk could not extinguish it with water."[52] With a puff of air, he sends the fire back into the sky, so nothing but steam and smoke remain.

In the fourth and final event of this magical contest, once again, the little Red Jew offers the monk a choice: pointing to a gigantic tree that had been growing there since Noah's generation, he asks whether the monk would prefer to start by bending its massive trunk or to hold it afterward. The monk begins whining and moaning; indeed, without his demonic allies, he has no magical powers. This display provokes his adversary to taunt him: "Why are you taking your time and making these people here wait?"[53] The monk, we learn, is in no laughing mood (in contrast, we might note, to the amused reader); wishing that he were already dead, he has no choice but to opt for keeping the tree down, knowing this to be impossible without aid from the demons. At the grand finale of the magical contest, the reader is repeatedly invited to join the audience metaphorically and observe what transpires there: "Before everyone's eyes," the little Red Jew bends the enormous tree like a twig. When the monk, feeling uneasy, refuses to step forward to hold the tree down, the Red Jew exclaims: "Noble king and all the lords, see what a daring magician this is!" Shamed and terrified, the monk finally approaches the tree as the little Red Jew yells: "See if he holds it—then I will let go!"[54] Helpless, this formerly fearsome magician is killed when the tree snaps upright. Depending on the version, his head is knocked off or bursts open. The force of that impact catapults the monk's body into the air, where he is impaled by the steel pole between the two millstones, which propel him to a far-off desert, exactly as the little Red Jew had predicted.[55]

The reliability of sight is challenged in this story because, despite his physical appearance, the little Red Jew emerges victorious from the series of four magical tasks, for what you see is not always what you get. Significantly, the decisive tournament is staged in an arena—a panopticon—where spectators watch from all sides. The entire audience, comprised of both Jews and Christians, would have seen an ill-equipped combatant for the champion as he entered the scene. Ironically, Christian spectators should have enjoyed a commanding view of this event, since they were watching from the tribune, whereas the Jewish audience was standing at ground level.[56] The story's positive resolution, however, belies the expectations of this oppressive and purportedly superior Christian gaze. Despite their privileged position, these Christians misunderstand what they see—just like the subordinated Jews.

*Ma'aseh Akdamut* offers a sophisticated reclaiming of vision on behalf of the Jews and sets out to impart correct sight to its Jewish audience. By depicting Christians as dependent on superficial vision and oblivious to intrinsic truths, the tale mirrors and refutes the relentless Christian topos that Jewish eyes are shrouded by blindness. Indeed, in premodern Europe, along with other forms of physical disability, impaired sight was perceived as a spiritual handicap and its restoration as a metaphor for redemption.[57] Analogous to the allegedly misshapen and ailing Jewish body, Christian polemics asserted that this presumed blindness rendered Jews' sinful state outwardly visible, much as the wizened and feeble Red Jew in *Ma'aseh Akdamut* would have appeared to Christian eyes. Jewish caricatures in medieval Christian art often "rehearsed the Jew's role as original and eternal blind witness to Christian truth, and helped its viewer explore that truth," as Sara Lipton has aptly demonstrated.[58] Just as these works of art present vision and religious knowledge from a Christian perspective, *Ma'aseh Akdamut* demonstrates the power of the little Red Jew. Now let us consider what the Yiddish eye perceived when it imagined this tale of a wizard battle.

## Teaching Proper Sight to the Yiddish Eye

The Red Jews reminded the Jews of Ashkenaz of their promised future, when the oppressed would triumph over their persecutors. However, the Red Jew called to assist is not the prototypical hero that anyone familiar with Jewish or Christian images of the Ten Tribes would have expected. The Red Jews were known in both German and Yiddish as a nation of formidable warriors. Whereas in early modern Yiddish literature they are collectively called *rote yudn* (Red Jews) without a diminutive form,[59] in *Ma'aseh Akdamut*, the red savior is referred to as a little Red Jew. He is presented as a frail figure, ostensibly impeded by old age and physical disability. It reads as if Jeremiah's prophecy of an ingathering of the remnant of Israel has been grafted onto this Yiddish story: "I will bring them in from the northland, Gather them from the ends of the earth—The blind and the lame among them" (Jer. 31:8).

The tale of a physically impaired savior from beyond the Sambatyon has no precursor in medieval Hebrew literature nor in German sources; this theme is a uniquely Yiddish innovation. The hero who single-handedly defeats a mighty foe, however, has a precedent in the Eldad the Danite literature. Eldad ha-Dani's account was instrumental in sealing the image of the Ten Tribes as proud heroes and brave fighters from an invincible kingdom in the Middle Ages. He reports on the tribes' impressive cavalry and infantry that number in the tens of thousands and were constantly at war with other distant nations. Depending on the version, Eldad boasts that one warrior from the tribe of Ephraim or Manasseh could overcome one hundred or even one thousand enemies.[60] Whereas later echoes of this motif, which evokes Leviticus 26:8 and Deuteronomy 32:30, in Hebrew and Yiddish accounts consistently emphasize the prowess of the Ten Tribes,[61] the Yiddish Red Jews tradition foregrounds the apparent disadvantages of their singular representative. Rather than being portrayed as a warrior capable of subduing a multitude, the Yiddish version calls attention to its hero's limitations: he is simply a little Red Jew.

As this outwardly fragile fellow promises Jewish survival, the Yiddish legend compellingly illustrates the theme of the weak conquering the mighty that is common in international folklore.⁶² In Jewish lore, this asymmetrical balance of power is epitomized by the famous biblical encounter between young David and the Philistine giant Goliath.⁶³ In its reformulation of the Christian tale of the Red Jews, the Yiddish version utilizes the structure of David versus Goliath. The imposing Christian monk is cast in the role of Goliath, who challenged the Israelites to send one of their fighters to battle with him. The little Red Jew mirrors David, the shepherd boy who appears inferior to his enemy in every respect, setting the stage for a seemingly lopsided competition. The popular Yiddish *Shmuel-Bukh*, the late medieval biblical epic based on the Book of Samuel, emphasizes David's petite physique (especially in comparison to Goliath) by calling him "the little one." In a striking parallel, David in the *Shmuel-Bukh* and the little Red Jew in *Ma'aseh Akdamut* are referred to as "small little dwarf" (קליינש ווילבטעליין) and "small little man" (קליין מענכין, קליין מענדליין), respectively, epithets that do not occur in the biblical text.⁶⁴ Another battle scene in the *Shmuel-Bukh*, in which David spars with another giant named Goliath and which has no clear model in the original biblical text, even involves motifs reminiscent of *Ma'aseh Akdamut*: a pole that is broken to pieces like a willow twig.⁶⁵ Despite the little Red Jew's physical disadvantages, Davidic lineage assures his victory in this struggle. He achieves the putatively impossible task of overpowering a magician in his own discipline, echoing David, who defeated the heavily armed Goliath with a stone and his slingshot.⁶⁶

The motif of a diminutive hero who fights a mighty magician also appears in *Viduvilt*, another well-known late medieval (likely fifteenth-century) Jewish chivalric romance, a Yiddish adaptation of the Middle High German *Wigalois*.⁶⁷ In *Viduvilt*, a lady from a distant land arrives at King Arthur's court to plead for help to liberate her country from the giant that has overthrown its leadership. Armed with sorcery, this giant killed the king and claimed his dominion but the castle, where the queen and the princess are held captive, so far resists his spell. The unmistakable parallels to the biblical legend of Goliath distinguish the Yiddish version from its German model. Whereas Wigalois is the first to volunteer for this mission, Viduvilt only commits himself to this long and precarious journey after the Arthurian knights all react to her account with fear. As the youngest knight, Viduvilt is affronted by his elders' cowardice and feels obligated to uphold his king's honor, much like David, who steps forward after hearing Goliath taunt the armies of the God of Israel and witnessing Saul's warriors quake with fear before the giant Philistine.[68] Viduvilt's preparation for battle also nods to biblical lore. Where the German tale elaborates on how Wigalois dons his knightly armor, the Yiddish narrative focuses on the young knight's request for a helmet that is small enough to fit him. This is reminiscent of David's inability to move in battle garb that was made for an adult rather than his teenage stature.[69]

The Yiddish romance unfolds with an unsurprising plot: as in the German version, King Arthur and the female envoy initially doubt the abilities of this sixteen-year-old lad due to his youth and lack of experience. This sentiment is dramatically amplified in the Yiddish version, replete with a scene where the youth's father offers to accompany his son for protection, which the future hero declines; the German romance includes no such scenario.[70] Friends and enemies alike repeatedly attempt to dissuade him from this quest; they advise him to return home throughout his journey, even just before he confronts his final opponent.[71] Time and again, following the logic of the biblical account and with greater emphasis than the German version, his youth is the locus of criticism. First, the ambassador compares Viduvilt to "a babbler, a child, who—even with seeing eyes—is blind"; later, one of his gallant opponents initially considers it improper to fight a youngster, but he would rather give him "a whipping on his behind."[72] Similarly, throughout the Yiddish rendering of the Book of Samuel, David is consistently referred to as a boy. When Goliath mocks David, he even calls him an unweaned child.[73] Nevertheless, the reader follows Viduvilt on the road and witnesses his successes against knights, giants and their infuriated mothers, as well as dragons and other malicious creatures, until his courageous victory is rewarded with marriage to the beautiful princess whom he liberated. It becomes evident that all have underestimated this unexpected hero. In the outset of his adventures, he told the female emissary who dismissed his offer to rescue her land: "Who knows how weak I may be." As the story unfolds, the lord of a castle remarks: "I considered you a child. I may well have been blind."[74] That insight encapsulates the message of this tale: it was not Viduvilt who misjudged his abilities but everyone else who underestimated him.

The Yiddish reevaluation of the Red Jews that revolves around the smallness of their hero is anchored in the association of David with the color red. In the biblical source, David's ruddy complexion signals his purported weakness. In our Yiddish myth, the redness of the Red Jews is thus imbued with new vitality, for this trait is not derived from Edom, as in the Christian identification, but from the valiant David. The Bible attributes redness to two protagonists, Esau and David, who are each described as *admoni*. This term is noteworthy for appearing only three times in Scripture and offering one of the rare physiognomic descriptors of dramatis personae in the Hebrew Bible, but also for serving as an essential plot device. Indeed, "the *adom* element and its derivatives form an important element of the etiological story of Jacob vs. Esau, Israel vs. Edom," the biblical topoi that have informed Jewish-Christian relations for centuries.[75] The further appearances of *admoni* refer to the young David, with similar dramaturgical significance: when he was initially brought before Samuel, it is written, "he was ruddy-cheeked"; and his ruddiness is noted when he approaches Goliath. When David confronts Goliath, the Philistine can hardly believe his eyes upon seeing whom King Saul has sent into battle. He shows disdain toward his combatant, "for he was but a boy, ruddy and handsome."[76] By assuming that this handsome youngster was necessarily inexperienced, the Philistine felt assured of an easy victory when David approached.

Several Jewish Bible commentaries and midrashim address the redness that characterizes both David and Esau by comparing its antithetical reading for each of them.[77] *Midrash Rabbah* weighs the significance of this shared feature: when Samuel first saw David, he feared that this future king of Israel might be another Esau, mistaking David's ruddiness as a mark of brutal determination; however, God assured Samuel that David would reserve punishment for convicted transgressors.[78] Much as David's appearance initially fooled Samuel and Goliath, so too did the sorcerer and audience for the wizard contest in *Ma'aseh Akdamut* misjudge redness.[79] Rashi also contrasts Esau's redness, which is taken as a sign that he will spill blood,[80] to the ruddy good looks of David. In two passages, Rashi understands redness (*adom*, *admu*) together with white skin to define the physical beauty of a ruddy complexion (equated with *admoni*).[81] David Kimḥi similarly interprets David's ruddy appearance to indicate the handsome, not yet weathered face of a youth, in contrast to a warrior whose skin bears battle scars and signs of exposure to the elements year after year.[82] Both commentaries were available to Ashkenazic Jewry; an abridged vernacular translation of Rashi's commentary also appeared in a Yiddish edition of the liturgical Bible, first printed in 1560.[83]

Youthful beauty, a delicate physical stature, and external signs of weakness are qualities that stand in stark contrast to the gigantic and grotesque portrait of the Red Jews conjured in the Christian imagination. Christians too would have differentiated David's redness from red as associated with

Esau and the Red Jews. Jewish and Christian traditions both ascribe a decidedly positive character to King David, corroborating general European views of the body according to which, as a rule, a virtuous soul was thought to reside in an attractive body and ugliness signified a wicked character.[84] Accordingly, David is rarely depicted with red features in medieval Christian art, in contrast to maligned figures—including Jews, Judas, and Cain. It is David's beauty that plays an important role in iconographic renderings of this biblical story in Christian art, while Jewish illuminations emphasize his youth by depicting him without armor.[85]

Steeped in biblical color symbolism, Old Yiddish literature enlisted the contrasting interpretations of the redness that were interculturally associated with David and Esau to negate the features that Christian narratives ascribed to the Red Jews. The Yiddish tale restores its protagonists' standing as heroes by recasting the myth of the Red Jews according to the David versus Goliath trope. This reframing substitutes the Christian notion of the Red Jews as a force that would perish with the Antichrist at the time of Jesus's Second Coming with an emphasis on Davidic lineage, thus repositioning the Red Jews as messianic victors. This cycle of symbolism is completed by the Jewish tradition that David was born and died on Shavuot, the festival when Ashkenazic communities would recite *Akdamut Milin* in synagogue, as if to celebrate the little Red Jew as a *David redivivus* (new David).[86] The Yiddish tale of the Red Jews transformed a Christian nightmare into a Jewish salvation myth, reaffirming the traditional role of the Ten Tribes, which the Christian depiction of the Red Jews had distorted. The two groups observed the same legendary tribe with red features, but they interpreted its coloring differently.

## Visual Delusions

Teaching the Yiddish eye proper sight, *Ma'aseh Akdamut* attests to the primacy of vision. This sensualism rang familiar to its audience; the language of Torah and the rabbis is highly sensory and sight is central to traditional Jewish epistemology, as Yael Avrahami, Daniel Boyarin, and Rachel Rafael Neis have aptly demonstrated for Scripture and rabbinic literature, respectively.[87] Yet even as our Yiddish story underscores that sight is important for understanding the world, it also advises against unconditional reliance on this physical faculty, which is inevitably susceptible to error. This myth cautions that physical sight can be deceptive, and, therefore, the inner eye, which can perceive the imprint of the soul on the body, provides more trustworthy counsel. I argue that *Ma'aseh Akdamut* evokes both the traditional and new meanings of seeing, in particular when highlighting the shortcomings of absolute reliance on sensory perception. Visual illusions had become the subject of vigorous debate first during the thirteenth and fourteenth centuries and increasingly characterized early modern approaches to vision.[88] *Ma'aseh Akdamut* displays conversance with the tandem messages that encompassed the crisis of vision in early modern Europe, which was closely entwined with the empiricist approach to knowledge.

In the early modern period, firsthand experience and observation became ever more important factors in the fields of science and philosophy.[89] David Ruderman has shown that select Jewish intellectuals embraced empiricism and a firm reliance on the sensorium that paralleled the trends of the scientific revolution.[90] Although such support for these innovative methodologies was still a minority opinion, the primacy of sensory experience in cognition achieved strong currency among audiences that extended beyond the educated elite of early modern Jews and Christians alike. According to Ruderman, by the mid-seventeenth century, expanding traditional emphases, Jewish culture had generally become "fully attuned to seeing and hearing rather than cogitating."[91] J. H. Chajes, for instance, has examined a popular level of Jewish religious discourse that was shaped by early modern scientific theories of vision. He demonstrates that the concept of the evil eye had to be revised in response to Johannes Kepler's optics for, with the replacement of a haptic understanding of sight, the evil eye became a supernatural belief.[92]

Prominent Jewish thinkers emphasized empirical methods for describing natural phenomena without claiming that science could convey the comprehensive truths that were reserved for divine revelation. They deemed sight suspect for an additional reason that resembles the arguments of Christian philosophers and scientists: human investigation was curtailed by the unreliability of sensory perception for attaining veridical knowledge of the material world. Observation was vulnerable to the fallibility of the senses, which could yield errors, distortions, and illusions.[93] *Ma'aseh Akdamut* too expresses doubts about the reliability of sight. It focuses on the sensory illusions performed by magic and displays an awareness that the devil, the archetypal deceiver, could subvert vision and thereby manipulate cognition, echoing notions that were a major expression of the European visual crisis.[94]

*Ma'aseh Akdamut* begins by describing how the devil and his minions brought destructive magic to the world. A wheel of fortune was created, with seats for ten persons who sought to become disciples of this sorcery. The devil would select one of them to do with him whatever he wished, while he would tutor the remaining nine in his dark arts, ultimately to be dispatched into the world. These protégés, the reader is informed, have been covertly ruling the world from their castles and monasteries, with the most sinister and formidable in their ranks camouflaged as monks. The black monk of *Ma'aseh Akdamut* is one of those elect sorcerers who were schooled on the wheel of fortune.[95] He only appears to be a great magician in the first two rounds, however, when the demons who support him are manipulating the competition. As we have seen, this charade unravels once the little Red Jew eradicates the demons, thereby eliminating the monk's purported magical talents.

This depiction of visual illusion reads as a cautionary tale against the lure of illegitimate magic. Among early modern European Jewry, magic was ubiquitous in myriad forms. These practices, especially the invocation of divine names, but also appealing to angels and demons (permissible under certain conditions) for assistance, were often inseparable from Kabbalah, science, and medicine.[96] Such traditions could be traced to ancient lore, having been preserved by generations of rabbinical scholars, then augmented by medieval and early modern esoteric teachings and customs. This knowledge and its application were complemented by the popular magic of miracle healers and diviners, who prescribed remedies and exorcisms, charms and amulets. Nevertheless, Jews in this period were also suspicious of esoteric beliefs; their doubts dovetailed with issues of practitioner reliability. While Jewish tradition endorsed magic by adepts, its performance was forbidden among uninitiated community members. Naturally, illicit forms of magic were prohibited without exception.[97]

The reluctance to offer broad access to esoteric wisdom may be reflected in *Ma'aseh Akdamut*, where anyone who was interested in becoming an apprentice to the devil's arts could simply sit on the wheel. This legend recounts a Jew who wished to learn magic, so he approached the wheel and took a seat. When the devil was about to choose his next servant, that Jew panicked and began to recite the *Shema Yisra'el* (Hear, O Israel). The devil could not tolerate the sound of this prayer and, in his fury, smashed the wheel of fortune and inadvertently slayed the nine non-Jews seated there. This episode, where a Jew became the inadvertent catalyst for the destruction of the wheel of fortune, was the source of the monk's animosity toward the Jewish people.[98] In other words, the calamity being recounted in *Ma'aseh Akdamut* originated with unrestricted access to (dark) magical knowledge. By contrast, the Red Jews in our story stand for those who are most qualified to engage in magic. This perspective is consistent with the teachings of certain rabbinic authorities, such as the *Ḥasidei Ashkenaz* (German Pietists) in the twelfth and thirteenth centuries and rabbis in Renaissance Italy, that magical activity complements sincere piety and perfects the individual practitioner.[99] After all, Jewish tradition views the Ten Tribes, and by extension the Red Jews, as exceptionally pious Jews who lead lives of untarnished holiness.[100]

The single character in *Ma'aseh Akdamut* who clearly belongs in the category of an unauthorized magician is the monk, because he chose a tutor who trained him in pagan witchcraft. The tasks in this legend's sorcery contest impart the binary polarization between evil and holy magic: the Red Jew, with his knowledge of the divine names, sends and retrieves objects to or from heaven, whereas the activities of the monk, who communicates with demons, are earthbound: sinking an item into the ground and creating something else from clay. Even if the monk and the little Red Jew perform the same feats, the actions of the monk are considered illicit. The story thus warns of the lure and inefficacy of the dark arts. Nevertheless, *Ma'aseh Akdamut* does not address forbidden magic per se; rather, what we have here is primarily a case of religious Othering.[101] In this context, "magic" is a pejorative code for the religious practices of the Christian Other, implying that Christianity was an expression of foreign worship (*avodah zarah*), whose strength was derived from idolatrous forces, exemplified by the monk's dependence on Satan for his prowess.

## The Church and Visual Trickery

The Fürth edition of *Ma'aseh Akdamut* adds an important detail that further defines Church ritual as a harmful magic spell: we are told that the monk kills Jews with a touch to the forehead.[102] According to some versions of the story, his victims number 30,860.[103] This lethal contact may echo the Christian canard that Jews in general, and the Red Jews in particular, would pollute whatever they touched.[104] The Yiddish narrative turns this accusation on its head: "I will not touch you," the little Red Jew assures the fearful monk.[105] By acting in opposition to the monk, who kills through touch, the

Red Jew subtly defies Christian polemics: it is not Jews but the Church that operates in the carnal realm rather than relying on the spirit.[106] Most importantly, these particulars add another specifically Jewish-Christian dimension to the tale, drawing intertextually on Ezekiel 9:4 and the New Testament's interpretation of this verse in Revelation 7:2–4. Revelation reads Ezekiel's "mark upon the foreheads" of those righteous believers that God will spare when punishing Jerusalem as the salvation of the Jews by conversion to Christianity (as in *Ma'aseh Akdamut* a specific number is given). The Yiddish story, in contrast, bluntly equates baptism with black magic that causes the death of those marked with "the seal of the living God," the very opposite of salvation. Redemption here is instead effected by the Jewish savior (the little Red Jew) who foils the monk's grand plan to obliterate the Jews.

It is particularly noteworthy that this biblical mark on the forehead is also often identified with the tau cross used by the Antichrist to brand his followers—illustrated, for instance, by marking the Red Jews in the Frankfurt Antichrist window. In Revelation, the list of the twelve tribes of Israel that follows omits the tribe of Dan, which is one of the reasons that Dan came to be exegetically associated with the Antichrist, as the tribe from which Christ's archenemy would spring. Ostensibly in sync with its rival Christian interpretation of the Red Jews as the Antichrist's henchmen, the Yiddish story's eponymous red hero is named Dan.[107] Viewed from another perspective, however, this name undermines the Christian view since, in Jewish tradition, this tribe would be crucial for messianic redemption: not only was this tribe fabled as the bravest and most experienced in combat among the Ten Tribes,[108] but Dan is anticipated as the maternal line of the Jewish Messiah.[109] Whereas the Christian version saw the Red Jews as faithful allies of the Antichrist, the Jewish reading in fact transferred this fateful role to the sorcerer monk, as a closer look at the protagonists in *Ma'aseh Akdamut* reveals.

As the personification of evil, the Antichrist is the notorious charlatan of Christian tradition and the master of illusion who, at the end of time, is prophesied to establish his global reign with terror and feigned miracles.[110] By Christian logic, this false savior would delude the blind Jews who would accept him as their Messiah.[111] This identification of the Jewish Messiah with the Antichrist seeped into vernacular literature, as featured in the medieval plays by Hans Folz (1435/1440–1513), one of Germany's most popular authors of that era. In *Des Entkrist Vastnacht* (The Antichrist's carnival) Folz portrays Jews as the first to succumb to the Antichrist's deceit, followed by

Christian rulers and clergy. His late fifteenth-century work, *Spil von dem Herzogen von Burgund* (The play about the Duke of Burgundy), similarly exposes the Jewish Messiah as the Antichrist and Jews as his eager followers.[112] Interestingly, in this play, a wheel of fortune is the instrument that tests whether the Antichrist is the true redeemer. While we cannot know if the author of *Ma'aseh Akdamut* was familiar with the link between the *rota fortunae* and the Antichrist-Messiah in German literature, Jews in Germany were undoubtedly aware of anti-Jewish teachings about the Antichrist. Distinct parallels exist between the medieval Antichrist legend and *Ma'aseh Akdamut*: for example, the Antichrist was believed to induce fire to rain from the sky, reminiscent of round three in the tournament.[113] Other Jewish polemical works, first among them the famous retelling of the life of Jesus, *Toldot Yeshu*, also ascribe to Yeshu many of the ominous traits that Christian lore associates with the Antichrist, such as depicting him foremost as a false Messiah and master of dark arts.[114] The Antichrist was a model for Yeshu no less than the monk. *Toldot Yeshu* may have in fact informed *Ma'aseh Akdamut*.

*Toldot Yeshu* has an elusive textual lineage; the nucleus of its narrative dates to the middle of the first millennium, and several versions of this work have reached us.[115] Due to its subversive content, this folk narrative was primarily transmitted orally (though manuscripts do exist), as both Jewish and Christian sources corroborate.[116] Numerous references in Christian (and, to a lesser degree, Jewish) texts show that *Toldot Yeshu* had become immensely popular among Jewish readers in Christian Europe by the High Middle Ages. With the exception of Aramaic fragments from the Cairo Geniza, the earliest extant Hebrew texts were copied in the fifteenth and sixteenth centuries. An early Yiddish translation can be traced to the seventeenth century.[117]

In this alternative biography, Yeshu is presented as a magician-impostor. Rather than being born to a virgin, he is portrayed as an illegitimate child. Since his father is allegedly impotent, his mother, Miriam, does not conceive until she commits adultery. The family moves to Egypt, where her gifted son Yeshu studies both Torah and witchcraft. Upon their return to the land of Israel, Yeshu, the self-proclaimed Son of God, attracts a group of disciples and leads a scandalous life. Various episodes from his immoral and heretical behavior are detailed: for instance, he steals the ineffable name from the Temple for use in magic. Sorcery has a major place in this narrative, which describes Yeshu performing miracles that are reminiscent of the New Testament, such as turning water into wine and feeding a multitude with a single loaf of bread. While the gospels teach of Jesus working wonders to benefit others, exercising his supernatural gifts to heal the sick and even resurrect the dead, in this Jewish diatribe, Yeshu boasts of an ability to inflict death. Yeshu's own life ends after his shameful loss in a sorcerers' duel with Judas Iscariot, when he is arrested and hanged.

The parallels between *Toldot Yeshu* and *Ma'aseh Akdamut* are striking. Beyond featuring a villain who wields sorcery to commit murder, in fact or by threat, both tales employ similar elements in their decisive magical contest between the forces of good and evil: massive items are lifted with ease; objects are fashioned from clay and tossed to incomparable heights; a millstone is featured in both legends; a tree seals the aggressor's downfall; and Yeshu and the sorcerer monk, respectively, take flight or are launched in the air when they ultimately confront defeat.[118] In the end, like the monk in *Ma'aseh Akdamut*, Yeshu is thwarted. In both cases, failure is an inevitable consequence of exercising ill-gained magical skills. Both meet their demise when stripped of their supernatural powers; Yeshu loses command over the ineffable name when his contender urinates or ejaculates on him (depending on the version), while the little Red Jew disarms the monk by burning his demonic sponsors. By contrast, the champions both succeed because they act with divine sanction and rightly invoke the divine names.[119]

Significantly, upon realizing that he has lost his demons, the monk cries and laments his fate, saying: "How have you abandoned me, beloved masters?" This phrase closely resembles Jesus's loud call, reported in the Gospel of Mark, "My God, my God, why hast thou forsaken me?" (Mark 15:34). Further playing on the Christian doctrine of Jesus as God's son, the little Red Jew responds to the monk's distress by inquiring whether his laments were prompted by a death, perhaps his father or mother?[120] The conclusion of *Ma'aseh Akdamut* when the monk is catapulted into the sky, caught between two millstones, and cast toward the desert, enacts another verse from this gospel: "And whosoever shall offend one of these little ones that believe in me, it is better for him that a millstone were hanged about his neck, and he were cast into the sea" (Mark 9:42).[121]

Jewish coding thus subtly equates the vicious monk in *Ma'aseh Akdamut* with none other than a mocking portrait of Jesus as the Antichrist. This analogy is supported by the little Red Jew's repeated efforts to show spectators, within and outside the frame of the story, that this monk lacks divine authority. When the monk conjures two millstones, the Red Jew remarks, "You said you have created them. It is no wonder to me that I cannot create them, because I am no God."¹²² In the next round of their contest, after the monk conjured a spring that fuels rather than quenches the fire, the Red Jew delivers an incisive comment: "Let it burn for a little while longer, so that it will burn the well that you conjured and people will not say that you are God and created this source."¹²³ *Ma'aseh Akdamut* adopts a quality that Eli Yassif has identified in *Toldot Yeshu*: this polemic is devoted to countering Christian assertions that Jesus's ability to effect marvels, which persuaded many followers, had divine rather than magical origins. "He [Jesus] would lose the awe-inspiring aura of mystery stemming from divinity, and would become a regular human being performing magic tricks of the sort that anyone clever enough to learn the secrets of sorcery could imitate."¹²⁴ In the language of the ancient rabbis, this was *aḥizat einayim*, literally, "seizing the eyes," by conjuring a deceptive display that "is only concerned with the aesthetics of the performance," in contrast to "an act resulting in transformational changes" that was caused by divine forces.¹²⁵ Consequently, the above-cited speech given by the Red Jew concludes with questioning Jesus's ascension: "But I say to you that you will as likely go to heaven as a cow into a mousehole."¹²⁶ Similar to the way in which Yeshu is exposed in *Toldot Yeshu*, *Ma'aseh Akdamut* reveals that the monk is a deceiver.

The one who uncovers the alleged hidden truths in *Toldot Yeshu* binds this composition even more closely to the universe of the Red Jews: he is none other than Judas, the prototypical redheaded Jewish traitor of Christian lore.¹²⁷ Both of these Jewish stories transform a negatively cast red figure into a hero: Judas and the Red Jew become redeemers in these works. This literary device succeeds precisely because the events themselves are not at the heart of Jewish-Christian dispute but, rather, their interpretation. Indeed, Christian traditions name Judas as the lone Jew who knows the truth about Jesus, as Ora Limor and Israel Yuval have shown in their comparative reading of this character in *Toldot Yeshu* and two medieval Christian legends.¹²⁸ Both in *Toldot Yeshu* and *Ma'aseh Akdamut*, the protagonists reveal secrets that their narrator wants the audience to see clearly. Parallel with the little Red Jew in *Ma'aseh Akdamut* who blows the monk's cover, Judas discloses Yeshu as an imposter in *Toldot Yeshu*. He is the first to uncover that Yeshu's miracles are based on illegitimate powers since he acquired the divine name unlawfully, an incident that is proven publicly by his defeat in the sorcery contest. Subsequently, Judas announces this crime once more when Yeshu returns to Jerusalem in secret, probably in hopes of restoring his magical powers. After his death, Yeshu is unmasked as an impostor a third time.

In an effort to prevent his disciples from feigning that Yeshu had risen from the dead by stealing their master's body from his grave, Judas hides Yeshu's body in his garden. This dual motif of concealing and revealing is a meaningful Jewish innovation that does not appear in the New Testament, as Limor and Yuval emphasize. Visual delusion and its disclosure are the paired themes that drive plot development in both *Toldot Yeshu* and *Ma'aseh Akdamut*.

Another original detail turns Yeshu into a direct model for the monk in *Ma'aseh Akdamut*: when Judas eventually reveals to the sages where he hid Yeshu's corpse, they "took him by the hair and tried to pull him out of the hole. But the hair remained in their hands and his head was left bald. And that is [why] the priests make for themselves bald pates on their heads, in memory [of this]."[129] Tinged with anti-monasticism, the secret order of sorcerer monks in *Ma'aseh Akdamut* may well reflect broader epistemological suspicions that impostors were posing as priests and friars.[130] Indeed, it is possible that the magical Othering in *Ma'aseh Akdamut* was influenced by Reformation-era efforts to discredit the purported miracles of the Catholic Church, which may also have informed Augusti's criticism discussed at the opening of this chapter. In a way similar to that of the Yiddish tale, Protestant critiques of miracles often conflated Catholicism with the Antichrist, as a means of denouncing its alleged hypocrisy. Efforts to demonstrate their mendacious nature were part of a quest to prove that so-called "papists" were aligned with the Antichrist, the master of deception who could fool even the most devout Christians.[131]

Might the articulation of a possibly anti-Catholic posture in a Jewish text explain the surprising fact that *Ma'aseh Akdamut* was not censored, despite its anti-Christian stance and prominently featuring a monk as its antagonist? Like *Toldot Yeshu*, the transmission of this polemical work was probably predominantly oral, not only because this modality typified folklore but to shield its sensitive contents from Christians.[132] Unlike *Toldot Yeshu*, however, *Ma'aseh Akdamut* was printed several times between the sixteenth and eighteenth centuries. All extant early modern editions conspicuously stem from cities that had embraced the Protestant Reformation: Fürth, Amsterdam, and Frankfurt am Main. The lost editio princeps from Cremona appeared in Catholic Habsburg lands; however, Cremona in the territory of Milan was known for printing Jewish books that had difficulty finding publishers elsewhere. The authorities in Milan initially opposed the papal bull of 1553, which demanded that the Talmud be burned, and again resisted pressure from the Holy Office to enact that edict four years later. In 1559, the Inquisition was finally orchestrated for tens of thousands of Jewish books to be burned in Cremona. Nonetheless, the Christian publisher Vincenzo Conti, who also printed *Megiles Reb Meyer*, continued to release Hebrew and Yiddish books.[133] It is tempting to speculate about Protestant censors and subversive printers in Cremona who were bemused by the anti-Catholicism of this Yiddish parody and allowed its printing for their own reasons.

Anti-Catholic or not, in any case, the devastation of the sorcerer at the hands of the little Red Jew in *Ma'aseh Akdamut* symbolizes a sweeping metaphorical victory over Christianity. The black monk stands for the Church and its incessant oppression of Judaism, bolstered by allusions to Jesus, the Antichrist, and Goliath, and further intensified by his association with wicked Edom. As noted before, in Jewish thought, Edom was a code for Christendom.[134] As Edom's typological twin, Esau was midrashically known as a magician in Jewish tradition.[135] That polemical reading of the monk as Edom is supported by King David's subjugation of the ancient Edomites early in his reign.[136] The midrashic collection *Lekaḥ Tov* further details that messianic retribution against Edom will be exacted by one who is as red as his royal ancestor "who is called 'ruddy-cheeked and bright-eyed.'"[137] Genesis Rabbah also foretells that the destroyer of Edom, "the red one," would likewise be "clad in red."[138] Simon Lazar has previously argued for this midrash as a source for the Yiddish expression "Red Jews." He identifies the red avenger as a member of the Ten Tribes because rabbinic literature equates them with the fire through which "Esau's seed would be delivered only into the hands of Joseph's seed for it is said, 'And the house of Jacob shall be a fire and the house of Joseph a flame, and the house of Esau for stubble, etc.'"[139]

God's attribute of severe judgment is often cast in red hues. According to Isaiah 63:1–6, the divine avenger will emerge on the day of retribution, clad in red apparel; David Kimḥi explains that his red garb is saturated with Edom's lifeblood. This interpretation that red represents the blood-soaked garments of the One who unleashes his wrath against Christian oppressors found its way into *Tsene Rene* (Go forth and look, first published in Hanau, 1622). This widely popular Yiddish homiletical Bible translation by Jacob b. Isaac Ashkenazi of Janow from the early seventeenth century, which weaves the biblical passages that are read in synagogue with various medieval Bible commentaries and midrashim, explicates these verses from Isaiah as follows:

The prophet compares the Holy One to a great warrior who has killed many people. His garments are besmeared with the blood of the people that he has killed. Thus, will Israel also be in the days of the Messiah, and the Holy One who will kill many nations. Who is this that comes from Edom with besmeared red clothes . . . ? The Holy One responds: I spoke with justice. I am taking vengeance now, for I have much strength to help Israel. . . . Their blood sprayed my clothes and I have smeared my clothes. . . . I will trample the nations and crush them with My wrath. I will bring down their strength to the ground.[140]

As we have seen, Jewish messianic expectations were based on biblical prophecies about the fall of Edom; redemption would follow its demise. The little Red Jew's conquest thus foreshadows the anticipated messianic triumph of Israel over Edom. *Ma'aseh Akdamut* fittingly attaches the epithet "sons of saviors" (*bnei moshi'im*) to the Red Jews. As recited in Jewish daily morning prayers, these liberators "shall march up on Mount Zion to wreak judgement on Mount Esau; and dominion shall be the Lord's."[141] That is to say, Jews in Ashkenaz longed for the Red Jews as eschatological avengers as much as in the role of messianic saviors.

Not incidentally, this verse follows the liturgical recitation of *Shirat ha-Yam* (Song of the sea; Exod. 15:1–18), in which Moses and the Israelites praise God after successfully escaping enslavement in Egypt.[142] The preceding contest between Moses and Aaron against Pharaoh's sages and wizards that in the biblical account determined the release of the Israelites (Exod. 7:9–12) may in fact also have been a typological model (in addition to the Goliath narrative) for liberating a weaker party from its mighty oppressor. The Song of the Sea describes the utter defeat of Pharaoh and his troops at length. Referring to the deep fear that befell Edom and other nations upon hearing about the might of the God of Israel, this hymn foretells the apocalyptic destruction of Edom. It concludes with a confident assertion that the people of Israel will return to its land and build the holy sanctuary.

Thus, the Red Jews become part of the ancient quarrel between Jews and Christians over the identity of the vanquished Edom. In the Yiddish story, the desired self-identification as his righteous brother Israel is conversely embodied in the little Red Jew's physical disadvantages. Although a Christian perspective interprets his limp as an association with the satanic Antichrist,[143] his asymmetrical gait also connects him to Israel. In the biblical narrative, Jacob was named Israel after he prevailed in wrestling with God and men; during this fight, his hip was injured, causing him to limp.[144] His impairment was therefore not a sign of weakness but of courage. *Ma'aseh Akdamut* thus not only undermines the Christian apocalyptic construct of the Red Jews but also overturns the Christian claim that the Church is the true Israel. This Yiddish narrative primarily sought to bolster accusations that the Church was tricking the eyes. In *Ma'aseh Akdamut*, as in *Toldot Yeshu*, Christianity's failure rests on its flawed relationship to sight. Christian eyes were blind to the fraudulence of the sorcerer's tricks and, by extension, to seeing that the Christian Messiah's miracles were as contrived as those enacted by the Antichrist. From this position, the Church was entirely false, was purportedly without substance, merely a grand illusion. It becomes evident that, just as the sorcerer monk in *Ma'aseh Akdamut* fails, so too the Church never superseded the Jews as God's chosen people. The authentic, "old" Israel remains personified by the elderly little Red Jew. The result is a polemic deconstruction of the Christian narrative of identity and an affirmation of the Jewish self-understanding as a partner in an enduring covenant.

## Observers in the Yiddish Panopticon

To conclude this chapter, let us consider the vantage point of the audience in the Yiddish Red Jews legend more closely. We could reasonably ask how uneducated readers (and listeners) could grasp the nuances of this sophisticated counterstory. I would contend that the Yiddish audience did not have to be conversant in Christian theology to appreciate its subversive message. Nor was detailed knowledge of the German legend of the Red Jews a prerequisite for delighting in its Yiddish version. Simply put, not all readers would have been aware that the tale undermined specific Christian ideas. Jeremy Dauber, in his analysis of Old Yiddish literature, argues that their capacities for complex comprehension were "not necessarily dependent on conventional markers of audience sophistication such as textual education or linguistic knowledge." He shows that the efficacy of a parody need not rely on an extensive or direct encounter with original sources.[145] Rather, general familiarity would suffice: at a minimum, understanding and enjoyment of the Yiddish Red Jews as a polemical satire required a recognition of this

Christian expression for the Ten Tribes and the terror that its mention generated among Christians.

It is safe to assume that the average Ashkenazic Jew was familiar with this level of Christian parlance since shared literary material among Jews and Christians tended to be the rule rather than the exception.[146] Furthermore, various scholars have demonstrated that, in medieval and early modern Ashkenaz, Jews and Christians were cognizant of many aspects of the other group's texts, beliefs, and practices, and informal conversation was commonplace.[147] Amid the atmosphere of end-time anxieties in 1523, Jews and Christians followed the sensational news of the Red Jews' alleged appearance and debated its political implications. In that year, as discussed in the previous chapter, several German pamphlets claimed that the Red Jews had breached their confines and were heading for Jerusalem. Michael Kramer, a Protestant pastor in Kunitz (near Jena), published his exchange with Jacob of Brucks, a Jewish merchant whom he encountered in an inn. Among other topics, the two men spoke of the Red Jews. Kramer was unsettled by the prospect that these Jewish tribes would reconquer Jerusalem, whereas his Jewish interlocutor was confident that these tidings signaled imminent messianic redemption for Jews and a return to the land of their ancestors.[148]

Above all, general access to the myth of the Red Jews was facilitated by its visual qualities. Much as visualization and color symbolism were convenient techniques for reaching the German audience at large, seeing and imagining also instilled its Yiddish counterpart with the Red Jews' subversive message. The color code for the fierce inhabitants beyond the Sambatyon rendered their destined role visible. The Red Jews swathed hope for apocalyptic retaliation in red. As the color of blood and an intercultural symbol of the warrior, here red represents the blood-soaked garments of the One who unleashes his wrath against Christian oppressors. Whereas the Red Jews assumed the role that the Ten Tribes had traditionally held in Jewish messianism, the terminology differs in tone and polemical import, comparable to their adaptation into Christian parlance.[149] By adopting this fearsome German epithet, the Yiddish Red Jews conveyed the anti-Christian twist in the redemptive myth of the Ten Lost Tribes of Israel *expressis verbis*, underscoring their retributive promise in Ashkenazic messianism. Polemic becomes a visual pursuit in particular by reenvisioning the sinister Red Jews of German lore in the image of the Yiddish story's Davidesque little hero: this retelling scoffs at Christian fears of this nightmarish people. *Ma'aseh Akdamut* accommodates various comic elements that climax in the wizard battle when the little Red Jew constantly taunts the formidable adversary who engineered this competition to determine the fate of the Jews but ironically is made conspicuous by his absurd performance.[150] The Yiddish term "Red Jews" thus becomes anti-Christian ridicule made visible.

Humor as another form of nonverbal language was in fact a key ingredient in the resounding success of the Red Jews' story in Yiddish culture. Surreptitious laughter at the dominant societal stratum played an important cultural role in the story, born from a sense of powerlessness in Christian society. Homi Bhabha observes the potential for mockery and, by extension, menace that is implied when a marginalized group copies elements from the dominant culture. Mimicry disrupts the authority of the majority by disclosing a social mechanism that defies its control.[151] In the case of the Red Jews, narrative reappropriation represents a subtly rebellious gesture: the Yiddish revision of the Christian account of the Red Jews mimicked the storyline of the German version in a way that overturned its essence, explicitly countering that rival usage by employing the identical phrase. The product is a literary fantasy of liberation spun by those who lack conventional social and political power. By envisioning the destruction of their oppressor, resistance is cultivated through fantasy and memory.[152]

The Red Jews provided a release for otherwise quietly held anti-Christian sentiments, such as hatred, anger, and a desire for vengeance. Elisheva Carlebach has argued that such polemical expressions are particularly evident in Yiddish writings from this period.[153] Indeed, the magical contest concludes with a vivid scene of ruthlessness: the monk is decapitated and impaled. These graphic images of brutality surely increased the story's entertainment value and popularity. It shows that Jewish audiences, no less than their Christian peers, could derive positive meaning from tales of cruelty toward the Other. The often sarcastic depiction of the magical contest binds imagined violence and laughter closely together as a means of emotional diversion to deflect aggression.[154] The myth of the Red Jews thereby represented a vital strategy for spiritual and social persistence within a hostile and seemingly invincible Christian society.[155]

Beyond providing a cathartic form of resistance to Christian hegemony, laughter fosters a bond among those who share a joke.[156] Shared humor strengthens solidarity and group identity and, therefore, may bolster a vulnerable or embattled community. An inside joke necessarily excludes others, especially when laughter targets a particular Other, reinforcing social boundaries and, in the case of religious groups, inhibiting apostasy. Medieval and early modern Jewish polemics, among them *Ma'aseh Akdamut* and *Toldot Yeshu*, employ irony to portray the Christian religious and political elite as ludicrous. In these texts, Christianity does not merit respect nor should its beliefs be entertained as a credible alternative to Judaism.[157] It is thus no coincidence that mockery and violence in *Ma'aseh Akdamut* are directed specifically against the malevolent monk, who alone caused the Jews' distress. The Church is highlighted as the primary danger for Jewish society.

Another Old Yiddish tale that is preserved in a late sixteenth-century Italian manuscript transmits a related phenomenon. This narrative belongs to the earlier manuscript tradition of the famous collection of Yiddish stories, *Mayse Bukh* (A story book; first print Basel, 1602). In this legend, the pope has declared that Jews must annually deliver two young boys whom Christians would sacrifice to atone for the Jews' alleged responsibility in the death of Jesus. This demand is nullified when the medieval Jewish philosopher and Bible commentator Abraham ibn Ezra magically conjures Jesus, who intervenes with the pope and his cardinals. Jesus seeks an end to the persecution of Jews, arguing that it adds to the sinful actions by Christians for which he continues to suffer. The pope realizes that he erroneously believed that Jesus would delight in the oppression of Jews and, as a corrective, discontinues this vindictive practice.[158] Christian condemnation of Jews is presented by the Yiddish narrator as an inaccurate interpretation of Christianity's basic tenets by religious authorities. In an argument closely resembling traditional Christian polemics against the harmful influence of the rabbis, the Church is responsible for false indoctrination, resulting in hostile attitudes and behavior toward Jews.

The message of this story is similar to that of *Ma'aseh Akdamut*: the Church, represented by its monastic clergy, is identified as the driving source of hostility between the two religious communities by preaching and enforcing an anti-Jewish position. Even comparatively benign secular rulers are impotent to resist its power, like the king in *Ma'aseh Akdamut*. When the monk audaciously kills two members of the Jewish delegation in his presence, the Jews rightfully doubt whether the sovereign is capable of defending them.[159] This scenario is particularly telling given the ascriptions to sight in this period: a just government was equated with watchful oversight. The eyes of the ideal magistrate, like God, were all-seeing.[160] The sovereign's failure to protect the Jews whose lives were being threatened before his eyes thus questions the legitimacy of his reign. This episode patently exposes his constricted authority within the royal palace and, by extension, his kingdom vis-à-vis the Church.

In the end, both stories evoke the aspiration for harmonious coexistence between Jews and Christians. As distinct from other versions of the story, the *Mayse Bukh* tradition about ibn Ezra as an intercessor is not resolved by a reversal, where Jews settle the score with a call for revenge for the yearly execution of their children. Rather, it effects reconciliation. *Ma'aseh Akdamut* explicitly stresses that the little Red Jew's victory offered relief to society as a whole, for the monk had also instilled fear among the Christian majority, from commoners to kings: "And the king and all the king's judges and all the people became friendly towards the Jews due to the wonders that the little Jew performed."[161]

In this context, the focus in the Jewish version of the myth on the individual Red Jew rather than the collective is significant. In the early modern European imagination, newly encountered peoples in distant lands were often assumed to be threatening in the aggregate whereas an individual might be deemed a "noble savage."[162] So too the Red Jews were collectively cast as an intimidating, aggressive horde in both Jewish and Christian tradition whereas, in *Ma'aseh Akdamut*, a lone little Red Jew is the compassionate savior whose victory over the monk liberates both his diasporic counterparts and the Christians among whom they dwell. Much as contrasting depictions of violent tribes and the "benevolent savage" reflect early modern European fears of war and rebellion and a desire for peace, the Red Jews' story addresses turbulence in Jewish-Christian relations, while despairing of this woeful conflict.[163] This Yiddish myth therefore served as more than a literary expression of spiritual resistance and an emotional outlet or a buttress for in-group identity; its concluding image also conveys a desire for societal acceptance.

This manifold cultural function accounts for the generic shift of the Red Jews from Christian to Jewish culture, predominantly into the realm of narratives. And yet, these Yiddish stories by no means fictionalized the Red Jews. On the contrary, they worked as reassuring fantasies because Ashkenazic Jews, like their Christian contemporaries, did not doubt their existence. The Red Jews were eagerly anticipated at the end time. While *Ma'aseh Akdamut* could be read as an allegory for redemption, it would not be understood by its readers as a work of fiction but rather as a historical account, as the title page of almost every print assured the reader: A beautiful tale that is the historical account of Rabbi Meir, the little Red Jew, and the black monk (*Ayn sheyn mayse dos iz di geshikhtnis fun Reb Meyer un fun den rotn yudlayn un fun den shvartsn minkh*).¹⁶⁴ Indeed, rather than merely emphasizing fantasies of a splendid future, Old Yiddish literature ushered the Ten Tribes from an unknown land and a distant future into the current Diaspora in the guise of Red Jews. Ultimately, we will see, the little Red Jew became a role model for powerful Jewish agency in exile.

Chapter 3

# The Little Red Jew
## A Vernacular Icon of Ashkenazic Identity

*Tsin a roytn yid darf men hobn a roytn yid.*
(For a Red Jew it takes another Red Jew.)

—Yiddish saying

Jews and Christians projected mutually exclusive hopes and fears on the shared myth of the Red Jews, polemically using their rival portrayal against the Other. The analysis of *Ma'aseh Akdamut* has demonstrated how the Yiddish Red Jews exposed Christian misconceptions regarding the role of their German counterparts and, more broadly, satirized Christian beliefs and notions of identity. As the Red Jews were recast within a distinctly Jewish framework, the Christian apocalyptic scenario morphed into a reassuring Jewish legend of deliverance, cultivating spiritual resistance. This Yiddish reworking, however, did not restrict red coloration to the realms of religious competition and literary subversion, nor eschatology; rather, it translated the salvific potential of the Red Jews from a future promise into a desire for immediate Jewish agency.

While hopes for the messianic future could offset the experience of oppression, persecution, and suffering that had marked Jewish history for centuries, providing a buffer against life's harsh realities, the Yiddish myth of the Red Jews offered an alternative form of succor. In contrast to the Ten Tribes' eschatological escapism, the Yiddish legend of the Red Jews gave voice to deliverance in this world. The earlier stigma of redness became the embodiment of Jewish self-assertion in exile. The color red, in other words, was transformed from a badge of denigration into an emblem of Jewish empowerment. This chapter traces the usage of the image of the Red Jews within Jewish culture once the myth had been reappropriated. It shows how the Red Jews took root as a vernacular icon of a confident Ashkenazic identity that exploited the mnemonic utility of visual cues. While stories about the Red Jews were hugely popular, we will see that their message of how to navigate diasporic reality became contested within various strata of Jewish society, entwined with gender conflict and discussions of class and race.

## Red Warriors

The tale of the Red Jews shared its core message with the legend of the Ten Lost Tribes of Israel who represented everything that a politically subaltern and socially oppressed diasporic Jewry could desire.[1] Jews who lived in dire straits found comfort in the vivid image of a Jewish community dwelling in freedom, holiness, and abundance, in stark contrast to their own experience. By depicting an autonomous Jewish kingdom that was thriving in the far reaches of the world beyond the Sambatyon River, the myth countered Christian claims that God had abandoned his people and thus fulfilled an important psychological function in Jewish culture. This message of safety and autonomy explains the popularity of reports about the Ten Tribes and the Red Jews during the Middle Ages and early modern period. The convert Friedrich Albrecht Augusti incisively explicates: "When great need makes it necessary, and the entire Jewry or ten *Landesrabbiner* (rabbis with territorial jurisdiction) give permission, a number of *shtadlanim* (intercessors) cross the river, and stay with the Red Jews for a time, to form a precise impression of their happiness, and to write about it and make all that they have seen and heard known to scattered Israel beyond the Sambatyon for its comfort."[2]

A sixteenth-century Yiddish source likewise stresses the significance of such journeys across the Sambatyon, albeit in the opposite direction: Red Jews who educated Diaspora Jewry about the idyllic Jewish life in their country "did much good for the poor people who were there." In their own land, the Red Jews lived amicably; their lives were free of jealousy and infighting, illness and harsh winters, and they were sheltered from assaults by any king on earth.[3] In 1815, Christian August Vulpius, the author who included an excerpt from Augusti in his booklet *Curiositäten* (Memorabilia), reports that every so often, Jewish vagabonds would appear and claim to be Red Jews.

Stories of their purported homeland apparently drew great interest among European Jews, especially in Poland.[4]

In Yiddish literature, the military prowess of the Ten Tribes, known from medieval and early modern Jewish lore, is painted in particularly vibrant and exaggerated terms, stressing their wild and violent nature. This emphasis reflects the standard practice for culling material from the Hebrew corpus to be translated for the widely inclusive spectrum of Yiddish readers: revisions of Hebrew writings and original Yiddish compositions tended to focus on tangible imagery, making them accessible—and more enticing—to the least sophisticated strata.[5] One of the most elaborate accounts of the Ten Tribes as a formidable armed force appears in *Kol Mevaser* (The heralding voice), a compilation of documents on the Ten Tribes, first published in Hebrew by the book collector Isaac Akrish (Constantinople, ca. 1577) and followed by numerous Yiddish versions that appeared from circa 1600 onward.[6]

Akrish attributes one selection in the appendix of this book to a certain Moses ha-Kohen Ashkenazi of Candia (Crete), whose identity remains unresolved. He may be the emissary (by the same name) from the Holy Land, who was dispatched to the Ottoman Empire in the final quarter of the fifteenth century and is generally considered the author of the Yiddish *Shmuel-Bukh*.[7] This supplementary account figures prominently in the Yiddish translations of *Kol Mevaser*. It was eventually incorporated into the body of the text and even its advertisement. The title page of an undated Yiddish edition from Amsterdam thus promises a "beautiful and true tale of the Jews who live beyond the Sambatyon River or the Red Sea . . . how they wage war against other kings . . . who cannot harm the children of Israel because they are strong and skilled and they are seasoned warriors."[8] The lengthy passage from this Ashkenazic informant does not actually use the Red Jews terminology, but the generic phrase "Ten Tribes" may safely be equated with the Red Jews, particularly since certain motifs from the Red Jews' tradition are clearly represented, reflecting a particular version of the Red Jews' tale (which we will read closely below).

First of all, the title page locates the Ten Tribes near the Red Sea. This notion has parallels in the trope that the Red Jews live on an island in the midst of the Red Sea, which emerged in Christian thought in the late fifteenth century and is also evidenced in later Jewish sources.[9] For example, the first Yiddish cosmography, *Sefer Tela'ot Mosheh* (Book on the trials and tribulations of Moses; Halle, 1711)—by Moses Drucker (also known as Moses b. Abraham the Proselyte or Moses b. Abraham Avinu), a convert to Judaism and printer in Amsterdam and Halle, among other places—asserts that the Ten Tribes inhabit an island kingdom in the Red Sea. In this description of world geography, Drucker focuses on the legendary locale of the Ten Lost Tribes, which he primarily bases on Abraham Farissol's well-known Hebrew geography *Iggeret Orḥot Olam* (Treatise on the ways of the world; Venice, 1586) but also non-Jewish geographical works that may have informed his Red Sea association.[10] According to Drucker, the Ten Tribes are enclosed by insurmountable mountains in Turkey (as per their traditional location in the Caucasus), but they may also be encountered in "India," where the Red Jews are confined. It remains somewhat unclear whether this author distinguishes between the Ten Tribes and the Red Jews, or understands the Red Jews as one group among the Ten Tribes.[11]

Steeped in medieval imagination, in *Tela'ot Mosheh*, "India" denotes a territory with blurry borders that encompasses the Arabian Peninsula. The notion that "India" was a vague designation that signified vast lands at the southeastern margins of the known world continued into the early modern period, though it slowly receded as geographical knowledge became ever more precise and economic ties with the Far East became stronger. Drawing on information from Farissol's geography, which divides the Ten Tribes between India (north of Calcutta) and the fictive Chabor Desert of Arabia, Drucker thus envisioned the Ten Lost Tribes and the Red Jews to have been scattered from one end of "India" to the other, from Calcutta to the Red Sea. He identifies Chabor as the desert through which the biblical Moses led the Israelites and locates it near the Red Sea, purportedly named for the red sands on its shores.[12]

Drucker places discrete groups from the Ten Tribes (the Red Jews?) on islands in the Red Sea. Here, he blends Farissol's description of these islands (without Jewish inhabitants) and Jewish populations on islands in the Indian Ocean, with a report from the Dutch geographer Petrus Bertius's *Tabularum Geographicarum* (Amsterdam, 1600). The Yiddish text offers the misleading impression of being based on the Latin original, but, in fact, Drucker used an expanded German translation that first appeared in Frankfurt am Main in 1612. Since Drucker resided in Amsterdam, it is plausible that his source was the 1650 reprint issued there. Bertius here writes of the "Island of the Samaritans" in the Red Sea, which he claimed was populated by descendants of the Northern Kingdom of Israel, progeny of the nation that ultimately became the exilic Ten Tribes.[13] Drucker, following Farissol, describes the magnetic fields of certain islands: these were detrimental to ships crossing the Red Sea, which were uncontrollably pulled toward them. This notion also appears in the German work by Fischart (printed a good ten years before Farissol's *Iggeret*), which depicts the Red Jews as a capable seafaring nation, who, in order to avoid the dangerous magnetic fields, used ropes made from palm trees instead of iron nails to construct their vessels.[14]

Apart from the explicit link to the Red Sea, various objects in the relevant part of *Kol Mevaser* relating to the Ten Lost Tribes are cast in red, to complement the symbolic coloring of the Red Jews themselves known from other sources: they fight with red lances, and on the Sabbath their king illuminates his castle with a glowing carbuncle.[15] The readers who were enticed to purchase the book would not have been disappointed by its wondrous contents, which included giant-sized Jewish kings; fiery horses that could run nonstop for three days after feeding on meat and wine; and heavily armed Jewish warriors who would slay any uninvited intruder who attempted to ford the Sambatyon River into their territory while marauding Jewish battalions plundered the neighboring kingdoms for months on end.[16]

The details of this watery border, which demarcates the Red Jews' territory, in the account by Moses Ashkenazi in *Kol Mevaser* are unique. In accordance with the well-known myth of the Sambatyon, this passage explains that the river cannot be crossed during the six weekdays because of its roaring waters and the stones, sand, and rubble that they stir. It is placid only on the Sabbath, when religious law bars Jews from traveling. Not until messianic times would God quiet the turbulent guardian of the Lost Tribes and permit them to traverse the Sambatyon. However, the Ashkenazic source describes a brief, weekly window when the Red Jews can cross the otherwise impassable Sambatyon. Two hours before the Sabbath starts, the river begins to calm, making it possible to cross. The Red Jews frequently seize this opportunity before the day of rest arrives to journey from their land and delight in terrorizing the peoples on the far bank.[17]

This document includes one of the most detailed accounts of the tensions between the Red Jews and one of their neighbors, the fabled Christian king Prester John. Christians imagined the Ten Tribes as the vassals of this priestly monarch. This legend originated with the famous letter Prester John had allegedly written to a Byzantine emperor. The popularity of Prester John's famed correspondence was not limited to European Christians, but it was also translated and printed in Hebrew since it conveyed information about the whereabouts of the Ten Lost Tribes.[18] By contrast, Jewish sources exhibit a markedly different balance of power. *Kol Mevaser*, for example, claims the Red Jews subjected many peoples in their vicinity to taxation and any resistance was swiftly subdued.[19] Furthermore, it indicates how intimidated Prester John was by the Jewish tribes: whenever a young Red Jew challenged one of his subjects to a duel, the king would intervene by weighing that Red Jew and paying him his weight in gold. After all, their child-princes, in the truest sense of the term "little Red Jews," were capable of cutting down a legion of enemies.[20]

Several decades later, this description of aggressive and war-loving Jews who routinely raid neighboring settlements was included in the Yiddish *Gelilot Erez Yisra'el* (The regions of the land of Israel; first printed 1635, followed by numerous editions). For this travelogue, Gershon b. Eliezer Segal Yidls of Prague copied the Yiddish translation of *Kol Mevaser* and augmented it with further details.[21] He adds, for example, that Prester John assigned guards to patrol the banks of the Sambatyon to prevent Jewish hordes from invading his territory and tormenting his subjects.[22] Furthermore, he states that two of their young princes could vanquish one thousand foes, thus exponentially increasing the number of enemies that a single member of the Red Jews could defeat.[23] *Gelilot Erez Yisra'el* also reports that the bellicose tribes beyond the Sambatyon would import iron from the Ottoman Empire to produce weaponry. He claims to have overheard that they would trade one centner of gold for an equal measure of that precious resource.[24]

## Imminent Rescue

These accounts of the Red Jews had contemporary currency because, in semantic terms, they operated in the Ashkenazic present. Drucker's cosmography conveys up-to-date geographic and ethnographic knowledge, while Akrish and Yidls claim to transmit contemporary eyewitness reports.[25] As we have seen, *Ma'aseh Akdamut* places historized events from medieval Europe at its center. The second of the two main versions of the story about the Red Jews that were available in the early modern period, a Yiddish epistle from Safed, similarly heightens its realism, albeit using different devices.[26] Besides the use of authentic geographic and personal names, temporal points of reference, and direct speech, the realistic flavor of this source is above all bolstered by its claim to document current events.[27] This letter purportedly records news of remote Jewish communities that was shared by Samuel and Asher—two Jewish travelers from Susa, Persia—while visiting Safed in 1579.

They are said to have informed the Jews of the Galilee about the circumstances of Jews in their home country as well as other kingdoms in Asia and Africa, including Prester John's realm and the Red Jews, much like the medieval description of the Ten Tribes by Eldad ha-Dani.

Sara Zfatman has noted that the epistolary genre augmented the account's credibility. Not only did news of the Ten Tribes often circulate in letters throughout the Jewish world, but the letter before us is attributed to a local rabbi, a certain Jacob b. Eliezer from Ober-Ashkenaz (Upper Ashkenaz), who allegedly recorded these tidings. This likely fictitious writer is associated with correspondence about the Tribes elsewhere. Jacob b. Eliezer is mentioned in the roughly contemporaneous collection *Kol Mevaser*, which in fact displays numerous commonalities with the present source, among them the names of peoples and places.[28] Rabbi Jacob claims to have translated the Persian travelers' updates, conveyed in Hebrew, and dispatched the news in Yiddish letters to Ashkenazic Jews outside the land of Israel, a standard practice at that time.[29]

Most importantly, non-Jews in the Safed letter are portrayed as contemporary European Christians, rather than historicizing the plot elements in their non-European countries. Notwithstanding its uncharted setting, the ethnographic report is laden with anti-Christian symbolism, peppered with color: one of the kings mentioned is named Rot Hut (red hat), a German nickname for a cardinal, due to his red cap.[30] His subjects are called "white Kushites" (*vays morn*, lit. "white blacks") and are described as appalling to observe. Both early modern Jewish and Christian sources characterize these paradoxical beings as repulsive freaks, albinos too pale to be considered praiseworthy with red eyes (some texts add that they have red hair).[31] Their physical anomaly is compounded by blindness. However, as with smallness for the Red Jews, this ostensible deficit equips them with an unexpected ability: they are blind by day but capable of sight in darkness and, thus, see sharply when others cannot.

Unsurprisingly, this monarch Rot Hut is cast as an evil oppressor of Jews (and enemy of the Turks), unlike another king, the pious Muslim Kyzyl— perhaps referring to a city in Siberia by that name and meaning "crimson" in many Turkic languages—whose Jewish subjects thrived: they were known to be wealthy and, more importantly, highly educated in religious matters and "other books which are not [available] here in your lands," to such an extent that most royal advisors were Jews.[32] Jerold Frakes has observed an analogous politicization in early Yiddish Purim plays, where the characters in the story of Esther would not be "historically plausible inhabitants of the Persian Empire of the fifth century BCE: Jews are portrayed simply as Jews contemporary with the play itself, while the non-Jews are not the ancient Persians of the biblical narrative, but rather more or less contemporary, early modern, European Gentiles, that is, Christians."[33]

In line with these anachronistic references, which translated an originally apocalyptic legend into a mundane matter of urgency, the letter from Safed seems if anything to neutralize the messianic impulse. Much of this epistle is devoted to an incident in Prester John's kingdom that involves the Red Jews, supplying background information to the Christian ruler's anxiety mentioned above in *Kol Mevaser*. We are told that Prester John rules over a country whose numerous Jewish inhabitants live in peaceful coexistence among an ethnically and religiously diverse populace. One day, the priestly king rides through the *Judengasse* (Jewish street) in one of the cities in his empire. One of the princes in his entourage has studied many Jewish languages "like a rabbi," and he is fluent in Yiddish (*yudash*, lit. "Jewish").[34] When the royal retinue passes a Jewish school, they overhear a teacher reciting the opening of Deuteronomy 32:30 with his young pupils: "How could one have routed a thousand, Or two put ten thousand to flight?"[35] Being as puzzled as he is displeased by this teaching, which he considers false, Prester John orders the rabbis and community elders to appear before him. These Jewish leaders have to prove that one of them can overcome one thousand men, and two of them ten thousand. If they fail to bring qualified candidates before him within one year, he will execute the number of Jews that matches their boast.[36]

The community sends its two most accomplished Torah scholars to the Red Jews for help. A heavenly voice reveals to the Sanhedrin, the highest rabbinical court in the Red Jews' kingdom, that God will send them two angels to defeat Prester John's entire realm: a boy and girl, both seven years old.[37] Following the rabbis' advice, King Daniel of the Red Jews recruits a pair of clever seven-year-olds for this task, whom the Sanhedrin trains in magic, using the divine names. Eventually, a strong wind rises and carries the two little Red Jews together with the emissaries back to the city in Prester John's empire. The community elders announce to Prester John that they have identified two Jews who can defeat his troops by the promised numbers. As expected (and analogous to *Ma'aseh Akdamut*), Prester John becomes enraged when he sees the children, assuming that the Jews are mocking him.

However, the Jews rejoice upon the little Red Jews' arrival and declare that Prester John will soon witness a divine miracle.[38]

When the boy and the girl ride onto the battlefield that has been prepared for this contest, Prester John's heavily armed, mounted warriors await them with such an imposing presence that the royal couple and all of their subjects quake at the sight. The children draw their swords and, like a battle cry, they shout a variety of divine names, then begin to slay the soldiers. The massacre continues until the king begs the Jewish elders to stop them. The young heroes of this tale thus defeat Prester John's mighty forces, armed solely with their knowledge of the divine name, in a sweeping victory. As in *Ma'aseh Akdamut*, here too, the audience's eyes are opened to the truth of Jewish power, the spectators in the story and its early modern Yiddish readers alike. Accordingly, the episode closes with the children announcing to Prester John that they journeyed to his land only to show "you that the living God, blessed be his name, is with Israel."[39] The narrator affirms: "The king and queen and all the princes of the kingdom have seen this. Thus, the king lifted his eyes to the sky and said: 'Now I see that a living God exists and I see well that all his wonders are true.'"[40] Analogous to the harmonious ending of *Ma'aseh Akdamut*, Prester John eventually learns his lesson and the Jews can go on living under his dominion in peace.

Here the tale of the Red Jews departs bluntly from traditional messianic lore about the Ten Tribes because deliverance is not dependent on the Messiah. The Yiddish myth asserts that, whenever a Jewish community is in grave danger, as a last resort, instant assistance can be sought from the Red Jews. Augusti indicates that, through the mid-eighteenth century, German Jews believed that the leaders of the Red Jews would occasionally grant permission to individuals among them to cross the Sambatyon when Jews in the Diaspora desperately needed their aid. Under such circumstances, it was permissible for the Sabbath to be desecrated when Red Jews embarked on this journey.[41] In the early modern Yiddish legend of the Red Jews, the designated hero was liberated from their prison beyond the Sambatyon if their unique skills were urgently needed. In stark contrast to the Ten Tribes, who had to wait until the end of time before crossing the Sambatyon and could only leave their confinement as a collective, Red Jews were able to intervene as rescuers in times of crisis before their assigned role in the Last Days. Alongside the Messiah, they would lighten the burden of exile in the future; however, individual Red Jews were on call to offer a glimpse of liberation long before. They were authorized to provide rescue from the everyday hardships suffered by their diasporic peers, an imperiled minority living in a hostile environment—anywhere from the heartland of Ashkenaz to remote outposts, like Prester John's kingdom. Thus, the Red Jews personified hope for salvation in its broadest sense and ensured Jewish survival in the Christian world until the Messiah would bring about ultimate redemption from exile. This is not to suggest that Ashkenazic Jews had relinquished their messianic beliefs. The Red Jews simply highlight a pragmatic position in the interim that would have been no less invigorating for their readership.

Early modern Jews often asserted that, if not for the Sambatyon, "the Red Jews would have come long ago and liberated us."[42] This claim roused Christian mockery, as illustrated by this retort, cited by Victor von Carben in the early sixteenth century:

> Are you not ashamed of your evident lies when you say that the Red Jews cannot come across on Friday or Saturday and you cannot cross the wild sea to them? How many Jews have traveled since time immemorial from all countries to Jerusalem, and [while en route] have often been forced on account of unfavorable winds to remain at sea, day in and day out, for half a year, and [thus] to break their Sabbath. It is no shame or sin for them, so how much less would it be shameful for the Red Jews to break one Sabbath and come across [the Sambatyon] to redeem you and regain the Holy Land? Everything you say is nonsense and against all honesty.[43]

Jews surely pondered this same argument. Would not *piku'aḥ nefesh*—the Jewish legal principle that preserving a life overrides virtually any other religious commandment—justify the suspension of Sabbath laws and, thus, enable the Red Jews to ford the Sambatyon to rescue their vulnerable fellows? Although Halakhah does cite certain prohibitions that cannot be subordinated to *piku'aḥ nefesh*, keeping the Sabbath is not among them. The Yiddish myth of the Red Jews, who could be summoned in cases of emergency, offered a response to the conundrum of the Ten Tribes' continued imprisonment.[44] In *Ma'aseh Akdamut*, the Jews wonder how it was possible to call on the Red Jews because "who will desecrate the Sabbath and have no part in the World to come because of this? The Red Jews will judge him [and execute him by stoning]; and for one who endangers his own life, it is difficult to enter the Garden of Eden."[45] The narrator, however, explicitly states that the Red Jews did not condemn Meir Shatz for violating the

Sabbath when he crossed the Sambatyon since he acted on a matter of life and death.⁴⁶ Yet, he was not permitted to cross the river a second time to return home to his family; thus, he had to stay with the Red Jews for the rest of his life. This concern of traversing the sabbatical river is niftily circumvented in the Safed letter; instead, the protagonists soar through the air from place to place, never even approaching the Sambatyon.⁴⁷

Another legitimate reason for venturing into the land of the Red Jews on the Sabbath was to request sanctuary in that haven for downtrodden Jews. *Kol Mevaser* reports that, when an individual reached the territory beyond the Sambatyon in search of permanent refuge, the king would administer a Hebrew exam to verify whether that petitioner were indeed Jewish. Furthermore, he would inquire what hardship had justified the Sabbath violation which crossing the Sambatyon entailed. An acceptable answer took this form: "This was not enacted willfully. Since we are slaves, imprisoned among the nations, we escaped here in order to save our life. We fled to you due to mortal danger (סכנת נפש), for we heard that you were Jews and that you would fulfill the verse: 'You shall not turn over to his master a slave [who seeks refuge with you from his master]' (Deut. 23:16) on our behalf."⁴⁸ Any Jew who reached the Red Jews' realm was indeed fortunate since, based on this biblical prohibition against expelling refugees, asylum would be granted to any Jew who wished to live among them and, as *Kol Mevaser* describes, each new arrival was welcomed with gifts and a bride.

## Powerful Agency

The Yiddish tales about the Red Jews convey a keen awareness of the precarious social and political status of Ashkenazic Jews in premodern Europe. With the Red Jews' ability to provide instant relief, this Yiddish story runs counter to the ubiquitous image of unabated suffering, coupled with hope for a future divine deliverance. A pronounced expression of such a stance in religious literature through the ages appears in rabbinic interpretations of Isaiah 53, which identify the suffering servant as the people of Israel, whom God elected to endure hardship for their own sins and, vicariously, the sins of the nations.⁴⁹ In the myth of the Red Jews, resistance to this identity as suffering servants emerges: a close reading of the central tales of the Red Jews affirms that the Yiddish legend challenges acquiescence to exilic conditions while patiently awaiting messianic redemption. In contrast, the Red

Jews boldly encouraged diasporic Jews to take the initiative when they were in jeopardy and defend themselves rather than merely trusting in the coming of the Messiah. They emphasized the potential for active protest, as symbolized by petitioning for support from beyond the Sambatyon.

This novel aspect of agency in the tale of the Red Jews is alluded to in the Safed letter. After the incident with Prester John is resolved, every year during the ten days of repentance from Rosh ha-Shanah to Yom Kippur, King Daniel would ride to the Sambatyon and pray for the river to calm down, enabling him and his Red Jews to cross it and liberate Israel. One year, he hears a heavenly voice calling: "Go back, O king, it is not yet time! Israel is not sufficiently pious to be worthy of redemption."[50] *Ma'aseh Akdamut* is more explicit on this point. When the imperiled German Jews discover that only a Red Jew can successfully confront the evil monk, they ask: "Since God, blessed be he, wants to help us with a Red Jew, why does He not give us a sign, making him come here for us, that we should not need to travel there and desecrate the Sabbath?" The answer arrives: "You are not worthy of such a sign and that the ways of the world should be changed for your sake, making him fly here."[51] Such divine intervention is reserved for the end of time, when God would liberate the Lost Tribes from captivity and permit them to traverse the dry Sambatyon en masse. Until then, if Jews need help from beyond the Sambatyon, they must send a messenger. The title of the printed letter from Safed even uses this message to market itself as a booklet that shows how God watches over those who summon his aid.[52]

Significantly, the Yiddish myth does not interpret this plea for God's mercy traditionally, namely through expressions of increased piety and repentance. At first, these stories reenact typical Jewish strategies for coping with oppression. Confronted with a threatening enemy, the Jews in *Ma'aseh Akdamut* initially appeal to the sovereign, who is the protector of this minority in his realm. When the Christian ruler cannot shield them, the Jews desperately pray that the monk will die. Throughout the land, they fast, wear sackcloth, and give charity.[53] Similarly, in the Safed letter, after an unsuccessful attempt to appease Prester John with precious stones, the Jews repent—in vain: "The elders prayed to God, blessed be he, [for a response]. What should they do? On account of our many sins, we are now in exile where it is not possible [to enact Deut. 32:30]. No prayer helped."[54] Here, this practice is taken to such an extreme that even the Red Jews participate. When King Daniel hears about the calamity, he reflexively adopts the standard diasporic Jewish instruction: he immediately declares a fast throughout his country, then he convenes his counselors, who seclude themselves for several days of prayer and fasting.[55] When he finally consults the Sanhedrin, he admits his limited strategies: "Give me some advice, dear rabbis, on what can be done to save them. Unfortunately, I have not found a way other than [reliance on] your prayer and your learnedness."[56] In both narratives, the two initial attempts to avert mortal threat eventually fail: reliance on royal protection proves to be as ineffective as repentance and prayer. Instead, the stories answer to their protagonists' vicarious shiftlessness by calling for Jewish empowerment over supplications for divine intervention. This reinterpretation of postures to suffering takes up a central motif found in Isaiah 53: whereas this biblical depiction of the suffering servant is replete with imagery of disability and disease,[57] these tropes have markedly different purposes in our Yiddish myth. Indeed, the decision to introduce its little red heroes—an elderly man with a limp or a boy and girl aged seven years old— by describing their physical disadvantages and meek appearance signals a crucial shift in perspective. The spotlight shines on these Jewish protagonists who actively use their powers to rescue Israel.

This Yiddish myth is essentially a subversive narrative about power that challenges widely held assumptions among Jews and Christians alike regarding the weakness of the Jewish minority in the Diaspora. Demeaning depictions of Jews as fearful and incapable of self-defense, much less combat, coexisted with Christian conceptualizations of Jews as violent, even physically robust. Predictions of the Red Jews as allies of the Antichrist as well as accusations of blood libels illustrate such concerns regarding the danger that Jews represented. The obverse notion was equally persistent in the Middle Ages and the early modern period. The work of Johann Jacob Schudt, an orientalist in Frankfurt am Main, which claims to present empirical observations, exemplifies this tendency to assert that Jews are inferior. In his theological interpretation of Jewish history, *Judaeus Christicida gravissime peccans et vapulans* (The Messiah-murdering Jew's most intense sin and punishment; 1703), he writes: "There is no worse insult for any honest man than to be called a Jew. Among all the two-legged earth-dwellers, these are the most disgusting, abject and contemptible creatures . . . of an abject and broken spirit that makes them shiver of fear at the lightest occasion, cowardly and anxious."[58]

Jews were aware of these common allegations, as *Kol Mevaser* exhibits. Akrish reports that, upon hearing of a forceful Jewish people, Sultan Suleiman the Magnificent was reputed to have responded that they could only possess half that strength if indeed they were Jews.[59] Jewish timidity could even be strategically exaggerated for political purposes, as displayed by the seventeenth-century Venetian rabbi and scholar Simone Luzzatto in *Discorso circa il stato de gl' hebrei* (Discourse concerning the condition of the Jews), where he aims to convince his Christian audience that Jews lacked political aspirations. He states that, being "a nation of a most debased and weak spirit,"[60] they were incapable of exercising governance.

Juxtaposed with this disparaging imagery of the meek Jew, rabbinic culture developed a more nuanced approach to Jewish manhood. The gentle and bookish Talmud scholar (*talmid ḥakham*), who values words over actions, offered a positive counter to the gentile ideal of the muscular and forceful soldier. It was a desirable alternative to the bellicose masculinity of hegemonic discourse in the Roman world and, later, in Christendom, which remained influential well into the modern period.[61] Daniel Boyarin has pointedly argued that Jewish resistance in the Diaspora has primarily been characterized by evasive tactics.[62] Various literary forms of Jewish counterhistory—the imagined nation of the Red Jews among them—manifest this trend; each polemic conveys the resentments of the marginalized who despise the strong.[63]

Fantasies of violence played an important role in European Jewish history, as Israel Yuval and Elliott Horowitz show in their studies of the Middle Ages and the early modern period, respectively.[64] This phenomenon is not limited to the tradition of messianic vengeance, detailed above, and expansive retellings of great warriors of the past, such as King David. Violent anti-Christian hostility found symbolic expression in ritual and prayer and Old Yiddish epics such as the highly popular *Bovo d'Antona* by Elye Bokher and the romance *Viduvilt* feature chivalric knights as the protagonists in plots that center on fierce confrontations.[65] And yet, despite having triumphed over his adversaries, the Jewish knight Viduvilt is depicted as vulnerable with equal frequency in the same account: for instance, he narrowly escapes death several times; when sparring with the mother of the giant that he is pursuing, she beats him twice; after fighting a dragon, he faints and, while unconscious, is robbed and left naked.[66]

Yiddish stories like those about Viduvilt and the Red Jews convey a dissonance between the well-established view that power can only be exercised by those who wield conventional force and the fantastic victory of a most unlikely hero. They indicate that although Jews (in these tales as in life) may not have appeared strong to the casual observer, they were far from powerless. To the contrary, despite their manifest limitations, the heroes in the myth of the Red Jews display remarkable, ostensibly physical, strength in the various competitions. As we saw in the Safed letter, two children wage an offensive that leads a cavalry to surrender. Similarly, the little Red Jew in *Ma'aseh Akdamut* performs extraordinary feats: he easily raises a heavy steel pole and throws it into the sky; he bends a gigantic tree as if it were a twig; and he grinds two millstones into powder with his bare hands. It is no coincidence that the latter echoes Samson, who exhibits his supernatural might by lifting two mountains and crumbling them like clods of earth.[67]

This Yiddish fable deliberately contrasts the valiant Esau (the Christian enemy) with David the warrior (the little Red Jew) rather than Jacob, his mild brother. The Yiddish Red Jews thus defy the traditional Jewish dichotomy between these biblical twins, with Jacob signifying the domestic realm and Esau representing the typically masculine domains of the field and the hunt.[68] Rather, they embody compatibility between the idea of the scholarly Jew and the skilled fighter. The little Red Jews compensate for their frailty by harnessing strength from a source that is neither corporeal nor visible, but that could even beat their rivals at their muscle-flexing game: magic based on the divine names. Their physical might flows from the holy power of letters, connecting the intellectual ideal with the aspiration for Jewish forcefulness. Their opponents, Prester John and the monk, respectively, hint at a similar notion in Christian culture: Christian clerics were excluded from bearing arms in battle but their vigor remained unchallenged, for their masculinity was derived from spiritual combat against the forces of evil.[69] The myth of the Red Jews thus exposes a thread of Jewish vernacular culture in early modern central Europe that did not fully accept the ideals of communal resignation to the trials of exilic existence and of Jewish men who spurn violence.

## (Red) Jews Out of Control

While medieval and early modern Jewish religious and ethical norms continued to propagate this picture of Jewish manhood, as prescribed by rabbinic Judaism, several Yiddish accounts display a conflict over two dissonant modes of response to the threats posed by the Christian majority. This tension is exemplified by the story of a magical goose in the collection of Yiddish tales about Jewish life in Worms that were compiled by the sexton and scribe Yuzpa Shammes and posthumously published by his son in Yiddish as

*Mayse Nissim* (Account of wonders; Amsterdam, 1696). This narrative recounts events in 1349, when Jews were charged with having poisoned the city's wells and allegedly causing a plague. In retaliation, the Christians of Worms set out to kill their Jewish neighbors. When the bishop refused to intervene, these Jews resolved to steer their own fate by lashing out against their tormentors. On the very day when the Jews were to be executed, their community elders assassinated the entire city council, less notable Jewish men engaged in combat with Christians in the streets, and Jewish women set fires around the city. Ultimately, this brave response failed; most Jews in Worms perished. The fortunate few that survived were not those who fought back but those who were concealed in the homes of compassionate Christians. When searching for these hideouts, Christians pursuers enlisted an enchanted goose that flew to each house where a Jew was being sheltered. As a result, more Jews were slain. Force could not quell this hostility, which continued unabated until a learned Jewish visitor, who was disguised as a priest, tricked the Christians into questioning that goose.[70] While read by earlier scholarship as a simple tale of Jewish resistance, Iris Idelson-Shein has recently considered this account in the context of Old Yiddish works that tend to discourage violence in opposition to persecution and advocate silence as the preferred course. She highlights how Yuzpa's tale seems to suggest that violent resistance against the Christian majority is pointless, even counterproductive.[71]

Diametrically opposite advice for Jewish behavior under duress appears in a tale from the *Mayse Bukh*.[72] Astrid Lembke's analysis of this narrative shows the use of literary techniques that resemble those discussed above in accounts of the Red Jews.[73] In this case, a pious rabbi is transformed into a ferocious werewolf by his cunning wife, and he begins to run wild through the forests, devouring humans. As in the Red Jews' story, this narrator equivocates regarding the suitable means for Jews to ensure their survival: intellectual acumen versus physical aggression. Here too, a combination of these capacities eventually proves successful. The rabbi-werewolf regains his human form by writing a Hebrew message in the snow, urging his king to help him retrieve the magical ring that his wife used to transform him. By relying on his human ability, the rabbi seems to prioritize scholarship; however, his plea concludes with a lethal threat to the king if he withholds support.[74] In the end, the rabbi rescues himself by exercising violence as a werewolf. Even though we are informed early in this story that the rabbi is well-versed in seventy languages, he chooses to communicate with the king in Hebrew.[75]

The rabbi thereby wills the king to summon his advisors to translate this message. By using the holy tongue, the rabbi uncompromisingly foregrounds his Jewishness; by deliberately avoiding Yiddish, he adamantly demonstrates his refusal to bend to the surrounding Christian majority and their authorities, not even to use a language that would facilitate mutual comprehension.

Another parallel with the Red Jews' story is apparent in the deceit enacted by the werewolf who had previously accompanied the king like a loyal dog. Lembke accurately stresses that the rabbi's transformation unmasks the ferocious potential hidden beneath his human skin. Christians may have mistaken Jews for servile dogs, but this story tells its audience that, in fact, Jews are wolves who will succeed, by force if necessary. This narrator thereby takes up the derogatory association of Jews as dogs that had been widespread in Christian Europe since the Middle Ages and replaces the dog in that insulting analogy with its noble lupine relative.[76] In all three stories, deception is a common means for revealing each narrative's message: the rabbi-werewolf, the disguised Jewish visitor who undermines trust in the goose, and the little Red Jew all trick the eye with an outward appearance cloaking a Jewish ideal that becomes clear to the reader as the plot unfolds. Despite their shared elements, these tales utterly differ regarding how such individuals achieve their goals. While the diplomatic visitor clearly favors the amicable option, the werewolf and the Red Jews stand for a confrontational approach toward the majority society.

The popularity of the latter two tales may reveal dormant aspirations of Jews in Ashkenaz. Yuval has suggested that such narratives "reflect how Jews of the early modern period wished to see themselves." He claims that this assertive, early modern vision contrasts sharply with the medieval Jewish inclination to defer revenge to the messianic future.[77] While I take issue with this neat chronological partition—the stories analyzed here most certainly circulated in oral tellings long before their first written versions, and parallel tales of armed resistance are documented in medieval Jewish literature[78]—these contrasting forms of behavior highlight a fundamental conflict over strategies for addressing social tension and organizing life in the Diaspora. The Yiddish narrative tradition that includes the Red Jews and the rabbi-werewolf offers a variant that did not conform to the acquiescent principles of proper conduct advanced by rabbinic and lay leadership as well as the Old Yiddish tradition, where the story of the goose originated, namely: rise up and act.

Adam Teller's analysis of sources related to the 1648–49 Chmielnicki uprising in Ukraine, with its rampant massacres of Jews, is highly instructive for the realities and representations of violent empowerment.[79] Natan Notte Hannover, who chronicled these events in his *Yeven Mezulah* (Book on the abyss of despair; Venice, 1653), describes the brutal killings of Jewish victims in graphic detail.[80] He underscores another aspect of these assaults in his description of Tulczyn, where Jews and Polish soldiers and nobles initially joined forces and bravely fought against their common enemy. However, when the Polish aristocrats plotted to betray their Jewish allies to the Cossacks in an attempt to save themselves, the "Jews understood the deception and wanted to oppose and kill the nobles first, because they had been the ones to betray the pact." But the head of the yeshiva in Tulczyn, Rabbi Aaron, pleaded: "Listen, Brothers and Fellow Jews. We are in exile among the nations. Should you lay a hand on the nobles, and the Christian kings hear of it, they will extract vengeance from all our brothers in exile, Heaven Forfend. So, if it has been decreed in Heaven, we will accept our judgment with pleasure."[81]

This rabbinic leader rejected his community's advocacy of vigilante action, which challenged the moral and social norms that tacitly guided the precarious life of Jewry, as a dangerous precedent that would ultimately be self-defeating in a hostile Christian environment. Whether historically accurate or imagined, this account certainly suited Hannover's efforts to establish a Polish-Jewish identity that emphasized Jewish suffering and martyrdom.[82] With similar reasoning, Jewish community authorities in early modern Germany cautioned against anti-Christian animus at times of messianic ferment.[83] Given the incendiary potential—even if only fantasized—they also objected to an openly polemical Purim play; it was regarded "de facto as political action that required a very specific kind of control and policing."[84] The tales about the Red Jews and their activist tone were prone to provoke the Jewish elite's fear of losing communal control as well. From their perspective, the blurred categories in the Yiddish stories threatened established hierarchies because, instead of relying on guidance from communal leaders, the Red Jews opted for populist agency.

Rabbinic leaders tended to assume a vigilant posture toward Yiddish publications; although this language was tolerated as a necessary means for furthering religious education, vernacular literature also posed a threat to the elite's monopoly on learning and authority. The invention of the printing press precipitated an inexorable spread of information, as Hebrew and Yiddish books became available to an expanding readership.[85] Yiddish printing, in particular, gave less educated men and women unprecedented access to knowledge, without being mediated by a teacher, and participation in intellectual and societal discourse that had previously been beyond their reach. The authors, editors, translators, and producers of Yiddish books had an unparalleled role in shaping this phenomenon and its content.[86]

The letter from Safed offers unique insight into this tenuous balance of power and the role of Yiddish literature in negotiating the boundaries of permissible action within the exilic community. In contrast to *Ma'aseh Akdamut*, the line of attack here is aimed less at the Christian majority than the Jewish authorities. At critical moments in the story, Jewish leaders are depicted as weak, even indecisive, as illustrated by King Daniel, who quickly transfers responsibility for handling the situation to the rabbis. Earlier in that narrative, the head of the community and the rabbis who went before Prester John are not cast in a more favorable light: the rabbis are imprisoned, and the community elders achieve a nominal success in their audience with Prester John, convincing him to grant them one year to prove the veracity of the biblical verse that he overheard. The elders merely manage to defer the threat, whereas the rabbis remain in prison until the two little Red Jews explicitly request their release after having defeated Prester John's army.[87] The Safed letter thus reveals lacunae in the leadership of the Jewish community.

As the story unfolds, the Jewish elite seems to fare better, especially when Prester John honors King Daniel by journeying to visit him, thereby acknowledging the superiority of both the king of the Red Jews and his country's wealth. Daniel accepts an oath that Prester John will improve the standing of his Jewish subjects, and he will even dedicate their taxes to support their synagogues and impoverished Jews. Having negotiated a peace agreement on the basis of these terms, Prester John returns home and offers an awestruck report on the splendor of this Jewish kingdom.[88] The tale could have concluded with this scene, which seals Prester John's defeat. However, the first in a series of codas draws the reader's attention to a letter that King Daniel sent with Prester John for the Jews of his country. Upon his return, Prester John delivers this correspondence to the *parnassim* (Jewish community elders), which instructs the Jews in his realm to obey their Christian king, for he agreed to improve their treatment. It ends with the call: "And be pious and serve God the Lord, so you will fare well."[89] Daniel's letter is enthusiastically received by the Jews.

This addition surprisingly tempers the Jewish triumph that was catalyzed by tenacious individuals, thereby wedging this tale back into the framework of traditional community politics. I would posit that this insistence on the rabbinic dictum that "the law of the country is the law" (Aramaic, *dina de-malkhuta dina*), meaning that local law is binding for Jews, reflects Jewish leaders' fears of losing social control. The letter that is attributed to King Daniel discourages disobedience among the broad populace, including autonomous actions, thus preserving the integrity of communal authority. In another attempt to restrain the revolutionary message of the Red Jews' myth, these same *parnassim* command the two children to cease their attack on Prester John's army; the Jewish elders alone have the power to bridle the little Red Jews gone wild. This intervention by the established Jewish leadership ultimately makes it possible for peace to be brokered between the two kings and ensure the continued thriving of a Jewish community in the Christian realm. These interjections seem to represent a secondary conservative message that is interwoven into the legend of the Red Jews, perhaps at a later stage, as its position in the epilogue suggests.

Much like this early modern understanding, from the vantage of Jewish historiography too, power has usually been viewed as a collective venture.[90] David Biale, who pioneered the systematic study of Jewish power, focuses on its political aspects, which he defines as "the ability of a people to control its relations to other peoples as well as its own internal political, cultural, religious, economic and social life. . . . Power can only be exercised by a collective, a political body whose members recognize its authority and whose legitimacy is recognized by others." He terms power as "the attempt to exercise strength and authority in a collective framework, informed by conscious political goals."[91] In her aforementioned study on *Viduvilt*, Lembke too considers power to be communal in nature, stressing that the Jewish knight is positioned as a hero within his community, for his status depends on its support and acceptance. Even when this hero reaches the apex of the hierarchy as its sovereign, unlike in the medieval German romance, he remains a *primus inter pares* (first among equals).[92]

In stark contrast, the Red Jews act unilaterally. In legends of the Ten Tribes, hope traditionally focuses on the collective, whereas the Red Jews in our Yiddish tale do not act as a group. Rather, they pick one from their ranks to intervene in times of distress. These little Red Jews are singular actors.

Similarly, the rabbi in the werewolf story operates as a proverbial lone wolf, not the leader of a pack. Thus, these rebellious Yiddish narratives discuss autonomous action for the benefit of the collective. The imperative to support the community also underlies the tale of the werewolf, for this triggers the entire plot: the rabbi used his magical ring to amass money, which he donated to charity; appalled, his wife wants him out of her life and hexes him.[93] As Lembke has observed, the rabbi trusts no one, not even his disciples or the benevolent king, who seeks his friendship: "The readers are told, one must trust solely in God, keep one's own council, and ultimately maintain independence."[94]

Whereas the rabbi-werewolf is part of the learned elite, in the legend of the Red Jews no specialized knowledge or outstanding skills are needed to become a hero. In *Ma'aseh Akdamut*, the Red Jews decide whom to send to Ashkenaz by casting lots. This inclusive reading is bolstered by the game-changing dream of many pious men, simultaneously with a wise sage; these dreamers represent the full spectrum of the community of learners, not only its intellectual or social elite. In the Safed letter, two children are randomly picked to be trained for their task. Let us consider the unusual representation of children as heroes more closely. The printed version states: "If it is performed by the children, the miracle will be even greater."[95] What then is their singular role besides being little? Irrespective of their social background, children are not accorded authority in communal political structures. To the contrary, children were expected to obey their parents. In *Kol Mevaser*, the youngest son of King Aaron, king of the Red Jews, wants to join their military campaign. Enraged, his father objects, citing his youth. However, seeing his older friends armed for battle, the prince dons his armor and rides swiftly across the Sambatyon. On the other side, he encounters eighty enemies and kills them all. Upon his safe return, rather than chastising his impetuous son, the king lauds his extraordinary strength.[96] Thus, this youthful rebellion is retroactively sanctioned. This motif has a parallel in the Safed letter, in a scene in which King Daniel's nephew seeks permission to cross the Sambatyon. In contrast to *Kol Mevaser*, rather than flatly denying the lad's request, his royal uncle only stipulates that no Sabbath laws be violated.[97]

The observances of social and religious standards would typically be enforced by the communal leadership who guided the Jewish populace toward a righteous path, akin to parents overseeing their offspring. This system of societal governance is described in the portrait of Susa early in the letter from

Safed: anyone who violates the law is held to account by the rabbinical court, whose judges "constrain the people with the law," thereby ensuring that they live according to the Torah.[98] The stories of the Red Jews suggest that extreme circumstances might justify an otherwise unthinkable course of action, together with questioning the rigid power structure of the community and altering the hierarchy of cultural norms. Significantly, the little Red Jews do not even belong to the vulnerable community in need of defense; they are outsiders, from beyond the Sambatyon. The rare discussion of children among the tribes beyond the Sambatyon River has an additional dimension: Chone Shmeruk has shown that Passover *haggadot* refer to Israelite children's participation in the events in Egypt, to nurture the younger generation's engagement with the holiday and placing themselves in the exodus drama.[99] Similarly, the tales of the Red Jews may have been designed to convey a pedagogical message to young audiences.

The stories about the Red Jews and related tales convey a strongly subversive message by highlighting resistance, not only against the outside Christian oppressor but also against restraints from within the Jewish community. The recurrent theme of powerful Jewish agency in these narratives challenged the established implications of Diaspora life, meaning acquiescence until messianic redemption brings release and indiscriminate acceptance of the present social structures. Whereas the utopian myth of the Ten Lost Tribes of Israel promises to supplant exile, the Red Jews question current conditions, traditional social organization, and ethical values. The little Red Jew represents the Diaspora itself. That individual and autonomous hero offers a model of agency that every Jew can activate to relieve the straits that typified minority existence—irrespective of erudition and social status. Indeed, different sources of power are presented as complementary in a society to which all members contribute according to their abilities.

## Gendered Perspectives on Class

In order to discuss class, these stories about the Red Jews approach female roles, much like childhood, with complexity. Jewish men who primarily read Yiddish because of their limited Hebrew proficiency could hardly embrace the conventional approach to Jewish masculinity, which was synonymous with erudition. For men who would never become rabbinic scholars, a different type of ideal was needed. Paradoxically, these men were often cast in feminine terms by Yiddish authors and book producers, who categorized them as "men who are like women."[100] As this equation seems equally displeasing for the male majority of Yiddish readers, the Red Jews and similar Yiddish texts provided a contrast to that disparate characterization.

Medieval Christian theology and science deprecatingly likened male Jews to women when characterizing them as "unmanly." This quality was complemented by descriptions of their alleged carnality, feeble intellect, and lack of faith. Early modern Christian sources manifest this portrait of the "effeminate" Jewish man.[101] The French Roman Catholic priest Henri Grégoire, better known as Abbé Gregoire, actually linked this "womanish" weakness to red hair in the late eighteenth century, when he voiced popular opinion that Jewish men "have almost all red beards, which is the usual mark of an effeminate temperament."[102] In contrast, imagery of the effeminate Jew in Jewish culture underscored the positive rabbinical ideal of manhood. David Kimḥi, for example, embraced the ascription of feminine traits—evidenced by an absence of aggression—to Jewish men as a spiritual model for exilic life.[103] Iris Idelson-Shein has persuasively demonstrated that such feminization of Jewish men appears in early modern Yiddish compositions as well. She analyzes gendered role reversal in one story, retold by Glikl of Hameln, a German Jewish merchant whose life spanned the late seventeenth and early eighteenth centuries, in which a pious Jew is coerced into marrying a "savage" woman who brutally rapes him.[104]

Stories about the Red Jews, in contrast, explicitly affirm that the attribution of feminine norms to Jews and forceful Jewish agency were in no way mutually exclusive. It is hardly coincidental that the manuscript collection Ms. Opp. 714, which features the two main versions of the tale of the Red Jews and the empowerment story of the rabbi-werewolf, also includes a Yiddish version of the apocryphal Book of Judith. This heroine similarly takes matters into her own hands when she decapitates the enemy general Holofernes, thereby saving the people of Israel from another seemingly unstoppable threat when her male counterparts were so terrified that even their trust in God's deliverance had waned.[105] Even though depictions of extraordinary women may have appealed to a certain segment of Yiddish readers, the primary image in this collection is the unexpected triumph of the Jewish man, who is pejoratively viewed as womanish by his own peers, rather than the vindication of female agency. The gender preference in the letter from Safed suggests the generic mention of female figures: the boy from the land of the Red Jews is consistently mentioned before the girl; he takes the offense by instigating the fight with Prester John's troops (in the printed version); and only he speaks to the king (in the manuscript). The girl, by contrast, merely follows his lead and never acts independently.[106] While the addition of women to the plot effectively heaps insults on the enemies' injury, the heroic team is more male than female.

In addition to the tastes of the majority of consumers of Old Yiddish literature, we need to take into consideration the role of men as its primary creators. Although these authors acknowledged the traditional roles of women in Jewish society and were attentive to their worries, they often treated women as inferior.[107] This ambivalence is exemplified by the narrator of *Ma'aseh Akdamut*, who introduces the wives of the main protagonists, Meir Shatz and Dan, the little Red Jew. He strives to reveal the terrible price that these women pay when, after completing their mission, their husbands cannot cross the Sambatyon and return home: they are each left an *agunah*, a deserted wife who may not remarry for halakhic reasons because her husband disappeared without granting her a divorce (neither Meir nor the little Red Jew can write a divorce document on the Sabbath). This detail reflects the contemporary problem of *agunot* in the Jewish communities of early modern Europe when travel was dangerous, especially in times of war, and communication was limited. Despite the urgent demand that the congregation take care of these abandoned wives and support them financially, *Ma'aseh Akdamut* does not include much of an internal critique of this reality of Jewish society. In fact, the *agunot* issue clearly supports the male-centered tendency of this empowerment tale. The happy ending is limited to its male heroes: Meir and Dan each take a new wife, moving on and starting a new life, while their first wives remain chained into passivity, unable to improve their dire situation. In fact, Dan marries the daughter of Meir Shatz (in parallel, Meir marries Dan's daughter), and his wife from the Rhenish city of Worms, soon afterward, gives birth to a son.[108] In the end, the exilic community welcomes the triumphant hero into their fold, claiming that the lineage of the Red Jews extends into diasporic Jewry through the male line. The conclusion of *Ma'aseh Akdamut* thus indicates that their heroism can be replicated in exile. Liberating agency becomes an option for men, in contrast to their female counterparts.

This subordination of female protagonists is hardly surprising, since the agency of women was generally considered suspect in early modern Jewish society. Not unlike contemporaneous Christian culture, rabbinical and lay leadership challenged the role of women in the public arena as an exclusively male space and attempted to confine women to the domestic and private sphere (though not always successfully).[109] Elisheva Carlebach and Debra Kaplan argue that the general increase in regulation of daily life in early modern Europe affected women in particular, since the domestic sphere had previously not been subject to such formal regulation.[110] The retreat of women from public life and the restrictions imposed on their social and religious scope were paralleled by suspicions regarding feminine power that are ubiquitous in Jewish literature from that period, in both Hebrew and Yiddish.[111] In his work on Old Yiddish Purim plays, for example, Jerold Frakes has demonstrated that Mordechai saves the Jews in these dramas, whereas minimal initiative is credited to Esther.[112] Similarly, the moral of the werewolf tale signals that a man who confides in his wife is a fool. The version of this story in the printed *Mayse Bukh* elaborates on the unworthiness of women by detailing the disaster that a cunning wife brings to the rabbi. She ultimately meets the fate she deserves and is transformed into an ass, implying that punishment and ridicule await any rebellious woman.[113] While the werewolf is a symbol of active resistance, this tale bears a misogynist message similar to that of the myth of the Red Jews: if a Jew speaks up in exile, that daring role is for a man, not a woman. Yet, the brave standing of Mordechai and the rabbi-werewolf—members of the social and intellectual elite, respectively—suggests that gendered criticism in Old Yiddish literature is regularly linked to the reinforcement of male-dominated social power structures and general fears of revolt.

## A Proud Self-Image

The Red Jews propagated a self-confident version of a Jewish identity, impressing their pride onto the diasporic collective memory. "Seeing" a Red Jew while reading or hearing their legend served as a visual mnemonic. The audience would retain the heroic message more readily due to visual associations.[114] Rachel Rafael Neis has demonstrated that visuality had an analogous function in rabbinic literature, as exemplified in the Jerusalem Talmud in tractate Shabbat 1:2, 47a: "One who recites a tradition in the name of one who said it should see the tradition's author as if he were standing before him." According to Neis's interpretation, the sight of that sage, whether in person or envisioned, would become a reminder of his halakhic rulings and thus guarantee the authenticity and longevity of their transmission.[115] Similarly, the evocative image of the Red Jews drew on the efficacy of optical recall.

While red signifies the potent warrior, as noted above, crimson and purple are traditionally the colors of royal dominion across cultures.[116] In the Bible, given its relatively sparse use of color terms, the red-purple range dominates, often with reference to the splendor of the Temple.[117] Accordingly, for early modern Yiddish speakers, the Red Jews provided vividly colored proof of the continued existence of an independent Jewish society beyond the Sambatyon River. In a written repudiation of Judaism, the convert Paul Joseph, who served as a rabbi in Poznań prior to his conversion in 1611, explicates this use of color. He refers to a locus classicus in Jewish-Christian debates on Genesis 49:10: "The scepter shall not depart from Judah, nor the ruler's staff from between his feet, until Shiloh come; and the homage of peoples be his." According to the classic Christological understanding of Shiloh as the Messiah, this verse ostensibly validates Jesus's messianic claim, for Israel lost its political sovereignty close to his lifetime and has been in exile ever since.[118] Jewish refutation of this interpretation would usually refer to the Ten Tribes, saying "that they still have their scepter that is across the river Sambatyon. Therefore, the Jews of that country are called the Red Jews."[119] Over a century later, another convert, the aforementioned Augusti, in his book on the Red Jews, offers the same explanation for this unparalleled expression for the Ten Tribes in Yiddish, stating that the name Red Jews "is highly esteemed and glorious... both on account of the red and lively color of their faces and the exquisite purple clothes, which they wear as a free people in order to distinguish themselves from all other [Jews] living in misery." A footnote explains to the German reader: "Neither European nor Asian Jews are allowed to wear red garments because they are still mourning the [destruction of the] Temple and the city of Jerusalem. The color red is a sign of freedom and of the greatest joy among Jews. Royal children were privileged [to wear red], a color that distinguished them from others. The Red Jews, however, so they say, have experienced no *galut*, no *ḥorban*, i.e., no captivity and no destruction. These Jews wear the most beautiful purple, and no one can forbid them [from doing so]."[120]

Indeed, it was customary for Jews in premodern Christian Europe to wear dark colors (black, gray, brown, and dark blue). The Jewish leadership considered it improper for Jews to wear colorful fabric and, especially, bright colors. Such clothing was deemed unethical, not least because it was thought to be an ostentatious display that was unfitting for life in exile.[121] The preamble to ordinances by the Jewish community of Fürth in 1770 underscores this value by advising its members to desist from dressing like non-Jews and acting cheerful.[122] The rabbinical authority Moses Isserles—in his glosses on the legal code *Shulḥan arukh* (The set table; Venice, 1565)—likewise objects to the adoption of gentile conduct in order to avoid any blurring of religious boundaries. He rules that Jews are forbidden from embracing gentile norms if they bear traces of the immoral practices associated with idolators (עובדי כוכבים), such as dressing in red, which characterized noblemen.[123] In contrast, paralleled in Christian perspective, the colors of common people and societal outsiders were to be dark.[124] A letter to the Jews of Germany, dated to the first half of the fifteenth century and attributed to Yitzhak Zarfati, the Chief Rabbi of Edirne, points to a corresponding Jewish dress code: "In Christendom . . . you dare not even venture to clothe your children in red or in blue, according to our taste, without exposing them to the insult of being beaten black and blue, or kicked green and red, and therefore are ye condemned to go about meanly clad in sad colored raiment."[125]

The free Red Jews thus deliberately rejected black garb, preferring instead their red wardrobe. The abovementioned account in *Kol Mevaser* tells that Jews beyond the Sambatyon "had all kinds of beautiful clothes made from wool and silk, from silver and gold, of all kinds of pretty colors. These Jews did not wear black garments."[126] This source reports that a young Red Jew was once seized by Prester John's forces. Hesitant to execute such a handsome, vigorous warrior, despite the fact that this Red Jew had killed many of his own subjects, the famed Christian leader tried, in vain, to persuade this prisoner to convert by promising him riches and sovereignty over his people. The captive justified his past actions as self-defense, since Prester John's soldiers had raided the Red Jews' territory, and by observing that the priestly king would have done the same. Prester John was convinced by this argument. Not only did he let him live, on the condition that henceforth he would never again harm members of his nation, but this Red Jew was sent home with specially prepared (presumably kosher) provisions and an escort of forty knights to protect him until he reached the Sambatyon. Before his departure, Prester John presented him a black silk robe interwoven with gold, but the young man refused this gift because it violated his people's dress code. Neither would he accept a red robe, however, for he considered it unclean, probably—reflecting Isserles's argument—because Jews were not permitted to wear anything that was associated with Christianity.[127]

The Red Jews' bright palette was a bold reinterpretation of Jews' attire in the lands on the other side of the Sambatyon, as described in earlier Hebrew sources. Jewish geography often situated two groups, each identified with a particular color, in the vicinity of the Ten Tribes: *Bnei Rekhav* and *Bnei Mosheh*.[128] On the one hand, Benjamin of Tudela reports that the Rechabites, "mourners of Zion," dress in black and fast to commemorate the destruction of the Temple.[129] According to an early modern Yiddish translation of this account, these pious men in black never partake of meat or wine, not even on the Sabbath and festivals. Day and night, they are devoted to sacred texts in study halls. They do not have houses, but they spend their entire lives in caves, weeping over the Temple's demise and pleading with God to bestow mercy on the people of Israel.[130] On the other hand, Eldad ha-Dani describes the lush red-linen robes worn by the Sons of Moses, who personified a very different expression of that same grief. The Sons of Moses were identified as Levites who had been carried to safety on a cloud after the destruction of the First Temple. Eldad clothes their descendants in red garments, reminiscent of the historical robe worn by the High Priest.[131] The Yiddish Red Jews adopt this color of a glorious past but without its melancholic aftertaste: for them, red symbolizes the exuberance of freedom that replaced the sorrow of exile. The name "sons of saviors" (*bnei moshi'im*) for the Red Jews, which appears in Jewish sources from early modern Ashkenaz, possibly represents a phonetic link to *Bnei Mosheh*.[132]

This assertive self-image is enhanced by affirmations of the Red Jews' exceptional beauty, which is most pronounced in the tale of the handsome warrior who was seized from their ranks in *Kol Mevaser*. This narrative was pleasing to the eye and the ear alike. *Kol Mevaser* introduces a unique soundscape to the sensory world beyond the Sambatyon by reporting on the mellifluous voice of this Red Jew. Upon being released from captivity and before departing with his escort, the knights ask Prester John to invite the youth to perform a song, "as the Jews sing." He performed so beautifully that all who heard him were moved to tears.[133] Like their scarlet dress code, this detail contradicts the motif that Jews are continually mourning their exile (as symbolized by the Levites refusing to sing at the rivers of Babylon) by emphasizing vocal happiness over silent lamentation.

The depiction of a physically attractive and musically talented Red Jew in fact countered Christian allegations that Jews were ugly and not musical. The long-standing accusation that Jews created dissonant sounds, by contrast with the idealized claim that Christians produced vocal harmony, was compounded by contemporaneous Christian imagery of "the ugly Jew."[134] Jews were acutely aware of this negative portrait that featured dark red and black hues to denigrate Jewish skin color or hair. They likewise understood and accepted the European standard of white beauty and the unaesthetic connotations of dark or black skin, as demonstrated in a talmudic story in the *Mayse Bukh*. This vernacular compilation translates the Hebrew phrase אדם אחד שהיה מכוער ביותר (an exceedingly ugly person) in the Talmud (BT Taʾanit 20a) as איין גרושיר שווארציר מאן (a big black man) in Yiddish. Accordingly, in the Talmud, Rabbi Elazar asks whether everyone in that man's town is as ugly as he is; whereas, in the *Mayse Bukh*, the rabbi inquires if the people of the town are black like him.[135]

Like their Christian counterparts, prominent medieval Jewish thinkers such as Rashi and Kimḥi interpreted darkness as a punishment for transgression, often based on the suffering servant figure in Isaiah.[136] The Talmud (BT Sanhedrin 92b) claims that any young Israelite men who were forced into exile were executed because gentile women went wild over their extraordinary handsomeness. These earlier manifestations of Jewish beauty were thought to have vanished with the dispersion of the Jewish people, only to be restored in messianic times. The anonymously authored manuscript *Sefer Vikuʾaḥ Teshuvah la-Minim* (A book of responses in debates with the gentiles), presumably copied in Germany in the sixteenth century, states: "Before our Temple was destroyed we were more beautiful. . . . When our Temple was destroyed, that beauty was taken away. . . . And God is going to return us our beauty."[137] In *Sefer ha-Niẓẓaḥon*, probably written in Prague circa 1400, Yom Tov Lipmann Mühlhausen also predicts that "in the messianic age, we will all be good-looking." This statement was written as a counter to Christian ridicule toward Jews who are recognizable by their physical appearance, likely suggesting that they could be identified by their unattractive features.[138] Until the arrival of the Messiah, physical beauty could not be maintained in the harsh conditions of exile, which one medieval exegete from northern France compared to the sun that unrelentingly burns the skin of those who are exposed to it for too long. He explains Jews' dark complexions thus: "Because we are in exile, as it is said in Song of Songs (1:6): 'Don't stare at me because I am swarthy, because the sun has gazed upon me. My mother's sons quarreled with me, they made me guard the vineyards; my own vineyard I did not guard.' But when I kept my own vineyard I was most beautiful, as it is written: 'Your beauty won you fame among the nations' (Ezek. 16:14)."[139]

Such commentaries demonstrate medieval and early modern Jews' interpretation of their own identification as being dark and ugly by European standards. This stance was both defensive and offensive, since these authors proudly reappropriated darkness as a signifier of piety and chosenness, not inferiority. In the eighteenth century, for example, both Jonathan Eybeschütz, a rabbi in Hamburg, and Abraham b. Elijah, son of the Gaon of Vilna, proudly tout dark skin as an indication of genealogical purity, proving that Jews had remained separate from gentiles.[140] In contrast to the conflation of the beautiful with the good, and the imperfect with the immoral, the unaesthetic became imbued with transcendent valence, identified with moral principle and spiritual distinction. This form of cultural reappropriation is expressed most explicitly in an oft-quoted passage from the anonymous *Nizzaḥon Yashan*, which concurred with the emergence of the Christian myth of the Red Jews. Its author, who compiled polemical arguments, directly responds to a common Christian perspective when he is asked why most gentiles are fair and handsome but most Jews are dark and unattractive. His reply: "This is similar to a fruit; when it begins to grow it is white but when it ripens it becomes black, as is the case with sloes and plums. On the other hand, any fruit which is red at the beginning becomes lighter as it ripens, as is the case with apples and apricots. This, then, is testimony that Jews are pure of menstrual blood so that there is no initial redness. Gentiles, however, are not careful about menstruant women and have sexual relations during menstruation; thus, there is redness at the outset, and so the fruit that comes out, i.e., the children, are light."[141] Relying on a medieval biological theory that explained Esau's and, by extension, Christians' redness by their alleged conception during menses,[142] *Nizzaḥon Yashan* thus accepts European Christian conventions that fair coloring indicates beauty but inverts their spiritual aesthetics; ugliness is counterbalanced by menstrual and, thus, moral purity. *Toldot Yeshu* extends this reasoning to its anti-hero, Yeshu: although his beauty is a topos in Christian iconography, this polemic claims that he was actually conceived during menstruation.[143]

The portrayal of the Red Jews in Old Yiddish literature departed meaningfully from these long-established responses to the notion of Jewish deformity. Rather than supplying an apologetic response, the Yiddish narrative inverts Christian aesthetic claims regarding Jewish appearances by recasting red features as beautiful. This myth bases its positive image of Jews on two sources. First, unsullied Jewish beauty was reputed to have survived among the Lost Tribes beyond the Sambatyon, where all Jews were well-built and had attractive facial features, and women were exceptionally passionate beauties.[144] Second, it evokes the biblical David, the poet and musician par excellence, whose ruddiness translates into handsomeness, as we have seen in Chapter 2. In the medieval and early modern period, *admoni* as an indication of David's good looks appears to have signified the rosy coloring of a healthy complexion in accordance with European ideals of beauty. Early modern physiognomic works that were written in Hebrew also articulate a Jewish preference for light skin with a rosy tone. *Shoshanat Ya'acov*, for instance, defines a pretty face as "white with red."[145] With their Davidic lineage, the Red Jews' visage fits the positive connotations of a rosy complexion, in contrast to the redness that derived from the sexual impurity of the red nation, Christian Edom.

In an extension of the Ten Tribes' tradition, the Red Jews' myth offers a fresh perspective on Jewish existence. Rather than grieving for what was lost in exile, tales of the Red Jews emphasize all that thrives across the Sambatyon, beyond the reach of persecution. There, Jews collectively flourish in spiritual harmony, exercising political independence and military prowess; and, individually, they exude physical and artistic eminence. The Red Jews' appearance thus regaled their audience with externally visible beauty that matched the proud awareness of their resources and strengths.

## Becoming by Seeing

The Jewish self-confidence that the Red Jews embodied was thought to have a qualitative influence on their audience's worldview and understanding of social conduct. I would posit that the Red Jews became icons of identity with a practical aim. Neis has pointed out that the rabbinic sages of late antiquity strove to stylize themselves as exemplars of religious praxis to facilitate their disciples' commitment to cultivating their own worthy qualities. This is no less a process of emulating a role model than becoming by seeing.[146] The sensory perception evoked by the Red Jews operated similarly. The Red Jews were positive visual objects designed to shape Yiddish readers' thoughts and actions. To "see" a Red Jew suggested becoming like him (to some degree). This mythic people's appearance and power had a magnetic effect, as a Yiddish adage suggests: "For a Red Jew it takes another Red Jew" (*Tsin a roytn yid darf men hobn a roytn yid*).[147]

The Yiddish adaptations of selected narratives from the Talmud and midrashim in the *Mayse Bukh* contribute to understanding the practical function of the myth of the Red Jews in Jewish culture. On the one hand, these rabbinic *aggadot* stress the importance of internal rather than corporeal attributes. The abovementioned tale of an ugly, swarthy man criticizes arrogance toward unsightly people, which leads them to be judged unworthy on the basis of their physique.[148] On the other hand, the *Mayse Bukh* is full of good-looking men and women of impeccable character and piety.[149] Most famously, Rabbi Yochanan is described as the *beau idéal* because of his exceptional looks. His splendor was so dazzling that it could illuminate an entire room. Rabbi Eliezer wept at the mere thought that such beauty would cease to exist upon this sage's death.[150] A parallel appears in *Tsene Rene*: when a righteous man dwells in a town, he is its beauty and light, but when he leaves, that beauty and light depart with him.[151] Another text states that Rabbi Yochanan would sit beside the entrance to a mikveh so the women who immersed in this ritual bath would behold his radiance before returning home to their husbands; as a result, they would give birth to sons who were similarly handsome and gifted as students of Torah.[152]

The depictions of Rabbi Yochanan from rabbinic sources that were transmitted in early modern Yiddish convey a significant lesson: his idealized appearance radiates and benefits anyone in his proximity. Other examples from Jewish culture confirm that despite any reservations, outer beauty was often pragmatically harnessed for sociopolitical purposes. Although the great medieval philosopher and rabbinic scholar Moses ben Maimon laments such simplistic correlations in his *Guide for the Perplexed*, he also explains that, in reference to Temple service, physical and moral perfection were deemed synonymous. Lest doubts be cast on the greatness of the ancient Israelite Temple, priests were selected according to their flawless physiques and were required to wear the most impressive dress.[153] Likewise in the eighteenth century, in *Amudei beit Yehudah* (Pillars of the house of Judah; 1766), the Lithuanian physician Judah Horowitz joins Maimonides in condemning this persistent conflation in his discussion of an alleged "savage" who is assumed to be immoral and uneducated since he does not dress like a gentleman or a prince, as if integrity and wisdom come with an elegant wardrobe. If so, he ironically asks, perhaps the reverse is also true, imagining a well-dressed mule with a necklace of golden bells.[154] Such repeated criticism reveals that the popular confusion of external beauty with virtue proved resilient.

Theories of vision that hinged on blurring the one who sees and the entity or thing being seen have been documented in Jewish and Christian culture throughout the Middle Ages and the early modern period. Images, colors, and shapes were thought to modify human feelings and behavior. This concept was applied to both positive and negative visual objects. By looking at a favored person or item, the one who sees would profit from the subject of his or her gaze, while unattractive visual input was thought to have a detrimental effect. Maimonides lauds the practice of viewing beautiful pictures, among other pleasant sensory stimuli for the eyes, ears, nose, and tongue, for their beneficial effects on the body and mind. When he ascribes healing powers to architecture, nature, music, and visual art, he likens exposure to these elements to rousing the appetite of a sick person who feels no hunger, positing that a dose of aesthetic stimuli can cure melancholy.[155]

The power of images, both real and fictive, also permeates folk culture. It underlies a notion that was commonly accepted in both Jewish and Christian premodern cultures: parents' visual encounters leave a mark on their offspring. Accounts of the physical influence that the visual stimuli or thoughts that parents, especially the mother, experience during intercourse or pregnancy have on a fetus abound in ancient, medieval, and early modern Hebrew and Yiddish texts, as in non-Jewish literature.[156] The tale of Rabbi Yochanan stationed near the mikveh is one such example. The author of *Nizzaḥon Yashan*, in his discussion of the ugliness of the Jewish body, refers to the impact of images in similar terms. He posits that Christians are so immoral that they have intercourse during the daytime, when they can see attractive faces on pictures, which explains why they give birth to such beautiful offspring.[157] The *Mayse Bukh* includes two versions of a related folktale. One speaks of a handsome, white royal couple to whom an unattractive, black baby is born; this event is explained by a painting of a Moor that hangs on the wall above the couple's bed. A variant on this story presents a black couple who gives birth to a white child, whose appearance is also ascribed to a visual stimulus. The latter telling also found its way into the immensely popular Yiddish ethical work *Simḥat ha-Nefesh* (Delight of the soul; Frankfurt am Main, 1707) by Elhanan Henle Kirchhan.[158]

Through such didactic tales, the ancient tradition that the senses decisively influence moral character and behavior reached a wide audience. Hebrew and Yiddish *musar* writings elaborated on this subject more abstractly. The opening chapter of the anonymously translated Yiddish edition of *Sefer Shevet Musar* (Book of the rod of admonition; Wilhermsdorf, 1725; first Hebrew printing, Constantinople, 1712), authored by the Ottoman Rabbi Elijah ha-Kohen Itamari, explains that "God created man with cavities. On the outside, he made sockets for his eyes so he could see. He created eyelids (lit. eyebrows) so he could close his eyes when he sleeps and avoid seeing bad events, as the prophet Isaiah said: '[He who walks in righteousness, speaks uprightly . . .] shuts his eyes against looking at evil.'"[159] The instruction here is to shut oneself off from negative influences, lest they enter through the eyes. Around the same time, Aaron of Hergershausen wrote in his *Liblikhe Tefile* (Lovely prayer; Frankfurt am Main, 1709): "The heart can do nothing without the five senses (lit. forces, כוחות)."[160] Here Aaron paraphrases the introduction to the anonymous ethical treatise *Orḥot Ẓaddikim* (The ways of the righteous; probably Germany, fifteenth century), originally written in Hebrew. The latter became one of the most popular books of ethical literature, printed in numerous Hebrew and Yiddish editions. Its first Yiddish publication was an abridged version, *Sefer ha-Middot* (A book of ethical qualities; Isny, 1542). The full Hebrew text appeared in Prague in 1581.[161] Echoing his source, Hergershausen focuses on practical behavior, offering guidance for religious life and the attainment of moral perfection. He explains that the heart, which arbitrates moral decisions, operates through the senses: since they transmit all stimuli to it, every thought and action necessarily follows that communication. He cautions that if the senses are not properly engaged (i.e., without a deeper understanding of what the ears hear and what the eyes see), the heart cannot discern and, therefore, signal what is good or harmful.[162]

Various Jewish and Christian sources attest to the notion that a colored object emanates the characteristics inherent in that particular hue. In parallel to early modern color theory, Jewish thinkers discuss the power of color to affect passions.[163] In *Pardes Rimonim* (An orchard of pomegranates), his encyclopedic synthesis of kabbalistic thought, Cordovero writes that colors channel the activities of their respective divine emanations. The *sefirah* of *gevurah* (the divine emanation of might; or *din*, judgment) is depicted in red, both verbally and in diagrams, since it symbolizes blood, cruelty, and wrath. Thus, everything red stimulates these qualities, much as wearing a red garment invokes judgment and a red face arouses associated emotions and actions.[164]

Analogously, the Red Jews' sensuous qualities relied heavily on the carefully crafted color symbolism that we have examined. The effect of the Red Jews' appearance on the mind's eye was intended to forge a proud Ashkenazic identity in exile. In *Ma'aseh Akdamut*, the narrator's choice of the figure of Rabbi Meir Shatz as a protagonist is hardly coincidental: "Me'ir" is the Hebrew word for "one who illuminates" or "enlightens." Occasionally, Meir Shatz would therefore be called Nehorai (the illuminator), like his namesake, the second-century Rabbi Meir, who was known as Rabbi Nehorai. This renowned sage was so handsome that, like Rabbi Yochanan, his countenance brightened any chamber.[165] Much like these classical rabbis, Meir Shatz introduced a spark of beauty—the little Red Jew—to illuminate his exilic community. Like Yochanan, who positioned himself outside the mikveh in his town, Meir Shatz draws readers' imaginary gaze to their glorious cousins beyond the Sambatyon. The description of the Red Jews' typological model David in 1 Samuel 16:12, as "ruddy-cheeked, bright-eyed, and handsome" (lit. goodly to look upon), is essential to fully comprehending this myth. Not only was this future king's attractive rosy mien associated with his eyes, but, more importantly, he was "goodly to look upon"—so Yiddish readers were being invited to do just that.

This self-assured visual message was deeply entrenched in Ashkenazic Jewish culture. Relics from the Red Jews were displayed in synagogues and Jewish homes in early modern Europe: small vessels filled with water or sand from the Sambatyon River that allegedly swirled throughout the week, only to cease when the Sabbath was about to start, indicating that the day of rest had begun, when the boundary between the Red Jews and Diaspora Jewry became less insurmountable.[166] To some degree, this fascination with the Red Jews may be compared to the veneration of saints and the experience of seeing icons in medieval and early modern Christianity. Indeed, Neis identifies the Christian cult of saints in Palestine as a major factor in the rabbinic search for corporeal manifestations of the sacred.[167] These portable renderings of Christ, the Virgin Mary, and saintly relics were all believed to be imbued with divine grace. Through visual piety, Christian saints and their relics were therefore conduits of the sacred. Rather than solely serving as reminders of saints' past deeds, worshippers anticipated an actual response, in the form of assistance in daily life from the sacral image or object of veneration that was encountered as a proxy for the historical figure that it represented.[168]

This immediacy was fortified by the fact that the myth of the Red Jews became anchored in the annual liturgy for Shavuot, the festival for which Meir Shatz composed *Akdamut Milin*. Just before Shavuot, Jewish communities in the Rhineland would commemorate the anti-Jewish pogroms of the First Crusade. Israel Yuval argues that local fast days which memorialized the martyrs of 1096 were intended to invoke divine wrath and spur God to finally destroy Edom and bring forth the Messiah. According to Yuval, the blood of these martyrs served as evidence of Christian guilt that must be atoned for when the Messiah arrives.[169] Jeffrey Hoffman has considered the history of *Akdamut* in the context of the Crusade massacres. He notes that the longevity of this piyyut in the Ashkenazic rite may be attributed to the importance of commemorating the events of 1096, for the catastrophes of the First Crusade gave additional meaning to this poem and thus strengthened its message of comfort for later generations.[170] It seems that in fact, among early modern Ashkenazic Jews, a sense of eschatological efficacy was attributed to the recitation of *Akdamut Milin* on Shavuot. This may be inferred from a statement by Isaac Wetzlar, a learned and well-traveled Jewish businessman from Celle (Lower Saxony). This eighteenth-century religious critic of Jewish society was heartened that this piyyut was recited in synagogues throughout Europe.[171] Yet he bemoaned the rejection of another mystical hymn, *Shir ha-Yiḥud* (Hymn of unity), recitation of which was likewise needed for the coming of the Messiah. Wetzlar was dissatisfied that most scholars refused to recite *Shir ha-Yiḥud* and, in some communities, it had been abolished entirely.[172]

In addition to the placement of *Akdamut Milin* in the Ashkenazic liturgy, Shavuot became the occasion for recounting the story of Meir Shatz and the Red Jews. *Ma'aseh Akdamut* was read in Jewish communities across Ashkenaz on Shavuot, presumably in domestic settings. In the sixteenth century, the Italian Jewish intellectual Abraham Yagel reported that some congregations had a special scroll for this reading, which he had witnessed in Mantua. During his visit, Yagel probably saw a copy of the first print of *Megiles Reb Meyer* from Cremona.[173] Celebrating the little Red Jew's triumph on Shavuot thus typologically anticipated that God would respond to the prayers for messianic retaliation.[174]

Many communities incorporated a "second Purim" into the festival cycle to commemorate their own deliverance from persecution, modeled after the Purim festival, which celebrates Queen Esther having saved the Jews of ancient Persia from the notorious Haman. A special megillah was normally composed for this local or regional holiday, which recounted those events in the style of the biblical Scroll of Esther. For example, in *Megillat Vinz*, the Jews of Frankfurt commemorated their return to the city after a temporary expulsion during the Fettmilch uprising of 1614–16. The Yiddish version of this scroll was read at home, whereas the Hebrew was recited in synagogue, much like *Megillat Esther* on Purim.[175] One of the major sources for *Ma'aseh Akdamut*, *Toldot Yeshu*, also seems to have been read, or even performed, as a megillah, called *Ma'aseh Tolah* (Tale of the hanged one), perhaps on Christmas Eve or the Jewish fast on Tevet 9 (or 10).[176]

In contrast to these other megillot, *Megiles Reb Meyer* and the Red Jews' tale as such do not limit themselves to historical (or historicized) events. Rather, they are present and future oriented. Much as on Passover, when Jews reading the Haggadah are invited to experience the Exodus as if they too had been brought out of servitude in Egypt, remembrance of a miraculous salvation by the Red Jews impressed the immediate potential of deliverance on annual gatherings of readers and listeners through its incorporation into Ashkenazic ritual. Most importantly, the Red Jews' bold reinterpretation of Jewish postures in exile, coupled with resistance to its conditions, highlighted Jewish agency rather than divine providence. In that sense, this Yiddish myth echoes the model megillah, the biblical Book of Esther, which makes no mention of God (whereas rabbinical commentaries on *Megillat Esther* take pains to attach theological significance to this text).

The Red Jews in early modern Yiddish literature introduced unique elements that are without parallel in earlier Hebrew sources. Their role as saviors extended beyond eschatology. In stark contrast to the Ten Tribes, who are confined beyond the Sambatyon River until the Messiah arrives, the Red Jews in this Yiddish variant can traverse those waters before then. Drawing on the utilitarian practicalities of vision, their imagined crossings were designed to transfer power from the Red Jews to exilic Jews by allowing them to think about self-propelled agency in the face of Christian oppression rather than waiting patiently for God's deliverance. The analysis of the language and imagery of the Red Jews and their cultural functions opens a portal onto how Ashkenazic Jews saw themselves and articulated their societal aspirations from a vernacular vantage point. These same stories that they read, heard, and retold inform us about tensions regarding order and control within early modern Jewish society, when the popular desire for more active political participation clashed with the elites' interest in preserving their long-standing leadership and the precarious balance of Jewish life amid an overwhelmingly Christian society. Red Jews crossing the Sambatyon River thus signified traversing established boundaries.

Chapter 4

From West to East and Beyond Yiddish
The Transmission History of *Ma'aseh Akdamut*

> Civilized nations and civilized people have long felt strange about color—meaning bold colors—being drawn to them, yet at the same time uneasy, even repelled, wanting them less wild, less bold, and less free to wander away from the ghettos of "men in a state of nature," where they can be regarded from afar and enjoyed—from afar.
>
> —Michael Taussig, *What Color Is the Sacred?*

The Red Jews roamed freely within the early modern Yiddish world, from Amsterdam to Lviv. With the decline of Yiddish as a medium for cultural creativity in western and central Europe in the closing decades of the eighteenth century, the legend was sustained by Yiddish speakers in eastern Europe. However, the image of the ruddy-faced Jews in red garments from beyond the Sambatyon River remained unique to vernacular language and literature. This chapter examines the story's travels from western to eastern Yiddish, as well as its transformations in Hebrew translations and adaptations. As noted above, we have no evidence of Hebrew reception of the term "Red Jews." When this narrative ultimately extended beyond its original Yiddish speech community from the seventeenth century onward, it lacked the idiosyncratic expression "Red Jews," together with their potent coloration, and had a limited scope.

In the following, I will explore the dynamics and boundaries of the trajectory of this Yiddish folktale from its medieval Yiddish origins, across cultural borders, into multilingual early modernity, with particular attention to the effects of the printing revolution and Jewish geographic mobility. The expulsions and migrations within and beyond Europe that were a signature of the early modern period prompted cross-cultural engagement among Jews from diverse spaces. The unprecedented intensity of these encounters naturally incorporated literary exchanges, for narrative traditions accompanied European Jews wherever they went, whether in the form of physical volumes or orally transmitted tales and ideas. As a result, books took on lives of their own: often being written or edited in one location, produced in another, then purchased and read elsewhere. Each phase yielded translations of meaning.[1] The Yiddish tale of the Red Jews showcases early modern adoption of vernacular material in new cultural settings.

## Yiddish Transmission from West to East

The printing press contributed to the immense popularity that the myth of the Red Jews achieved throughout the Yiddish-speaking Diaspora. While manuscripts remained prevalent and oral transmission predominated during the early modern period, starting in the 1470s, Hebrew printing expanded the availability of texts to ever-growing circles of readers. Yiddish printed books were first produced in Cracow in 1534–35, and Yiddish printers soon sprang up in cities across Poland-Lithuania, northern Italy, and Germany, as well as Prague and Amsterdam, which became the two unrivaled centers of Yiddish book production in the seventeenth and eighteenth centuries.[2] The early print history of the legend of the Red Jews illustrates the mobility that characterized Yiddish printing up to the Haskalah, the Jewish enlightenment, when these mythic protagonists moved eastward. Multiple editions were released in the centers of Yiddish printing, reflecting the chronology of their prominence: this story was initially produced by printing houses in northern Italy, select German cities, and Amsterdam from the mid-sixteenth through the eighteenth century. From the beginning of the nineteenth century, publication only continued in Poland-Lithuania through the early twentieth century. That turning point is identified with 1805, when the last printing was issued in Amsterdam and the first of three Yiddish editions is produced in Lviv.

As noted earlier, in the early modern period, two primary versions of the story of the Red Jews were in circulation: *Ma'aseh Akdamut* and the letter from Safed. The sole extant manuscript (Ms. Opp. 714) features both versions, thus supporting them as the most popular tellings in the sixteenth century. Judging from its abundant printed editions, *Ma'aseh Akdamut* enjoyed far greater popularity than the correspondence from Safed over time: the latter is included in one printed edition (Prague, ca. 1660), not as a separate volume but bound with letters about Isaac Luria, the renowned sixteenth-century mystic from Safed.[3] *Ma'aseh Akdamut* appeared in numerous stand-alone prints from the sixteenth century onward. In addition to its manuscript version, we can identify up to eight printed Yiddish editions of *Ma'aseh Akdamut* during the long early modern period, up to 1805. These works were produced under various titles, with the presumed editio princeps from circa 1560 Cremona and a 1660 reprint from Amsterdam (neither are extant) released as *Megiles Reb Meyer*. Other editions are titled *Mayse fun ayn glik rad* (A tale of a wheel of fortune) and, most frequently, *Geshikhtnis fun Reb Meyer un fun den rotn yudlayn un fun den shvartsn minkh* (A historical account of the little Red Jew and the black monk).[4] In addition to the early modern printings enumerated by Isaac Rivkind and Sara Zfatman, the scholars who initially studied this story many decades ago, I traced two more fragments of this tale in the geniza of Reckendorf (near Bamberg, in Franconia).[5] They provide evidence of two editions of *Ma'aseh Akdamut* that were previously unknown or had been considered lost. One was likely produced in an Amsterdam print shop and presumably dates from the second half of the seventeenth century (possibly from the lost 1660 edition).[6] The other fragment was probably printed during the eighteenth century in or near Frankfurt am Main.[7]

The extraordinary popularity of *Ma'aseh Akdamut* among publishers and readers alike may be attributed, at least in part, to its connection with the piyyut *Akdamut Milin* and its famous composer, Meir Shatz of Worms. The piyyut provided a liturgical context that prevented this narrative from slipping into oblivion, because its annual recitation gave its etiological story a status that heightened the motivation for retelling it.[8] Beyond this liturgical anchor, the narrative markers that echoed the realities of the Ashkenazic Diaspora furthered the resilience of *Ma'aseh Akdamut*. As demonstrated above, the success of the Red Jews was primarily derived from its readers ability to relate to the story through the details of their daily lives. The situational framework, wherein a Jewish community is suddenly endangered through no fault of its own, would be all too familiar for Jews living in a predominantly Christian milieu. Indeed, *Ma'aseh Akdamut* constructs a convincing backdrop in premodern Ashkenaz by situating the endangered Jewish community under the reign of a certain king named Martin von der Lanze (Martin of the lance). In the Fürth printing of 1694, he bears the title "emperor and king,"[9] referring to the Holy Roman Emperor, who was first elected to the German monarchy and subsequently crowned emperor. The manuscript and Fürth edition both cite a specific year (1360/61 and 1401, respectively) when the events allegedly occurred.[10] The tale in the letter from Safed too is infused with direct and indirect references to Ashkenaz as the homeland of its audience, through terms such as "here" and "in your lands."[11] Its printing moved our narrative linguistically even closer to the everyday speech of Ashkenazic Jews by substituting most Hebrew-Aramaic elements found in the manuscript with Germanic equivalents.[12] By contrast, however, this narrative takes place in an exotic locale, namely the mythic realm of Prester John, and thus it lacks major validating elements that played on the audience's sense of spatial familiarity.

And yet, the hometown of the protagonist of *Ma'aseh Akdamut*, Meir Shatz of Worms, is not explicitly mentioned. He is simply introduced as "Rabbi Meir Hasan (of the Germans)."[13] Rather than depicting him as a historic personage from the Rhineland, he is identified by generic qualities: erudition, righteousness, and piety.[14] This hero is thus transformed into an ideal Ashkenazic Jew who could have lived anywhere in the Yiddish-speaking world. Similarly, the scheming monk threatens Jews throughout the entire land, that is, Ashkenaz.

The printing press reinforced the capacity to appeal to a wide audience and, therefore, emerged as a key factor that elevated *Ma'aseh Akdamut* over other tellings of the tale of the Red Jews. As David Rotman has noted, the very process of printing conflicts with the multiplicity that characterizes folk literature. Even though this means of literary reproduction did not inhibit oral transmission, a printed edition would reach larger circles of readers and could thereby become the dominant or even single form that later generations would preserve.[15] With the rise of print, marketing strategies came to play an ever more important role in shaping narratives and plot development; Yiddish editors and printers, who catered to the entire Yiddish Diaspora, formulated stories that were designed to satisfy a majority of readers, with the aim of maximizing sales.[16] Further omission of details that would tie the narrative in *Ma'aseh Akdamut* to a certain Ashkenazic community may have resulted from such editorial considerations. Although many other printed narratives that became highly popular are situated in a specific site—

for instance, many tales in the *Mayse Bukh* occur in the land of Israel—in the case of our tale, the publishers opted for delocalization.

The anonymization of markers in *Ma'aseh Akdamut* during the age of printing especially stands out when the extant manuscript is compared with the print editions from Fürth (1694) and Amsterdam (1704, 1805), which are almost identical, with orthographic differences). While in the manuscript Martin von der Lanze "ruled over many lands," the printed version from Fürth deliberately casts the monarch as sovereign over a vast empire: "Germany, Italy, Poland, Bohemia, Russia, Hungary, that means a part of Turkey."[17] This fictional territory substantially exceeds the boundaries of the Holy Roman Empire (even inclusive of the Italian and Hungarian domains of the royal house of Habsburg, which produced the emperor during this period), especially by its eastern expansion into Poland-Lithuania and Russia. Thus, this realm encompasses the entirety of Yiddish-speaking Ashkenaz-Polin, following the Jewish cultural map. By the time *Ma'aseh Akdamut* later appeared in Amsterdam, contextualizing details were almost absent: except for a precise date (1401), neither a specific ruler nor location is named.[18] In the Amsterdam editions, the tale's setting in Europe may be inferred solely from broad references, such as an anonymous emperor/king, Christian populations, and a notorious monk. Editorial efforts clearly tailored the narrative to facilitate its applicability to any location in the Ashkenazic Diaspora, from west to east.

The Red Jews enjoyed enduring popularity in western Yiddish culture through the eighteenth century. As late as 1800, two Yiddish *purim-lukhes* (Purim papers) from Amsterdam treat the Red Jews as shorthand for a Jewish people from a remote, unnamed land. In another twist, a contemporaneous almanac from Amsterdam mentions the Green Jews of Greenland,[19] signaling a loss of their original cultural role, akin to the decline of this myth among German speakers two centuries prior.[20] A roughly contemporaneous anonymous Hebrew work about the Sabbatean messianic movement, *Sippur Ḥalomot Keẓ ha-Pela'ot* (The tale of dreams: The end of wonders, also titled *Me'ora'ot Ẓvi*), which originated in the last decades of the eighteenth century, followed by several printings throughout the nineteenth century, identifies the Jewish tribes beyond the Sambatyon similarly as "little green and red Jews" (גרינע אונד רוטע יודלך), who have either green- or red-colored complexions.[21]

As the printing history of *Ma'aseh Akdamut* indicates, this tale remained popular among Jews in eastern Europe: in Lviv, several Yiddish editions were produced in the nineteenth century.[22] Judging from its form and content, which essentially stayed constant, the image of the Red Jews remained quite stable during their transition from western to eastern Ashkenaz. The Lviv prints are almost identical to the Amsterdam editions, only the alleged year given for the reported events is updated to 1701.[23] Additional associations may have augmented the allegorical meanings of red coloration in the eastern European context. For instance, in Russian, as in other Slavic languages, *krásnyj* means both "red" and "beautiful";[24] this linguistic influence would have lent itself to the image of the Red Jews detailed above.

## Visual Failure Outside Yiddishland

The legend of the Red Jews spread not only to eastern Europe but also beyond the Yiddish-speaking world, albeit to a limited extent and with a transformed profile. One translation of *Ma'aseh Akdamut* into Hebrew, which closely follows the extant Yiddish versions, has reached us from the early modern period; it stems from northern Italy, 1630, and is preserved in a manuscript. In addition, three tersely written Hebrew adaptations, which render the basic plot and select tropes from *Ma'aseh Akdamut* quite freely, were composed by Italian, Sephardic, and Mizrahi Jewries from the seventeenth and eighteenth centuries. The collection of the Israel Folktale Archives (IFA) at the University of Haifa also includes a number of orally transmitted variants on the motif of a member of the Ten Lost Tribes who miraculously rescues an imperiled local community. Like most material collected by the IFA, these tales, which were probably originally told in Judeo-Arabic or Ladino, were recorded in Hebrew during the latter half of the twentieth century by immigrants to Israel, primarily from Yemen and Greece.

With the exception of select modern texts that were prepared by and for Yiddish speakers in eastern Europe (like a Hebrew edition from 1916 Lviv), which translate "Red Jews" literally as *yehudim admonim* (or *adumim*), none of these versions use the peculiar term.[25] This appellation remains virtually exclusive to Yiddish. In the Hebrew tales, the unparalleled term "Red Jews" is replaced by familiar phrases that denote this group, such as the generic "Ten Tribes" or "Sons of Moses," and, occasionally, simply the "Sons of Israel" beyond the Sambatyon. Even the Italian Jewish scholar Yagel, in his brief remark about *Megiles Reb Meyer* cited earlier, does not mention the Red Jews as such; he refers to the Ten Tribes (עשרת השבטים).[26]

Why was the highly evocative term "Red Jews," having been literally and metaphorically imbued with color, not regularly translated into Hebrew and other Jewish languages? Why were translators reluctant to adopt their redness, so omitted it instead? After all, the biblical symbolism of King David as *admoni* would have been readily accessible to all Jewish cultures. We have observed a similar phenomenon with respect to the Christian linguistic sphere. While the motif of the menacing Ten Tribes was known throughout late medieval Europe, Middle High German alone assigned a specific name and color to these villains. This appellation was not known outside German-speaking regions, although the widely held negative connotations toward the color red could feasibly have evoked similar responses across Europe. Moreover, the Red Jews appeared only in the German vernacular, never in Latin writings.[27]

I contend that the visually potent Yiddish idiom "Red Jews" proved untranslatable into other cultural milieux because its roots are distinctly German. We have seen that the term and image first developed in a shared (albeit contested) cultural and linguistic space in the German lands. The initial reappropriation of the Red Jews from German into Yiddish alone seems to have succeeded on pragmatic and utilitarian grounds. Terminology tends to be shaped by cultural encounters in an attempt to cultivate mutual understanding.[28] The debate over the significance of the Red Jews in premodern Germany required the determination of a common phrase among Jews and Christians in their respective vernaculars. Most importantly, by adopting this appellation, Jews could reconfigure a negative symbol that the majority culture had imposed on them. Once the reappropriation of the Red Jews proved successful, they became an organic element of Ashkenazic vernacular culture. The anonymization of spatial references detailed above replicated the patterns that Rotman has observed regarding the transformation of medieval Hebrew folktales in the early modern period: the print narratives fostered communities of readers that shared collective memories and literary tastes.[29] This trend has been documented even more dramatically among vernacular narratives. As we have seen with the Yiddish legend of the Red Jews, a regional Jewish language, in conjunction with influences from local, non-Jewish traditions on the Jewish folk repertoire, formed a geographically defined community of readers despite the loss of its original setting.[30]

This common Ashkenazic literary culture was not available to Jews from other vernacular and cultural backgrounds. By contrast, the need for linguistic reappropriation of the expression "Red Jews" did not pertain to the

Hebrew translators of this Yiddish tale: the well-established Hebrew equivalent *aseret ha-shevatim* (the Ten Tribes) offered a universally recognized option for their anticipated readership. Translators would have weighed the question: Why break with convention by introducing a new expression? On the one hand, in a Hebrew text for a non-Yiddish-speaking audience, "Red Jews" would have been an acontextual neologism that would certainly have been confusing. Furthermore, phonetics may well have inhibited the use of a term like *yehudim adumim* (or *admonim*) in Hebrew, for it would always resound with the negativity of Edom rather than convey a positive tone. On the other hand, Jews who were fluent in Yiddish and familiar with the Red Jews' lore would automatically read their qualities into any mention of the Ten Tribes, even if the term "Red Jews" were missing, as demonstrated above. This option is illustrated by the Israelis with Eastern European backgrounds who recorded tales about the Red Jews for the IFA: in Hebrew, they used the expression "Ten Tribes" rather than "Red Jews" although, in their communities of origin, the story was surely told in Yiddish with its standard vocabulary.[31]

The Red Jews, as a name and a legend, only proved viable in *loshn Ashkenaz*, the tongue of Ashkenaz, with a distinct regional cultural heritage that was shaped during the Middle Ages and continued in the early modern period but was not readily visible in other languages and cultures. While the early modern intensification of relationships among members of diverse Jewish communities facilitated the distribution of vernacular narratives among Jewries, permeating regional borders, each transfer into a new linguistic environment reduced their geographic and cultural specificity. The further they traveled from their points of origin, the more their signature traits fell away.[32] The trajectory of the Red Jews showcases the challenges of translating singular aspects of Jewish vernacular culture beyond their linguistically defined terrain, and even the immobility of certain vernacular literary motifs.

Early modern Hebrew translations and adaptations of the legend of the Red Jews seem to have been significantly less popular than their Yiddish counterparts. In comparison with the overwhelming success of the Yiddish myth, based on the surviving literary evidence, its Hebrew versions were conspicuously few in number, appearing fairly late and scattered in time and space.[33] These Hebrew translations were not issued in print editions, with the exception of modern and contemporary publications of *Ma'aseh Akdamut*, which have all been published in Yiddish-speaking environments, where familiarity with this myth is a given. While Yiddish tales tend to enjoy greater popularity than Hebrew stories, simply due to their linguistic accessibility, I would suggest that the failure of the myth of the Red Jews to gain currency in early modern Jewish literature beyond Yiddish largely results from the omission of the moniker "Red Jews" and other visual material.

Let us consider how sight is treated in the Hebrew translation of *Ma'aseh Akdamut* from 1630 by Israel b. Abraham Kohen, a Ferrara-based copyist, which usually stays close to the version preserved in the late sixteenth-century Yiddish manuscript Ms. Opp. 714.[34] If it were based on a printed edition, that would likely have been the Cremona imprint, the only known release prior to 1630. First, the production of this text requires our attention. Kohen, who was not a Yiddish speaker himself, writes that he produced this Hebrew text from an intermediary translation into French that he requested from "a learned man who knew the Ashkenazic script." Nothing is known of this auxiliary translator and no record remains of his French version; however, we learn from Kohen that, in his view, it was not rendered in elegant language. He reports that he attempted to create the most literal possible Hebrew translation, but he also admits that he found it difficult to understand his French source at times.[35] If the French translator had not substituted *dix tribus perdue* for "Red Jews," for want of an established French idiom, the Red Jews may have lost their redness in this process of secondary translation and apparent misunderstandings, from Yiddish to French to Hebrew. Had the anonymous translator chosen the direct meaning, *juifs rouges*, Kohen might have opted for *aseret ha-shevatim* rather than its literal rendering, because he may simply have been confounded by this strange phrase.

Israel Kohen was targeting an audience that, like himself, was not familiar with Yiddish; therefore, each occurrence of the uniquely Yiddish expression "Red Jews" was removed in the process of translation into Hebrew. Kohen explains that he identified the need for a new Hebrew version of this tale since, with the rare exception of Hebrew variants in a few old *mahzorim*, this legend was only available in Yiddish; therefore, he decided to make it widely available to his fellow Jews in the holy tongue (perhaps to be printed and sold in the international market).[36] However, he may have misjudged the demand for his translation, for the question remains: Who are the Hebrew readers who would be drawn to such a tale? Yiddish speakers who were literate in Hebrew were unlikely to consume a Hebrew translation of *Ma'aseh Akdamut*. While the intended audience may have included Ashkenazic Jews in northern Italy, among whom Yiddish declined as a vernacular at the end of the sixteenth century (to be replaced by Judeo-Italian),[37] this most popular version of the myth of the Red Jews, as the origin story of *Akdamut Milin*, would have garnered little interest outside the Ashkenazic community, where this piyyut was not included in synagogal rites.

Beyond Kohen's marketing aspirations, however effective they may have been, the omission of the Red Jews reveals a literary agenda. Besides the loss of the Red Jews' color, deviations from the original are primarily related to visual content. Without any reference to color, a biblical quote was inserted to draw the analogy between the colorless hero from beyond the Sambatyon and David's apparent weakness compared to Goliath.[38] This rendering also eliminates the highly symbolic, stratified placement of Jews and non-Jews in the arena during the sorcery contest. The erasure of visual keys is most stark during the final round of the sorcery competition, when the little Jew shouts to the audience, "Listen, this so-called master of magic will not be able to hold the tree down."[39] By contrast, the Yiddish audience is invited to look rather than listen.[40] Once translated, this uniquely Yiddish creation was stripped of the visual code that animated the original. Without even the mental image of its ruddy heroes, this and other Hebrew versions of the story of the Red Jews lose the most basic graphic that stimulated the mind's eye and, consequently, evoked an array of visual associations that contributed to its enduring popularity among Yiddish speakers.

## Domesticating Red Jews

The editor of the 1630 Hebrew translation of *Ma'aseh Akdamut* modified its presentation not only stylistically but also thematically, as determined by his linguistic choices. This version is considerably more conservative than its Yiddish source: the visually oriented self-empowerment was thoroughly excised. The Red Jews thus lost much of their original subversive force in Hebrew. The divergence is evidenced by the texts' attitude toward crossing the Sambatyon and whether this was inevitable, despite its inherent desecration of the Sabbath. We have seen that this question is crucial in the Yiddish tale and therefore debated at length, then resolved to dispatch a pre-apocalyptic envoy to the Red Jews, rather than waiting for heavenly intervention. This exchange with its proactive solution is entirely missing from the Hebrew, which succinctly cites the primacy of *piku'aḥ nefesh* and supports fording the river to avert mortal danger.⁴¹ Indeed, the rebellious option to exercise Jewish agency is effectively removed and replaced with divine protection: Kohen advertises this Hebrew story as an account of God's mercy and the miracles performed for Israel.⁴² Accordingly, the (formerly red) elderly Jew from beyond the Sambatyon serves solely as an instrument of divine salvation. Whereas the little Red Jew in the Yiddish original readies himself for the magical competition by washing his hands, signaling preparation for human action, his pious Hebrew counterpart prays for God to ensure support from benevolent forces and grant him victory.⁴³

The more conventional image of the Red Jews found in Kohen's translation, which differs markedly from the Yiddish transmission, is confirmed by a comparative reading of other international adaptations of *Ma'aseh Akdamut*. Let us look more closely at the early modern Hebrew variants of this tale (which are not translations in a narrow sense like Kohen's) and compare them to each other and the Yiddish versions. All these additional renderings are characterized by a brevity that is blunt in comparison with the elaborate plot and polished language of its Yiddish versions.

A first variant is included in a collection of exempla from the seventeenth century written in Sephardic script.⁴⁴ By contrast to thirteen folio pages in the Yiddish manuscript, in little more than three folios this compiler tells of a Polish king who is induced by a wizard-monk to issue a decree stating that, in one year, his Jewish subjects must either convert to Christianity or suffer death or expulsion. The community beadle is designated to seek assistance from the Children of Moses beyond the Sambatyon, since they are famed for their knowledge of practical Kabbalah. The Sons of Moses respond by sending their own sexton to Poland, who then declares that he will kill the monk if this edict is not revoked. The monk refuses to cause the king to rescind the law, which leads the Jew and the monk to hold a magical contest before the king. In the final round of their competition, the Jew strikes the ground, causing the monk to sink into it up to his ankles. Once more the Jew asks the monk to instruct the king to retract the order, but again he refuses. The sexton then strikes the ground seven times and, with each blow, the monk sinks deeper into the earth, until he disappears from sight. Frightened by this spectacle, the king abolishes the edict. The timidity and political weakness of this monarch build on a motif in the Yiddish original: not only is a representative of the Church responsible for persecuting Jews, but their sovereign ruler is reduced to serving as the monk's puppet. However, only a faint reminder of the original message of empowerment of the otherwise unheralded community members remains: both beadles are suggestive of the every-Jew heroics of the Yiddish myth.

Another Hebrew adaptation of *Ma'aseh Akdamut* appears in northern Italy, in a narrative collection copied in Lugo, in the province of Ravenna, in 1785.[45] The story is transported from medieval Ashkenaz to the land of Israel (sometime after the destruction of the Temple) and, thus, is not told as the etiological tale of the piyyut, depicting the messenger as a tzaddik from Jerusalem instead of Meir Shatz. A savior from the Ten Tribes arrives from their distant home to save the Jewish community of Jerusalem from a mighty sorcerer-priest. This sinister figure is portrayed with language that echoes the biblical account of David and Goliath in the Book of Samuel—as an imposing man whose malevolence is explicitly compared to the infamous Philistine—who demands that the Jews provide an opponent for a duel, then the plot unfolds according to the Yiddish original. As in the Hebrew translation from 1630, this narrator curtly states that, for the sake of *piku'aḥ nefesh*, a messenger may traverse the Sambatyon on the Sabbath once. The savior, who is chosen by lot, is "a lame, hunchbacked dwarf."[46] It is hardly surprising when the Jerusalemites skeptically react with concern: "How can this fellow save us?" This question is a quotation from 1 Samuel 10:27 that, interestingly, was articulated by Israelites that doubted King Saul, who towered over everyone else (1 Sam. 10:25). How much more so for this hobbling little Jew!

The sorcery detailed here differs from the Yiddish source, although some objects are retained. First, the monk tosses seeds of wheat on the stage, which instantly mature into sheaves ready for harvest; in response, the Jew conjures roosters who devour all of the ears of wheat. Next, the Jew magically produces two massive trees that appear to have sprouted from the stage and he asks the priest to bend them earthward. The sorcerer complies, but as he strains to bow the trunks till they almost touch the ground, the trees spring up again and split the monk's body, with half of his corpse hanging from each one. The Jew then causes two millstones to materialize in midair; the two halves of the corpse fall on them, and they are ground into powder until the sorcerer has vanished.

Significantly, by contrast with the Yiddish original, none of the little Jew's tricks seem to demand physical effort (e.g., he neither flexes the tree trunks nor crumbles millstones in his bare hands). This frail hero does not feign to exceed the expectations of a stock Jewish morality tale. From the outset, his abilities fall squarely within conventional Jewish parameters: after being introduced as a limping midget, he is henceforth called "the wise Jew" (היהודי החכם), and, much like in the 1630 translation, he serves as an intermediary for the divine. The story's message is unequivocal: this little Jew from beyond the Sambatyon has carried out God's will, thereby demonstrating that God acts "not by might, nor by power, but by My spirit" (לֹא בְחַיִל וְלֹא בְכֹחַ—כִּי אִם־בְּרוּחִי). This quotation from Zechariah 4:6 recalls a phrase in 1 Samuel 2:9: "for not by strength shall man prevail" (כִּי־לֹא בְכֹחַ יִגְבַּר־אִישׁ).⁴⁷ This Hebrew tale seems preoccupied with asserting God's protection instead of reliance on personal initiative, human agency, and physical vigor, as the Yiddish by contrast suggests.

All Hebrew renderings of *Ma'aseh Akdamut* strictly tamed the activating message, which had been a salient characteristic of the original Yiddish myth of the Red Jews. This is not to say that Yiddish sources, simply by virtue of their language, reflect a unified transhistorical vernacular worldview, as opposed to Hebrew texts. Indeed, it is quite possible that the extant Hebrew versions of *Ma'aseh Akdamut* continue a different strand of vernacular transmission, which simply is not documented in early modern Yiddish. In modern Eastern European Yiddish, in contrast, we do find suggestive traces of parallels, for example, the motif of the threat of forced conversion. Significantly, an oral version in the IFA is close to the muted Hebrew tale from eighteenth-century Ravenna.⁴⁸

In any case, when the story of the Red Jews spread beyond Yiddishland, the focus was on the Ten Lost Tribes of Israel as divine helpers, adding a new, non-apocalyptic variant to this corpus of Jewish legends. David Rotman's findings confirm that in Hebrew literature from the late fifteenth century onward the Ten Tribes were reduced from a nation of redeemers to one lone savior. According to Rotman, this portrait is first documented in Moses Ashkenazi's account in *Kol Mevaser* discussed earlier and reached its conclusion in the early modern period, specifically in Hebrew renderings of Yiddish sources, most prominently *Ma'aseh Akdamut*.⁴⁹

These narratives' focus on God's deliverance in daily life through the assistance of a mediator is intensified by a tradition that identifies Meir Shatz, the hero of *Ma'aseh Akdamut*, with Rabbi Meir Ba'al ha-Nes (the master of miracles, also known as Nehorai), the second-century Palestinian sage, who is cited in the Talmud and whose grave is located in Tiberias (by the Sea of Galilee). The tomb of Meir Ba'al ha-Nes became a holy site in Judaism and, since the medieval period, thousands of Jews have made pilgrimage there to pray for protection, healing, and help in matters large and small. The cult of this rabbi as an everyday savior escalated in the eighteenth century when collection boxes inscribed with his name, for funds that would support impoverished Jews in the land of Israel, became a fixture in virtually every Jewish home in the Diaspora. These charitable efforts symbolized assurance of aid during personal crises.⁵⁰ Since miraculous deeds were ascribed to both of these rabbis named Meir, their identities were apparently merged at some point. The insertion of the talmudic Rabbi Meir into *Ma'aseh Akdamut* seems to be known among Yiddish speakers, at least during the twentieth century. In his interview with the IFA, an informant from Poland recalled that while some say that Meir Shatz resided beyond the Sambatyon for the rest of his life and died there, others say that he immigrated to the land of Israel and was buried in Tiberias. According to this man, his burial place was known as "the grave of Rabbi Meir Ba'al ha-Nes."⁵¹

I found this conflation also in a Persian manuscript from the seventeenth or eighteenth century, which contains a story that combines motifs of *Ma'aseh Akdamut* and the letter from Safed.⁵² Here an Aramaean king announces to the Jewish population of an Israelite city that he would convert to Judaism if they could demonstrate the superiority of Moses over Jesus. If they failed, they would all be slain. The Jews, who have twenty days to prepare, begin to fast until one of their elders mentions that he knows a boy in Tiberias, named Meir, who could meet this challenge. This child, henceforth called Rabbi Meir, is brought before the king with the help of *kefizat ha-derekh* and performs wonders by uttering the ineffable name: he causes soldiers' hands to wither and conjures a serpent that incinerates many of the king's men. The final and most powerful feat eventually convinces the king to accept the superiority of the Torah: Meir conjures a personage of Jesus who exudes a stench so noxious that it proves lethal to many people; then he summons Moses and instructs him to bring perfumes from paradise to cure them.

## Entering Judeo-Arabic and Ladino

Through the two major versions of the Yiddish tale of the Red Jews its heroes reached other Jewish communities in Muslim countries. An eighteenth-century Mizrahi manuscript collection of diverse literary genres that incorporates select motifs from *Ma'aseh Akdamut* into a slightly more detailed adaptation of the Safed letter differs from the restrained Hebrew tales discussed before, instead celebrating forceful heroics.⁵³ A Jewish convert (presumably to Islam) informs his king that the Jews in his realm are boasting that any one of them could vanquish ten thousand people. To prove his accusation, this convert escorts the monarch to the synagogue, where students can be heard reciting Deuteronomy 32:30. Infuriated, the king calls on the Jewish teacher to explain that passage. The instructor reassures him that it refers to the Israelites who were freed from Egypt, not contemporary Jewry. Nevertheless, the sovereign commands his Jewish subjects, as the Israelites' descendants, to substantiate this claim within one year, or else they will all be killed or driven from the country. After six months of fasting and weeping, a Jew steps forward and proposes that he will recruit one of the Children of Moses, who could demonstrate that the verse still applies. In contrast to the Yiddish versions, this messenger returns with a young girl from the Sons of Moses. The two Jews approach the king together and announce that they are ready to provide the required evidence; therefore, he should assemble his troops. The king complies and, with allusion to *Ma'aseh Akdamut*, the girl asks him for two heavy millstones. They are formed of stone from a nearby mountain and, upon pronouncing the name of God, the girl lifts the millstones into the air and uses them to pulverize the entire army. Having completed her mission, the child departs for her home beyond the sabbatical river. For this author, unlike his Ashkenazic counterparts, to violate the Sabbath by crossing the Sambatyon, even a second time, raised no concerns.

The climax of this story is remarkable: upon witnessing the instant demise of his army, the king recognizes the veracity of the verse that had been recited at the synagogue and he declares: "If this can merely be done by word of mouth, how much greater the power when done by hand?"[54] This variant seems to build on a remnant of the Yiddish legend, by manifesting its message about the latent might of Jews. Another revealing detail in this story does not appear in Yiddish lore: during her encounter with the king's army, the girl is disguised as a man. Whereas the reader knows her true identity, the king and his army see what they expect, namely a male warrior. The efficacy of forceful masculinity in response to persecution is thus underscored.

A number of tales that were recorded for the IFA during the 1940s to 1980s, as related by Israelis from the Judeo-Arabic speaking community of Yemen and also from Greece, clearly hark back to the tradition of the Yiddish Red Jews.[55] Based on the original legend, in which the weak triumph over the strong, these later variants are often designed as commentaries on Deuteronomy 32:30, inspired by the Safed version of the Red Jews myth.

Occasionally, they weave in additional strands from *Ma'aseh Akdamut* (such as the savior's marriage with a local spouse at the conclusion). The emissary from the distant tribes consistently has surprising physical features, though the specific conditions vary: these compromised heroes frequently include young women and men with bodily limitations.

One tale from Yemen, for example, portrays a rabbi who saves his people with the help of the Ten Tribes when the imam who rules the country demands that the Jews justify Deuteronomy 32:30 as part of their Scriptures. If they fail, he will obliterate any memory of Judaism in his land. Reminiscent of our Yiddish tale, this account describes how the Jews of Yemen fast and pray until a rabbi eventually reaches the Sambatyon, where the Levites and the tribe of Dan live together. Those distant tribes dispatch a hero, who is blind in one eye, together with his sister to rescue their endangered kin. These two saviors uphold the biblical verse by defeating the imam's enormous army.[56] In all parallel versions from Yemen, including some that follow the plot of the Yiddish original more closely (such as the inclusion of a king who overhears the recitation of this verse when he passes a Jewish school), the savior from the Ten Tribes is a girl who acts alone.[57]

In 1943, Moshe Attias—one of the earliest collectors of Sephardic folklore, who was born in Salonica when it was still under Ottoman rule then lived in Jerusalem—recorded an instructive variant. In this story, which would presumably have been transmitted in Ladino, the Sons of Moses are all described as "very tall, courageous, and dauntless," yet their representative who is sent as a savior has one arm and is blind in one eye.[58] However, as in the Yemenite tale, and in striking contrast to the Yiddish versions, his appearance does not prompt any doubts about his qualifications. Nevertheless, his diminished vision is a central element in this legend. Similar to the Yiddish message of the Red Jews, this sense is used to refute the Christian perspective of Jews as spiritually blind.

We have seen that religious thinkers throughout history expressed reservations about relying on the sense of sight. Paradoxically, some therefore argued for the merits of blindness. Sight was inherently vulnerable, for misconceptions such as moral corruption could enter through the eye, whereas blindness offered freedom from sinful temptations. Being sightless—literally or by closing one's eyes—could thus lead to an unoccluded understanding of the divine.[59] It is therefore particularly noteworthy that in Attias's story, on their journey to the imperiled community, the helper asks the Jewish messenger, who had crossed the Sambatyon to seek assistance, to shut his eyes.

When the rescuer permits him to open them again, they have miraculously returned to his hometown (presumably by *kefizat ha-derekh*). Similarly, in the Yemenite version discussed earlier, the rabbi rides on his rescuer's back, closes his eyes, and prays to God for a successful mission as they fly back to Yemen, where he opens his eyes again.[60] Immediately upon arrival, the one-armed and half-blind man exhibits tremendous physical strength by toppling buildings in order to widen the street and ease his entrance into the city. The king, fearing that this Jewish visitor will destroy the entire city, acknowledges the essence of Deuteronomy 32:30, namely that Jewish might is indeed incomparable.[61]

With its arrival in Muslim lands, the tale of the Red Jews once again embraced the reassuring message of its Ashkenazic origins. Like the Yiddish original, these later versions emphasize salvation from the precariousness of minority existence by an individual who emerges to be strong despite his or her misleading looks. The emphasis on sight and hidden meaning is sealed when the king in Attias's story confirms "with my own eyes I have seen" the power of the Jews.[62] And yet, the myth was further appropriated to accommodate novel cultural, social, and political conditions. Dina Stein, for instance, emphasizes the comical endings of two tales from Yemen, which, in sharp contrast to *Ma'aseh Akdamut*, focus on domestic misunderstandings following the marriage of the Danite savior with a local Jew: these heroines from beyond the Sambatyon prove mismatched for everyday life and the couples divorce either childless or after their offspring die at birth. Stein explains that these variants reflect the disappointment experienced by Yemenite Jews when the mundane realities of life in Israel fell short of the ideal of a melting pot for Jews from all ethnic backgrounds.[63] This conclusion in fact contradicts the fairy-tale ending of the Yiddish story where the little Red Jew's successful marriage with Meir's daughter epitomizes the messianic promise that the twelve tribes of Israel would be reunited, to be followed by a golden age of universal bliss on earth, an age of peace and prosperity, of justice and joy.

# Chapter 5

# Into Modernity
## The Wandering Jew in Bright Red

> You wander about aimlessly, you lie in a daze . . . !
> . . . Get up, brothers! It's time!
> You've been lying in the mud for two thousand years already,
> and you don't sense how miserable you are!
> —Sholem Aleichem, *The Little Red Jews*

The image of Red Jews continued to thrive in various literary and artistic forms in eastern European Jewish culture well into the twentieth century. The transition of the Yiddish Red Jews into modernity is characterized by both the survival of the Old Yiddish legend and a radically new interpretation of this motif in modern Jewish literature. Two new, opposing interpretations emerged in the late nineteenth and early twentieth centuries, in works by central figures within modern Yiddish and Hebrew literature: the Wandering Red Jew and Muscular Red Jews. On this journey through time, the mechanisms at work were similar to the changes that occurred when the Red Jews were introduced as a literary motif into early modern Hebrew. While some authors reinterpreted the activating image of the Red Jews in response to changing political perspectives, it seems that in Europe the tamed version of *Ma'aseh Akdamut* made it into the modern era, irrespective of the language of transmission.

Interestingly, another transformation occurred with regard to how Yiddish speakers envisioned the ruddy features of the Red Jews. While this mythical tribe had been ruddy-faced and pictured in red garments in premodern Jewish imagination, by the nineteenth century, Yiddish authors largely characterized the Red Jews by their signature red hair (in rare cases, we find blond girls among them or handsome men with long black hair).[1] Their red skin came to the fore only when the Red Jews were occasionally identified with Native Americans in the Jewish press.

## Iterations in Modern Yiddish

The unwavering popularity of *Ma'aseh Akdamut* is attested in several Yiddish and Hebrew printings that appeared in Lviv between 1805 and 1916.[2] Even in their traditional narrative, however, the Red Jews were viewed differently in modern Yiddish culture. The title that was given to two Yiddish editions of *Ma'aseh Akdamut* from Lviv (1839, repr., 1850s) suggests a change in their reception. Much as the more subdued myth in early modern Hebrew, their title *Ma'aseh Gvurat ha-Shem* (A tale about the strength of God) emphasizes God's role over human agency in this tale of salvation. Accordingly, the title page of the Hebrew translation from 1916, which closely follows the Yiddish original on the whole, advertises this as a story of Meir Shatz who rescued the Jews of Ashkenaz with the help of God. The Red Jews are absent from this plot description; rather, the hero is this rabbi who acts in the name of the divine. In this light, the main text is slightly altered: whereas the Yiddish prints from Lviv convey the Jewish quest for a magician who can stand up to the monk, this Hebrew version seeks someone imbued with "the spirit of God" (רוח אלקים).[3]

This reversal in the Red Jews' message in modern Eastern European Jewish culture is also evident in other written records and oral traditions. For example, an oral version in the IFA, *The Jerusalemite Sorcerer and the Savior from Afar*, recorded in 1958 by Dov Noy, who had immigrated to Palestine from Poland twenty years earlier and later became Professor of Folklore at the Hebrew University of Jerusalem, likewise emphasizes divine providence. Interestingly, this tale is parallel to an earlier Hebrew version that has been preserved in an eighteenth-century manuscript from northern Italy (discussed above).[4] A late tradition that can be traced to the turn of the twentieth century firmly situates *Ma'aseh Akdamut* in the religious realm rather than in social conflict with the dominant majority. A succinct Hebrew summary of this story is included in *Sefer Akdamut* (The book of Akdamut; Warsaw, 1902), a commentary on the piyyut *Akdamut Milin*, which Moses

b. Abraham Boman collated from the writings of several rabbis from Polish Sokhachev.[5] In this abstract, the helper from beyond the Sambatyon is recruited for a religious disputation with a priest, not a sorcery competition. The role of magic is limited to a prelude to the disputation, merely as entertainment for the king. The main battle should have been an intellectual contest to determine which of the two religions is superior. However, before it begins, the monk who had tossed two millstones in the air is catapulted between them, a familiar scene from the Old Yiddish tale.

Among Hasidic groups, this version of *Ma'aseh Akdamut* is still produced by publishers in Brooklyn and Jerusalem, albeit omitting the term "Red Jews."[6] These booklets, in Yiddish or Hebrew, which are often intended for children, combine a translation of the piyyut with the story of its author. The illustrated editions anachronistically depict all Jews in traditional Hasidic attire (fig. 22). These tales feature the major plot points of Boman's version, in greater detail but without the rebellious potential and eye-play that mark the early modern Yiddish tale: no longer set in Europe, this drama has been relegated to a distant kingdom in Asia, close to the Sambatyon River. This country is ruled by a benevolent king who protects his Jewish subjects, in contrast to the ubiquitous Christian persecution of Jews in other lands. When a priest starts murdering Jews with a glance, reasoning that it is his duty to kill these rivals of Christianity, the king calls for a debate to resolve this conflict. If the Jews are defeated, they would all be required to convert (or be sentenced to death if they refuse). The community rabbi allows Meir Shatz to traverse the Sambatyon on account of *piku'ah nefesh*, hoping that he will find a candidate among the Sons of Moses who is learned and a skilled magician capable of withstanding the priest's evil eye. A tailor, a prototypical uneducated Jew, is charged with this responsibility.

In stark contrast to the original *Ma'aseh Akdamut*, his abilities are never doubted; he is welcomed with great enthusiasm by the endangered Jews. The disputation is introduced by the abovementioned show of magical skill, in which the priest is soundly defeated, and here the Christians—who celebrate this tyrant's death together with the Jews in earlier Yiddish versions—turn their eyes away in shame. The happy ending differs too. Here, the tailor marries the ex-wife whom Rabbi Meir divorced prior to his departure, recognizing that he would not be able to return. Unlike the prior Yiddish tellings that create two *agunot* who cannot remarry, these modern ultra-Orthodox renderings circumvent this halakhic complication.[7]

This conservative variant has also reached us in oral form. The narrative was recorded for the IFA by Efraim Tsoref, originally from Poland, in 1958 and 1960.[8] Both times, he told the story from memory, as he claimed to have heard it in his native country. These two versions differ slightly: in one, Meir Shatz is a native of Worms; in the other, he is erroneously situated in Mainz, where he allegedly studied with Rashi. According to Tsoref's telling, a Christian priest in Ashkenaz condemned the Torah before his king, who then issued an evil edict against the Jews of his realm. The king convenes a debate with Jews on matters of religion; if they win, he will rescind his decree. The most conspicuous difference between these oral tellings and all other extant Yiddish versions of *Ma'aseh Akdamut* is the absence of Red Jews, Sons of Moses, or Ten Tribes. Meir Shatz is selected to represent Jewry for his erudition, rather than serving as a messenger to petition for support from beyond the Sambatyon. When he ventures beyond the sabbatical river (he dips a foot into its roaring waters, which suddenly become calm, so he can safely swim to the other shore), he simply prays for the abrogation of anti-Jewish orders before the contest begins. Upon his return, Rabbi Meir wins the contest by acclaiming the wonders of God's creation that may be witnessed in the world, as he would write in his famous piyyut.[9] This retelling of *Ma'aseh Akdamut* reinforces earlier efforts (highlighted in the 1916 Lviv print) to elevate Meir Shatz as the sole, divinely ordained hero, thereby displacing the Red Jews. Another shift in the role of this rabbi is also highly instructive: whereas in the early modern Yiddish tale he enlightens his readers on how to respond proactively to exile, in the variant in the IFA, Meir Shatz relies on God to illuminate his path to success.[10] Thus, by modern times, the unique tradition of the Red Jews in Yiddish had been watered down almost beyond recognition.

This altered portrayal is epitomized by the name the Red Jews acquired in modern Yiddish: whereas Old Yiddish culture highlighted the power of one unimpressive representative, for the first time, this entire nation is collectively called "little Red Jews" in modern Yiddish literature.[11] Accounts of the little Red Jews culled from the early modern *Gelilot Erez Yisra'el* enjoyed wide currency among eastern European Jewish readers: in addition to numerous reprints of this complete work in both Yiddish and Hebrew, several Yiddish chapbooks from the early twentieth century include excerpts.[12] At the same time, a certain Shamir produced three booklets in Warsaw and Vilnius that were advertised as *Mayse fun die Royte Yudlekh* (A story about the little Red Jews). Although none of them mentions the Red Jews (rather, they are in fact reprints of a story about two brothers: one poor but learned and righteous, and the other a rich business man), a fourth booklet is a collection of classical sources on the Ten Lost Tribes—such as Eldad ha-Dani and Abraham Farissol—in Yiddish translation.[13] Mislabeling the content of his works was not the only trick this author played on his target readership. By using the pseudonym Shamir, he sought to fool potential buyers into believing that this work was written by a prolific author of Yiddish novels with a similar pen name, Shomer (Nokhem Meyer Shaykevitsh, 1849?–1905). That well-known Shomer was disparaged in intellectual circles as a writer of *shund* (junk novels), but he was highly popular among a mass Yiddish readership.[14] Apparently it was profitable to sell purported tales about the famous Red Jews, and even more so if Shomer wrote them.

The label "little Red Jews" remained the name of the Ten Lost Tribes of Israel in modern Yiddish ever since. Along with the diminutive effect of this idiom, the distinctive subversive heroism of this mythic people was reduced. Indeed, Shamir's actual text about the Red Jews emphasizes traditional features of the Ten Lost Tribes, namely political independence, physical strength, and a life of wealth and piety, rather than individual agency. When the Red Jews ultimately became established as a motif in modern Yiddish literature in the late nineteenth and early twentieth centuries, to negotiate emergent challenges to Jewish life and culture, their standing as a symbol of empowerment would be entirely lost.

## Classic Yiddish Fiction

The founders of modern Yiddish fiction—Mendele Moykher Sforim (Sholem Yankev Abramovitsh), Sholem Aleichem (Solomon Rabinovitch), and Y. L. (Isaac Leib) Peretz—all featured the little Red Jews in several works. Let us assess the treatment of this imaginary people in their oeuvres. Mendele's novel *Kitser masoes Binyomin hashlishi* (The brief travels of Benjamin the third), first published in 1878, represents the first appearance of the Red Jews in modern Yiddish literature.[15] Presented as a travelogue, this volume describes the adventures of Benjamin of Tuneyadevka (the town of idlers), who sets out in search of the legendary red nation. By embarking on this quest, he emulates two historical namesakes, the twelfth-century traveler Benjamin of Tudela and the mid-nineteenth-century Romanian explorer Israel Joseph Benjamin;

thus his designation as "the third." In his preface, Mendele claims that this Benjamin achieved renown among Jews and Christians across Europe. Jewish periodicals as well as English and German newspapers allegedly reported on the travels of this small-town Polish Jew to lands that even the greatest British explorers had not reached, and, thus, the Royal Geographic Society of London awarded him a medal for his unprecedented discoveries.

The account itself, however, casts Benjamin as an unsophisticated fellow from a parochial Jewish town; its inhabitants were simple, credulous, and mostly poor, while being content with their lot and steadfast in their faith in both divine providence and the future arrival of the Messiah. Like everyone else in town, Benjamin assumed that "beyond Tuneyadevka ... the world came to an end, nor was there a better or sweeter place anywhere."[16] But after a visitor told him about the wonders in the land of Israel, he began to seek out tales of other distant locales, among them the adventures of Eldad ha-Dani and Benjamin of Tudela. Through Benjamin's exploration of texts, Mendele's knowledge of the Old Yiddish background of the myth of the Red Jews is evident. He consciously plays on these historical tropes when Benjamin plans to speak with the Red Jews in their own vernacular language, which he identifies as Aramaic, the language of *Akdamut Milin*, allegedly composed by Eldad ha-Dani, himself a Red Jew.[17] Here Mendele merges *Ma'aseh Akdamut* with the famous story of this ninth-century traveler. As Benjamin immerses himself in the fantastical books about the Red Jews, "his imaginings flew far away to the ends of the inhabited earth. He crossed mountains, valleys, and deserts ... he reached the lands of the Ten Lost Tribes."[18] Tuneyadevka was becoming too small for him, so he decided to journey to the Red Jews with his companion Sendrel. Despite Benjamin's aspirations, their exploits were not as "exotic" as he had hoped. To the contrary, Mendele sardonically reports that he and Sendrel got no further than several *shtetlekh* (lit. small towns) from home when they were kidnapped and sold into military service, only to be discharged after a medical examination disqualified them due to madness.

Mendele posits that the inability, or perhaps unwillingness, to leave the familiar typifies traditional eastern European Jewry in the late nineteenth century. In his memoir, he wrote about his childhood in Kopyl (near Minsk), where he was raised in a traditional Jewish family, in terms that echo his description of Benjamin, "being innocent, like the chick in the egg, I thought this was the whole world and beyond Kopyl a desolate desert with mountains of darkness and the Sambatyon River with strange weird creatures."[19]

Mendele employs the traditional location of the legendary Ten Lost Tribes who, according to Jewish literature, are trapped beyond the mountains of darkness as a metaphor for the closed sphere of the eastern European synagogue and *beit midrash* (study house), characterized by unquestioning acceptance of rabbinical dogma and unsubstantiated folk beliefs.[20] When Mendele became an adherent of the Haskalah in his youth, like other Jewish intellectuals in eastern Europe of his time, he sought to foster Enlightenment values among its predominantly traditionally religious Jewish society, encouraging his coreligionists to emerge from the proverbial mountains of darkness.

Although in his parody of the narrow-mindedness of his small-town Jewish neighbors the Red Jews represent Benjamin's desire to broaden his cultural horizons, they are paradoxically as isolated as their counterparts in Tuneyadevka. In fact, Benjamin and Sendrel are mistaken for Red Jews by the equally naive Jews of nearby Glupsk (Dumbsville).[21] As its name suggests, in this neighboring town of fools, the two simpletons meet their "true equals . . . thousands of other Jews."[22] The travelers' unfamiliarity with the topography and populace beyond their town confirms their ignorance of the world around their circumscribed Jewish community. By journeying to the Red Jews, rather than escaping from the dreary realities of Jewish life in the Russian Pale of Settlement, Benjamin actually exchanges one insular Jewish society for another. He shows an awareness of this parallel but it does not deter him: Benjamin tells Sendrel that they need to practice Aramaic; by contrast with eastern European Jews, the Red Jews do not know a word of Yiddish, the key to communication not only with other Jews but also with non-Jews, given its similarity to German.[23] It is significant that Benjamin himself knows Aramaic, the old-fashioned language of the Talmud and other religious compositions, but not Ukrainian, the spoken language of his non-Jewish neighbors.[24] Thus, the association of Red Jews with the Diaspora life offers a through line from Old Yiddish into modern Yiddish literature, despite the differences in their prompts to enact change in the real world rather than being content with the status quo.

Whereas the first edition of *Benjamin's Travels* primarily served as a vehicle for Mendele's criticism of his contemporaries in the spirit of the Haskalah, the Hebrew translation from 1896 advocates Zionist activism, which attracted the author later in life.[25] In the intervening years, violent pogroms against Jews in Russia during the 1880s and restrictive tsarist politics had cast doubt on the likelihood that enlightened education would improve the stagnant conditions of Jews in the Pale of Settlement. From 1881 onward, Jews began to emigrate en masse to various destinations: many to the United States, and significant numbers to the land of Israel. Amid these changing political circumstances, Mendele translated and republished his novel with minor emendations in 1896, the same year that Theodor Herzl's *Judenstaat* (Jewish State) was released.[26]

Against this turbulent backdrop, Benjamin's quixotic search for the splendid land of the Red Jews reads like a reflection on the growing statelessness of modern Jews within the emergent nations of Europe. In his prologue (included in the original Yiddish edition from 1878), Mendele captures the impoverished conditions of Jews in eastern Europe with the Yiddish idiom "go over the houses" (געהט איבער די הייזער), meaning that, like beggars, they go from door to door trying to eke out a living.[27] Irrespective of their efforts, they were spurned at every turn; by the time of the Hebrew translation, their sole option was a return to the ancient Jewish country, the land of Israel. In the novel, Mendele alludes to the Torah portion *Lekh-lekha* (Go forth; Gen. 12–17), applying God's promise of land to Abraham as a relief from the misery that Jews in Russia endured. After all, in traditional Jewish messianic thought, the rediscovery of the Ten Tribes is a prelude to the restoration of Israel, in contrast to achieving salvation through cultural integration and political emancipation.

Indeed, Mendele gives his flawed hero a second chance to locate the Red Jews. The epilogue in the second Hebrew edition of this novel, published in 1911, informs readers that Benjamin had embarked on another attempt to reach their realm. Due to his prior experience, he was appointed to lead an expedition by the Torah Exploration Society, which was initiated by a group of kabbalists in Jerusalem, to find the Sambatyon River. From the perspective of this epilogue, Benjamin was still en route, engaged in battle with Prester John, an indication that he was very close to his goal.[28] In 1898, a circle of mystics in Jerusalem had actually published a pamphlet that called for such an excursion, and, in response, Mendele swiftly grafted Benjamin's fictitious travels onto this contemporary framework in two Hebrew texts, published in 1903: *Aggadot ha-Admonim* (Tales of the red ones) and *Midrash va-Yera* on the Torah portion "And He Appeared."[29] These satires are styled as critical editions of midrashim that Mendele concocted, mimicking the scholarship of nineteenth-century *Wissenschaft des Judentums* (The science of Judaism). This mockery targets the edition of Eldad ha-Dani's account published by Abraham Epstein in 1891 and a collection of Hebrew documents on the Ten Lost Tribes edited by Adolf Neubauer, which appeared in *Kobez al Yad* in 1888 (the journal of the Berlin-based *Ḥevrat Mekizei Nirdamim*, The society of those who wake the slumbering) and in an English version in the *Jewish Quarterly Review* (1889).[30] With *Midrash va-Yera*, Mendele feigned to unveil a previously unknown midrash that Benjamin purportedly brought back from his successful encounter with the Red Jews.[31] He thus camouflages sharp criticism of romanticized or utopian perspectives on the Red Jews, whether academic or religious, in an intellectualized lampoon.

The translated reprint of Benjamin's first voyage from 1911 seems to apply the same critique to early Zionist activity. His unsuccessful first attempt to reach the Red Jews demonstrates that the "urgencies of the mundane 'real' quickly supersede the manifestly naïve longings of the heroes," as Sidra DeKoven Ezrahi observes.[32] The ironic presentation of Benjamin's command in a second expedition does not make a different outcome seem likely. Mendele's multilayered satire thus also warns against simply equating Jewish nationalism with the fulfillment of messianic hopes, without serving as a catalyst for tangible progress. The pressure to implement effective solutions grew ever more urgent after the Kishinev pogroms in 1903 and 1905, when violent anti-Jewish riots again erupted in Russia, as international efforts for Jews to flee from persecution by resettling in a new Jewish homeland increased.

The dissonance between Zionist utopia and political realism was also discussed by Mendele's younger contemporary, Sholem Aleichem. Shortly before the Kishinev pogroms, while promoting Zionism, Sholem Aleichem expressed a similar concern that competing political factions within eastern European Jewry would impede nationalist hopes for solving the threats to Jewish existence in Europe, especially for the Jews of Russia.[33] In two humorous stories—*Di Royte Yudlekh* (The little Red Jews), published in the bimonthly *Der Yud* (The Jew) in 1900, and its sequel, *Meshugga'im* (Lunatics), in the Zionist Organization paper *Di Velt* (The world) in 1901—he describes the Red Jews, who live "far, far away from our areas, somewhere beyond the Mountains of Darkness, on the other side of the Sambatyon River."[34] As in Mendele's portrayal, the Red Jews have been transformed from heroes in Old Yiddish to a symbol of backward traditionalism. In Sholem Aleichem's fiction, "the red Little Jews, who consider themselves very grand and high and mighty people, and who are very sensitive about the respect due to them,"[35] are in fact unaware that they live in misery. The quasi-ethnographic introduction of "The Little Red Jews" describes their coarse behavior in terms that mirror contemporaneous Maskilic critiques of Jewish life in the Pale of Settlement. The Red Jews have essentially abandoned Jewish practice, as exemplified by their ignorance of Hebrew; they lack education and they live in poverty; and their allegedly grand capital is actually a mudhole.[36] Even the language of the narrator belittles them as *royte yudlekh* or *royte yidelekh* (little Red Jews), respectively, and pities them as "poor little brethren" because of their shortcomings, which are not countered by any heroic act.[37] Sholem Aleichem thereby negates the popular fantasy of the mighty Red Jews by casting this as *ayn oysgetrakhte zakh* (a fictitious account), as the subtitle of "The Little Red Jews" asserts. Upon closer examination with the innovative tools and methods of ethnography in Europe, this legend did not satisfy its claims.[38]

In "Lunatics," the little Red Jews experience an analogous sense of disillusionment. In this short story, Sholem Aleichem inverts the ethnographic lens: here a Red Jew reports on his exploration of the wondrous lands on the other side of the Sambatyon, where all Jews have black hair.[39] The Red Jews, among whom red hair was the norm, "couldn't even imagine a Jew with no red hair—what a freak!"[40] This traveler brought high expectations, informed by extravagant rumors of happiness and great wealth in that distant land, whose streets were strewn with gold that everyone could freely take. Sholem Aleichem seems to borrow from the early modern Yiddish legend when he describes how the Red Jews would pray for God to bring a miracle that would ferry them across the Sambatyon, even if only for a day, to gather as much gold and silver as they could carry. "But to pick yourself up and go there yourself—nobody liked that idea!"[41]

Once, Moshe the beadle secretly crosses the river, leaving everyone wondering about his disappearance. Upon his return, this aptly named "lost Moshe"—a combination of the identification of the Red Jews as Lost Tribes and more specifically the Sons of Moses—pens a comprehensive account of his journey and publishes it as a book. He reports on the fortunate Jews who dwell in the land of lunatics: unlike the little Red Jews, they are tall and proud, dressed in the finest black garments, and display impeccable manners. However, he considers their behavior peculiar and he details the aspects of their material culture and lifestyle that he finds quite strange: electricity and telephones; an orchestra; a synagogue that is led by a clean-shaven cantor and a rabbi who earned a doctorate, whose services include an organ and choir; Jewish high schools where students of both genders study together; secular education for laborers; Jewish athletic clubs; girls chatting in Hebrew; and women reading newspapers and frivolous books in the folk library. The Red Jews who read this travelogue are disappointed: "Nothing to it! . . . Wasn't worth waiting all this time to find out!" They reject the traveler as a charlatan since his observations contradict cherished lore: "The whole story is a lie! He invented the lot! Out of his own head!"[42] The cosmopolitan culture on the other side of the river seemed outlandish to the traditionalist Red Jews. Most disturbing was its enthusiasm for a Jewish state in Palestine that would equal all other nations: their distant coreligionists collected money for that purpose, founded agricultural colonies that would build the country, and trained a Jewish army, all without waiting for the Messiah; moreover, they planned to liberate the poor little Red Jews and resettle them there.[43]

We learn more about these Red Jews' attitudes toward the land of Israel in *The Little Red Jews*. A Zionist enthusiast, "one of the Black Jews . . . from the other side of the Sambatyon,"[44] comes to their land with the tidings of their impending salvation: they can finally return to their ancestral homeland to "become decent human beings" and cease from being "the laughingstock of all nations." In this narrative, however, rather than eagerly waiting for a new Moses who would lead them to the Holy Land, the Red Jews find it all quite odd. The messenger decries their isolation: "You pray, but you don't know what you're praying! You talk, but you don't know what you're saying! You're sick, but you don't know what's wrong with you! You wander about aimlessly, you lie in a daze, and you sleep badly! . . . Get up, brothers! It's time! You've been lying in the mud for two thousand years already, and you don't sense how miserable you are!"[45] He explains that Jews in the Diaspora had behaved similarly in the past, singing sweet songs about the messianic age for solace in the face of dire conditions. Taking up the Old Yiddish theme of the Red Jews as an emblem of self-empowerment, Sholem Aleichem writes that their diasporic counterparts finally realized "that help was purely in our own hands, and that no one would help us if we didn't help ourselves."[46] In preparation for the task of building a Jewish state, they eventually shed the spiritual narrowness of the ghetto by becoming educated in both Jewish and secular subjects, raising funds, and holding meetings that called for resettlement.

The visitor's arguments in favor of Zionism among the Red Jews prove futile in the end. The Red Jews are unwilling to change, even for the hope of a better life. Incapable of imagining this potential, they thwart the great promise of Zionist activity in lengthy debates between competing political and social factions—the Orthodox, the socialists, and the Maskilim—

without progress. Even those who do not object to Zionism in principle and who agree to the urgent need for a solution to the "Jewish problem" cannot envision a practical mechanism for resettling an entire nation in a new homeland: "The Red Jews had long been looking forward to the arrival of the Messiah. . . . And now suddenly, they were supposed to think about the Holy Land too!"[47] Such a departure from tradition was unthinkable. After their pointless discussion of the visitor's strange proposal, everyone goes home, and the status quo remains.

This outcome reflects Sholem Aleichem's skeptical assessment of the political scene of his generation. In the aftermath of the Kishinev attacks and anti-Jewish riots during the Russian Revolution of 1905, he appended *The Little Red Jews*.[48] This addendum explains that, following an ancient law, whenever danger arises, the Red Jews would gather in synagogue, deliberate, repent, and wait for the Messiah.[49] Even amid the dire need for relief from increasing levels of anti-Semitic violence, the Red Jews convened committees that fervently debated possible approaches to emigration to ameliorate their distress but without moving from words to action. The novel closes with a letter from one of these Red Jews, which was allegedly discovered by a historian many years later. Writing from Egypt, where he had fled in search of freedom and happiness, this Red Jew was utterly disappointed. Here "Egypt" seems to serve as code for both the land of Israel and North America. Indeed, after a period of meandering throughout central and western Europe, Sholem Aleichem left Russia for the United States in late 1906; the following year disillusionment led him back Europe, but he ultimately settled in New York City.[50]

Sholem Aleichem further develops the theme of unproductive quietism in his satire *Revolutsye oyf yener zayt Sambatyen* (A revolution on the other side of the Sambatyon), first published in 1906.[51] In this novella, he projects criticism of tsarist despotism on the society of the Red Jews who, despite priding themselves on being a free nation, are ruled by an autocratic *parnas ha-ḥodesh* (elder of the month). Ironically, on their side of the Sambatyon, this is a hereditary position with a lifelong term (despite its sardonic title), whereas Jewish communal leadership rotated among appointed elders among diasporic Jewry. Moreover, the Red Jews are submissive to this elder; they bow before him, lavish him with presents every Sabbath, and expect punishment if their offerings fail to please him. His cronies are "privileged" to eat the leftovers from his meals; therefore, the author nicknames them derogatorily as *telerlekers* (plate lickers).

Given that the abortive Russian Revolution failed to advance the Jewish struggle for full citizenship, Sholem Aleichem harnesses humor and metaphor to critique the revolutionary forces in Russia by ridiculing the Red Jews. When an uprising threatens to erupt beyond the Sambatyon, in an attempt to avoid a putsch, the elder of the month proposes the creation of a parliament and a constitution. The *telerlekers* fear that their leader will still be overthrown and, by extension, their prestigious standing will be lost, resulting in their need to "go over the houses" to support themselves. Under the battle cry "Plate lickers throughout the land: Unite!"[52] this abject elite convinces the Red Jews to petition the elder to retract the modest concessions to democratization.[53] The Red Jews are grateful that their political and social conditions will remain untouched, confident that they dwell happily and in freedom. The gullible Red Jews are duped into favoring an ostensibly quiet and secure life over the opportunity to improve their situation by demanding equal rights.[54] Their staunch defense of tradition guarantees that nothing will ever change.

A similarly ironic preference to a static world is the leitmotif of Sholem Aleichem's lesser-known story *Alemen Glaykh* (All are equal), which appeared three years prior, in 1903.[55] Subtitled "A Utopia," the story envisions a socialist society whose members all have a single socioeconomic rank. This tale begins with a Red Jew who writes a letter in form of a prayer (*gebet brif*) to God; reminiscent of *Akdamut Milin*, he begins by praising the divine attributes of might and mercy. He then describes the social and economic injustices that pervade the world and petitions God to redistribute wealth equally throughout the earth, so envy, hatred, and war will end and peace will prevail. God answers his prayer, causing all money to be collected and reallocated equally to each person.[56] As a result, everyone has the wealth of a noble, but unanticipated sorrows follow: people all stop working and, consequently, basic human needs are disrupted—from food supplies to medical care—and social institutions like education and religious communities come to a halt.[57]

In another allusion to *Ma'aseh Akdamut*, a certain Rabbi Meir is the first to grasp the difficulties that have been caused by the new fiscal equality. Known as the town fool and ironically nicknamed *bal moyekh* (the clever one), he alone takes action while the others drift into the new status quo. Since shoemakers no longer work, Meir repairs his own boots. He questions whether this new social order is really an improvement, since nothing is available for purchase with their riches, so people have begun to steal and even commit murder to obtain food. This Meir the Clever observes that the flow of capital keeps a society running, despite its inherent inequities. He concludes that people cannot yet operate within a purely altruistic framework.[58] The tale concludes when its narrator awakens, revealing that this dystopian scenario was just a nightmare. Rather than lodging an anti-socialist critique, this satire mocks naive notions of redemption that cannot even succeed in a dream. As in the Old Yiddish tradition about the Red Jews, here too humanity is not yet ready for a messianic resolution so—as Meir the Clever demonstrates, despite being dismissed as a fool by his peers—proactive adaptations to turbulent historical circumstances are imperative.[59]

Around the same time, Y. L. Peretz published *Dray Khupes* (Three wedding canopies; 1901); his novella about the Red Jews appeared in *Der Yud*, the periodical where Sholem Aleichem's *Little Red Jews* had first appeared.[60] Like Mendele and Sholem Aleichem, this author of classic Yiddish fiction also rejects the eschatological escapism of eastern European Jewry. Peretz terms the Red Jews' home Wonderland, a pristine country of lush landscapes and impressive cities, crowned by its capital, Faithstone, and peaceful coexistence between humanity and nature. When a prediction by a fortune teller is misinterpreted, the royalty of this land—King Solomon and his daughter, Princess Shulamite with "flashing red hair"[61]—leave this paradise only to wander as beggars. The narrator explains: "The hardest thing for us Jews, the punishment that a Jewish penitent has to suffer for the worst sins—wandering, 'the sorrows of exile'—was a very easy matter in Wonderland and brought a great deal of pleasure. In a land where people are good, everything is good. You feel at home anywhere. . . . The houses are open, like the hearts of the inhabitants! . . . But even Wonderland comes to an end."[62] Whereas these two vagrants are treated with compassion in Wonderland, across the border, "every door is guarded, at every gate people glare at you suspiciously."[63] By juxtaposing the idyllic vision of Jewish traditional lore with the harsh realities of life in the Diaspora, Peretz details its grim qualities: people labor ceaselessly but without joy and care for themselves alone without helping peers in distress, much less showing mercy toward the poor. When the king and the princess seek directions to Wonderland, they are mocked for believing the *bobe-mayse* (grandmother's tale) of this fantastical place: "There's no 'Wonderland' in any geography book!"[64] It is laughable to believe in such fairy tales; instead, they give a pamphlet titled "Help yourself!" to these two beggars.

Peretz makes his position clear: all beliefs in a messianic kingdom, with their promise of fulfillment to be dispensed from heaven without human efforts, are without foundation.⁶⁵ His interpretation of the Old Yiddish tradition about the Red Jews comes full circle when Solomon and Shulamite finally return to Wonderland from their undeserved exile.⁶⁶ Their arrival is replete with rabbinic imagery: they are welcomed with a festive procession and the sounding of the shofar, whose trumpeting blasts will herald the Messiah, and a great feast that foreshadows the future messianic banquet. However, the story ends with the musings of a wise crow, who wonders whether this salvation will succeed. The crow explains that it has already witnessed failed attempts toward deliverance. It refers to two distinct populations that inhabit the novella's world, unmistakably inspired by the Old Yiddish legend: dwarfs who live underground and lead a scholarly existence, known for their small bodies and big souls; and the marauders and murderers, with small souls and big bodies, who live aboveground. Symbolic of the Jewish minority and Christian majority in Europe, respectively, these two types of humans are engaged in ongoing battles to see which will prevail, physical strength or the soulful intellect. Time and again, the dwarfs tried in vain to make peace with the mighty ones by appealing to those in command. At the end of our story, during the festivities for the royals' return and the princess's wedding, they dispatch a new delegation to King Solomon, hoping that he will finally forge peace.⁶⁷

Neither Mendele, Sholem Aleichem, nor Peretz could predict how the various proposals addressing the "Jewish question" would determine the future of Russian Jewry. Despite the uncertainties, they were confident that determined action against their oppression should replace patiently awaiting messianic salvation. These three Yiddish writers expressed their generations' complicated relationship to late nineteenth- and early twentieth-century life in the Diaspora by reappropriating the Red Jews and their activist tropes from Old Yiddish and applying them to contemporary ideologies and trends: Haskalah, Zionism, and emigration to America.

## Chagall's *Jew in Bright Red*

The Russian Jewish painter Marc Chagall, who embraced modern Yiddish literature, drew from the innovative literary interpretation of the Red Jews, as in the stories by Mendele, Sholem Aleichem, and Peretz. Chagall's paintings often "speak" Yiddish⁶⁸ and, indeed, his famous *Jew in Bright Red* (fig. 23) translates a textual depiction into a pictorial icon, much as the idiom "Red

Jews" renders language visible in the mind's eye. This monumental oil painting from 1915 links exile and Jewish identity on canvas: an elderly Jew with red hair and a red beard embodies the entire Jewish people, whose existence has been marked by suffering.[69] Akin to contemporaneous Yiddish authors, Chagall reappropriates the anti-Jewish figure of the Wandering Jew, which originated with medieval Christian polemics and persisted into modernity, as a symbol of Jewish self-awareness to overlay his fate on the Red Jews.[70]

Chagall's Eternal Jew, weary from ceaseless movement, sits on a bench in front of several houses with his hands resting on his legs. One of his hands is white and the other green, referring to *The Jew in Red* (fig. 24) and *The Jew in Green* (fig. 25), respectively; these two paintings from 1914 similarly portray the Wandering Jew who is destined to be an eternal beggar. *The Jew in Red* underscores this pervasive image of eastern European Jewry by featuring symbols of Diaspora: a walking cane and a traveler's sack. In Yiddish, *trogn zayn pekl* (to carry one's pack) is also a figurative expression for *shlepn dem goles* (to bear exile; i.e., enduring the afflictions of exile).[71] The model for *The Jew in Green*, whom Chagall identified as the Maggid of Slutsk, an impoverished itinerant preacher, bears a strong resemblance to the subject of *The Jew in Bright Red* with respect to their features and posture: both have careworn faces, similarly shaped beards, and sidelocks visible on one side; they sit hunched with hands flaccid on their lap, wearing identical caps. Each has one eye open and the other closed. The shut eye signifies exhaustion, and perhaps the approach of death.[72]

Surprisingly, the many interpretations of *The Jew in Bright Red*, with the sole exception of Sabine Koller, fail to acknowledge its subject's roots in the Yiddish literary symbolism of the legend of the Red Jews.[73] Having grown up in a traditionally observant, Yiddish-speaking family in the Pale of Settlement, Chagall surely knew legends about the Red Jews. He also must have been familiar with their portrayals in contemporary Yiddish fiction since he read Yiddish literary classics and especially admired Sholem Aleichem, who had already become renowned.[74] Koller notes in her interpretation of Chagall's oeuvre that *hobn ayn oyg bay got* (to have one eye with God) stands for trust in God;[75] on a related theme, I would posit that Chagall turned the tables, visualizing his Red Jew as partially blind to the options of human action. Mirjam Rajner's reading of this painting supports this understanding: she connects the Red Jew's closed left eye with life in the Old World shtetl, structured by traditional religious laws and faith: "In contrast, the character's right half presents a modern, contemporary Jew firmly rooted in the outer world. He is open-eyed and wears the short jacket of a maskil—an enlightened, secular Jew. He lacks external religious symbols such as a sidelock, his skin color is a neutral white and he sits comfortably on the stool, whose leg is visible in this case. Moreover, next to him is a little blooming tree signifying spring and thus a new beginning and optimism."[76]

The historical context for the production of his three monumental paintings of Wandering Jews is indicative, for they were created during World War I, when Jews were caught as victims amid the surrounding events. In fact, the ink drawing *The War* from 1914 links these three paintings, though in different colors: it depicts a figure much like the subject of *The Jew in Bright Red* and *The Jew in Green*, who carries a traveler's pack as in *The Jew in Red*, and appears to be a motionless witness to all that transpired around him, without the ability to control causes or effects.[77] One major occurrence at this time was the displacement of 1.5 million Jews on the Russian-German front; they were forced to flee their homes within hours.[78] *The Jew in Bright Red* appears to be on the verge of leaving the shtetl behind him, for the next phase of his exile. The Hebrew text written in the background of this painting suggests its directive: *Lekh-lekha*, the abovementioned Torah portion that opens with God's call for Abraham to leave his home to settle in the land of Israel, which is promised to the Jewish people. However, the Yiddish phrase, *lekh-lekho*, is equated with *gey dir avek* (get out) and refers to the expulsion of Jews rather than messianic redemption. Scholars have especially pointed to Sholem Aleichem's series of Yiddish short stories about Tevye the Dairyman as a literary parallel to this painting; the final collection, written from 1914 to 1916, is titled *Lekh-lekho* and focuses on Tevye's banishment from his village.[79] More importantly, Sholem Aleichem and Mendele place their narratives about the little Red Jews in the context of the pogroms and forced migration of Jews in Russia in the late nineteenth and early twentieth centuries, as we have seen, suggesting these stories as the most obvious literary inspiration for Chagall's *Jew in Bright Red*, which reflects sorrow and criticism of the long, difficult history of Jewish survival in exile.

Despite deriving from the Old Yiddish myth, the representations of the Red Jews in modern Yiddish literature and, by extension, in Chagall's painting should also be considered with respect to the persistent European stereotype that Jews have red hair, which was fixed in Jewish and Christian imagination. Alongside the tendency to associate curly dark hair and dark skin as Jewish features that dominated European perceptions of race from the late eighteenth century onward,[80] the roster of redheaded Jewish characters in nineteenth- and twentieth-century literature is extensive, including the extremely popular German novel *Soll und Haben* (Debit and Credit; 1855) by Gustav Freytag.[81] Analogously, the Austrian Jewish writer Joseph Roth asserts that Jews living in the eastern provinces of Austria-Hungary must trace their ancestry to the legendary Chazars, descendants of the Ten Tribes, on account of their stereotypical red hair. He describes these "frontier Jews" in *Radetzkymarsch* (Radetzky March; 1932) as follows: "The hair flamed from their heads. Their beards were as torches. On the backs of their nimble hands red wires bristled up, like tiny spears. Their ears were veiled over by rank tufts of fine red wool, the after-glow, perhaps, of fires smouldering in their brains."[82] Most Jews, of any descent, in this novel are in fact described as red-haired.

At the turn of the twentieth century, the German scholar Friedrich Hottenroth produced illustrated volumes on German folk costumes that bolstered this persistent image (fig. 26). Jewish redheads also appear frequently in paintings from the first quarter of the twentieth century, roughly contemporaneous with Chagall's work. For example, the Jewish artists Isidor Kaufmann and Reuven Rubin (figs. 27, 28) produced a number of portraits of eastern European Jews with red beards. In 1901, the Polish painter Edward Okuń rendered a classic Red Judas in his painting with that same name (fig. 29). The redheaded and red-bearded Wandering Jew by S. C. Dumont provides an infamous exemplar of red coloring in anti-Semitic iconography: this colored woodcut, based on an artwork attributed to the French painter Gustave Doré, appeared on the cover of the satirical *Journal pour Rire* (June 1852; fig. 30) and was later displayed in *Der Ewige Jude* (The eternal Jew), a major exhibit of Nazi propaganda that toured Germany and Austria from 1937 to 1939. As with the emergence of the Red Jews' myth in Old Yiddish, the visualization of the Wandering Red Jew by Dumont and Chagall share many features, notwithstanding their divergent interpretations. These contrasting depictions of this legendary redheaded and red-bearded personage signaled a renewed struggle over the status of Jews in society, here too expressed through color symbolism.

## "Red Indians"

Again in search of belonging, modern Jewish perspectives on the Red Jews took yet another path, and their redness was occasionally related to Native Americans. From the turn of the twentieth century through its high point in the 1930s, Native American history, ritual, and folklore was a recurrent theme in the Jewish press in eastern Europe and the United States.[83] A prominent motif in these publications was the identification of American Indians as Red Jews. This association continued a theory that had gained popularity among Christians and Jews in Europe and America alike during the seventeenth and eighteenth centuries. This millenarian notion claimed that among the indigenous populations in the western hemisphere were descendants of the Ten Lost Tribes of Israel who had reached those lands.[84] While I am not aware of any early modern source that connects the American Indians, who were considered "red-skinned" as early as the sixteenth century,[85] with the Red Jews via their complexion, Menasseh ben Israel, the mid-seventeenth-century Sephardic scholar from Amsterdam who had a key voice in this discussion, makes several references to the Lost Tribes' alleged red hair when he identifies them in South America. For Menasseh, auburn hair and white skin were marks of beauty that distinguished them from the Incas' dark complexions and hair. He claimed that these Jewish tribes had arrived in America long before the American Indians.[86] Admittedly, despite having collected a wealth of material on the Ten Tribes to bolster his hypothesis, from rabbinic literature to writings from his own generation, Menasseh had no knowledge of the Red Jews or their legend.[87] Not until the early twentieth century did "red Indians" become Red Jews, when the "coincidence of language certainly facilitated identification," as Rachel Rubinstein shows in her study on Native America in the Jewish imagination.[88]

One of the more political Jewish articles about Native Americans was written by the poet and journalist Elijah Haim Sheps (1892–1968; better known by his pseudonym, A. Almi), who emigrated from Poland to the United States in 1912. When he was still living in Warsaw, Almi participated in a project that collected Yiddish folk songs and tales, under the leadership of linguist and folklorist Noah Prilutski (1882–1941). Prilutski's publications include songs that Almi gathered from members of his family. The Red Jews as heralds of the Messiah's arrival are mentioned in a Hasidic melody of the Havdalah prayer *Got fun Avrom* (God of Abraham) contributed by his seventy-four-year-old grandmother Chaya, who had learned it from her grandmother.[89] In the summer of 1945, Almi composed *Di Royte Yidelekh*: a four-act Yiddish musical plus prologue and epilogue about the Red Jews. Since this play has been lost, we cannot determine its content.[90] However, given its English title, *The Red Skinned Little Jews*, it may likely have had a novel American setting.

Indeed, Almi adapted legends from his childhood to his new cultural context in an essay, *Tsvishn Indyaner* (Among Indians), published in 1919 in the Jewish daily newspaper *Der Moment* (The moment) in Warsaw, where he served a contributing editor. He describes his encounters with native tribes of "the red race" during his travels across North America, which reminded him of the lamentable state of the Jewish people in exile. To Almi, the words of one young Native American man reminded him of a Jewish voice speaking with "the same sorrow and bitterness . . . and the same consoling messianic yearning" that prevented the indigenous tribes from losing hope in a better future and enabled them to foresee an autonomous American Indian republic. It was "our messianic yearning," Almi writes after their conversation, "A Red Messiah! A certain legend, unbidden sprang to mind—that the Indians were of the ten lost tribes. . . . Running muddled through my head the entire time was: 'Red Jews . . . Red Messiah . . . Red Messiah . . . Red Jews.'" Against the backdrop of hardships that European Jewry endured during World War I, Almi feels a sense of kinship with the Native Americans of his chosen country. He conceived of a bond between these two peoples, both "in exile in their own land," joined by their experiences of displacement and destruction as well as their aspirations for political independence.[91]

## Red Muscular Judaism

The Red Jews became newly politicized in Zionist poetry. These writers revived the original empowerment that cultivated the emergence of the Red Jews in Old Yiddish, in opposition to their function as Wandering Jews. These two interpretations were expressed by members of the same literary circle in late nineteenth-century Odessa. The city's flourishing Jewish intellectual scene included luminaries such as Mendele and Sholem Aleichem, as well as the Zionist thinker Ahad ha-Am (Asher Ginzberg), the publisher Yehoshua Ravnitzky, and the distinguished historian of the Jews, Simon Dubnow. In his autobiography, Dubnow recalls that his close friend Mendele teased Ravnitzky and Ahad ha-Am, calling them "little red-haired Jews," referring to both their reddish hair color and their organization *Bnei Mosheh*.[92]

Ahad ha-Am founded *Bnei Mosheh* in 1889 as a quasi-secret society comprised of a Jewish nationalist elite—modeled after a Masonic lodge—in response to what he considered the ideological and practical shortcomings of *Ḥovevei Ẓion* (Lovers of Zion), whose groups promoted Jewish immigration to Palestine. For nearly a decade, the few but committed members of *Bnei Mosheh* endeavored to instill Jewish national awareness among young Jews, in accordance with Ahad ha-Am's teachings on cultural Zionism. Rather than opening with the political ambition for a sovereign state, this approach prioritized its spiritual aspects, fostering a renaissance of the heritage of Judaism. A revival of Hebrew culture was at its core: all members of *Bnei Mosheh* had to become fluent in Hebrew.[93] Ahad ha-Am distanced himself from Yiddish, which he considered less desirable.[94] Being from a Yiddish-speaking Hasidic family and certainly knowing the legend of the Red Jews, he would hardly have appreciated Mendele's implication that these heroes of Yiddish literature were eponymous for his group, especially not as depicted in modern writing. To the contrary, *Bnei Mosheh* was intended to evoke the biblical Moses worthy of emulation.[95] Indeed, these young Zionists' self-perception differed sharply from their colleague's wry comment, in which Red Jews were tainted by a reputation for idleness and unproductive activity.

To this effect, Naphtali Herz Imber and Uri Zvi Greenberg, well-known Hebrew poets of that period who shared a Zionist worldview, ushered the Old Yiddish concept of the heroic Red Jews into modern Jewish politics. This pair of prominent intellectuals reveal that, among eastern European Zionists, the Red Jews of Old Yiddish lore were considered agents of change who would return the Jews to their ancestral home in Palestine. The Zionist movement transformed Jewish heritage into the enterprise to create a national culture that drew from earlier demonstrations of "courage, physical prowess, political independence." The Hebrew term *gevurah* (heroism) was applied to this active and courageous life.[96] This word choice was deliberately chosen to counter the prevailing exilic sentiment of defeat and to instill a positive reading of Jewish history that fostered a bright vision of the future, especially among Jewish youth. The proud reputation of the legendary Ten Lost Tribes and the role traditionally ascribed to them in Jewish messianism suited this secular narrative of national redemption.[97] To a limited extent, their Yiddish parallel, the Red Jews, were also used to revive national consciousness by restoring the image of triumphant Jewish heroes. I argue that the Red Jews' coloration is a major factor in their inclusion. As we will see, their signature redness served as a visible badge of Zionist activism in the Yiddish poetics within this movement in eastern Europe.

Imber, the celebrated author of *Ha-Tikvah* (The hope), the poem that would become the Israeli national anthem, lived in Palestine for several years in the early 1880s, where he became a singer in early pioneering settlements.

He subsequently returned to Europe, then settled in New York City, where throughout that time he continued to publish poems and prose pieces on Jewish national themes, primarily in English and Yiddish but occasionally in Hebrew. In the first years of the twentieth century, he published Yiddish poems that expressed aspirations for national restoration in the land of Israel in various Jewish newspapers and periodicals in America.[98] These pieces invoke the biblical prophets' assurance that the exile would soon end, while charging his readership to act courageously for freedom, rather than endure suffering until redemption comes. For Imber, national rebirth required a new Maccabee who would lead the Jewish people in a revolt against their ongoing persecution. In a brief, witty poem, *A lakhediger grus tsum lakhedign puk* (A funny greeting to the funny puck), which appeared in the humorous weekly *Der Yudisher Puk* (known in English as *The Hebrew Puck*) in 1895, Imber accuses typical Jewish laments over exile of futility. Instead, he proposes that sticking their tongues out and laughing in the faces of their enemies would be more effective.[99]

After the Kishinev pogroms, Imber dedicated several poems to these attacks and, more broadly, he intensified his call for violent opposition. In 1904, he published *Barkai ha-Shlishi o Go'el ha-Dam* (The third barkai or the blood avenger), a collection of poetry that prophesies the downfall of Russia. It includes a series of militant poems that lash out against the vicious nation of "Ivan the terrible," which he identifies as a contemporary manifestation of ancient Edom, Israel's age-old nemesis. First, the Hebrew poem *Masa Yavan*—titled "To Iwan the Terrible" in the author's English version—predicts that the tsar's "throne will be smashed to the ground" by the valiant and fierce army of a distant nation: "Japan and China's hordes / Will cast upon thee their swords, / And set free all thy slaves."[100] Next, the bilingual Hebrew-English poem, *Le-Milḥamah* ("On to War"), explicitly denotes Japan as the rod of God to avenge for the Jewish blood that was spilled in Kishinev. This poem ends with the messianic hope that "to Zion [God] will give, the sword of my pride."[101] Accordingly, Imber dedicated his volume to Emperor Mutsuhito of Japan, better known as Meiji, who had been battling the Russian Empire since earlier that year. The sole Yiddish poem in this collection, *Tsu di yapaneser* (To the Japanese), addresses this people, encouraging them to bravely wage war, buoyed by God, who had given Japan the sword of revenge to smash Russia's dark power.[102] Indeed, Jews of that era looked hopefully toward Japan. Notably the American Jewish financier Jacob Schiff issued a loan for two million dollars to the

Bank of Japan in 1904, which supported Japan's victory against this powerful adversary.[103]

The proactive tone of the original Old Yiddish legend of the Red Jews suited the poet's aspirations for the Jews of his own time. In *Bnei Mosheh o ha-Yehudim ha-Adumim* (The Sons of Moses or the Red Jews), a solemn Hebrew poem from his collection of poetry published in 1900, Imber presents the Red Jews as a model for modern Diaspora Jewry. Here the poet recalls reading about these heroes—skilled fighters and swift horsemen—who dwelled beyond the Sambatyon in the Arabian desert.[104] He expresses a longing to fly like a bird to their distant home, so he could live among the Red Jews, who would instruct him in the arts of warfare. There he would perform his songs about the bitterness of exile, detailing how their brethren among Edom are scorned and persecuted, to persuade the Red Jews to rush to their aid. His dream of returning to the land of Israel would not be heard, however, for its time has not yet come. Still, invoking Jeremiah's vision of national restitution for all Israel, even the weakest among them, Imber "will sing unto the blind and the lame." They will be like Jacob (and, by extension, the physically compromised little Red Jew in *Ma'aseh Akdamut*), who "will slowly walk, limping because of his hip," and, with cleverness, Israel will eventually reach its destination.[105]

The final stanza hints at the region where Imber expects to find the Red Jews: Yemen.[106] Even earlier, in *Ha-Teimanim* (The Yemenites), a poem written during his sojourn in Palestine in 1883, he explicitly identifies its protagonists, the Jews of Yemen, as the Sons of Moses and the Ten Lost Tribes beyond the Sambatyon.[107] Here Yemenite Jewry and the Sons of Moses are described with parallel attributes, sometimes with identical language. These robust heroes of the Arabian desert, especially famed for their cavalry, alone can save Israel. Once more, we see the hyperbolic image that originated with medieval tales of the Ten Tribes and is reiterated in stories of the Red Jews: one from their ranks could chase one thousand, and two could send ten thousand to flight.[108]

The theory that the Jews of Yemen descended from the Ten Tribes flourished in the nineteenth and early twentieth centuries.[109] Like Imber himself, Yemenite Jews were among the earliest to come to the land of Israel in significant numbers in the nineteenth century; they began to arrive in 1881, shortly before the initial wave of immigration from eastern Europe. Imber's encounters with members of this relatively isolated community made a lasting impression on him. In his popular column "Imber's Picture Gallery" that featured various Jewish groups in the *Reform Advocate*, a Jewish magazine in Chicago, he wrote about the Jews from Yemen in 1908.[110] Here and in a Yiddish article in the Sukkot 1902 issue of *Minikes's Monthly*, both titled "The (little) Red Jews," Imber informed the American Jewish public about this unfamiliar Jewish community.[111] These portraits lavish unreserved praise. His tone is strikingly different from the ambivalence that typified European Jewish views of Yemenite Jewry, which described them using the same terms that were applied to indigenous peoples during that era of colonization: "noble savages" who were close to nature and an original, spiritual religion but comparatively "primitive" and thus inferior to the Ashkenazic leaders of the Zionist revolution.[112] By contrast, Imber highlights the positive traits of Yemenite Jews, thereby identifying them as the legendary Red Jews whose tales animated his early childhood and captured his imagination from a young age.[113] He depicts them living a simple agrarian life without striving for luxury, and as pious but neither fanatical nor fundamentalist. He underscores their incomparable messianic belief; they would be the first to follow the Messiah to the promised land: when they "heard, that the Messiah had appeared and so, they come too, to aid him in his great task to gather all the Jews from the world and to bring them into their promised land."[114]

Imber derived their name, "red little Jews of Yemen," from their purportedly uniform looks, tapping into Yiddish literary tradition: they are "all redheaded and of the same color their beards were."[115] These "pygmies," as Imber calls them, "are weak and little, but talented with an arduous strength, like the strength of the entire Jewish people."[116] Contemporaneous Jewish travelers recorded similar impressions of the Jews they encountered in Yemen: "they are not very tall, rather thin, very erect; with fine features, dark, ruddy skin."[117] Interestingly, Imber compares Yemenite Jews to the Japanese: "In stature, they may be called, the 'Japanese Jews,' for in size they resembled the little brown men."[118]

The occasional association of the Ten Tribes with Japan, which began in the early modern period, regained currency in the last decades of the nineteenth century and received greater attention in both the Jewish and non-Jewish press in Western societies at the turn of the twentieth century.[119] Imber's reason for equating these two groups is unique. Rather than focusing on analogous customs or linguistic features, he bases his position on the Red Jews' delicate stature and the Japanese reputation for working diligently. In Imber's opinion, the Jews of Yemen were superior to European Jewry on account of that same work ethic. He claimed that Sephardic Jews could be lazy, and he accused Polish and Russian Jews of devoting their energies solely to mercantile or financial professions; by comparison, he states that Yemenites "are very industrious and every one of them knows a trade."[120] The Yiddish version of this profile details that Yemenite Jews either engage in agriculture or they are artisans; thus, they have mastered crafts needed for a country to prosper.[121] Moreover, his praise for them as invincible warlords who had also made and supplied weaponry to the Arab tribes for centuries brings to mind Imber's poem about the Japanese army battling against Russia.

As the antithesis of the standard image of European Jewry, these Red Jews from Yemen were a model for the new Hebrew people that Zionism promulgated. These muscular Jews became reconnected with the biblical past, distancing themselves from their weak and oppressed diasporic counterparts. In the process of transforming the Yiddish legend into Zionist ideology, Imber turned the Red Jews in the guise of Yemenite Jews in Palestine into paradigmatic pioneers of redemption who were actively participating in rebuilding the new Jewish homeland. "They are the pure race of the old Hebrews," according to Imber.[122] All of these authentic Jews, who had not been damaged by exile, even the women, were fluent in Hebrew and Aramaic. Curiously, he notes that they speak Hebrew with an Ashkenazic accent, just like Polish Jews.[123] Journalism was a major tool for propagating Zionist interpretations of Jewish culture;[124] thus, through these populist articles in American Jewish periodicals, Imber influenced how Yiddish heritage would be understood in the new secular-nationalist context.

From the next generation of Zionists, Uri Zvi Greenberg, born in eastern Galicia, similarly engaged the Red Jews in his writings for the pioneering community. Having personally experienced the brutal pogrom in Lviv that marked Polish victory over Ukraine in 1918, and narrowly escaping execution together with his family, Greenberg became convinced that Europe would eventually murder its Jewish population. He boldly expressed this conviction in his apocalyptic Yiddish poem *In malkhes fun tseylem* (In the kingdom of the cross), first published in 1923, which radically proclaimed Zionist emigration as the only resolution for the "Jewish question" in Europe.[125] The necessity to turn their backs on accursed Slavic Europe is reflected in Greenberg's own choices: *In malkhes fun tseylem* was his last epic Yiddish poem; in late 1923, he left Europe for Palestine, where he switched to writing almost exclusively in Hebrew.

Greenberg compared the promised land, the alien Orient for most Europeans, to the mysterious region beyond the Sambatyon River—subjects of

Figure 1. Redheaded Jews, Russian matryoshka dolls.

Stefan Scholl, "Hau doch ab in dein Gelobtes Land!" *Frankfurter Rundschau* 72, no. 33 (February 9, 2016): 21.

Figure 2. The Red Jews beyond the Sambatyon River, panel in the Antichrist window at St. Mary's Church, Frankfurt an der Oder, ca. 1370.

Brandenburg State Office for the Preservation of Monuments and the State Archaeological Museum, Zossen, photo archives, no. s II 4b (photo: Peter Thieme/Florian Profitlich, 2006).

Figure 3. Alexander imprisons Gog and Magog behind the Caspian Mountains, colored woodcut in Pseudo-Methodius, *Revelations* (Basel, 1498).

Herzogin Anna Amalia Library, Weimar, Inc 300, fol. b4r.

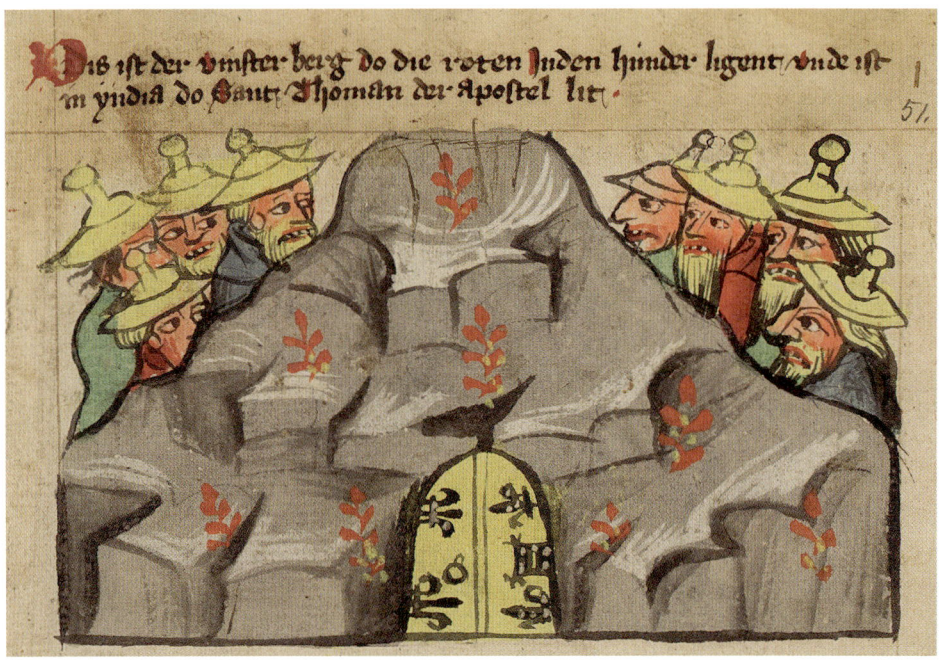

Figure 4. The Red Jews beyond the mountains of darkness, in a medieval book of heraldry, Strasbourg, ca. 1401–1425.

The Carl von Ossietzky State and University Library Hamburg, Cod. in scrin. 90 B, fol. 51r. https://resolver.sub.uni-hamburg.de/kitodo/PPN1047126273

Figure 5. Alexander encloses the Red Jews, in a historiated Bible, fifteenth century.

The manuscript and early print collection of the Prussian Cultural Heritage Section, Berlin State Library, Ms. Germ. 2° 565, fol. 531v.

Figure 6. "Today's Costume of the Jews of Worms," in Marcus zum Lamm, *Thesaurus picturarum*, late sixteenth century.

University and State Library Darmstadt, Hs 1971, vol. 23, fol. 121.

Figure 7. *The Jews' Entrance with Their Messiah*, undated colored reproduction from Dietrich Schwab, *The Jewish Disguise* (Mainz, 1619).

Historical Museum, Frankfurt am Main, C 10154.

Figure 8. *The Last Supper*, detail of an altarpiece by Bertram of Minden, 1391–1400. Lower Saxony State Museum, Hanover (photo: Artothek).

Figure 9. Gog and Magog break free from the Caspian Mountains, colored woodcut in Pseudo-Methodius, *Revelations* (Basel, 1498).

Herzogin Anna Amalia Library, Weimar, Inc 300, fol. b5r.

Figure 10. The rulers of the world submitting to the Antichrist, including the Red Jews and the Amazon queen, in *Antichrist and the Fifteen Signs of the Final Judgment*, Franconia/Nuremberg[?], ca. 1450 (no later than 1467).

Otto Schäfer Library, Museum Otto Schäfer, Schweinfurt, OS 372=Xylo.-A, fol. 7v.

Figure 11. The Antichrist with the Red Jews beside the Sambatyon, panel in the Antichrist window of St. Mary's Church, Frankfurt an der Oder, ca. 1370.

Brandenburg State Office for the Preservation of Monuments and the State Archaeological Museum, Zossen, photo archives, no. s II 4c (photo: Peter Thieme/Florian Profitlich, 2006).

Figure 12. The Antichrist resurrects the dead, panel in the Antichrist window of St. Mary's Church, Frankfurt an der Oder, ca. 1370.

Brandenburg State Office for the Preservation of Monuments and the State Archaeological Museum, Zossen, photo archives, no. s II 6b (photo: Peter Thieme/Florian Profitlich, 2006).

Figure 13. A Red Jew accepts the Antichrist, panel in the Antichrist window of St. Mary's Church, Frankfurt an der Oder, ca. 1370.

Brandenburg State Office for the Preservation of Monuments and the State Archaeological Museum, Zossen, photo archives, no. s II 4a (photo: Peter Thieme/Florian Profitlich, 2006).

Figure 14. The Holy Roman Emperor accepting the Antichrist, panel in the Antichrist window of St. Mary's Church, Frankfurt an der Oder, ca. 1370.

Brandenburg State Office for the Preservation of Monuments and the State Archaeological Museum, Zossen, photo archives, no. s II 5c (photo: Peter Thieme/Florian Profitlich, 2006).

Figure 15. The Red Jews being identified with the Turkish threat, in Justus Jonas, *The Seventh Chapter of Daniel* (Wittenberg, 1529).

Bavarian State Library, Munich, 4 Exeg. 406, fol. A1v. urn:nbn:de:bvb:12-bsb00024135-2.

Figure 16. The Red Jews emerging from beyond the mountains, frontispiece of a German pamphlet, *Concerning a Great Multitude and Host of Jews* (Augsburg, 1523).

Herzog August Library, Wolfenbüttel, A: 131.1 Theol. (27).

Figure 17. The land of the Red Jews, enclosed in the Caspian Mountains and proximate to nations of cannibals, on Andreas Walsperger, *Mappa mundi* (Konstanz, 1448). Detail in lower-left corner.

Biblioteca Apostolica Vaticana, Pal. lat. 1362 b.

Figure 18. *The Last Supper*, detail of Hans Holbein the Elder, predella of the Frankfurt Dominican altarpiece, 1501.

Städel Museum, Frankfurt am Main.

Figure 19. The Antichrist causes fire to rain down, panel in the Antichrist window of St. Mary's Church, Frankfurt an der Oder, ca. 1370.

Brandenburg State Office for the Preservation of Monuments and the State Archaeological Museum, Zossen, photo archives, no. s II 6c (photo: Peter Thieme/Florian Profitlich, 2006).

Figure 20. The Red Jews in league with the Amazons, in an illuminated German manuscript on the Antichrist, Bavaria, fifteenth century.

The manuscript and early print collection of the Prussian Cultural Heritage Section, Berlin State Library, Ms. germ. fol. 733, fol. 3v.

Figure 21. The Red Jews in the Red Sea, Gog and Magog behind the Caspian Mountains, on Hans Rüst, *Mappa mundi* (Augsburg, ca. 1480). Details in upper-left and lower-right corners.

The Morgan Library & Museum, New York, PML 19921 (photo: The Morgan Library & Museum).

Figure 22. A Jew from beyond the Sambatyon bends a tree to the ground during the magical prelude to the disputation, in a Hebrew-Yiddish booklet for children, *Beyond the Sambatyon* (Jerusalem, n.d.).

National Library of Israel, Jerusalem, 95 A 4479, p. 16.

Figure 23. Marc Chagall, *The Jew in Bright Red*, 1915.
State Russian Museum, St. Petersburg. © VG Bild-Kunst, Bonn 2022.

Figure 24. Marc Chagall, *The Jew in Red*, 1914. Collection Im Obersteg, Kunstmuseum Basel. © VG Bild-Kunst, Bonn 2022 (photo: Hans Hinz, Artothek).

Figure 25. Marc Chagall, *The Jew in Green*, 1914.
Private Collection, Switzerland. © VG Bild-Kunst, Bonn 2022 (photo: Hans Hinz, Artothek).

Figure 26. Jewish garb in Worms, second half of the sixteenth century, in Friedrich Hottenroth, *German National Costumes* (first edition, 1898–1902).

Friedrich Hottenroth, *Deutsche Volkstrachten: Vom XVI. Jahrhundert bis zum XIX. Jahrhundert,* pt. 1: *Süd- und Südwestdeutschland*, 2nd edition (Frankfurt am Main: Heinrich Keller, 1923), pl. 7. University Library, Frankfurt am Main, 86.930.46.

Figure 27. Isidor Kaufmann, *Man with Fur Hat*, ca. 1910.

Collection of the Jewish Museum, New York, Gift of Lisl Weil Marx in memory of her husband Julius Marx and his brother Rudolf Marx.

Figure 28. Reuven Rubin (1893–1974), *Red-Bearded Jew*, 1923, oil on canvas. Collection of the Rubin Museum, Tel Aviv.

Figure 29. Edward Okuń, *Red Judas*, 1901.
Private collection.

Figure 30. S. C. Dumont, *The Wandering Jew*, colored wood-engraving based on Gustave Doré.

*Le Journal pour Rire* 36 (June 5, 1852), cover. National Library of France, Paris, FOL-LC2-1681.

Figure 31. Reuven Rubin (1893–1974), *The Poet Uri Zvi Greenberg*, 1925, oil on canvas.

Courtesy of the Rubin Museum, Tel Aviv.

Figure 32. Michal Levin, *Shrine to the Red Jews*, 2012.
Refrig-Curator #4, B&AB Project Space, Brooklyn, New York.

profound longing but nearly impossible to reach.[126] Tamar Wolf-Monzon has demonstrated that this poet's fiery charge to take possession of the land of Israel in order to settle and cultivate it with their own hands was received enthusiastically by the Yishuv of the 1920s. His target audience of pioneers, mostly comprised of farmers and members of the Labor movement, heard their frustrations and desires expressed in Greenberg's poems. These readers referred to his poetry as "red songs." In *Ha-Poel ha-Ẓa'ir* (The young worker), a poem that appeared in 1925 in the newspaper of the socialist organization with that same name, Greenberg too refers to his writing as such: "I was summoned to a feast of the poor—and I came. I did not bring a piece of bread. I brought a red song."[127] This metaphorical use of redness probably acknowledges this color as a sign of the international labor movement, which the author was affiliated with at that time.

Uri Zvi Greenberg later broke with Labor Zionism, criticizing its goals and efforts as inadequate; starting in 1930, he became a major activist for Revisionist Zionism, campaigning for a more assertive approach to gaining control in the region. He joined the Irgun, a guerrilla force that fought the British authorities in Palestine. Greenberg unequivocally articulates his radical stance in a poem, for which he returned to Yiddish, that first appeared September 1934 in the Zionist newspaper *Di Velt*: *Got vet kumen tsu hilf tsum bavafnetn folk* (God will come and help the armed people).[128] The concluding stanza promises that God will help those who plow the fields, bear arms, and grow stronger—not those who live dispersed among the nations as slaves. Significantly, Greenberg signed the poem as "Joseph Molkho," a nod to Solomon Molkho, a historical figure from the sixteenth century, whom Greenberg calls "my brother" in another Yiddish poem published in the same issue of *Di Velt*.[129] Their imagined kinship was based on their shared commitment to messianic enterprises, driven by a military campaign to regain the land of Israel for the Jews and led by Messiah Son of Joseph, who would fight the apocalyptic wars to prepare for the messianic kingdom. Molkho also appears in a Hebrew poem by Greenberg, where the author yearns to sit "in the court of the guard" together with him and his partner David Reuveni, who claimed to be from the Ten Lost Tribes that would join European Jews in their quest of freeing Jerusalem.[130] Much like Imber, Greenberg admits that this sovereign Jewish country, replete with triumphant armies and impressive fortresses, had always attracted him; he still hoped that it would become a source of help in distress. In 1949, the programmatic poem was printed in *Ḥerut* (Freedom), the eponymous daily newspaper of the right-wing nationalist political party which Greenberg then represented as a member of parliament.¹³¹

Given his proclivity for tapping into apocalyptic traditions, especially images of the Lost Tribes, it is hardly surprising that the Red Jews appear in Greenberg's oeuvre. In a lament written in 1947 for his friend Dov Shlonsky, the brother of the poet Abraham Shlonsky, Greenberg refers at length to the Red Jews.¹³² He portrays them with red hair and beards, dressed in white, dwelling in a wondrous land beyond the Sambatyon. Ever sitting in a tavern, drinking red wine from their own abundant vineyards; their goblets are never empty, they graciously welcome the newcomer and invite him to join them, as if they had anticipated his arrival. Greenberg compares himself to the Red Jews, because he was a redhead, as shown in portraits by the contemporary Israeli painters Sionah Tagger¹³³ and his friend Reuven Rubin (fig. 31). Here too, Greenberg refers to his poem as a "red song." Once he brings it to the Red Jews, they too will chant it, recognizing this ruddy bard as one of their own and his song as their tribal hymn.¹³⁴ We learn that "his song is red because it comes from the blood," written with bloody script in the sky,¹³⁵ a symbol of the destruction and death of Jewish life in Europe that reached a horrific climax in the Shoah. This grim image sparked the original Red Jews' call for bold and warlike action. Thus, as Greenberg entwines the Red Jews and Zionist political radicalism, red represents blood as well as the dawn of a hopeful future.¹³⁶

Close to the time when Greenberg wrote his elegy on Shlonsky, the Yiddish poet and novelist Isaac Perlow evoked the Red Jews, albeit from the perspective of postwar Europe. His essay *Royte Yidelekh* (Little Red Jews) appeared in March 1947 in the Yiddish newspaper *Undzer Veg* (Our way), published in a displaced persons (DP) camp in Munich.¹³⁷ Much like Greenberg, Perlow associates the name "Red Jews" with the color of blood. In this case, it is the blood of those who were murdered in the Holocaust, for he refers to DPs as "little Red Jews." He viewed the *sheyres-hapleyte*, the surviving remnant of European Jewry, as "a tribe, severed from the entire people of Israel, discarded beyond the Sambatyon, beyond the mountains of darkness."¹³⁸ They were left behind, forgotten amid German perpetrators whose hands were stained with Jewish blood. Perlow declared that neither the Jews who had found a safe haven, in the United States and elsewhere, nor the international community cared about the DPs; although political delegations and journalists visited these camps, they merely gazed at these survivors to report on their current state, often with disdain.

In the absence of support to escape from the country of their would-be murderers, Perlow imagines how the little Red Jews would take hold of their destiny by heroically leaping into the ever-churning rocks of the Sambatyon River. "With the greatest self-sacrifice and valor which is rarely to be seen among us civilized and cultured people," he writes, they would struggle to swim in the treacherous tide toward the land of Israel, home to their brethren.[139] Even in this fantasy, guardian angels attempt to discourage these desperate Red Jews from the dangerous undertaking, supposedly protecting them by warning that they would fare no better elsewhere. Thus, the DPs should stay in Germany rather than risk the unknown in Palestine. Perlow asks, if the efforts of the United Nations Relief and Rehabilitation Administration (UNRRA) and the American-Jewish Joint Distribution Committee (JDC) were hardly effective, what were their alternatives? This essay verbalizes most DPs' experience of being trapped in an utterly hopeless situation, where they were rejected as unwanted reminders of the Shoah. Despite their jeopardy, these little Red Jews are no less self-possessed and energetic than Greenberg's wine-producing countrymen.

The Old Yiddish image of the Red Jews provided a resource for poetic creativity toward the pioneering "new Jew" in the land of Israel prior to the establishment of the Jewish state. This legend thus served as an alternative source for revising muscular Jewishness (*Muskeljudentum*), a concept that was famously coined by Max Nordau to counter the centuries-old notion of the weak Jewish man with a mainstream masculine identity construct that would fit new political ambitions. Among fin-de-siècle Jews and non-Jews alike, the Jewish body was widely derided as degenerate, as we have seen. A life in European ghettos was primarily made responsible for the poor physical state of many Jews. The shared response proposed by Zionists and those who sought emancipation in the Diaspora was a new, muscular Jewish self.[140] Like Nordau, these thinkers and activists promoted a regimen of physical training and labor to create strong, healthy Jewish men and women. They were convinced that renewal of the Jewish body would revive the Jewish spirit and, eventually, alter discourse about Jews and their place in modern societies. Their views owed much to national movements that valued physical agility and stamina in nineteenth-century western and central Europe.[141] And yet, the Red Jews, much as heroic personae from biblical literature and antiquity, provided an authentic yet previously overlooked Yiddish heritage of virility, military prowess, and Jewish agency that the Zionist pioneering spirit could access.

The modern age produced contrasting interpretations of the mythic Red Jews. Their portrayals as divine helpers in modern printings of traditional stories and as Wandering Jews in classic Yiddish fiction reversed their premodern essence. The muscular Jews envisioned by eastern Jewish Zionist writers returned the Red Jews to their ideological origins of physical strength and martial skill. However, both readings were aligned with the Old Yiddish tale's message of proactivity. Mendele and Sholem Aleichem, Imber and Greenberg each adopted the popular literary motif of the Red Jews to shape a cultural model for Jewish behavior in a changing world, which—after the Haskalah and emancipation lost their promise—often meant a call for immigration to Palestine. Over the course of the nineteenth and twentieth centuries, the linguistic versatility of the Red Jews increased as well, reflecting the realities in new centers of Jewish life. With Hebrew emerging as the national Jewish language, the Red Jews now easily succeeded in Hebrew literature written by Yiddish speakers for a readership from the same background.

Epilogue

# An Old Yiddish Legend in a Brooklyn Fridge

> Now is it not fitting that even blind men should become sharp-sighted in their minds to such and similar things, being furnished with eyes by the most sacred words,
> ... and not to be limited to the mere understanding of the speech?
>
> —Philo, *De somniis*

The tale of the Red Jews is a myth that is decaying alongside the dying language that long sustained it. Since World War II, the Red Jews have occasionally made their appearance in works that were written in Yiddish in defiance of the annihilation of most Yiddish-speaking Jews in the Holocaust. The Polish Yiddish writer Yekhiel Yeshaye Trunk, who narrowly escaped the Nazis and settled in New York in 1941, continued to write Yiddish to commemorate this lost culture. His book *Khelemer khakhomim oder yidn fun der kligster shtot in der velt* (The wise men of Chelm, or, Jews of the wisest town in the world), published in Buenos Aires in 1951, draws from the widely popular folk tradition about the fools of Chelm and features a brief reference to the Red Jews.[1] In one episode from this novel, the Chelmites Reb Fayvush and Reb Leybush arrive in Prussia, where all houses have red roofs that make them look like "ridiculous turkeys"; thus, these travelers conclude that they must have crossed the Sambatyon into the territory of the legendary Red Jews. Trunk attempted to rescue the Red Jews from the destruction of Eastern European Jewish folklore. Paradoxically, by relocating the Red Jews to

Prussia and leaving their identity ambiguous—Fayvush and Leybush regularly confuse Jews and gentiles—he brought them back to Germany, their place of origin, and a country in which few real Jews survived.

In the scattered niches where Red Jews still dwell, their Old Yiddish origins are barely recognizable. A faint shadow of this figure survives where Yiddish remains a living language: ultra-Orthodox neighborhoods and their local bookshops in Israel and the United States that sell children's booklets retelling the *Akdamut* story in both Hebrew and Yiddish.[2] In 2012, the Old Yiddish perspective on the Red Jews was revived in Brooklyn when the artist Michael Levin presented his *Shrine to the Red Jews* as part of the Refrig-Curator exhibition at B&AB Project Space (fig. 32). Just as a refrigerator preserves perishable food, his installation is designed to conserve the concept of the Red Jews. In a video that accompanies this artwork, Levin explains that his shrine contains milk and honey as a food offering to the Red Jews, to commemorate their potential to obliterate oppressive Christian culture and civilization, and initiate a Jewish Golden Age.[3] It is emblematic that this artist moved to Williamsburg, where he has become an observer of its close-knit Hasidic world with increasing fascination and made them the subject of his artistic work.[4] However, Levin did not learn of the Red Jews through this encounter with Hasidism but through scholarship, such as Andrew Gow's *Red Jews*, while researching another topic.[5] Without awareness of the traces of this resilient Yiddish myth among his ultra-Orthodox neighbors, Levin inadvertently juxtaposed the legend's Germanic origins with current editions of *Ma'aseh Akdamut*.

Significantly, a visual artist became attracted to the Red Jews and used their defining color for his *Shrine to the Red Jews*, replete with red-carpeted walls and a string of red lights. In Levin's piece, red operates as a preservative, much as this eye-catching color contributed to the longevity of the myth in Yiddish culture that this volume has traced. The peculiar Yiddish coloration of the Ten Lost Tribes of Israel served as a universal language throughout Ashkenazic culture, which transcended social and educational strata, unrestricted by the formality of words. With their red hair and beards, faces, and clothing, the Red Jews created a visual idiom that distilled a complex message about Jewish self-definition into its monochromatic essence.

As I have argued, their redness lent the Red Jews a disruptive quality. In his book *Chromophobia*, David Batchelor argues that the power and autonomy that are inherent in color prompted suspicion to such an extent that he identifies a Western discomfort with color, which dates back to antiquity.

As a result, Batchelor asserts that color has often been associated with the Other whose motives may be suspect and considered a sensory threat to Western rationalism.[6] The German legend of the Red Jews exemplifies this visual othering. Drawing on medieval color symbolism, the term and image of *Rote Juden* embody an overarching Christian perception of the Jewish Other as a danger to Christendom. Once reappropriated from German language and culture, and posited against their Christian origins, the Red Jews indeed developed a number of subversive roles in early modern Yiddish culture, all anchored in their novel color interpretations. We have seen that the Red Jews spread a rebellious message among the Jewish populace that was directed against the ruling elite of both the Christian majority, particularly the Church, and Jewish society.

In an effort to encourage its audience to depart from acquiescent endurance by acting to influence their immediate situation, the Red Jews' myth utilized the sense of sight. In *Ways of Sensing*, David Howes and Constance Classen consider how people understand their surroundings through their senses, and how politics, social order, and culture are shaped by sensory practices and metaphors. These mechanisms are reflected in the majority treatment of minority groups as well as subaltern responses, as my analysis of the politics of seeing through the literary figure of the Red Jews has demonstrated. Reading about the Red Jews was itself a sensory experience, which first and foremost activated sight. These narratives were tailored to the concerns of their vernacular audience; thus, the Red Jews gave "visceral answers to intellectual questions"[7] and existential challenges in the form of a literal and literary spectacle. Their audience became witnesses, learning alongside the Jews who gathered in the arena in *Ma'aseh Akdamut* to watch the fateful sorcery competition.

The Red Jews' stories contrast critical seeing with blind acceptance of traditional approaches to exile and communal authority. Compliant listening—to God, *parnassim*, or rabbis—is juxtaposed with the benefits of self-reliant cognition, achieved through independent use of the eyes, that leads to autonomous and unconventional actions. The potentially detrimental outcome of aural primacy is highlighted by the catalyst for *Ma'aseh Akdamut*: reflexive recitation of the *Shema Yisra'el* triggers persecution in this tale. Significantly, this prayer concludes with a reminder to observe God's laws in tandem with a warning against following "your heart and eyes in your lustful urge" (Num. 15:39). In fact, it is customary to cover one's eyes with a hand while reciting the opening verse of the *Shema*. While this liturgical gesture, which had become an established practice by medieval times, is typically associated with heightened concentration,[8] our Yiddish story equates this central Jewish prayer with thoughtless adherence to authority. This narrative seeks to replace *gehorkhikayt* (obedience, in Yiddish)—which, like its Hebrew equivalent, shares the same root as "hearing" (געהארכיקייט from הערן, הארכן; משמעת from לשמוע)—with opening one's own eyes.

The Red Jews provided Ashkenazic Jews with an imaginative cultural resource for discussing Jewish experience amid dynamic social and political circumstances. A wide range of conditions became catalysts for the changing projections onto this image: from Jewry as an oppressed religious group in premodern Christian contexts and, in the late nineteenth and early twentieth centuries, when emigration to new destinations—such as the land of Israel and the United States—became ever more vital, concomitant with the assertion of Jewish life in the modern world. As prior scholarship has established sight as a crucial lens for understanding Jewish history, the present study has shown that this observation is particularly applicable to Yiddish culture and literature. The investigation of the "Yiddish eye" that gazed at the Red Jews deepens our understanding of how visualization in reading functioned in vernacular culture at large. As a unique Yiddish depiction, the topic of the Red Jews amplifies the Jewish vernacular voice by revealing visual sensibilities. The unparalleled Yiddish term, image, and myth of the Red Jews thus offer glimpses of attitudes held by Jews in the Ashkenazic realm, including those who rarely leave records of their ideas.

In addition to demonstrating how their coloration contributed to the Red Jews' popularity, I have also shown that this image defied ready translation into other sociocultural milieux despite the ubiquity of the color red in symbolic systems. The Germanic-Yiddish linguistic framework in which the Red Jews originated was not easily engaged by Jews from other vernacular backgrounds. Thus, the authors and publishers of Hebrew versions eliminated the emphasis on redness and, along with this color, they excised the anti-establishment message of empowerment that marks the Old Yiddish legend. This domestication persists in the current Hasidic editions of *Ma'aseh Akdamut*, which, even when written in Yiddish, lack the distinctive personae of the Red Jews. Rather, the protagonists are a colorless, traditionalist rendering of the Ten Tribes, in line with a conservative interpretation of our tale, tamed to invigorate unwavering faith in divine providence.

This complete neutralization of the subversive meaning of the Red Jews is underscored on the occasions that they appear in contemporary secular

Jewish literature. For example, Gilles Rozier, a French Jewish author born after the Holocaust, borrows the motif of the little Red Jews from Sholem Aleichem. In his short novel *Par-delà les monts obscurs* (Beyond the dark mountains; 1999), Rozier compares assimilated Jews in France with the "petits hommes rouges" (little red men), who are estranged from their Jewish heritage. In contrast to Sholem Aleichem, this author does not equate immigration to Israel with a path to fulfillment. Rather, his principal character eventually stays among the little Red Jews in France, whom she prefers over the "pays des surhommes juifs" (the nation of Jewish supermen), for only in the French Diaspora does she share a mother tongue with her compatriots, a cultural bond that she finds stronger than the political gathering of exiles in the Jewish state.[9] Rozier postulates that, rather than seeking a better life elsewhere, Diaspora Jewry should come to terms with their present reality, accommodating Jewish identity in their non-Jewish environment. In this French translation, the *petits hommes rouges* embrace a resolution that is diametrically opposed to Sholem Aleichem's interpretation, as much as it forgoes their original Yiddish counterparts' confrontational tone. And yet, inadvertently, the stance of Rozier's protagonist transports the concluding image of peaceful coexistence from *Ma'aseh Akdamut* to the twenty-first-century French Diaspora.

The legend of the Red Jews is used by this largely assimilated French Jewish author to create his Jewish identity afresh. As an adult, Rozier studied Yiddish and Hebrew, languages that he had not learned as a child. His growing interest eventually led him to earn a doctorate in Yiddish literature. Similar to the artist Michael Levin, the writer Gilles Rozier encountered the Red Jews through academic study. While both confirm the absence of the Red Jews in Jewish culture today, their artistic reconstructions, in a piece of French fiction and a Brooklyn fridge, respectively, erect a visible homage to the irrepressible roots of the Red Jews in Old Yiddish.

# Appendix

## *Ma'aseh Akdamut*

(Bodleian Library, Oxford,
Ms. Opp. 714, fols. 21v–34v)

A story about Rabbi Meir the Hazan which took place in the year which was written 121 [1360/1]. There was a great commotion in the world which God, blessed be His name, sent to the world, in the days of a [22r] king named Martiano (!) von der Lanze, who ruled over many lands. In his days the wheel of fortune was made and so too in his days it was destroyed. As I will tell you.

In his times there was much sorcery. There was a wheel which people called the wheel of fortune because whoever was upon it could accomplish whatever he wished through [the help of] demons. However, the payment which the demon required was that there must be ten of them sitting on the wheel and he [the demon] takes one of the ten and plays with him however he wants, according to his desire and will, and teaches the others what they desire. Thus there were many apprentices and black magicians in the world. Until at last there came a Jew who likewise wanted to learn and to sit on the wheel with the other nine. This Jew saw that the demon came, wanting to take one and choose one from the ten, and he went around the wheel of fortune until the Jew began to doubt and think to himself, "Do I want to surrender to the demon and lose this world and the world to come?" So he [22v] became frightened and began to recite the *Shema* and the demon could not bear to listen to it and in his anger the demon killed the nine non-Jews and destroyed the wheel of fortune. And no other was created in the world, nor any sorcery, and henceforth they [the sorcerers] made themselves castles and monasteries and lived therein, fearing the king who did not favor sorcery; otherwise he would have killed them in their sleep.

They led the world at that time, and it could not be known who they were; they were able to draw to themselves all the most beautiful women and maidens whom they desired and some of them made themselves monks with cassocks and became the greatest sorcerers in the world.

In those days, there came a black monk who sought to take revenge on the Jews. When he saw a Jew, he ensured that he would not remain alive. When he simply [23r] touched him or gave him only a blow or a flick, then the Jew went home to his house and died. In this way he killed thirty thousand and eight hundred and sixty, until the wise men approached one another, saying, "We will all die from this black monk!" and complained to the king.

Thus the king sent for the monk and he came before the king, saying, "Honored king, what is your request?" So the king answered, "The Jews complain that you have killed many of them and here they stand behind you," so he turned around and saw them. And he said, "You should know, I am only touching you out of curiosity," and thus he touched three of the Jews and he drew away their strength. And as soon as they arrived home, they died. Therefore the Jews cried out to the king again: "Gracious highborn king, if we deserve to be killed rightfully let us not die by the hand of the black monk, [23v] let us die by another death," because they feared that he would not be able to protect them, considering that the monk killed them in his presence.

Thus the king spoke to the monk, "By my crown, if you will obey my command and enjoy my favor make the three Jews healthy again and do not cause them any more harm." So the monk replied, "I will gladly obey your command and profess my loyalty and bring the Jews back to life. However, inform your Jews that they must present to me in one year's time a person that can compete with my magic, then I will do nothing. Yet if, in one year, I see that they cannot present any such person, I will kill them all. I do not do this for my own sake, but because I have harbored a hatred of them for a long time due to the magic. If they agree to this, I will be loyal, as you ordered, but if not [24r] I will kill them all, even if I risk my life in so doing."

So the king told him that he should leave. Thus he departed from the king's palace and then the king called the Jews, informing them, "Dear people, what can I answer you? If you will acquiesce to this, I will inform him of it. Then he will wait until the year is over and do nothing to you." The Jews answered swiftly, with great fear and trembling, "We will accept the appointed time of one year" because they thought that perhaps the monk would die within the year. "Therefore we will repent." So the king ordered that the monk be called and said to him, "The Jews will present one who can compete with your magic, therefore you must swear that for one year you will do nothing." And indeed, he swore accordingly. Then he departed, and the Jews began to repent, pray, and give charity and donned sackcloth, from the youngest to the oldest, and sent out [messages] to all the distant lands in which Jews reside, asking them to repent so that the monk may die and not kill all the Jews, and the Jews repented, wherever they were.

There was a wise sage who fell asleep over his learning [24v] and dreamed a dream, together with other pious men, and the master of dreams spoke to him, saying, "Beloved children you are praying in vain for the monk's death. He will not die this year, only immediately after the year is over will he die. Therefore seek good counsel, because the Holy One Blessed be He will not strike back against his malice because your sins are great against Him. Yet if you will remain pious, as you have begun to be, and not stray from Him, then the Holy One blessed be He will not ignore your calls but will help and will send someone, a magician who can protect with angels and not through sorcery. No one else can withstand the monk, so search as best as you can."

When the men awoke they wondered, "Beloved Lord God, what can this be, what can be the meaning of this dream?" until, however, they fell asleep again over their books on the second night, then this dream came [again] and they thought, "What can this dream be?" and they did not want to sleep in the middle of the night, saying, "Maybe God, may His name be praised, is informing us how we can save our [25r] lives. He also gave signs to our forefathers." Then they prayed, saying, "When we give testimony of this [dream], then people will take it for a [mere] dream before long. Therefore, beloved almighty God if You want to show us a sign of wonder, reveal them to us while we are awake." So each one said, "Therefore, in order that we may know and speak the truth to our brothers. And we may find help in this way." And God, blessed be His name, was merciful and sent them the master of dreams during waking hours and he spoke to them as was written above.

So they quickly dispatched letters to one another, because the master of dreams told each one, "I have also informed your companion, and I spoke in this way to the one dwelling in that city." So they said, each one in his city, and each one brought proof from another who was more than a thousand miles away, who wrote swiftly and sent out messengers.

Then the Jews recognized that this must be true, so they all consulted with each other, the pious men and all the men, and no one knew [25v] who could withstand the monk.

There was one among them who said, "Beloved brothers, our God, blessed be His name, has warned us that we must search for a magician who can do magic well and we know of no one. Yet there must indeed be such a person, because He ordered us to search for him. So be pious and continue to pray. We will all, therefore, beg that God, blessed be His name, will reveal to us who the great magician is and his place of residence."

So they all consulted with each other and obeyed the wise man, repenting and praying and giving charity, until again the master of dreams descended one night. And he came to them as before and said to them: "Beloved brothers and children, you will not find anyone in this land, and likewise not in the Land of Israel, but rather you must cross the River Sambatyon, which does not rest all week long, except on the [26r] Sabbath. Whoever wishes to cross it during the week sinks into the river, be he Jew or non-Jew (pardon the comparison), because it flings stones from the riverbed up on high, breaking the ship and everything which travels upon it. So you must fetch someone from the tribes who were driven there because they are *ba'alei shemot* [wonder workers]. Thus they will come to your help. When the exile will come to an end, they will also come to our aid, and they are called Sons of Saviors (*bnei moshi'im*), as the verse states: 'For liberators shall march up on mount Zion to wreak judgment on the Mount Esau' (Ovadiah 1:21). This means they will help us in Zion to judge Gog and Magog. They cannot cross over the River Sambatyon until God, may His name be blessed, will show them a way to walk on the dry ground." So they said to the master of dreams, "Since God, blessed be He, wants to help us with a Red Jew, why does He not give us a sign, making him come here for us, that we should not need to travel there and desecrate the Sabbath?" The master of dreams answered, "It is true, you are right, but you [26v] are not worthy of such a sign and that the ways of the world should be changed for your sake, making him fly here." So they said to him, "Who will desecrate the Sabbath and have no part in the world to come because of this? The Red Jews will judge him [and execute him by stoning]; and for one who endangers his own life, it is difficult to enter the Garden of Eden."

So the master of dreams said, "The Sons of Saviors will worry about what to do with him. Thus it will be." And because they all agreed, they sent to advisors to search for someone to make the journey, then they all recommended [sending] Rabbi Meir [Shatz of Worms] because he is a great sage and a pious man and constantly served the community for good. They gave him sufficient provisions and three pious rabbis to accompany him.

So they set out in God's name and reached the River Sambatyon [27r] on a Tuesday, eight days before the end of the year that the monk had stipulated, and they waited by the River Sambatyon until the Sabbath. And Rabbi Meir sat in a ship and said to his brothers, "Beloved brothers, wait here, why should we all desecrate the Sabbath? It is sufficient for me to do so and to risk that they will judge me." So his brothers remained over the river and he crossed it alone, arriving there on the Sabbath and declaring, "I have a letter from Israel." They immediately ordered that he be thrown into prison because he had desecrated the Sabbath. Yet they had the letter opened by those with whom they trade, giving them grain and pepper in return. And when they heard the meaning of the letter, that a terrible decree was hanging over their brothers, they released him from prison and said, "Who among us will cast off the Sabbath?" And they drew lots among themselves, whoever's name would be pulled out, and the lot fell upon one called Dan, who was old and lame.

Therefore, they said to Rabbi Meir, "Impart [27v] what you wish to say to your wife and your children because you will not desecrate the Sabbath again. You will stay here with us, leaving your wife to live as a pious widow, because you may not write her a writ of divorce. Similarly, this Dan must leave his wife because in another eight days the [appointed] time will pass, and each one can take another wife and leave the widow thus. So God, blessed be His name, requires it."

Then Rabbi Meir, *shali'aḥ ẓibbur* (cantor, lit. emissary for the community), imparted for his home everything that had happened to him, as I will write for you shortly, with God's help. And the little Red Jew sat in the ship and traveled over the river. There he found the three rabbis and they were very frightened when they did not see Rabbi Meir. They inquired about Rabbi Meir and he told them everything. And the three rabbis were very afraid and wondered, "How is it possible that such a small, lame little man will withstand the monk? What has Rabbi Meir done to us, how has he brought about the destruction of the entire nation of Israel?"

When they saw how the small little man walked, [28r] with a limp, they thought that they must guide him and show him the way. However, he led the way and arrived at their destination within two days and two nights because he chose shortened ways. Or he reached the place by invoking divine names. Thus the appointed day and time arrived and the Jews were in great sorrow, crying, "Rabbi Meir, Rabbi Meir, what have you done to us, how have you endangered yourself for our sake?"

Thus they were crying and wailing until they came to the place which the monk had specified, where they were to go on the same day. When they saw the small little man, they were even sadder that they had sent Rabbi Meir and that he had brought for them such a lame and small person and had not come himself, because they did not know anything and they thought, "Almighty God, how can it be that a small little man can withstand such a monk, who is so strong and so mighty and uses sorcery and demons?"

[28v] So they were placed in a large square, where the Jews stood underneath, around the square, and the others above, because a structure had been constructed above in order that immediately following the defeat of the Jews, the monk could kill them all, as had been determined before the king. Now the monk stood opposite them and said, "Look how the Jews are making a mockery of me! With what have they presented me? A small shaking little man with whom to do magic?" So all of Israel were very afraid, but the messengers who had seen how he had led them through a shortened way, they shouted in the square and said, "You magician, you have not seen tomorrow! You will see that he will make the world too small to contain you."

The speech of the messengers calmed the Jews a little.

Then the monk began and he commanded all the demons to bring him a great steel pole with which he intended to beat the little Jew to death. He took the pole, which was so heavy that not even an entire army could carry it, and threw it with the strength of the demons into the earth and the earth [29r] covered it. Then he cried out to the little Jew, "Now pull it out, otherwise you will cause me to kill all the Jews. Because you have angered me, I will have no mercy on anyone, it is just as though you had murdered them." So the small little man quickly answered the monk with cunning, "You should not have thrown it so deep in the earth. How can I possibly take it out again?" Directly, he took a receptacle filled with water, cleaning himself and washing his hands, and said, "See, beloved brothers, Jews and non-Jews, excuse the comparison, and pagans, watch carefully. And you, monk, speak up, how you can stand up to me? I tell you that, no doubt, whatever is down in the earth is better than you. You threw this pole under the earth and I will pull it out from under the king's chair."

The king was amazed by the speech of the little Jew and watched as he took his little finger and dug a hole, pulling it out with no effort and throwing it up so high that it could barely be seen [29v], leaving it hanging in the air. He said to the monk, "Now you reach it! I did not hide it and if you cannot reach it everyone will see that your head will be stuck on the pole today and I will drive it into the desert where no one may set foot, and you and your teachers will have no power over me."

The monk sought to reach the pole using his magic but he was unable to do so. It was so high that no demon could hover there. And he could not reach it and stood ashamed. So he said to the little man, "We will show another trick," expecting that he would forget about the pole, and he made two millstones, saying, "I have created them." Then he proceeded directly to grind them between the hands, just as one grinds flour or stones to bits of lime and chalk.

Then the little Jew answered him, "You said [30r] you have created them. It is no wonder to me that I cannot create them, because I am no God. But I am hoping for God's aid, that He will help me also to create them in such a way." His prayer was followed by a wind that would blow together all the pieces. And as soon as it started to blow, the pieces were formed into two masses, just as someone would knead clay, he formed two stones out of it, much bigger than those that the monk had made, because the wind mixed in a big heap [of additional material]. Right away the Jew took the two millstones, without any effort and ground them to dust, without any effort, [and remade them] and made a wind come and let the wind carry them up on high to that same pole. Then everyone saw that he could not reach or grasp it and he was filled with shame.

Then the little Jew said, "How long will I have to trouble myself with you, you cannot stand against me. Now I will do more magic. Now either you respond [to my magic], or [30v] initiate [magic of your own]. I will make flames of fire come down from the sky: you put it out. Or you kindle it and I will put it out."

So immediately, the monk thought, "What a piece of magic this is. I will put it out." Thus the little Jew made a great fire shoot down from the sky, writhing like a snake, as though the fire was burning the forest and the grass and herbs but they were not consumed [by the flames]. So everyone was amazed. Then the little Jew said to the monk, "Put it out, it has burned long enough." The monk conjured from below a stream which shot out of the earth, to extinguish it. But the fire went over it in the sky and burned the water, burning more fiercely than before.

Then the monk said, "I do not know how to put it out." So the little Jew said, "Let it burn for a little while longer, so that it will burn the well [31r] that you conjured and people will not say that you are God and created this source. But I say to you that you will as likely go to heaven as a cow into a mousehole. If you have something to send to the next world you may tell me. Do not think that you will protect yourself with your magic because you cannot any longer. Because I brought this fire from the firmament. I saw them [the demons] all hovering and I burned them all."

The monk looked up and saw that none of his teachers remained and he completely despaired. He became pale and trembled, begging the Jew: "I will gladly serve you, let me live."

To this the Jew replied, "I will not take your life. I will not touch you, although you killed so many of my brothers. It would be befitting to kill you with harsh violent deaths."

So the Jew approached the fire and said, "See what people use to make fire—with that I will extinguish it while the monk could not extinguish it with water." Now [31v] the Jew blew once into the fire, a big blow, with his cheeks. And the fire directed itself up high, and went up higher, and they saw it no more, only steam and smoke. And there was no more fire because it had shot up to its place. [When the people saw it] they all fell on their faces.

Now the little Jew said, "Why should I show many tricks, I must drive out the pole and the millstones which are in the sky above so that people will not say that you are God." Then he said to the monk, "This tall tree is thick. It has not been cut down since Noah made the Ark. He cut one down and since then this one has grown in its stead. I will bend it down to the ground. And you will hold it down once I have bent it down to the ground so that it will not straighten again or I will hold it and you will bend it down."

Then the monk thought that he would again perform magic [32r] with the help of demons. But he could no longer see them and cried and lamented his fate. And he said, "How have you abandoned me, beloved masters?" However, thus spoke the little Jew with mockery, "Why do you cry, did your father or mother die?" But the monk did not laugh. He wished he had been dead for a long time because he did not know how to bend the strong tree. He started to scream. Then the little Jew said: "Why are you taking your time and making these people here wait? Say what you can do. Tell me, do you want to hold it, that it will not straighten again? I trust in

God, blessed be His name, in His power to bend it." So said the monk, "You bend it, I will hold it down so that it will not straighten again."

So the little Jew bent the tree like one bends a little stick, before everyone's eyes. Then the Jew said, "Now hold it so that it will not straighten again. Because I have bent it." The monk did not want to do his part and did not approach.

Then the little Jew cried, "Noble king and all the lords, see what [32v] a daring magician this is!" The monk was ashamed. "Because it was not his intention that I could bend it, therefore he said that he would hold it down so that it should not straighten again. Just as he cannot bend it, so he will not be able to hold it, he thought. But when he saw that I can indeed bend it, he did not approach to hold it down. And this gives him shame." Therefore he was forced to come forward, seeing that death was approaching, and in great shame he advanced toward the tree.

So said the little Jew, "Do not touch me and hold on fast to the tree without touching me," and he cried, "See if he holds it—then I will let go!" The monk held on tightly and the little Jew let it go. Then the tree snapped back and hit the monk with great force, knocking his head off, and everyone saw that he flew high into the heavens with terrible power and remained impaled on the pole and his body came between the two millstones and the millstones [33r] rotated on the pole and flew with him into the desert, as the Jew had said before.

So God blessed be He, saved us and all of Israel and this king Martin von der Lanze and other king[s] and all the peoples, they saw all the wonders and then everyone went home calmly and happily, they no longer needed to fear the monk. And the king and all the king's judges and all the people became friendly toward the Jews due to the wonders that the little Jew performed.

Then Rabbi Meir's wife came to inquire with the little Jew and the messengers concerning the fate of her husband Rabbi Meir: had he died, why he had not returned? The little Jew informed her, that the situation was such, "because the Sons of Saviors would not allow him to desecrate the Sabbath on purpose; they will also not allow me to travel home again. I may take a wife in this land and you must remain a widow all your days. He wanted to give you a writ of divorce, but he could not [33v] write it on the Sabbath. When he crossed the river Sambatyon the time appointed by the monk had arrived, so I also could not give my wife any writ of divorce." And it was time to pray, "and everything that he (R. Meir) asked me to impart I will say in the synagogue before all the holy community."

And the little Jew said, "Thus imparted Rabbi Meir *shali'aḥ ẓibbur* to you: Because on your behalf he was forced to leave his wife and his children and all his brothers, so people must provide his wife with food, he also asked you to treat her well, comfort and nourish her. And make a wedding for his daughter with a husband who is a wise scholar. And before I left he became my son-in-law because I have given him my daughter."

Therefore, all of Israel answered, "What is more righteous in all the world, considering that the saint and pious man risked his body and life for our sake—should we not grant his request?! Even if he had requested [34r] a limb from our bodies—it would only be befitting to give it, and not withhold it. But we also find it befitting that you should be gracious with this pious and righteous man, just as he did for you. He took your daughter—so you, too, should take his daughter, because how can we find a more precious person than you?"

So he accepted and Rabbi Meir's wife was pleased with this son-in-law when she heard that he agreed. Straightaway she went to her daughter and said, "Your father arranged for you [to marry] a wise scholar." And she told her how everything came about. So with happiness the little Jew became a bridegroom and this was on the eve of Shavuot. Thus he said, "As he accompanied me, he composed a tune in his name while walking. And he also requested that I ask you to say it in his name. So it is signed, Rabbi Meir son of Rabbi Isaac, great in Torah and good deeds, amen, be strong and brave."

"It is befitting that [34v] for his sake, and the sake of his name, you shall say it and that his name shall be remembered for generations. Therefore, I will write down the song, with God's help." So they accepted upon themselves that they will say it. The song begins *"Akdamut milin"* which is said on the first day of Shavuot, so that all the generations may know the story and deeds which happened to him and his generation and everyone's heart will rejoice in it. And also others will be worthy of God's reward and receive good recompense from Him. And this is the song that they say he wrote, so we will also be worthy of the redemption, in God's will. Amen. So may it be.

Finis.

# Notes

### INTRODUCTION

1. Adapted from the expression "rabbinic eye," coined by Neis, *Sense of Sight*, 7.
2. This follows the broad definition of visuality in Neis, *Sense of Sight*, 20n8. See also Neis, *Sense of Sight*, 22–23, 25. Cf. Mitchell, *Iconology*, chap. 1.
3. With the exception of select, literal equivalents of this phrase that appear in several, mostly later, direct translations from Yiddish to Hebrew, and German to Latin. See Chapters 1 and 2 for references.
4. Meier, "Colourful Middle Ages," 232–36; Suntrup, "Farbsymbolik"; Suntrup, "Liturgische Farbenbedeutung."
5. Leipold and Solms, "Farbbezeichnungen," 328–33; Wanzeck, *Etymologie lexikalisierter Farbwortverbindungen*, 50; Suntrup, "Farbsymbolik," 291; Lauffer, *Farbensymbolik*, 10–12; Wackernagel, "Farben- und Blumensprache," 196–98. See also Pastoureau, "Ceci est mon sang." On the symbolic use of blood in Judaism and Christianity, see Biale, *Blood and Belief*; Bildhauer, *Medieval Blood*; Bynum, *Wonderful Blood*; Matteoni, "Blood Beliefs."
6. On the contextual relativity of color symbolism, see Pulliam, "Color," 5; Gage, *Color and Culture*, 82; Meier, "Colourful Middle Ages," 234.
7. For Latin, Suntrup, "Farbsymbolik," 291; Meier, "Colourful Middle Ages," 249. For German, Leipold and Solms, "Farbbezeichnungen," 328–33; Rosenfeld, "Färberröte," 291–93; Jones, *German Colour Terms*, 398–99; Jones, *Historisches Lexikon*; Wanzeck, *Etymologie lexikalisierter Farbwortverbindungen*, 49–74.
8. Meier, "Colourful Middle Ages," 240–41; Ravid, "From Yellow to Red." On general links between clothing and social and personal identity, see Jones and Stallybrass, *Renaissance Clothing*; Jones, *German Colour Terms*, 133–41.
9. Mellinkoff, *Outcasts*, 43–47; Cassen, *Marking the Jews*. For sumptuary laws in Europe, see Schneider, "Peacocks and Penguins."
10. Mellinkoff, *Outcasts*, 37–43; Weber, "Antichristfenster," 86–87; Lipton, *Dark Mirror*, 7.
11. On classical humoralism and the theory of the four temperaments, see Nutton, "Humoralism"; Klibansky, Panofsky, and Saxl, *Saturn and Melancholy*. On the four temperaments in medieval and Renaissance physiognomy, see Reißer, *Physiognomik und Ausdruckstheorie*, 19–97. For a broad overview of medieval physiognomy, including theories of complexion, see Resnick, *Marks of Distinction*, chap. 1.
12. Leipold and Solms, "Farbbezeichnungen," 330–31, 335; Groebner, "Hautfarben," 8–9. See, e.g., the popular compendiums of physiognomy: *Phisionomi vnd Chiromanci*, 13; Indagine, *Kunst der Chiromantzey*, fol. 35r-v. Cf. Reißer, *Physiognomik und Ausdruckstheorie*, 35.

13. Rashi on Song of Sol. 5:10.

14. 1 Sam. 16:12; 1 Sam. 17:42.

15. Gen. 25:25. On Esau in Jewish and Christian thought, see Langer, *Esau*; Aminoff, *Esau, My Brother*.

16. Pastoureau, *Red*, 20, 105; Mellinkoff, "Judas's Red Hair," 31–32.

17. Mellinkoff, *Outcasts*, chap. 7; Mellinkoff, "Judas's Red Hair."

18. Mellinkoff, "Judas's Red Hair," 38.

19. For literary examples, see Chapter 5. On its contemporary persistence, see Levin, "Genetic Myths," 30.

20. Mellinkoff, "Judas's Red Hair"; Mellinkoff, *Outcasts*, chaps. 2, 7. Robert Jütte has recently included red skin, hair, and beard in his treatment of the Jewish body; Jütte, *Leib und Leben*, 58–59, 62–63, 77–83. For an unsystematic survey of the application of red and black color codes to Jewish figures in nineteenth- and twentieth-century German literature, see Lorenz, "Imaginierte Körperfarben." On the Jewish body in general, see also Gilman, *Jew's Body*; Eilberg-Schwartz, *People of the Body*; Gilman, Jütte, and Kohlbauer-Fritz, *"Der schejne Jid"*; and Diemling and Veltri, *Jewish Body*, as well as the collection of articles, edited by Myers, *Overcoming Matter*.

21. Gow, *Red Jews*. For the Yiddish version, see pp. 185–86.

22. Shmeruk, *Yiddish Literature*, 87; Shmeruk, "Prosa narrativa in Yiddish," 123–26; Zfatman, "Iggrot be-yidish"; Zfatman, "Yiddish Narrative Prose," 1:184, 207–217.

23. E.g., Gow, "Red Jews"; Petrovskii-Shtern, *Anti-Imperial Choice*, 88; Hoffman, "Akdamut." Accordingly, the Yiddish variant of the Red Jews has received negligible scholarly attention in the vast bibliography on the Ten Tribes in Judaism. For instance, the most recent study on the Lost Tribes, by Zvi Ben-Dor Benite, merely acknowledges the German myth of the Red Jews, citing Gow; Ben-Dor Benite, *Ten Lost Tribes*, 102.

24. See standard modern Yiddish dictionaries, such as Weinreich, *Yiddish-English Dictionary*; Niborski, Vaisbrot, and Neuberg, *Dictionnaire*; Beinfeld and Bochner, *Yiddish-English Dictionary*. Over a century ago, Simon Menahem Lazar erroneously surmised that this term's use was exclusive to Polish Jewry; Lazar, *Ḥidot*, 79.

25. Various explanations are listed in Lazar, *Ḥidot*, 79–80; Baron, *Social and Religious History*, 3:44; Posselt, *Geschichte des chazarisch-jüdischen Staates*, 44; Brook, *Jews of Khazaria*, 11–12, 212.

26. Zfatman, "Iggrot be-yidish," 249n35. I previously studied the dialogical formation of the myth of the Red Jews in Jewish and Christian culture in Voß, "Entangled Stories."

27. Such a model of reappropriation is described in Galinsky et al., "Implications for Social Identity"; Galinsky et al., "Reciprocal Relationship." These two case studies address the reappropriation of "queer" and "nigger."

28. Burke, "Cultures of Translation," 10.

29. Spivak, "Can the Subaltern Speak?" On the deliberate act of taking elements from the other culture in each direction, see Ashley and Plesch, "Appropriation"; Sponsler, "In Transit"; Füssel, "Kunst der Schwachen."

30. Marcus, "Imagining the Other," 210. See also Marcus, *Rituals of Childhood*, chap. 1.

31. Yuval, *Two Nations in Your Womb*; Epstein, *Dreams of Subversion*; Epstein, "Another Flight into Egypt"; Epstein, "Bestial Bodies." For a general treatment of the links between visual representations of the Jewish Self and the Christian Other in medieval and early modern Europe, see the articles in Frojmovic, *Imagining the Self*.

32. For early modern Europe, see, e.g., Bregoli and Ruderman, *Connecting Histories*; Idelson-Shein, *Difference of a Different Kind*; Kahana, *From the "Noda be-Yehudah" to the "Hatam Sofer"*; Kaplan, *Beyond Expulsion*; Teter, *Jews and Heretics*; Trivellato, *Familiarity of Strangers*; and the collected essays on overlapping spheres between early modern Jews and Christians in Germany, edited by Liberles, "Jews and Christians." For an overview of this trend of research, see Perry and Voß, "Approaching Shared Heroes."

33. The classic folklore study by Darnton, "Peasants Tell Tales," provides a model of examining fairy tales as a source on the mental world of peasants in late medieval and early modern France.

34. Turniansky, "Transmission of Knowledge," 13. Cf. generally, Zemon Davis, "Popular Religion."

35. Chartier, "Culture as Appropriation"; Chartier, *Cultural Uses*. The scholars of German literature Hans Robert Jauss and Wolfgang Iser apply a similar model to the reception of texts among various audiences; Jauss, *Aesthetic of Reception*; Iser, *Act of Reading*. The two-tiered model of "elite" and "popular" culture has long been abandoned as an artificial division. In the introduction to the third revised edition of his pioneering book, Burke, *Popular Culture*, 7–15 reviews various objections to "popular" as a defining categorization.

36. Chartier, "Culture as Appropriation," 231. Cf. a similar approach by the anthropologist William Christian; Christian, *Local Religion*, esp. 8, 177.

37. Stanislawski, "Popular Religion"; Stanislawski, "Yiddish Shevet Yehudah"; Stanislawski, "Yiddish 'Life of Jesus.'"

38. Turniansky, "Transmission of Knowledge," 8; Raspe, "Men and Women Reading Yiddish," 199. One of the first scholars to discuss the relationship between Hebrew and Yiddish was Weinreich, "Internal Bilingualism." More recent studies on Ashkenazic diglossia and the target audience for Yiddish literature are Turniansky, *Language, Education and Knowledge*, and Baumgarten, *Introduction*, chaps. 3–4. Early modern Yiddish literature was typically (and sometimes apologetically) addressed to the general public with the formulation "For women and for men who are like women," that is, the uneducated. Max Weinreich and Chava Weissler have argued that "women" was a label for a socioeducational cohort that included a less literate class of male readers; Weinreich, *History of the Yiddish Language*, 1:276–78; Weissler, "Construction of Gender." Dovid Katz has cautioned against dismissing the association of early Yiddish texts with women as merely formulaic because, for women, this represented the sole form of Jewish literature that takes their agency as readers into account; Katz, *Yiddish and Power*, 72–83. For a broader perspective on the multivalent relationships between languages and communities (e.g., religious, gender, occupational, regional, national) in early modern Europe, see Burke, *Languages and Communities*.

39. Turniansky, "Transmission of Knowledge," 14. Dauber, *In the Demon's Bedroom*, 22, terms this group the "slumming elites." Folklore has similarly been defined, not as the domain of "the simple people" but as a shared culture among varied societal strata; Ben-Amos, "Definition of Folklore."

40. Dauber, *In the Demon's Bedroom*, chap. 1. Admittedly, a reader's understanding, as it relates to individual personal, social, and cultural experience, is nearly impossible to discern. See, in general, Chartier, "Culture as Appropriation," 250.

41. Dauber, *In the Demon's Bedroom*, 7; Katz, *Yiddish and Power*; Berger, "Early Modern Yiddish," 284. With regard to the Red Jews, see my discussion in Chapter 3.

42. Saenger, *Space Between Words*.

43. On this secondary orality or, to quote Andrew Sunshine's coinage, "collaborative literacy," see Dauber, *In the Demon's Bedroom*, 14–18.

44. Shmeruk, *Illustrations in Yiddish Books*, chap. 3, esp. 39–40. See also recently Wolfthal, *Picturing Yiddish*, 139. Similarly, Katrin Kogman-Appel has argued that illustrated *haggadot* were marketed to a wide audience as an outcome of the visual language that had developed during the late Middle Ages; Kogman-Appel, "Audiences."

45. Arnheim, *Visual Thinking*.

46. Quotations from, respectively: Carruthers, *Book of Memory*, 16; Carruthers, *Craft of Thought*, 142. For the mnemonic role of visual aids during the premodern period, see also Yates, *Art of Memory*. Contemporary science and cognitive psychology emphasize the complex relationship between vision, memory, and verbalization; Rivlin and Gravelle, *Deciphering the Senses*, 53; Paivio, *Imagery and Verbal Processes*; Reed, *Cognition*, chap. 7.

47. On literary pictorialism and cognitive semiotics, see Zeman, "Ut pictura poesis." On the aesthetic experience of texts, see also the work of Niklaus Largier; Largier, "Applikation der Sinne." The close relationship between text and image in medieval German literature has been studied by Wenzel, *Hören und Sehen*, esp. chap. 6; Wenzel, *Spiegelungen*, esp. 9–63.

48. Habicht and Reich, "Farbe der Erinnerung."

49. See treatise 10, "On colors"; Cordovero, *Pardes Rimonim*, 4:36.

50. Bregman, "Aqedah." See also Neis, *Sense of Sight*, 22–23; Bregman, "Seeing with the Sages."

51. Bland, *Artless Jew*; Kogman-Appel, *Mahzor from Worms*; Epstein, *Dreams of Subversion*; Cohen, *Jewish Icons*. See also, among others, on vision and knowledge visualization in Jewish mysticism, Wolfson, *Speculum*; Chajes, "Kabbalistic Diagram."

52. For this classical ranking of the senses, see Classen, "Senses." An overview of Western attitudes toward sight from Plato through the Enlightenment, with additional bibliography, is offered by Jay, *Downcast Eyes*, chaps. 1–2. On the cultural history of the senses more broadly, see Classen, *Cultural History of the Senses*; Howes and Classen, *Ways of Sensing*; Jütte, *Geschichte der Sinne*.

53. Smith, *From Sight to Light*; Lindberg, *Theories of Vision*.

54. Scribner, *Religion and Culture*, 85–89, 115–16; Scribner, "Ways of Seeing," 97–99. On responses to art, see Kessler, *Spiritual Seeing*; Kessler, *Seeing Medieval Art*, chap. 3; Freedberg, *Power of Images*. More broadly on the place of vision and the visual in medieval theological thought, see Hamburger and Bouché, *The Mind's Eye*. Suzanna Biernoff examines the links between optical theory and theology in her monograph on ocular desire in the Middle Ages; Biernoff, *Sight and Embodiment*.

55. On the cognitive theory of emotions, see Nussbaum, *Upheavals of Thought*.

56. Several scholars have critiqued the suggestion that art may have served as a text intended for the illiterate, e.g., Duggan, "Book of the Illiterate"; Duggan, "Reflections"; Krüger, "Lesbarkeit von Bildern"; Curschmann, "Pictura laicorum litteratura." They all emphasize that imagery alone cannot fully transmit textual content.

57. Bale, *Feeling Persecuted*, 65, 185.

58. Bale, *Feeling Persecuted*, chap. 3; Mellinkoff, *Outcasts*, chap. 7. Alexandra Cuffel has shown how Jewish, Christian, and Muslim polemics were designed to evoke revulsion toward the Other; Cuffel, *Gendering Disgust*. Cf. Miller, *The Anatomy of Disgust*. For "the ugly Jew," see Lipton, *Dark Mirror*; Strickland, *Saracens, Demons, and Jews*; Bale, *Feeling Persecuted*, chap. 3; Gilman, "Die Rasse ist nicht schön."

59. Nirenberg, *Aesthetic Theology*, chap. 1.

60. Linares, "Kunst und Kultur im Mittelalter," 1:300, 303. On the use of color in medieval courtly literature, see, for example, the collected papers in Bennewitz and Schindler, *Farbe im Mittelalter*, 2:439–678. Brid Phillips investigates color words in Shakespeare as one method by which early modern drama engaged its audiences' emotions; Phillips, *Shakespeare and Emotional Expression*.

61. Linares, *Alles Wissenswerte über Farben*; Heller, *Wie Farben auf Gefühl und Verstand wirken*. On the social semiotics of color, see Leeuwen, *Language of Colour*. Linares, "Kunst und Kultur im Mittelalter," applies these insights from cognitive science and color psychology to medieval color semantics.

62. Schawelka, *Farbe*, 16, 84. See also Milner and Goodale, *Visual Brain*.

63. Batchelor, *Chromophobia*, 55, 75, 79, 81. On color as a universal language in arts, see Kessler, *Seeing Medieval Art*, 66, 172; Kessler, *Spiritual Seeing*, 121.

64. Linares, "Kunst und Kultur im Mittelalter," 1:299, 303–5, 309. Anna Wierzbicka has argued that color concepts are anchored in "universals of human experience"; Wierzbicka, "Meaning of Color Terms." Comprehensive studies on red are: Pastoureau, *Red*; Meier and Suntrup, "Zum Lexikon der Farbenbedeutungen"; Greenfield, *A Perfect Red*; Busuttil-Cesar, *Red*; Recio, *Essence of Red*.

65. Among the fundamental studies of color semantics and color symbolism are: Wackernagel, "Farben- und Blumensprache"; Pastoureau, *Figures et couleurs*; Gage, *Color and Culture*; Silva and Castelnuovo, *Il colore nel Medioevo*; Pastoureau, *Couleurs, images, symboles*; Gage, *Colour and Meaning*; Meier, "Colourful Middle Ages"; Pleij, *Colors Demonic and Divine*; Gage, *Colour in Art*; Petzold, "Iconography of Color." A wide-ranging collection of articles on color in the Middle Ages appears in the two volumes edited by Bennewitz and Schindler, *Farbe im Mittelalter*. A comprehensive compendium on the meaning of colors in the European Middle Ages on CD is: Meier and Suntrup, *Handbuch der Farbenbedeutung*. Osborne, *Books on Colour*, provides a bibliography of sources and secondary literature from about 1500.

66. Scholem, "Farben und ihre Symbolik," 1. On the alleged Jewish objections to iconography and, more broadly, the denigration of visuality in Judaism, see the historiographic overview by Bland, *Artless Jew*, chaps. 1–2.

67. Fine, "Menorahs in Color," 6–7.

68. Idel, "Kavvanah and Colors"; Idel, "Kabbalistic Prayer and Colors"; Idel, "Visualization of Colors I"; Idel, "Visualization of Colors II"; Sagiv, "Deep Blue"; Sagiv, "Dazzling Blue"; Sagiv, *Jewish Blues*; Fine, "Menorahs in Color"; Blech, "Parah Adumah"; Zabolotnaya, "Cosmology and Color Symbolism"; Ofrat, *Back to the Sea*, 167–212. On biblical color symbolism, see Brenner, *Colour Terms*; Gradwohl, *Farben im Alten Testament*.

69. For the nature of perception as a cultural and historical construct, see, e.g., Brennan and Jay, *Vision in Context*. A radical culturalist position is Wartofsky, "Pictures"; Wartofsky, "Picturing and Representing." Guy Deutscher and Beat Lehmann view color terms as a test case for the cultural conventions of language; Deutscher, *Through the Language Glass*; Lehmann, *ROT ist nicht "rot" ist nicht (rot)*. Cf. MacIntyre, "Tradition and Translation," 201, 210.

70. Kessler, "Shaded with Dust." Cf. Jütte, *Geschichte der Sinne*, 100–101.

71. Cited in Nirenberg, *Aesthetic Theology*, 67. On Bernard of Clairvaux's attitude toward medieval art and its reception, see in detail Rudolph, *The "Things of Greater Importance."* For a discussion of opposition to art in the medieval West due to the dangers that sensuality posed to religion, see Rudolph, "Resistenza." More broadly on Western chromophobia, particularly

on discomfort with and resistance to bright color, see Batchelor, *Chromophobia*; Taussig, *Color*.

72. Mann, *Jewish Texts*, 71–76, 109–11. The responsum by Isaac of Vienna has recently been analyzed by Shoham-Steiner, "Synagogue Decorations."

73. Clark, *Vanities of the Eye*, 337. On the preoccupation with vision that characterized the scientific revolution, see Chen-Morris and Gal, *Baroque Science*; Chen-Morris, *Measuring Shadows*. See also Pomata, "Observation Rising."

74. Clark, *Vanities of the Eye*, 12. Cf. Neis, *Sense of Sight*, 24, on critiques of vision as "bound up with coercion, power, and oppression." See also Haraway, "Persistence of Vision."

75. The term "Yiddishland" has been popularized by the work of Jeffrey Shandler and others in connection with Yiddishism and Diaspora nationalism that propagated Jewish cultural autonomy in eastern Europe at the turn of the twentieth century; Shandler, *Adventures in Yiddishland*, 33–34; Shandler, *Yiddish*, 35–36. Shandler defines Yiddishland as "the kingdom of the Yiddish word" and (modern) Yiddish literature, with reference to Sidra Ezrahi, as an "alternative sovereignty."

76. I am basing the term "counterstory" on Amos Funkenstein's concept of polemical counterhistory. By adopting the adversary's motifs while lending them new meaning, counterhistory aims to deconstruct the initial narrative, thus attempting to undermine its innovators' collective identity; Funkenstein, "History, Counterhistory, and Narrative"; Biale, "Counter-History."

CHAPTER 1

1. On this monumental work of artistry, see Knefelkamp and Martin, *Antichrist*; Rieger-Jähner, *Das spätgotische Antichristfenster*; and the editions by Karg, *Chorfenster*; Mangelsdorf, *Der gläserne Schatz*.

2. In medieval art, demons and the devil are often depicted in red clothing and with red features, including red beards and red faces; Pastoureau, *Red*, 61; Weber, "Antichristfenster," 86. On a medieval manuscript that includes an illustration of a Jew's red face as a demonic symbol, see Mellinkoff, *Antisemitic Hate Signs*, 53–54. Some sources also describe the Antichrist with red hair; Massyngbaerde, "The Physical Features of the Antichrist," 34, 37.

3. Gow, *Red Jews*, esp. chaps. 2 and 3. A concise definition of this term appears in Gow, "Red Jews."

4. On the concept of "vengeful redemption," see Yuval, *Two Nations in Your Womb*, chap. 3, esp. 93–109. For a broader treatment of messianic thought and activity in the early modern Ashkenazic world, see Voß, *Disputed Messiahs*. The development of the legend of the Ten Tribes is briefly outlined in Noy and Ben-Amos, *Folktales of the Jews*, 1:450–72. The classic work is Neubauer, "Collections" (English version: Neubauer, "Where Are the Ten Tribes?"). For two studies of this myth through the ages, with additional bibliography, see Ben-Dor Benite, *Ten Lost Tribes*; Parfitt, *Lost Tribes of Israel*. Barmash, "At the Nexus of History and Memory," discusses the actual history of the northern tribes after the Assyrian destruction of their kingdom.

5. Przybilski, *Kulturtransfer*.

6. For my detailed analysis of these early Jewish sources, see Chapter 2, 76.

7. Weber, "Antichristfenster," 87. On this interpretation, see Chapter 3, 111. On Eldad's writings in the Jewish and Christian imagination throughout the ages, see Perry, *Eldad's Travels*.

8. On Christian reactions to Jewish messianism, see in general Voß, *Disputed Messiahs*. Regarding Christian knowledge of the menacing Ten Tribes in particular, see Yuval, *Two Nations in Your Womb*, 274–91; Perry, "Imaginary War."

9. Since antiquity, Christian theologians have identified the Antichrist as the Jewish Messiah; see Gow, "Jewish Antichrist"; Cohen, "Antichrist." A brief overview is also in Trachtenberg, *The Devil and the Jews*, 32–43. On medieval and early modern portrayals of the Jewish Antichrist in Christian eschatology, see Voß, "Propter seditionis Hebraicae." The general literature on the Antichrist is vast; see, e.g., McGinn, *Antichrist*.

10. On Gog and Magog in Scripture, see Bøe, *Gog and Magog*. On their identification with "the barbaric peoples" in the Alexander Romance, see Anderson, *Alexander's Gate*, chap. 2, esp. 49–50.

11. Gow, *Red Jews*, 43–44; Anderson, *Alexander's Gate*, 58–86. See already Trachtenberg, *The Devil and the Jews*, 39–40. The identification of the Ten Tribes as the unclean peoples of the Alexander Romance contradicts the Jewish notion of the Lost Tribes living in a holy state of paradisiacal bliss; on this concept in Jewish thought, see, e.g., Yaniv, "Ḥevra utopit," 281–82.

12. Gow, *Red Jews*, 3.

13. Albrecht von Scharfenberg, *Der jüngere Titurel*, st. 6124–27.

14. Koppitz, *Göttweiger Trojanerkrieg*, 29:272.

15. For a discussion of the medieval and early modern sources, see Gow, *Red Jews*, chaps. 5–6.

16. On the rise of anti-Judaism in the Middle Ages, see Oberman, "Stubborn Jews." On blood libel and host desecration, see Langmuir, *Definition of Antisemitism*, 328–50. More broadly on demonization of the Jewish Other: Wistrich, "Devil."

17. On the optimism that Jews expressed in anticipation of the Mongol invasion, see Yuval, "Jewish Messianic Expectations"; Menache, "Tartars, Jews, Saracens"; Rosen, "Kazahrs." On the Christian view, see Schmieder, "Christians, Jews, Muslims and Mongols."

18. Lipton, "The Jew's Face"; Lipton, *Dark Mirror*.

19. Resnick, *Marks of Distinction*, 33. On the association of disease with sin, and the merging of medical discourse and religious polemic in the twelfth and thirteenth centuries, see Cuffel, *Gendering Disgust*, chap. 5.

20. On the legend of Jewish male menstruation, see Resnick, "Jewish Male Menses"; Johnson, "Jewish Male Menstruation"; Cuffel, *Gendering Disgust*, 168–82; Katz, "Shylock's Gender." See also Pomata, "Menstruating Men."

21. On the Wandering Jew, see Cohen, "Wandering Jew"; Sigal-Klagsbald and Cohen, *Juif errant*; Hasan-Rokem and Dundes, *Wandering Jew*; Anderson, *Legend of the Wandering Jew*.

22. Berger, *Nizzahon Vetus*, 159 (Hebrew), 224 (English), no. 238.

23. For examples, see Gilman, "Die Rasse ist nicht schön," 62; Gilman, *Visibility of the Jew*, 3; Strickland, *Saracens, Demons, and Jews*, 83–86, 249; Schorsch, *Jews and Blacks*, 180–81; Cuffel, *Gendering Disgust*, 162–64; Lipton, *Dark Mirror*, 10, 173, 175, 185, 205, 208, 241, 248; Resnick, *Marks of Distinction*, 294, 300–301. For the depiction of the "tormentors of Christ," see Mellinkoff, *Outcasts*, 1:122–30. See also Jordan, "Medieval Background."

24. Gow, *Red Jews*, 66–69.

25. Ziegler, "Text and Context"; Ziegler, "Physiognomy, Science, and Proto-Racism"; Reißer, *Physiognomik und Ausdruckstheorie*, 52–97; Porter, *Windows of the Soul*.

26. Resnick, *Marks of Distinction*, 319. On the 1613 Yiddish translation, see Geller, "Yiddish 'Regimen sanitatis Salernitatum.'"

27. Della Porta, *Physiognomie des Menschen*, 295, 140; cf. pp. 128, 191. Similarly, red eyes could signify anger and a hot temper; see pp. 251, 258.

28. E.g., *Phisionomi vnd Chiromanci*, 13. Cf. Jones, *German Colour Terms*, 73; Suntrup, "Farbsymbolik," 291; Wanzeck, *Etymologie lexikalisierter Farbwortverbindungen*, 54; Lauffer, *Farbensymbolik*, 10.

29. Della Porta, *Physiognomie des Menschen*, 93. Cf. Mellinkoff, *Outcasts*, chap. 7; Junkerjürgen, *Haarfarben*, 118; Jones, *German Colour Terms*, 76. For German, cf. also Grimm and Grimm, *Deutsches Wörterbuch*, 14:1296, s.v. "rot," 10:8–9, s.v. "Haar."

30. *Complexion der Menschen*, fol. A5v; *Phisionomi vnd Chiromanci*, 3, 5. On these volumes, see Reißer, *Physiognomik und Ausdruckstheorie*, 56–61. Otto Lauffer claims that evidence indicates that red hair and a red beard were increasingly viewed as signs of untrustworthiness in German folklore from the late twelfth century onward; Lauffer, *Farbensymbolik*, 13.

31. Junkerjürgen, *Haarfarben*, 46, 117, 118.

32. Pastoureau, *Red*, 49, 52.

33. For the importance of theology for the popularization of physiognomic conventions, see Resnick, *Marks of Distinction*, 29–31; Ziegler, "Text and Context," 164–66; Ziegler, *Use of the "New Sciences."* On horoscopes in calendars, see Brévart, "German Volkskalender," 317. Cf. Reißer, *Physiognomik und Ausdruckstheorie*, 207–11.

34. Such adages existed across German dialects. The quotations here and many other examples in Jones, *German Colour Terms*, 76; Junkerjürgen, *Haarfarben*, 117–22; Grimm and Grimm, *Deutsches Wörterbuch*, 10:9–10, 14:1300; Lauffer, *Farbensymbolik*, 14; Kuhn and Schwartz, *Norddeutsche Sagen*, 459, C435.

35. Grimm and Grimm, *Deutsches Wörterbuch*, 10:10, s.v. "Haar."

36. Kirchhof, *Wendunmuth*, 238–39. This story and various jokes about redheads also appear in *Fazetien* (Latin 1508, German 1558) by Heinrich Bebel; Bebel, *Fazetien*, bk. 1, nos. 39, 40, bk. 2, no. 143.

37. Mellinkoff, *Outcasts*, 153–54; Cuffel, *Gendering Disgust*, 164; Strickland, *Saracens, Demons, and Jews*, 122.

38. For Basel, see, e.g., Meier, *Verträumtes Basel*, 169; Gilomen, "Spätmittelalterliche Siedlungssegregation," 94. I thank Andreas Gehringer and Astrid Starck for this information.

39. Von Hutten, *Geschicht und Bekenntnis*, fol. A2v; included in Köhler, *Flugschriften*, no. 2313. Cf. Gow, *Red Jews*, 138–39; Trachtenberg, *The Devil and the Jews*, 82–83.

40. See Mellinkoff, "Judas's Red Hair," 45; Fontes, *Art of Subversion*, 185.

41. Profiles of Jewish robbers by the government of the prince-bishopric of Münster, 1752; city archives of Münster, Acta criminalia, no. 282; http://www.westfaelische-geschichte.de/med105. On the widespread practice among Jewish robber bands to disguise as Christians, see Kühn, *Jüdische Delinquenten*, 53; Geiger, "Vor hundert Jahren," 190. Additional examples, e.g., in Bierbrauer, *Beschreibung*, 32.

42. Thiers, *Histoire des perruques*, 29.

43. Edelman, "Which Is the Jew That Shakespeare Knew?"; Greenblatt, "Shakespeare and Shylock." Critically also Mellinkoff, *Outcasts*, 1:153.

44. Strickland, "Monsters, Demons, and Jews," 54.

45. This etching is a mirror-image replica on a single leaf. Cf. Schwab, *Jüdischer Deckmantel*, between pp. 2 and 3. On the *Judensau* motif that was especially common throughout Germany, see Shachar, *Judensau*; Fabre-Vassas, *Singular Beast*. Yuval, *Two Nations in Your Womb*, 127–28, discusses the Jews' sow as a satirical depiction of the messianic donkey. On Moses as a prototype of the Messiah, see Berger, "Typological Themes," 142–43.

46. Jonas, *Sermon*, fol. A5v. Cf. Kirchhof, *Wendunmuth*, 239: "rotfuchs, Judas Iscariot" (red fox, Judas Iscariot). On this iconic portrait of Judas, see Gubar, *Judas*, 14; Cohen, *Christ Killers*, 257; Mellinkoff, *Outcasts*, 1:51–52. See also Maccoby, *Judas Iscariot*. On the image of the redheaded Judas, see in particular Mellinkoff, "Judas's Red Hair"; Mellinkoff, *Outcasts*, 1:150–54; Bale, *Feeling Persecuted*, 84–89; Pastoureau, *Red*, 102–7; Baum, "Judas's Red Hair."

47. Mellinkoff, "Judas's Red Hair," 38. Hans Holbein the Elder's altarpiece also displays a red Judas; see 38. For additional examples of Judas with red hair and a red beard in European art, see Porte, *Judas Ischarioth*, 14, 16, 26, 34, 65, 67, 68, 85, 101–3. On performative settings for art, see Kessler, *Seeing Medieval Art*, chap. 7.

48. Mellinkoff, *Outcasts*, 1:47–48. Bale emphasizes that Judas's red hair was also a "bloody marker," since he too was associated with violence; Bale, *Feeling Persecuted*, 85. See Mellinkoff, "Judas's Red Hair," 32, on the fear of redheads as aggressors.

49. Bildhauer, "Blood, Jews and Monsters"; Matteoni, "The Jew, the Blood and the Body."

50. Brenz, *Türcken Büchlein*, fol. 10r: "Red Jews, that is, bloodhounds and murderers." Similarly Jonas, *Siebend Capitel Danielis*, fol. D4v; Nigrinus, *Jüden Feind*, fol. F4v. The bloodhound, a hunting dog that chases wounded game, was also termed a "red dog"; Wanzeck, *Etymologie lexikalisierter Farbwortverbindungen*, 52–53. Cf. Grimm and Grimm, *Deutsches Wörterbuch*, 2:184, 9:2466. Interestingly, della Porta compares a redhead to an animal, a dog in particular; della Porta, *Physiognomie des Menschen*, 302, 311.

51. *Neüwe Zeittung*, fol. 2ar. Edition and English translation in Gow, *Red Jews*, 274 (German), 277 (English). Details on the various editions of this pamphlet in Gow, *Red Jews*, 273n58. Cf. a pamphlet from 1596, based on this 1562 pamphlet, *Zwo warhaffte wunder seltzame neuwe zeitung* (VD 16 W 2562), 3; Gow, *Red Jews*, 288 (German), 292 (English).

52. Epstein, *Dreams of Subversion*, 16–38; Carlebach, *Palaces of Time*, 108–14; Horowitz, "Odd Couples"; Bale, *Feeling Persecuted*, 174–83; Offenberg, "Jewish Knight in Shining Armor."

53. Jonas, *Siebend Capitel Danielis*, fol. D3v. John Mandeville's travelogue also speaks of a fox that plays an odd role when the Red Jews breach the bounds of their captivity; Bremer and Ridder, *Jean de Mandeville*, 348.

54. Postel's personal copy of the ethnography of Jewish life and ritual that was authored by the convert Victor of Carben (originally published in German in 1508) is preserved in the National Library of France (BnF, A-2963 [5]); von Carben, *De vita et moribus Judaeorum*, fol. 78r; cited according to Margolin, "Sur quelques ouvrages," 128. For the exceptional verbatim translations that appear in Latin compositions by German speakers, see Gow, *Red Jews*, 69–70.

55. Gow, *Red Jews*, 75–76; further examples on pp. 77–80.

56. Jones, *German Colour Terms*, 398–99; Pfeifer, *Etymologisches Wörterbuch*, 3:1442, s.v. "rot"; Grimm and Grimm, *Deutsches Wörterbuch*, 14:1294–97, s.v. "rot." Cf. Gow, *Red Jews*, 67.

57. Jones, *German Colour Terms*, 399; Jones, *Historisches Lexikon*, 4:2312, s.v. "Rotjude," 4:2231, s.v. "rot." Cf. Jones, *Historisches Lexikon*, 1:147.

58. Wanzeck, *Etymologie lexikalisierter Farbwortverbindungen*, 69–70; Jones, *Historisches Lexikon*, 4:2309, s.v. "Rothure," 4:2231, s.v. "rot." While yellow remained associated with

prostitutes (and other social outsiders, including Jews) through the early modern era, they were also occasionally stigmatized by the need to dress in red, presumably as a symbol of their sin; Lauffer, *Farbensymbolik*, 23–25.

59. Batchelor, *Chromophobia*, 52.

60. Grimm and Grimm, *Deutsches Wörterbuch*, 9:1090.

61. Noted by Gow, *Red Jews*, 67. Cf. Girtler, *Rotwelsch*, 21–24; Cirkic, "Rotwelsch," 13–21.

62. *Von den Newen Juden*, fol. 3v (VD 16 ZV 23834), http://digital.onb.ac.at/OnbViewer/viewer.faces?doc=ABO_%2BZ207229909.

63. Gen. 25:25: "The first one emerged red, like a hairy mantle all over; so they named him Esau." The precise definition of *admoni* in its biblical context is not entirely certain. With respect to Esau, *admoni* might refer to the color of his hair or to his complexion; Brenner, *Colour Terms*, 127–28. The Latin vulgate, e.g., renders *admoni* as "rufus" (red, especially having red hair); Brenner, *Colour Terms*, 243n8. Cf. *Oxford Latin Dictionary*, s.v. rufus "red, ruddy, esp. hair, red-haired." Gesenius, *Hebrew and Chaldee Lexicon*, translates this adjective as "red, i.e. red-haired." He cites translations from the Vulgate and Septuagint to support this definition.

64. Gen. 25:30: "And Esau said to Jacob, 'Give me some of this red stuff to gulp down; for I am famished'—which is why he was named Edom."

65. The Jewish and Christian typologies of these biblical twins are discussed in Cohen, "Esau as Symbol"; Yuval, *Two Nations in Your Womb*, chap. 1.

66. Cited in Meier and Suntrup, "Zum Lexikon der Farbenbedeutungen," 423; Cohen, "Esau as Symbol," 264n43; Cuffel, *Gendering Disgust*, 167.

67. Schorsch, "Maoz Ẕur," 462. The popular Hebrew chronicle *Sefer Yossipon* (tenth century) cites the Arabic phrase *banu al-asfar* as proof for the identification of Edom with Christianity, which its author translates as "sons of the red one" and posits as the Arabic name for Christians; Stow, *Alienated Minority*, 78. Indeed, *banu al-asfar* (sons of the yellow, or ruddy, one) typically refers to Romans in Arabic sources. On this Arabic term in *Sefer Yossipon*, see Sela, "Genealogy of Sefo Ben Elifaz."

68. *Midrash ha-Gadol*, Gen. 25:25 (ed. Margaliot, 439); Rashi on Gen. 25:25. Cf. Berger, *Nizzahon Vetus*, 16 (Hebr.), 55 (Engl.), no. 19: "Esau's hands were always committing murder."

69. Berger, *Nizzahon Vetus*, 16 (Hebr.), 55 (Engl.), no. 18.

70. Jonas, *Siebend Capitel Danielis*, fol. D4r–v.

71. Nigrinus, *Jüden Feind*, fols. 4v–5r.

72. Cf. Yuval, *Two Nations in Your Womb*, 275, with this implicitly counterhistorical explanation of the term "Red Jews."

73. Gow, *Red Jews*, 13, 89–92.

74. The bibliography on early modern print culture is vast: for a general overview, see the classic study by Eisenstein, *Printing Revolution*; and Jones, *Nature of the Book*; Giesecke, *Buchdruck in der frühen Neuzeit*.

75. See Weber, "Antichristfenster," 86, 90–91; Weber, "Hanged Judas," 171, 175–77, 180–81. On the Antichrist as a theme in late medieval sermons, see Emmerson, *Antichrist in the Middle Ages*, 149. On dramas about the Antichrist and on liturgies for Advent and Christmas, see Aichele, *Antichristdrama*; and on plays about the last judgment, Flügge, "Vom Anfang und vom Ende der Welt," 94–95. On the general use of images in late medieval Christian spirituality, see, e.g., Großmann, *Spiegel der Seligkeit*; Schlie, "Erscheinung und Bildvorstellung"; Schmidt, "Kleben statt malen."

76. E.g., Musper, *Antichrist*, fol. 7r–v. Other edited and facsimile versions include: Pfister, *Puch von dem Entkrist*; Diemeringen, *Reisebeschreibung*; Boveland, *Antichrist*. Several editions are available online: https://www.bayerische-landesbibliothek-online.de/xylographa-werke#antichrist.

77. Besides Antichrist plays, the sources are: the *Antichrist vita* (ca. 960) by Adso of Montier-en-Der, and omens of the approaching end times that are detailed in sources such as Jacobus de Voragine's *Legenda Aurea* (ca. 1265); see Töppen, "Bildprogramm."

78. The Red Jews' skeptical response has been misinterpreted as a positive portrayal of Jews; Huber, "Endgericht-Fenster," 10; Mandel, "Bild der Juden." The anti-Jewish hostility conveyed in these scenes is unmitigated by the depiction of five men (including one Jew) who remain steadfast in their belief in Christ, which they demonstrate by kneeling before a crucifix (window s II 9b; Töppen, "Scheiben des Antichristfensters," 41).

79. On changes to the window during its renovation, see Töppen, "Scheiben des Antichristfensters," 44; Meinung, "Restaurierung," 55; Flügge, "Vom Anfang und vom Ende der Welt," 100; Weber, "Antichristfenster," 97n1.

80. See Töppen, "Scheiben des Antichristfensters," 37.

81. Jonas, *Siebend Capitel Danielis*, fols. Aiv, Cv. On the four monarchies in Daniel's visions, see Flusser, "Four Empires."

82. See Gow, "Gog and Magog," 68; Gow, "Kartenrand."

83. David, *Hebrew Chronicle*, 27, no. 19. For end-time expectations that were shared among Jews and Christians in the sixteenth century (including a discussion of the year 1523), see Voß, *Disputed Messiahs*.

84. *Von ainer grosse meng*. The term "Red Jews" appears on fol. 2r. VD 16 V 2686–89 lists the editions; three are included in Köhler, *Flugschriften*: Augsburg: Rudolf Steiner (no. 2636 = VD 16 V 2688); Augsburg: Rudolf Steiner, revised edition (no. 3374 = VD 16 V 2687); [Munich: Hans Schobser], without the woodcut title page (no. 4279 = VD 16 V 2689). VD 16 V 2686 [Nuremberg: Jobst Gutknecht] is printed in Clemen, *Flugschriften*, 1:342–44 (should be corrected to 442–44). English translation follows VD 16 V 2687 in Gow, *Red Jews*, appendix A, no. 19. On the various editions, see Kaufmann, "Flugschriftenpublizistik," 442n81; Gow, *Red Jews*, 148–49n58, 266n56.

85. For examples that include the Red Jews, *iudei clausi*, and Gog and Magog, see Gow, "Gog and Magog"; Gow, "Kartenrand."

86. We have no evidence that any of these maps have been preserved; therefore, see the reconstruction of Vienna-Klosterneuburg maps in Durand, *Vienna-Klosterneuburg Map Corpus*, plate 13. For the Ebstorf World Map, see van Duzer, "Hic sunt dracones," 407. Cf. Gow, *Red Jews*, 52; Strickland, *Saracens, Demons, and Jews*, 228–32. On the connection between Jews and accusations of cannibalism, see also Bildhauer, "Blood, Jews and Monsters." In general on grotesque peoples, see Friedman, *Monstrous Races*; on their depiction on early modern maps, see Davies, *Renaissance Ethnography*.

87. Gow, *Red Jews*, 4, 80–81. See generally, on depictions of Jews, in Bale, *Feeling Persecuted*, 68. For the function of emotions in medieval German epics, with special attention to rage and fear, see also Ridder, "Emotion und Reflexion."

88. On the importance of color for understanding medieval art, see Petzold, "Iconography of Color."

89. Carmassi, "Purpurismum in Martyrio," 1:252–54, 265; Tammen, "Rot sehen." In medieval Christian culture, red often symbolized the blood-stained garments of Christ and martyrs; Leipold and Solms, "Farbbezeichnungen," 332; Suntrup, "Farbsymbolik," 290; Meier

and Suntrup, "Zum Lexikon der Farbenbedeutungen," 429, 423–25. On the iconography of and devotion to blood, see Bynum, *Wonderful Blood*; Rubin, "Opfer und Erlösung."

90. On this retable, now at the Städel Museum, Frankfurt am Main, see Brinkmann and Kemperdick, *Deutsche Gemälde*, 388–428. The plates of the altarpiece may be viewed here: https://sammlung.staedelmuseum.de/de/werk/fluegel-und-predella-des-frankfurter-dominikaneraltars.

91. Frey, "Frankfurter Passionsspiel," 36–39; Frey, "Passionsspiel und geistliche Malerei."

92. Dieckmann, *Judas als Sündenbock*, 56; Büchner, *Judas Ischarioth*, 36–37.

93. Touber, *Donaueschinger Passionspiel*, v. 2697.

94. Toepfer, "Leiden Christi in Farbe," 769–70. Toepfer focuses on Jesus's red coat.

95. Frey, "Frankfurter Passionsspiel," 36, 38. Most notably, northern European artists in the late Middle Ages and the Renaissance consistently rendered Judas as ugly and deformed; Mellinkoff, "Judas's Red Hair," 31; Mellinkoff, *Outcasts*, 1:51–52. Cf. Westerhoff-Sebald, "Der moralisierte Judas," 14, 18, 22, 65–68, and, for examples of his unkempt hair, pp. 37, 47–48, figs. 22–25, 71. Analogously, foreboding portraits of the Other in Christian iconography included Jews and heretics who, like demons, were presented with unruly hair; Amishai-Maisels, "Demonization of the 'Other,'" 50. On the naturalistic style that is typical of visual arts from the Renaissance, see Smith, "Art, Science, and Visual Culture"; Kaufmann, *Mastery of Nature*.

96. In accordance with humoral theory, medieval Christian theologians claimed that Jesus had an exemplary complexion which signified his physical and moral perfection; Resnick, *Marks of Distinction*, 31–33.

97. Strickland, *Saracens, Demons, and Jews*, 234–35.

98. All quotes are from Koppitz, *Göttweiger Trojanerkrieg*, 272–74. For my English translation, see Voß, "Eschatological Avengers."

99. Marian Füssel has investigated the auditory qualities of early modern war and peace with the methodology of sound history; Füssel, "Schlachtenlärm und Siegesklang."

100. Frey, "Frankfurter Passionsspiel," 37–38.

101. This entry has only been preserved in one copy by a fifteenth-century compiler, so it may represent a later addition. The original German text appears in Ettmüller, *Jahrbücher*, 71–72, reprinted with English translation in Gow, *Red Jews*, 225–27. See also pp. 81–85. On the accusation that Jews in general were responsible for the plague, see Ritzmann, "Judenmord"; Ziegler, *Black Death*, 96–109; Horrox, *Black Death*, 207–26. For the deadly Jewish touch, see, e.g., Rothkrug, "Peasant and Jew," 62; Cuffel, *Gendering Disgust*, 157–58.

102. "Diese vnd dergleichen grewlichen thaten / haben sie gewißlich auß anregung des Satans / vnd auß ihrem mordlichen Haß zun Christen / oder auß anregung der rotten Juden . . . gethan"; Nigrinus, *Jüden Feind*, fol. K5v.

103. *Neüwe Zeittung*, fol. 3ar–v; Gow, *Red Jews*, 275 (German), 279 (English). Cf. *Zwo warhaffte wunder seltzame neuwe Zeitung*, 4; Gow, *Red Jews*, 289 (German), 293 (English); *Von den Newen Juden*, fol. 3v.

104. Schreckenberg, *Adversus-Judaeos-Texte*, 2:603–4; Schreckenberg, *Juden in der mittelalterlichen Kunst*, 254, fig. 10. A parallel motif appears in a Yiddish story about the Red Jews; see Chapter 2, 61.

105. Yidls, *Gelilot erez Yisra'el*, 85. These claims parallel testimonies by medieval Christian authors that the waters of the Jordan River, in which Jesus was baptized, were imbued with healing powers and could cure lepers who bathed in them; see Resnick, *Marks of Distinction*, 123.

106. Kelly, "Did Women Have a Renaissance?" For Germany, see Rublack, *Crimes of Women*. On the role of women in early modern Europe, see also Wiesner, *Women and Gender*; Wunder, *He Is the Sun, She Is the Moon*.

107. See the editio princeps of the German translation by Otto von Diemeringen (Basel 1480/81), edited by Bremer and Ridder, *Jean de Mandeville*, 347. Cf. Burger, "Endzeiterwartung im späten Mittelalter," 47–51. For earlier sources that present the Red Jews as the vassals of the Amazons, see Gow, *Red Jews*, 73–74. Cf. also Strickland, *Saracens, Demons, and Jews*, 235–36.

108. See Chapter 3. While the Amazons are often viewed as an intolerable challenge to patriarchy, Dror Wahrman presents a more nuanced view in his discussion of warrior women in the early eighteenth century: Wahrman, *Making of the Modern Self*, chap. 1.

109. "Doch wöllen wir vor die von Alexandro Magno mit Eisenbalcken versperrte Caucasische Clausen inn den Caspischen Gebürgen erbrechen, es kriechen darnach Teuffel, Türcken, Geschnäbelt Leut, blau oder Rot Juden oder was es will herauß." Fischart, *Geschichtsklitterung*, 328.

110. For a satirical alchemical text from 1608 that mocks the credulity of folk beliefs regarding the Red Jews, see Gow, *Red Jews*, 173–75.

111. The age of exploration was a catalyst for heightened interest in the Lost Tribes; Aescoly, *Jewish Messianic Movements*, 336–50; Gross, "Expulsion"; Gross, "Ten Tribes." For various peoples and places that have been identified as the Ten Lost Tribes and their lands, see, e.g., Neher, *Jewish Thought*, 119–48; Ruderman, *World of a Renaissance Jew*, chap. 11; Ben-Dor Benite, *Ten Lost Tribes*, chap. 5; Pollak, "Jewish Presence in Seventeenth-Century China." For similar discussions among Christians, see Rogers, *Quest for Eastern Christians*, 185–93.

112. Fraenkel-Goldschmidt, *Historical Writings*, 172–73; Ben-Dor Benite, *Ten Lost Tribes*, 154–55. On the myth of a Jewish-Turkish alliance as a threat to Christians, see Braude, "Myths and Realities"; Lewis, *Cultures in Conflict*, chap. 2. For a broader treatment of European perspectives on the expansion of the Ottoman Empire, see Kaufmann, *Türckenbüchlein*; Höfert, *Den Feind beschreiben*; Schwoebel, *Shadow of the Crescent*.

113. "Jn des nu solchs alles gehet, kompt im xx. Cap. auch her zu der Letzetranck, Gog vnd Magog, der Tuercke, die roten Juden, welche der Satan, so vor tausent jaren gefangen gewest ist, vnd nach tausent jaren wider los worden, bringet." Revised *Vorrede auff die offenbarung Sanct Johannis* (1530, reprinted 1546, original version 1522); Luther, *Werke*, Deutsche Bibel 7:417.

114. Luther, *Werke*, Schriften 30,2:224. Luther's view is discussed in Gow, *Red Jews*, 157–59.

115. Jonas, *Siebend Capitel Danielis*, fols. 3r–4r. Philipp Melanchthon accepts Jonas's interpretation; Köhler, *Melanchthon und der Islam*, 67–68. Cf. Brenz, *Türcken Büchlein*, fol. 9v. Other German Protestant thinkers continued to associate Turks with Gog and Magog but often without reference to the Jewish tribes. See, e.g., a sermon by the Lutheran theologian Heinrich Efferhen of Württemberg and the subtitle of *Weckglock*, a volume by Pastor David Rupert Erythropel of Hannover (1556–1626); Efferhen, *Christliche Predigten*, fol. e2r; Erythropel, *Weckglock*.

116. For a survey of Reuveni's activity, see Lenowitz, *Jewish Messiahs*, 103–23. The most recent study of Reuveni is Benmelech, "History, Politics, and Messianism." The standard work on this messianic movement remains the comprehensive and annotated collection of sources, including Reuveni's travelogue, with a new introduction, by Aescoly, *Story of David Hareuveni*. Based on those materials is Aescoly, *Jewish Messianic Movements*, 273–301, 357–436.

117. *Von ainer grosse meng*. Another pamphlet is also relevant here: Kramer, *Vnderredung vom glawben*, fols. 5v–6r; included in Köhler, *Flugschriften*, no. 1988. Another edition is in Clemen, *Flugschriften*, 1:323–40 (wrong pagination; correct to 423–40), partially reprinted with English translation in Gow, *Red Jews*, 255–57. I offer a detailed analysis of these pamphlets as sources on the Reuveni episode, including corroborating Hebrew letters, in Voß, *Disputed Messiahs*, 114–19. Their link to Reuveni had not previously been documented. Gow reads these pamphlets simply as generic representations of the Red Jews; Gow, *Red Jews*, 142, 150. By contrast, Scheiber and Tardy, "Echo de la premiere manifestation de David Reubeni," Rohrbacher and Schmidt, *Judenbilder*, 190, and Kaufmann, "Flugschriftenpublizistik," 444, have viewed them as historical indicators of a more complex reality.

118. On the demise of Reuveni and Molkho in Regensburg, see Voß, *Disputed Messiahs*, chap. 3.5, esp. 169–70. On Molkho, see the monograph by Benmelech, *Shlomo Molcho*.

119. *Verzeychnuß*, fols. D7v–8r, §79, F2r–v (VD 16 V 893).

120. Euling, *Chronik des Johan Oldecop*, 490.

121. *Neüwe Zeittung*, fol. 3av; Gow, *Red Jews*, 279.

122. See Gow, *Red Jews*, 273n58.

123. *Von den Newen Juden*, fol. 4r. Elsewhere, I erroneously dated the latter pamphlet to 1524; Voß, "Jüdische Irrlehre,'" 10. Scheiber and Tardy, "Echo de la premiere manifestation de David Reubeni," 597, cite its correct year, 1574.

124. Gow, *Red Jews*, 163–64. In 1570, e.g., Turks and Red Jews are also equated in Nigrinus, *Jüden Feind*, fol. F4v.

125. *Zwo warhafftige newe Zeittung* (VD 16 W 365); *Zwo warhaffte wunder seltzame neuwe Zeitung*. Printed with English translation in Gow, *Red Jews*, 281–93, here 283, 287–88. On similar reports of the Ten Tribes' conquests in the Muslim East that were concurrent with the messianic movement of Shabtai Zvi in the following century, see Scholem, *Sabbatai Sevi*, 332–54.

126. *Zwo warhaffte wunder seltzame neuwe Zeitung*, fol. 1v.

127. Gow, *Red Jews*, 160–68.

128. Analogously, in the thirteenth and fourteenth centuries, Christian political prophecy reassessed its view of the Mongols in the apocalypse: as their military threat to Europe lessened, rather than being equated with Gog and Magog, they were viewed in a positive light and considered potential brothers in arms against the Muslims; Schmieder, "Christians, Jews, Muslims and Mongols."

129. Resnick, *Marks of Distinction*, 300–317. For skin color as a medieval signifier of difference, see also Hahn, "Difference the Middle Ages Make"; Groebner, "Complexio/Complexion." On Jewish racial difference as a flexible category in the Middle Ages, see Kim, "Reframing Race."

130. 1 Sam. 16:12; 1 Sam. 17:42; Luther, *Werke*, Deutsche Bibel 9,1:239, 245. Biblical *adom* was applied to a far broader range of colors than our modern concept of "red," including shades of brown; Brenner, *Colour Terms*, 58; Gradwohl, *Farben im Alten Testament*, 26–27. Gradwohl similarly interprets *admu* (lit., they were ruddy) in Lam. 4:7 as light brown, suntanned skin (10); Against it, Brenner, *Colour Terms*, 79.

131. Gen. 25:25; Luther, *Werke*, Deutsche Bibel 8:109.

132. *Von ainer grosse meng*, fol. A2r–v.

133. Kramer, *Vnderredung vom glawben*, fols. Bv–B2r.

134. This link to the Exodus (via Exod. 14:13) appears in the story of the Sons of Moses in *Bereshit Rabbati* (ed. Albeck 125) and *Sefer ha-Zikhronot* (The book of memory; ed. Yassif 222). I thank Dudu Rotman for these references.

135. Concerning the extensive literature on the popular legend of Prester John, see esp. Ramos, *Essays in Christian Mythology*; Bejczy, *Lettre du prêtre Jean*; Hamilton and Beckingham, *Prester John*; Knefelkamp, "Priesterkönig Johannes." On Prester John and the Ten Tribes, see Chapter 3, 88–89.

136. Critical Hebrew edition and English translation by Adler, *Benjamin of Tudela*, 67. This edition is mainly based on a fourteenth-century Ashkenazic manuscript. According to Martin Jacobs, who discusses the complex and still largely unexplored history of the transmission of Benjamin's account (first Hebrew printing in Constantinople in 1543), textual discrepancies between the extant versions of Benjamin's travelogue are substantial; Jacobs, *Reorienting the East*, 32.

137. Schwarz (Nigri), *Stern Meschiah*, fol. 48v.

138. Fischart, *Geschichtsklitterung*, 325.

139. Gow, *Red Jews*, 281, 283, 289.

140. Cf. Chapter 3, 87.

141. Gow, "Gog and Magog," 71.

142. Durand, *Vienna-Klosterneuburg Map Corpus*, pl. 13.

143. Davies, *Renaissance Ethnography*, 296.

144. Gow, "Gog and Magog"; Gow, "Kartenrand."

145. Röhrich, *Folktales and Reality*; Ecker, *Legende*.

146. Gow, *Red Jews*, 80, 155–59.

147. On the "reformation of the eyes," see Clark, *Vanities of the Eye*, chap. 5. See also Miles, *Image as Insight*, chap. 5; Dyrness, *Reformed Theology*. On suspicions toward sight in late medieval worship, see Hamburger, "Seeing and Believing." On traditional religious criticism of the dangers posed by vision, see also Introduction, 15.

148. Quotes in Clark, *Vanities of the Eye*, 161. For visual aspects of late medieval worship, see Scribner, *Religion and Culture*, 83–145; Scribner, "Ways of Seeing." More broadly on the senses of sight and hearing in religious discourse, see Chidester, *Word and Light*.

149. See the nuanced studies on the significance of eyes and ears for perception in Protestant religious discourse and practice in early modern Germany by Friedrich, "Das Hör-Reich und das Sehe-Reich"; Baum, *Reformation of the Senses*. On the role of the senses in the religious transformations of early modern Europe, see also Boer, *Religion and the Senses*.

150. Toepfer, "Frühneuzeitliche Wende auf der Frankfurter Bühne," 151–55, 160–61.

151. The survival of a pictorial tradition that depicts Judas with red hair especially in predominantly Catholic southern Germany and southern Europe (primarily Spain) may be a parallel phenomenon; Junkerjürgen, *Haarfarben*, 47. See also Fabre-Vassas, *Singular Beast*, 109.

152. Jonas, *Siebend Capitel Danielis*, fol. D4r–v.

153. E.g., Augusti, *Geheimnisse der Jüden*, 27–28. For a discussion of this and other convert sources, see Chapter 2.

154. In the field of ethnology, the theoretical model of cultural appropriation describes such phenomena as "killing off the source"; Hahn, "Cultural Appropriation," 19, 30.

CHAPTER 2

1. Augusti, *Geheimnisse der Jüden*, 13–14. Until his conversion in 1722, Friedrich Albrecht Augusti had been known as Joshua b. Abraham Herschel. On his life and conversion, see Költsch, "Abenteuerliche Reise."

2. Von Carben, *Hier inne wirt gelesen*, fol. D4v. This work is better known by the title of its second edition, *Juden Büchlein* (n.p., 1550).

3. Margaritha, *Gantz Jüdisch glaub*, fol. b1r: "vnnd also hoffen sy gar vast / dise rotten Juden sollen kommen vnd sye erlösen / sy haben auch klaine Hebreische vnd teutsche [i.e., Yiddish] büchlin darinnen sy gar vil lugen vnd merlin von disen zehen geschlechten schreiben." Unless noted otherwise, quotations follow the editio princeps (March 1530; VD 16 M 972). A second, slightly revised edition appeared one month later (April 1530; VD 16 M 973).

4. For instance, in a pamphlet from ca. 1572, the convert Paul Staffelsteiner claims to quote an exchange between two Jews who were speaking of the Red Jews, among others; Staffelsteiner, *Seltzam vnd wunderbarlichs Gespraech* (VD 16 ZV 28386), fols. B6r, D5r. An anonymously authored German catalogue of blasphemies allegedly committed by Jews (ca. 1560) also mentions the Red Jews as the messianic army for whom Jews await; *Verzeychnuß*, fols. D7v–8r. This source refers to the Red Jews as *Rote Diebe* (red thieves); *Verzeychnuß*, fol. F2v.

5. Augusti, *Geheimnisse der Jüden*, 13–14; see also p. 7. Cf. Gerson, *Jüden Thalmud*, 391; *Verzeychnuß*, fol. D7v; BT Sanhedrin 98a.

6. Augusti, *Geheimnisse der Jüden*, 7, 15–19, 27, 42–47. On Wallich, see Böttrich, Kuhn, and Stein-Kokin, *Greifswalder Lehrsynagoge*. Claims of having seen or even possessed an hourglass with water or sand from the Sambatyon, which marked the onset (and end) of the Sabbath, abound in the early modern period; Voß, *Disputed Messiahs*, 88.

7. Clark, *Vanities of the Eye*, 163. Cf. Chapter 1, 49.

8. Clark, *Vanities of the Eye*, 5.

9. Neis, *Sense of Sight*, 24. See also Haraway, "Persistence of Vision."

10. Foucault, *Discipline and Punish*.

11. On this representation of sovereignty, see the contributions in Bredekamp and Schneider, *Visuelle Argumentationen*.

12. Bodleian Library, Oxford, Ms. Opp. 714 (IMHM F 20496), fol. 26r; edited in Rivkind, "Historical Allegory," 19. This text, *Ma'aseh Akdamut*, is analyzed below.

13. I have considered the Red Jews within the framework of Jewish messianism in Voß, "Entangled Stories"; Voß, *Disputed Messiahs*, chap. 3.1.

14. Gow claims that Jews, like Christians, accepted the association of red hair and red beards with Jewishness as a given, albeit without its negative valence; Gow, *Red Jews*, 67–68, citing Hebrew illuminated manuscripts included in Metzger and Metzger, *Jewish Life in the Middle Ages*. While I remain unconvinced by the evidence for this broad assertion, any historical assessment of these renderings is complicated by unresolved debates regarding the illuminators' identities (i.e., were they Jewish or Christian?) and the extent to which patrons and the intended audience influenced the Jewish content and symbolism in such illustrations. See Horowitz, "The Way We Were"; Epstein, *Dreams of Subversion*, 4–7; Epstein, "Another Flight into Egypt," 40–43; Suckale, "Anteil christlicher Maler."

15. Augusti, *Geheimnisse der Jüden*, 27–29.

16. Schäfer, *Mirror of His Beauty*, 147–48.

17. In contrast, Gow, *Red Jews*, 136–39, erroneously reads the use of this term in writings by converts as an uncomplicated reflection of Christian parlance. On methodological arguments for examining sources by converts for research on contemporaneous Jewish thought and practice, despite their polemical biases, see, e.g., Carlebach, *Anti-Christian Element*, 15; Deutsch, "Von der Iuden Ceremonien," 339; Diemling, "Anthonius Margaritha," 327.

18. Margaritha, *Gantz Jüdisch glaub*, fol. b1r.

19. See Chapter 3, 86.

20. The term *Ma'aseh Akdamut* was first introduced by Rivkind, "Megilat R. Me'ir Shaẓ." Accordingly, Dan, "Early Hebrew Source"; Dan, "History of 'The Story of the Akdamut.'"

21. Ms. Opp. 714, fols. 21v–34v; synoptic edition with a later Yiddish printing from Fürth (1694), in Rivkind, "Historical Allegory." See the Appendix of this volume for an English translation of the manuscript version, which serves as my base text in this chapter unless noted otherwise. An English translation of the Fürth printing is forthcoming on the online site *Early Modern Workshop*; Voß, "Sense of Sight." On the manuscript version, see Zfatman, *Bibliography*, 19, no. 8.2 (Hebrew numbers); Neubauer, *Catalogue of the Hebrew Manuscripts*, no. 2213,6; Steinschneider, "Jüdisch-Deutsche Literatur," 25, no. 5: 66, no. 410, VI. The terminus post quem for dating this collection is the year 1579 mentioned in the manuscript. Jacob Meitlis dates it to the beginning of the seventeenth century at earliest; Meitlis, *Ma'assebuch*, 99–100. Cf. Malachi Beit-Arié, who dates the manuscript to ca. 1600 on the basis of its watermark; Beit-Arié, *Catalogue of the Hebrew Manuscripts (Supplement)*, no. 2213.

22. On Meir Shatz, see Grossman, *Early Sages of Ashkenaz*, 292–96; Elbogen, *Jewish Liturgy*, 257–58; Zunz, *Literaturgeschichte*, 145–52.

23. Turniansky and Timm, *Yiddish in Italia*, no. *92; Zfatman, *Bibliography*, 30, no. 9; Romer-Segal, "Sifrut yidish," 783, 788n25; Shmeruk, "Prosa narrativa in Yiddish," 123–26, no. 2; Shmeruk, "Yiddish Printing in Italy," 173, no. 32; Friedberg, *Bet Eked Sepharim*, מ2927. Printed by Vincenzo Conti, who was active as a printer in Cremona from 1556 to 1567. Benayahu, *Hebrew Printing at Cremona*, no. 26, and Vinograd, *Thesaurus*, no. 32, propose 1561 as its printing date. On the censorial lists, see also Baruchson, *Books and Readers*, 156; Simonsohn, "Sefarim ve-sifriyot." Baumgarten, "Representation of the Body," 64, incorrectly claims that the Bible translation published by Conti was the sole Yiddish book printed in Cremona.

24. On the transmission of legendary material, see Raspe, *Jüdische Hagiographie*, 192–96; Yassif, "Rashi Legends"; Shmeruk, *Yiddish Literature*, 87. See also Meitlis, *Ma'assebuch*, 98. On the transmission of folklore from orality to writing, see Zfatman, *Marriage of a Mortal Man*, 24n27.

25. An editor in northern Italy justifies his new Hebrew translation of *Ma'aseh Akdamut* in 1630 because its sole extant version then was in Yiddish, except for Hebrew versions in rare *maḥzorim*; Yassif, "Early Versions," 218. On this early modern Hebrew version, see Chapter 4.

26. Margaritha, *Gantz Jüdisch glaub*, fol. b1r (note in the margin).

27. With the exception of several modern translations from Yiddish that render this phrase literally, as *yehudim admonim*, see Chapter 4, 126.

28. For the transmission history of *Ma'aseh Akdamut*, see Chapter 4.

29. E.g., Faierstein, *Ze'enah u-Re'enah*, on Deut. 32:26; Isa. 27:13; Jer. 31:8, 31:14; Kirchhan, *Simḥat ha-nefesh*, fol. 40r; *Yoẓerot*, Prague 1605, fol. 21–3v (Bodleian Library, Oxford, Opp. 4° 1298).

30. Bodleian Library, Opp. 8° 556 (10) ([Dessau, 1700?]); Bodleian Library, Opp. 8° 1056 (Jessnitz, 1723).

31. Benjamin of Tudela, *Masa'ot Binyamin*, fol. 64v; Bodleian Library, Opp. 8° 404. Cf. reprint, Frankfurt am Main 1711, fol. 21r; Bodleian Library Opp. 8° 1096. Similarly, "Ten Tribes" appears in the Yiddish edition of Menasseh ben Israel, *Mikveh Yisra'el*.

32. On Jewish physiognomic thought in medieval sources, see Meerson, "Physiognomy and Somatomancy"; Liebes, "Physiognomy in Kabbalah."

33. Ha-Kohen, *Ma'aseh Toviyyah*, fol. 75v. For a reddish face as a symptom of excessive yellow bile, see ha-Kohen, *Ma'aseh Toviyyah*, fol. 75r. The image of an avenger who bears a grudge as a snake does refers to BT Yoma 23a.

34. Abravanel, *Perush ha-torah*, 1:529–30, on Gen. 25:25. Cf. Melamed, *Image of the Black*, 35–36.

35. See the facsimile by Roth, *Haggadah von Sarajevo*, fol. 10.

36. ווער עש האט רוטי האר איז דער איין בעל קנאה ורמאי ורגזן; Galina, *Ḥokhmat ha-yad*, fol. 8v. שערות אדום (a fraud) is missing from the Yiddish. Cf. the Hebrew wording on fol. 8r: שערות אדום קנאי רמאי רגזן.

37. שערות אדום קנאי רמאי רגזן ולא טוב דבורו ולשון; Jacob b. Mordecai of Fulda, *Shoshanat Ya'acov*, fol. 3r. Cf. fol. 9v, on a red face as an indicator of anger.

38. Bernstein, *Jüdische Sprichwörter*, 256; Joffe and Yudel, *Great Dictionary*, 1:35. Cf. Wander, *Sprichwörter-Lexikon*, s.v. "Rother."

39. In modern Yiddish, *a geler* (lit. "a yellow one") became the common term for a person with red hair, with its pejorative meaning persisting; cf. Beinfeld and Bochner, *Yiddish-English Dictionary*, s.v. "gel," "geler"; Strack, *Jüdisches Wörterbuch*, s.v. "royt." By comparison, in early modern Western Yiddish, "yellowish hair" was apparently not read accordingly; see, e.g., Galina: ווער עש האט געלבליכי האר דר איז פרום און איין בעל מורא וחלש וחכם אבר ניט גליקליך; Galina, *Ḥokhmat ha-yad*, fol. 8v.

40. For the cinematic analogy, see Bregman, "Aqedah," [2].

41. Ms. Opp. 714, fols. 22v–24r; Rivkind, "Historical Allegory," 13, 15. Benedictine and, later, Dominican friars were often referred to as "black monks," in reference to their standard robes; Jones, *German Colour Terms*, 135–36.

42. Jay, *Downcast Eyes*, 15. On the assessment of dreams in the context of the early modern visual crisis, see Clark, *Vanities of the Eye*, chap. 9. The dream sequence in *Ma'aseh Akdamut* (the animal simile appears in the Fürth edition only): Ms. Opp. 714, fols. 24r–26r; Fürth 1694, fol. 2v; Rivkind, "Historical Allegory," 15–20.

43. Fürth 1694, fol. 3r; Rivkind, "Historical Allegory," 18.

44. The supernatural powers of the Ten Tribes across the Sambatyon is a popular motif in Jewish literature; Yaniv, "Moshi'a," 128. See Chapter 1, 40, on the Red Jews' magical skills in German lore.

45. In the Ashkenazic rite, recitation of *Akdamut Milin* precedes Torah reading on the first day of Shavuot; Davidson, *Thesaurus*, 1:332, no. 7314; Elbogen, *Jewish Liturgy*, 258. Text with English translation in Salamon, *Akdamus Millin*, 257–58. The Fürth edition includes a Yiddish translation of this piyyut.

46. Ms. Opp. 714, fol. 27r; Rivkind, "Historical Allegory," 21. Cf. the Fürth edition, fol. 4v; Rivkind, "Historical Allegory," 22. The term "little Red Jew" appears once in each version; Ms. Opp. 714, fol. 27v; Fürth 1694, fol. 4v; Rivkind, "Historical Allegory," 21–22. Thereafter, this Red Jew is referred to as "little Jew" or "little man."

47. Ms. Opp. 714, fols. 27v–28r; Rivkind, "Historical Allegory," 21, 23. On *kefiẓat ha-derekh* as a motif in Jewish folklore, see the bibliographical references in Yassif, *Hebrew Folktale*, 482. Since this magical shortening of paths creates a geographical continuum, Yassif reads it as a longing to live in a Jewish world, free of the disruptions caused by threats from the Christian majority; Yassif, "Local Identity," 45, 47.

48. Ms. Opp. 714, fol. 28r; Rivkind, "Historical Allegory," 23.

49. Ms. Opp. 714, fol. 28v; Rivkind, "Historical Allegory," 23.
50. All quotes Ms. Opp. 714, fol. 29v; Rivkind, "Historical Allegory," 25.
51. Ms. Opp. 714, fol. 30r; Rivkind, "Historical Allegory," 25, 27.
52. Both quotes Ms. Opp. 714, fol. 31r; Rivkind, "Historical Allegory," 27. This episode ends with: "[When the people saw it] they all fell on their faces." Cf. Lev. 9:24: "Fire came forth from before the Lord. . . . And all the people saw, and shouted, and fell on their faces."
53. Ms. Opp. 714, fol. 32r; Rivkind, "Historical Allegory," 29.
54. All quotes from Ms. Opp. 714, fol. 32r-v; Rivkind, "Historical Allegory," 29, 31.
55. Ms. Opp. 714, fols. 32v-33r; Fürth 1694, fol. 7r; Rivkind, "Historical Allegory," 31-32. Cf. parallel imagery of bending a tree whose branches tear off someone's head as it is being pulled toward the ground; ATU 1241. Cf. also the "bent tree test" as a motif, where a tree is released and smashes the antagonist to pieces when it snaps upright; Thompson, *Motif-Index of Folk-Literature*, H1522.1. Related motifs are G314 (death by the springing action of a tree) and K1112 (a bent tree rebounds and shoots someone into the sky).
56. Ms. Opp. 714, fol. 28v; Rivkind, "Historical Allegory," 23.
57. Isa. 35:5; Rom. 11:10, citing Ps. 68:23-24; Augustine, *De civitate Dei*, 18.46. On Jewish attitudes toward physical disabilities, see for the Middle Ages, Shoham-Steiner, *On the Margins of a Minority*.
58. Lipton, "The Jew's Face," 273.
59. A rare exception is *Tela'ot Mosheh* (Halle, 1711), which speaks of *rote yidlekh*; Drucker, *Tela'ot Mosheh*, fol. 3r. On this work, see Chapter 3, 86-88.
60. Two major critical Hebrew editions of Eldad's narrative exist in multiple recensions and versions: by Abraham Epstein, revised reprint by Abraham Habermann, and by David Heinrich von Müller; Epstein, "Eldad ha-Dani"; von Müller, *Eldad had-Dânî*. English translations in Adler, *Jewish Travellers*, 4-21. I quote from Epstein's edition of the Hebrew printings from Mantua 1480 and Constantinople 1519; these versions evidence both the interests and knowledge of Jews during the early modern period. Epstein, "Eldad ha-Dani," 52, 94 (Hebrew pagination); Adler, *Jewish Travellers*, 8. On the image of the Lost Tribes in Eldad, see Dan, *Hebrew Story*, 54-55.
61. This motif often appears in literature on the Ten Tribes; e.g., in a Hebrew account of the Alexander tradition, as transmitted in the medieval manuscript collection *Sefer ha-Zikhronot*, compiled in the Rhineland ca. 1325 (ed. Yassif, *Book of Memory*): When Alexander the Great encounters the Ten Tribes beyond the Sambatyon, he asks an elderly member of these tribes why they do not fear his massive army. That Jew responds: "Five of you shall give chase to a hundred, and a hundred of you shall give chase to ten thousand; your enemies shall fall before you by the sword." Reich, *Tales of Alexander the Macedonian*, 112-13, with Lev. 26:8. I thank Dudu Rotman for this reference. Additional examples are listed in Zfatman, "Iggrot be-yidish," 248-49n19. See also Chapter 3, 91.
62. Thompson, *Motif-Index of Folk-Literature*, L311. Cf. the types of folktales in ATU 327, 328. Cf. also the motif of unlikely heroes; Thompson, *Motif-Index of Folk-Literature*, L100-199. Among others, it could be an elderly man (L101.1) or a hero of unpromising appearance (L112), e.g., a very small hero (L112.2), a physically impaired (L112.3) or lame child (L112.8). Related motifs include help from a little man (N821), an old man (N825.2), and a child (N827). The attributes of the little Red Jew are remarkably similar to the descriptions of dwarfs in international, especially German, folklore. Beyond being described as very small (F451.2.1.1), parallels between Yiddish descriptions of the Red Jew and international folkloric portrayals of dwarfs are reflected in Thompson, *Motif-Index of Folk-Literature*, who describes dwarfs

as: wearing a red coat (F451.2.7.5); with a wrinkled face (F451.2.5.1); magicians (capable of flying through air, among other feats, F451.3.3); and, helpful, e.g., in performing tasks (F451.5.1).

63. 1 Sam. 17. On associated midrashic intepretations, see Noy, "Motif-Index."

64. References are according to the editio princeps of *Shmuel-Bukh* (Augsburg, 1544), facsimile edition by Falk and Fuks, *Schemuelbuch*; excerpts in Frakes, *Early Yiddish Texts*, 221, st. 327, p. 223, st. 339, p. 225, st. 360, p. 227, st. 370. English translation in Frakes, *Early Yiddish Epic*, 42, st. 327, 339, p. 44, st. 360, p. 45, st. 370. The phrasing regarding David's petite stature in *Ma'aseh Akdamut*: Ms. Opp. 714, fols. 27v–29v; Fürth 1694, fols. 4v–5v; Rivkind, "Historical Allegory," 21–25.

65. Falk and Fuks, *Schemuelbuch*, fol. 62v, st. 1091–97; English translation in Frakes, *Early Yiddish Epic*, 96–97, st. 1091–97. Cf. 2 Sam. 21:18–22. See Cohen Roman, "Chivalric Scenes," 16–17.

66. For a more detailed presentation of the motifs that this Yiddish story shares with the biblical account, whether explicitly or subtly, see Voß, "Entangled Stories," 23–26.

67. In the absence of a modern critical edition, see the often inaccurately transliterated texts (without the original in Hebrew lettering) in Landau, *Arthurian Legends*. A similarly problematic edition of the Cambridge manuscript is included in Linn, "Widwilt." Unless noted otherwise, I cite the English translation by Jerold Frakes, based on the Cambridge manuscript; Frakes, *Early Yiddish Epic*, 181–237. On the comparison between the German and Yiddish versions, see Linn, "Widwilt"; Dreeßen, "Zur Rezeption"; Dreeßen, "Wigalois—Widuwilt"; Jaeger, *Jüdischer Artusritter*; Lembke, "Ritter außer Gefecht."

68. For the Yiddish, see Frakes, *Early Yiddish Epic*, 200. For the German, see von Grafenberg, *Wigalois*, 42. Cf. 1 Sam. 17:24–32. Astrid Lembke has pointed me to another possible model for this scene in European courtly literature, the old French *Bel inconnu* (The fair unknown); Renaut de Bâgé, *Le Bel Inconnu*, st. 199–240. Susanne Knaeble, in contrast, reads this scene in *Viduvilt* as an ironic interpretation of the Christian Arthurian romance from a Jewish perspective; Knaeble, "Ironische Distanzierung," 98–101.

69. Frakes, *Early Yiddish Epic*, 200; von Grafenberg, *Wigalois*, 43–44. Cf. 1 Sam. 17:38–39.

70. Frakes, *Early Yiddish Epic*, 201; von Grafenberg, *Wigalois*, 44.

71. For advice that the hero abstain from fighting, see Frakes, *Early Yiddish Epic*, 205–6, 209–12, 230; Dreeßen, "Goliaths Schwestern und Brüder," 369–73.

72. Frakes, *Early Yiddish Epic*, 201, 207. Cf. the German version, which lacks metaphors for children: von Grafenberg, *Wigalois*, 45, 68.

73. ננון בישטו איין קינד אונ הושט נויליך גיזוגן; Frakes, *Early Yiddish Epic*, 225, st. 358. For another story about the Red Jews that picks up the motif of a child hero, see Chapter 3.

74. Frakes, *Early Yiddish Epic*, 206, 210. A similar motif is found in the German version: "Ein falscher Augenschein führt die Menschen oft ins Unglück" (a misinterpreted appearance often leads to disaster); von Grafenberg, *Wigalois*, 144.

75. Brenner, *Colour Terms*, 62. Cf. Meerson, "Physiognomy and Somatomancy," 581–82; Popović, *Reading the Human Body*, 277–78. On the Esau/Edom Jacob/Israel typology and its link to the etymology of the German term "Rote Juden," see Chapter 1, 31–33.

76. 1 Sam. 17:42. Cf. 1 Sam. 16:12: "He was ruddy-cheeked, bright-eyed, and handsome."

77. Early modern Yiddish Bible translations sometimes render the term *admoni* with different synonyms for "red" or "ruddy." E.g., רוט (Esau) in Adam, *Ḥamishah ḥumshei torah*; רויך (Esau) in Leb Bresch, *Ḥamishah ḥumshei torah*; ha-Kohen, *Ḥamishah ḥumshei torah*; ריטליך

(Esau) in *Magishei minḥah*; רויט and איין רוטר (David) in Ashkenazi, *Sefer ha-magid*; רוט (Esau), רוטליך (David) in Witzenhausen, *Torah nevi'im u-ketuvim*; ריטליך (Esau); רוטאקטיג in Blitz, *Ḥamishah ḥumshei torah*. The modern standard Yiddish translation of the Bible by Yehoyesh renders "א רויטער" for Esau and "גערויטלט" for David; Yehoyesh, *Torah nevi'im u-ketuvim*.

78. Genesis Rabbah 63:8 (ed. Theodor/Albeck 688). Cf. *Sefer Ḥasidim*: David may kill but he only battles against other nations; Wistinetzki and Freimann, *Buch der Frommen*, §175.

79. Another source that links David to deceit occurs in *Yalkut Mekhiri*: When David was conceived, his father, Yishai, mistakenly thought that he had had intercourse with a beautiful maidservant whom he desired. Due to this burning lust that was as hot as a flame, it is said that his wife gave birth to an infant that was completely red; *Yalkut Mekhiri* on Ps. 118:28 (ed. Buber 214). Cf. Ginzberg, *Legends of the Jews*, 2:911 with note 11.

80. See Rashi on Gen. 25:25 and additional medieval interpretations of Esau's redness in Chapter 1, 32–33. Accordingly, the Yiddish commentary in the eighteenth-century edition of the Bible with Rashi, *Magishei minḥah*, states: דז איז איין ביטייטונג דז ער ווערט איין בלוט פאר גיסר זיין. References to a red murderer are also found in the Zohar; Matt, *Zohar*, 4:418 (2:78a); and in some versions of the *Physiognomy of R. Yishmael*; Scholem, "Fragment zur Physiognomik," 192n102 (§33). On the other hand, the latter work states that everyone who has a red face is worthy of a crown or, at least, of eating with kings; Scholem, "Fragment zur Physiognomik," 184, §18.

81. Rashi on Song of Sol. 5:10 and Lam. 4:7. Cf. Gersonides and Joseph Karo on Song of Sol. 5:10. Rashi, like most other commentators, does not remark on *admoni* in Samuel.

82. David Kimḥi on 1 Sam. 17:42. Similarly, Joseph Kaspi. With regard to Esau, Kimḥi explains that most newborns have very red skin; Kimḥi on Gen. 25:25.

83. Leb Bresch, *Ḥamishah ḥumshei torah*. On this earliest comprehensive Yiddish translation of Rashi's Pentateuch commentary by Judah b. Moses Naphtali (better known as Leb Bresch), which was reprinted several times through the early seventeenth century, see Fram, "Preliminary Observations."

84. See Introduction, 4. For discussions of beauty in Old Yiddish literature, see Chapter 3. For Jewish physiognomic consciousness, see also descriptions of beauty and ugliness in apocryphal literature and the Qumran scrolls; Popović, *Reading the Human Body*, 286, 288; Popović, "4Q186," 247.

85. Zsengellér, "Judith as Female David," 200–204. Admittedly, isolated examples point to folkloric traditions (that follow the vulgate translation), which associate all of these figures with red hair; Mellinkoff, "Judas's Red Hair," 35. Cf. several descriptions of David having auburn hair in Steger, *David, rex et propheta*. On red hair as a sign of Jewishness, see Chapter 1, 28

86. JT Hagigah 2:3.

87. Avrahami, *Senses of Scripture*; Neis, *Sense of Sight*; Boyarin, "Eye in the Torah."

88. On the scholastic discourse on optics within debates about human cognition, see Tachau, *Vision and Certitude*; Denery, *Seeing and Being Seen*. On sensory illusion in writings of the medieval *Ḥasidei Ashkenaz*, see Shyovitz, *Remembrance of His Wonders*, chap. 4. See also Introduction, 15.

89. For anatomy, see, e.g., Kemp, "Vision and Visualisation"; Stolberg, "A Woman Down to Her Bones." For empiricist approaches to ethnography, see Chapter 1.

90. Ruderman, *Jewish Thought*. J. H. Chajes shows that kabbalistic illustrations of the cosmos relied on both anatomical rhetoric and astronomical conventions; Chajes, "Kabbalah and the Diagrammatic Phase."

91. Ruderman, *Jewish Thought*, 211.

92. Chajes, "Re-Envisioning the Evil Eye."

93. E.g., for Simone Luzzato's discussions of optical theory, see Ruderman, *Jewish Thought*, 164–65, 167, 175, 190. Cf. Clark, *Vanities of the Eye*, 22.

94. See Clark, *Vanities of the Eye*, chaps. 3–4.

95. Ms. Opp. 714, fol. 22r–v; Rivkind, "Historical Allegory," 13.

96. Chajes, "Magic, Mysticism, and Popular Belief"; Chajes, "Rabbis and Their (In) Famous Magic"; Idel, "On Judaism, Jewish Mysticism and Magic." The survey by Joshua Trachtenberg still merits consultation; Trachtenberg, *Jewish Magic and Superstition*. On the ineffable name as a magical device, see Trachtenberg, *Jewish Magic and Superstition*, 78–103.

97. On attraction to and rejection of magic, see Chajes, "'Too Holy to Print.'" During the seventeenth and eighteenth centuries, magic began to lose credibility due to its supernatural basis, a process that continued well into the nineteenth century; Henry, "Fragmentation of Renaissance Occultism"; Chajes, "Entzauberung and Jewish Modernity." Cf. also Clark, *Thinking with Demons*.

98. Ms. Opp. 714, fol. 22r–v; Rivkind, "Historical Allegory," 13.

99. Chajes, "'Too Holy to Print,'" 250; Chajes, "Magic, Mysticism, and Popular Belief," 476–77.

100. Yaniv, "Ḥevra utopit," 281–82.

101. Cf. Chajes, "Entzauberung and Jewish Modernity," 193–94.

102. Fürth edition, fol. 2r; Rivkind, "Historical Allegory," 13. On this translation, see Chapter 4.

103. Ms. Opp. 714, fol. 23r; Fürth edition, fol. 2r; Rivkind, "Historical Allegory," 13–14.

104. See Chapter 1, 40.

105. Ms. Opp. 714, fol. 31r; Rivkind, "Historical Allegory," 27.

106. On the polarized allegations of Jewish carnality versus Christian allegory and morality, see Abulafia, "Bodies in the Jewish-Christian Debate."

107. Ms. Opp. 714, fol. 27r; Rivkind, "Historical Allegory," 21. On the Antichrist being from the tribe of Dan, see Hill, "Antichrist"; Bousset, *Antichrist Legend*, 26, 171–74; Emmerson, *Antichrist in the Middle Ages*, 79–80; Jenks, *Origins and Early Development*, 77–79, 83–86, 183–84.

108. Dan, *Hebrew Story*, 55–57. See also Bin Gorion, *Born Judas*, vol. 2, no. 112, pp. 244–47.

109. Genesis Rabbah 97 (*shitah ḥadashah*) (ed. Theodor/Albeck 1218).

110. Bousset, *Antichrist Legend*, 175–83.

111. On equating the Antichrist with the Jewish Messiah, see Chapter 1, 23.

112. Von Keller, *Fastnachtspiele*, 1:169–90, no. 20; 2:593–608, no. 68. On these plays, see Ragotzky, "Fastnacht und Endzeit." For Folz's sharp anti-Jewish rhetoric, see Wenzel, "Judenproblematik."

113. Schreckenberg, *Adversus-Judaeos-Texte*, 2:603–4; Schreckenberg, *Juden in der mittelalterlichen Kunst*, 254, fig. 10.

114. On *Toldot Yeshu* as a classic counterhistory, Biale, "Counter-History."

115. The most recent studies of *Toldot Yeshu* are the collected volumes Schäfer, Meerson, and Deutsch, *Toledot Yeshu Revisited*; Barbu and Deutsch, *Toledot Yeshu in Context*. Editions and English translations of multiple Hebrew and Aramaic manuscripts in Meerson and Schäfer, *Toledot Yeshu*. These and additional texts are also accessible through an accompanying online database.

116. On *Toldot Yeshu* as a polemical *volksbuch* (folk book), see Yassif, "'Toledot Yeshu.'"

117. A partial list of the known Yiddish manuscripts appears in Meerson and Schäfer, *Toledot Yeshu*, 2:42–44. Preliminary studies of the Yiddish tradition, which had previously been almost completely neglected, are provided by Michels, "Yiddish *Toledot Yeshu* Manuscripts"; Rosenzweig, "When Jesus Spoke Yiddish"; Rosenzweig, "History of Jesus' Life"; Stanislawski, "Yiddish 'Life of Jesus.'" For the reception of *Toldot Yeshu* in Ashkenaz, see Carlebach, *Anti-Christian Element*, 13; Barbu and Dahhaoui, "Secret Booklet." Unless noted otherwise, I quote both a Yiddish manuscript, probably from the late seventeenth century, that is held at the Bodleian Library, Oxford, Ms. Rawl. Or. 37 (IMHM F 22740, Neubauer 2793), and the English translation of the Hebrew manuscript Ashkenazi A in Meerson and Schäfer, *Toledot Yeshu*, 1:167–84 (English), 2:79–95 (Hebrew). A German transliteration of the Yiddish text was published by Bischoff, *Jüdisch-Deutsches Leben Jesu*. For an edition of the Yiddish original, accompanied by an English translation, see Voß, "Sense of Sight."

118. Ms. Rawl. Or. 37, fol. 13r–v; Meerson and Schäfer, *Toledot Yeshu*, 1:170–74. Another manuscript, Ashkenazi B, likens lifting a millstone to the ease of picking apples; Meerson and Schäfer, *Toledot Yeshu*, 1:193.

119. Cf. 1 Sam. 17:50: David also confronted Goliath in the name of God.

120. Ms. Opp. 714, fol. 32r; Rivkind, "Historical Allegory," 29.

121. Cf. a type of international folktale where a millstone becomes a lethal weapon, by encircling the neck of someone who then drowns or by decapitating a character's head that was caught in its hole; ATU 1117, 1147. In *Toldot Yeshu*, Yeshu casts a millstone into the sea but, rather than sinking, it miraculously floats.

122. Ms. Opp. 714, fols. 29r–30r; Rivkind, "Historical Allegory," 25.

123. Ms. Opp. 714, fols. 30v–31r; Rivkind, "Historical Allegory," 27.

124. Yassif, "Toledot Yeshu," 125. See also pp. 121, 124. Cf. Deut. 13 for the warning against following false prophets who perform miracles.

125. Harari, "Ancient Israel and Early Judaism," 156. See also Alexander, "Talmudic Concept of Conjuring"; Veltri, *Magie und Halakha*, 53–65.

126. Ms. Opp. 714, fol. 31r; Rivkind, "Historical Allegory," 27.

127. Ms. Rawl. Or. 37, fol. 12r; Meerson and Schäfer, *Toledot Yeshu*, 1:173–74. In our Yiddish version, as in several other texts, Judah the Gardener replaces Judas Iscariot at a certain point; see Schäfer, "Agobard's and Amulo's Toledot Yeshu," 35.

128. Limor and Yuval, "Judas Iscariot," esp. 200–208.

129. Ms. Rawl. Or. 37, fol. 22r–v.

130. See Clark, *Vanities of the Eye*, 28–30.

131. See Clark, *Vanities of the Eye*, 178–82.

132. For warnings in Hebrew manuscripts that instructed readers to treat their sensitive contents with caution, see Deutsch, "Second Life of the Life of Jesus," 283–84. Such covert traditions, which circulated among members of a repressed group, have been referred to as "hidden transcripts"; Scott, *Hidden Transcripts*.

133. Milano and Francesconi, "Cremona"; Benayahu, *Hebrew Printing at Cremona*, 89–104.

134. Chapter 1, 32.

135. Thompson, *Motif-Index of Folk-Literature*, D1711.1.2; Noy, "Motif-Index," D1711.

136. 2 Sam. 8:14.

137. *Lekaḥ tov* 36:21–22 (ed. Buber 185) with a quote from 1 Sam. 16:12, near the end of the commentary on *Parashat va-Yishlaḥ*. This midrash identifies the Messiah, son of David, as the red avenger.

138. Genesis Rabbah 75:4 (ed. Theodor/Albeck 882).

139. BT Baba Batra 123b, cf. Genesis Rabbah 73:7 (ed. Theodor/Albeck 851). See Lazar, *Ḥidot*, 80.

140. From the critical English translation of *Tsene Rene* by Morris Faierstein, based on the edition Amsterdam 1711; Faierstein, *Ze'enah u-Re'enah*, 961.

141. Ms. Opp. 714, fol. 26r; Rivkind, "Historical Allegory," 19, quoting Obad. 1:21.

142. Elbogen, *Jewish Liturgy*, s.v. "Song of the Sea."

143. In Christian texts and images, the devil is often depicted with a limp, a physical feature that became an anti-Jewish stereotype; Jütte, *Leib und Leben*, 314–15.

144. Gen. 32:25–32.

145. Dauber, *In the Demon's Bedroom*, 2–3, 23–24.

146. On Yiddish adaptations of Christian literature, including folktales, chapbooks, and courtly literature, see Paucker, "Yiddish Versions." Among more recent works, see, e.g., the collection of articles in *Aschkenas* 25, no. 1 (2015), introduction by Lembke, "Aventiuren in Aschkenas"; von Bernuth, *How the Wise Men Got to Chelm*; Idelson-Shein, "Meditations on a Monkey-Face"; Rosenzweig, *Bovo d'Antona*; Timm, *Paris un Wiene*.

147. E.g., Baumgarten, *Practicing Piety in Medieval Ashkenaz*; Berger, "Mission to the Jews"; Carlebach, *Palaces of Time*; Idelson-Shein, "Rabbis of the (Scientific) Revolution"; Jütte, "Interfaith Encounters"; Kahana, "Sefer Meirav"; Marcus, *Rituals of Childhood*; Yuval, *Two Nations in Your Womb*.

148. Kramer, *Vnderredung vom glawben*, fols. 5v–6r. On the pamphlets that this debate references, see Chapter 1, 36, 43.

149. Gow, *Red Jews*, 88–89.

150. Yiddish speakers in modern-day Eastern Europe indeed regarded redheads as clever, as per the proverb "אַ געלער מאַכט ניט קיין פּעהלער" (A redhead does not make a mistake); Bernstein, *Jüdische Sprichwörter*, 62.

151. Bhabha, *Location of Culture*, 86.

152. Cf. Wolfthal, *Picturing Yiddish*, chap. 7, esp. 147, 149–50, 152. For additional examples of imagined Jewish violence against Christians, see, among others, Wolfthal, "Remembering Amalek." On fantasies of violence, see also Chapter 3, 97.

153. Carlebach, *Anti-Christian Element*, 18–19. For other examples of anti-Christian messages in Old Yiddish literature, see, e.g., Paucker, "Yiddish Versions," 162–63; von Bernuth, "Jischev fun Nar-Husen," 138.

154. Cf. Keil, "Kulturtransfer, Polemik und Humor," 114.

155. See generally Carlebach, *Anti-Christian Element*; Stow, "Medieval Jews on Christianity."

156. Keil, "Kulturtransfer, Polemik und Humor," 114–15. On the social functions of humor, see Auffarth and Kehrt, *Glaubensstreit und Gelächter*; Berger, *Redeeming Laughter*; Billig, *Laughter and Ridicule*; Classen, *Laughter in the Middle Ages and Early Modern Times*; Röcke and Velten, *Lachgemeinschaften*.

157. John Sewell has shown how *Sefer Niẓẓaḥon Yashan* and *Toldot Yeshu* use ridicule and embarrassment as tools for enforcing Jewish societal discipline in response to external pressure; Sewell, "The Son Rebelled." On *Toldot Yeshu*, see also Kattan Gribetz, "Hanged and Crucified," 168n28.

158. Editions of two versions of this tale, which was not included in any of the printed editions of the *Mayse Bukh*, appear in Timm, "Abraham ibn Ezra und das Maiśebuch."

159. Ms. Opp. 714, fols. 23v–24r; Rivkind, "Historical Allegory," 15.

160. Clark, *Vanities of the Eye*, 12–13.
161. Ms. Opp. 714, fol. 33r; Rivkind, "Historical Allegory," 31.
162. The concept of the "noble savage" became increasingly influential in seventeenth- and eighteenth-century Enlightenment writing. White, "Forms of Wildness"; Ellingson, *Myth of the Noble Savage*.
163. See the insightful discussion of eighteenth-century sources on "noble" versus "ignoble savages" in Idelson-Shein, *Difference of a Different Kind*, 95, 99, 101, 103.
164. According to the edition Amsterdam 1704; Bodleian Library, Oxford, Opp. 8° 1112. Cf. the other titles, Chapter 4, note 4.

CHAPTER 3

1. For the Ten Tribes in the Jewish imagination, see the surveys listed in Chapter 1, note 4.
2. Augusti, *Geheimnisse der Jüden*, 15–16.
3. Ms. Opp. 714, fols. 53v–54r, edited in Zfatman, "Iggrot be-yidish," 246. This text is analyzed in detail below.
4. Vulpius, "Wunder-Fluß Sambathjon," 534. This source is cited in Gow, *Red Jews*, 186.
5. On the guiding principles for the selection and presentation of the Yiddish literary corpus, see Turniansky, "Transmission of Knowledge," 10–11. For folklore in general, Yassif, "The Body Never Lies," 203.
6. The collection is often referred to as *Ma'aseh Beit David*, the name of a story about the Persian exilarch Bustenai that precedes the Ten Tribes' material. On *Kol Mevaser*, see Yaari, *Meḥkerei sefer*, 236–42.
7. Zfatman, "Iggrot be-yidish," 220n10; Baumgarten, *Introduction*, 149–52; Frakes, *Early Yiddish Texts*, 218.
8. Akrish, *Ma'asiyot ve-sippurim*, fol. 1r; Bodleian Library, Oxford, Opp. 8° 1103 (3). *Kol Mevaser* begins on fol. 5r, with the account by Moses Ashkenazi from fol. 6r onward. Mirjam Gutschow dates this print edition to the seventeenth or eighteenth century; Gutschow, *Inventory*, no. 34.
9. On Christian views, see Chapter 1, 46–47.
10. On Drucker and his cosmography, see Shmeruk and Bartal, "Tela'ot Moshe"; Pach, "Moushe's Choices"; Heller, "Moses Ben Abraham Avinu"; Sadowski, "Hebräischer Buchdruck." On Farissol's *Iggeret*, see Ruderman, *World of a Renaissance Jew*, chap. 11.
11. Drucker, *Tela'ot Mosheh*, fol. 3r; Bodleian Library, Oxford, Opp. 8° 1145. On the Ten Tribes in the Caucasus Mountains in Christian sources, see Chapter 1, 36. For contemporaneous Jewish perception, cf. von Carben, *Hier inne wirt gelesen*, fol. D4v.
12. See, e.g., Bertius, *Geographischer eyn oder zusammengezogener Tabeln*, 592. Augusti likewise describes the churning sand that flows in the Sambatyon; Augusti, *Geheimnisse der Jüden*, 18.
13. Drucker, *Tela'ot Mosheh*, chap. 4 (on the Ten Tribes), fols. 3v–6v, and chap. 6 (on the Red Sea), fol. 7v. Cf. Farissol, *Iggeret*, chap. 14 (on the Ten Tribes in Chabor, by the Red Sea), and chap. 24, esp. fols. 26v–28r (on the Red Sea and on the Jews of islands in India). With regard to the Island of the Samaritans, Drucker cites Bertius, *Geographischer eyn oder zusammengezogener Tabeln*, 593. He incorrectly refers to the Latin edition of "Berzius," bk. 3, p. 550. This reference to the Latin passage is accurate, but the Island of the Samaritans is only mentioned in the extended German version.

14. "Kommen wir ins Rot Mör zuschiffen, müssen wir kein Eisennägel in die Schiff geschlagen haben, die Diaimanten ziehen uns sonst zu sich: sonder müssen da von den roten Juden das Schiffschneiderhandwerck lehrnen, die Schiff mit Seylern von Palmen zusamen zubinden und zunähen." Fischart, *Geschichtsklitterung*, 325. Cf. Drucker, *Tela'ot Mosheh*, fol. 5v; Farissol, *Iggeret*, chap. 24.

15. Akrish, *Ma'asiyot ve-sippurim*, fols. 6v, 7v (Bodleian Library, Oxford, Opp. 8° 1103 (3)). The *Mayse Bukh* includes a parallel, where a carbuncle serves as a lamp in Rabbi Hanina's bedroom. All references to the *Mayse Bukh* are from the facsimile edition; Starck, *Un beau livre d'histoires*, no. 163, p. 431 (fol. 103v). English translations (sometimes with different numbering) are found in Gaster, *Ma'aseh Book*.

16. Akrish, *Ma'asiyot ve-sippurim*, fols. 6v–7v. The motif of marauding Jewish tribes also appears in Eldad and Benjamin of Tudela; Epstein, "Eldad ha-Dani," 38, 53 (Hebrew pagination); Adler, *Jewish Travellers*, 12, 16; Adler, *Benjamin of Tudela*, 47–48.

17. Akrish, *Ma'asiyot ve-sippurim*, fol. 7r.

18. The Latin and German versions of Prester John's letter are edited in Zarncke, *Priester Johannes*; Wagner, *Epistola presbiteri Johannis*. For its Hebrew translations, see Ullendorf and Beckingham, *Hebrew Letters of Prester John*. Several early modern printings in Hebrew, including the editio princeps from Constantinople 1519, are listed in Steinschneider, *Catalogus librorum Hebraeorum*, nos. 3596, 1369. The textual relationship between the Prester John and Eldad traditions is discussed by Perry, "Imaginary War."

19. Akrish, *Ma'asiyot ve-sippurim*, fol. 5r.

20. Akrish, *Ma'asiyot ve-sippurim*, fol. 7r–v.

21. A critical edition based on the original, Amsterdam 1723, is Yidls, *Gelilot erez Yisra'el*, 88. Zfatman, "Iggrot be-yidish," 221n14, has noted that this description of the Ten Tribes is entirely derived from Akrish. On this work as a whole, see Berger, "Diasporic Reading"; Aderet, "Itineraries in Yiddish," chap. 1.

22. Yidls, *Gelilot erez Yisra'el*, 84. Christian accounts claim that Prester John took numerous measures to prevent the Ten Tribes from escaping from their land; Perry, "Imaginary War," 12.

23. Yidls, *Gelilot erez Yisra'el*, 88. These passages seemingly prompted Jesuits in Warsaw to burn *Gelilot Erez Yisra'el*; Berger, "Diasporic Reading," 286.

24. Yidls, *Gelilot erez Yisra'el*, 84, 87. Cf. Akrish, *Ma'asiyot ve-sippurim*, fol. 7v. Eldad boasts about the wealth of these tribes, claiming that his own tribe lives "where there is gold," referring to the biblical land of Havilah (Gen. 2:11); Epstein, "Eldad ha-Dani," 38, 53 (Hebrew pagination); Adler, *Jewish Travellers*, 11, 15.

25. Moses Ashkenazi reports what a Muslim slave, who had frequently been taken on business trips to the Red Jews by his Christian master, told him in 1483; Akrish, *Ma'asiyot ve-sippurim*, fol. 6r–v.

26. This version of the story of the Red Jews is preserved in the same manuscript, which includes *Ma'aseh Akdamut* analyzed in Chapter 2; Ms. Opp. 714, fols. 41r–54r; and one print edition (Prague 1660s), *Tsvay maysim*, fols. 10r–19v (Bodleian Library, Oxford, Opp. 8° 1058 (4)). Vinograd, *Thesaurus*, 276, dates the latter to circa 1650. Cf. Zfatman, *Bibliography*, 20, no. 8.5 (Hebrew numbers), 48–49, no. 29b; Steinschneider, *Catalogus librorum Hebraeorum*, no. 3926; Cowley, *Catalogue of the Hebrew Printed Books*, 405; Neubauer, *Catalogue of the Hebrew Manuscripts*, vol. 1, no. 2213,9; Steinschneider, "Jüdisch-Deutsche Literatur," 25, no. 5: 67, no. 410, IX. Synoptic editions of both versions in Zfatman, "Iggrot be-yidish," 228–

47. Unless noted otherwise, all quotations follow the manuscript version. On this story, see also Zfatman, "Yiddish Narrative Prose," 1:207–12.

27. On specific data that locate legends in time and space, see Yassif, *Hebrew Folktale*, 319–20; Zfatman, "Yiddish Narrative Prose," 1:201–7.

28. Zfatman, "Iggrot be-yidish," 218n6, 221–25.

29. For early modern Yiddish letters from the land of Israel, see Assaf, "Mikhtavim be-idish."

30. Zfatman, "Iggrot be-yidish," 230 (fol. 42v). Cf. Grimm and Grimm, *Deutsches Wörterbuch*, 14:1310.

31. Zfatman, "Iggrot be-yidish," 230 (fol. 43r); Dapper, *Beschreibung von Africa*, 527–28. On this people, see also Idelson-Shein, *Difference of a Different Kind*, 118, 138.

32. Zfatman, "Iggrot be-yidish," 230 (fol. 43r-v).

33. Frakes, *Emergence of Early Yiddish Literature*, 100, cf. 87.

34. Zfatman, "Iggrot be-yidish," 232 (fol. 44v). The printing has לשון הקודש, the holy tongue, i.e., Hebrew; Zfatman, "Iggrot be-yidish," 233 (fol. 12v).

35. The Yiddish mistranslates רבבה (ten thousand) as "two thousand" in both the manuscript and printed version; Zfatman, "Iggrot be-yidish," 233 (fol. 12v), 234 (fol. 45r).

36. Zfatman, "Iggrot be-yidish," 232–36 (fols. 44r–46v).

37. This motif is paralleled in some Hebrew versions of Prester John's letter, which mention the nearby land of the Pygmies, whose adult populace is reported to be the height of seven- or eight-year-old children; Neubauer, "Collections," 12.

38. Zfatman, "Iggrot be-yidish," 236–42 (fols. 46v–50v).

39. Zfatman, "Iggrot be-yidish," 242 (fol. 51r).

40. Zfatman, "Iggrot be-yidish," 244 (fol. 51v), cf. 242 (fol. 51r).

41. Augusti, *Geheimnisse der Jüden*, 28–29n2.

42. Von Carben, *Hier inne wirt gelesen*, fol. D5v. Cf. Margaritha, *Gantz Jüdisch glaub*, fol. br.

43. Von Carben, *Hier inne wirt gelesen*, fols. D5v–D6r.

44. Daniel Stein-Kokin notes that the earliest explicit reference to a halakhic prohibition against crossing the still river on the Sabbath appears in the fifteenth century; Stein-Kokin, "Toward the Source of the Sambatyon," 2n2. Some texts attribute the tribes' inability to leave their dwelling place to additional barriers that were insurmountable at all times. Several Jewish sources describe them as natural wonders, such as fire, clouds, or mountains smooth as glass, wild animals, and fences constructed by Alexander; Stein-Kokin, "Toward the Source of the Sambatyon," 1–2; Zfatman, "Iggrot be-yidish," 236, nos. 36–40. In the Eldad narrative, only the Sons of Moses are actually enclosed beyond the Sambatyon, not yet the Ten Tribes; Perry, "Imaginary War," 10–13.

45. Ms. Opp. 714, fol. 26r-v; Rivkind, "Historical Allegory," 19.

46. Ms. Opp. 714, fol. 27r; Rivkind, "Historical Allegory," 21.

47. Zfatman, "Iggrot be-yidish," 246 (fol. 53v).

48. Akrish, *Ma'asiyot ve-sippurim*, fol. 8r. Also Yidls, *Gelilot erez Yisra'el*, 89.

49. See Schreiner, "Isaiah 53."

50. Zfatman, "Iggrot be-yidish," 246 (fol. 53r).

51. Ms. Opp. 714, fol. 26r-v; Rivkind, "Historical Allegory," 19.

52. *Tsvay maysim*, fol. 1r.

53. Ms. Opp. 714, fols. 23v–24r; Rivkind, "Historical Allegory," 15.

54. Zfatman, "Iggrot be-yidish," 234 (fol. 46r).

55. Zfatman, "Iggrot be-yidish," 236 (fol. 46v), 238 (fol. 48r–v). The printed version does not contain the first attempt to repent in Prester John's realm; Zfatman, "Iggrot be-yidish," 237 (fol. 14r).

56. Zfatman, "Iggrot be-yidish," 238 (fol. 48v).

57. Schipper, *Disability and Isaiah's Suffering Servant*.

58. Quoted according to Wilke, "From Deicide to Diaspora," 156. For premodern Christian imagery of the fearful Jewish man, see also Horowitz, "'Dangerous Encounter'"; Horowitz, *Reckless Rites*, chap. 7.

59. Akrish, *Ma'asiyot ve-sippurim*, fol. 5v.

60. Quoted in Horowitz, "'Dangerous Encounter,'" 347–48. For an additional example, see Resnick, *Marks of Distinction*, 49.

61. Boyarin, *Unheroic Conduct*. For the complexity of Jewish male norms and behaviors in the modern period, see the contributions in Baader, Gillerman, and Lerner, *Jewish Masculinities*.

62. Boyarin, "Masada or Yavneh." Contrary to the widespread perception that Jewish men are physically passive, throughout history Jews carried weaponry and defended themselves, both verbally and physically. For an insightful article on confrontational conduct and acts of physical aggression alongside the more conventional Jewish ideal of the pious Talmud scholar in early modern Ashkenaz, see Gotzmann, "Respectability Tested." For Jews and arms, see the special issue of *Aschkenas* 13, no. 1 (2003), and here, especially for early modernity, Litt, "Juden und Waffen"; Silber, "From Tolerated Aliens to Citizen-Soldiers."

63. See Chapter 2, 80.

64. Yuval, *Two Nations in Your Womb*; Horowitz, *Reckless Rites*. See also Rosenberg, *Legacy of Rage*.

65. Rosenzweig, *Bovo d'Antona*; von Bernuth, "Zwischen Kreuzrittern und Sarazenen." On Viduvilt, see Chapter 2, 64–65. Both Erika Timm and Claudia Rosenzweig have argued that, relative to European or Hebrew sources, the depictions of violence and cruelty were less severe in various Yiddish works written for entertainment; Timm, "Bovobuch," esp. 72; Rosenzweig, *Bovo d'Antona*, 87–92; Rosenzweig, "When Jesus Spoke Yiddish," 213. On anti-Christian curses, see Deutsch, "Anti-Christian Invectives."

66. Frakes, *Early Yiddish Epic*, 203, 221–24, 228–29, 231. See Lembke, "Ritter außer Gefecht," 75–78.

67. BT Sotah 9b, Leviticus Rabbah 8 (ed. Margaliot, 1:164–72). A connection between Samson and the Ten Tribes can be traced to the Eldad tradition, which identifies their strongest men as descendants of Samson; Epstein, "Eldad ha-Dani," 38 (Hebrew pagination); Adler, *Jewish Travellers*, 16.

68. On the continuance of these interpretations, see Horowitz, *Reckless Rites*, 209–10. See my discussion of the complex perspectives on the relationship between the Red Jews and Edom that appear in Christian sources (Chapter 1, 32–33) and Jewish polemics (Chapter 2, 76–77). For David, see Chapter 2, 64–66.

69. Resnick, *Marks of Distinction*, 50. Cf. Smith, "Saints in Shining Armor"; Rosenwein, "Feudal War and Monastic Peace."

70. Yuspa Shammes, *Mayse nissim*, fol. 17r–v, no. 10. Less than reliable translations are provided in Hebrew and English by Eidelberg, *Juspa*, 74–76 (Hebrew), 76–78 (English).

71. Idelson-Shein, "Kill the Hen That Crows Like a Cock." For the earlier interpretation, see Raspe, "Black Death in Jewish Sources," 473–74; Yuval, "'They Tell Lies,'" 87–88.

72. Starck, *Un beau livre d'histoires*, 716–39, no. 227. For an English translation, see Starck-Adler, "Mayse-Bukh and Metamorphosis," available online: http://journals.openedition.org/bcrfj/2092. A nearly identical version of the tale of the werewolf is transmitted in Ms. Opp. 714, fols. 9r–18r. See Meitlis, *Ma'assebuch*, 91–101; Meitlis, "Some Extant Folktales."

73. Lembke, "Raging Rabbi." For a comparison of this Jewish version with an international tale, rendered by Marie de France in the twelfth century in *Bisclavret*, see Lembke, "Das unwillige Untier."

74. Starck, *Un beau livre d'histoires*, 733 (fol. 179r).

75. Starck, *Un beau livre d'histoires*, 733 (fol. 179r), cf. 717 (fol. 175r).

76. Lembke, "Raging Rabbi," 209–10. On the association of Jews with dogs, see Stow, *Jewish Dogs*; Horowitz, "Circumcised Dogs." Jay Geller examines the Jewish self-identification with wolves that appears in another, though modern, Yiddish story; Geller, "'Der Volf.'"

77. Yuval, "'They Tell Lies,'" 87.

78. See Raspe, "Black Death in Jewish Sources," 485–87.

79. Teller, "Kill or Be Killed?" See also Teller, "'To Take Arms Against a Sea of Troubles.'" For an overview of the Chmielnicki uprising, see Raba, *Between Remembrance and Denial*.

80. Quoted in the Hebrew original and the English translation in Teller, "Kill or Be Killed?" 5–7. For a complete English translation of Hannover's chronicle, see Hannover, *Abyss of Despair*.

81. Quoted in Teller, "Kill or Be Killed?" 51 (English), 52 (Hebrew).

82. On Hannover's motivation, see Teller, "Jewish Literary Responses."

83. Voß, *Disputed Messiahs*, 40–42, 170–71; Yuval, *Two Nations in Your Womb*, 275–77. See also Voß, "Messias der Vergeltung"; Voß, "Propter seditionis Hebraicae."

84. Frakes, *Emergence of Early Yiddish Literature*, 97, cf. 94–95, 109.

85. On the printing press as a challenge to rabbinical authority, see Reiner, "Ashkenazi Elite"; Reiner, "Roots of the Urban Jewish Community"; Teplitsky, *Prince of the Press*, 133. Cf. David Ruderman's description of a crisis in the rabbinate in late seventeenth- and eighteenth-century Europe; Ruderman, *Early Modern Jewry*, chap. 4.

86. Shmeruk, *Yiddish Literature*, 9–13; Baumgarten, *Introduction*, 26–37, 58–62, 68; Berger, "Diasporic Third Space," 78. The subject of empowerment through Yiddish writings is discussed extensively in Katz, *Yiddish and Power*, esp. 45–71. For anxieties among the intellectual elite in response to the popularization of knowledge in early modern Yiddish literature, see the discussion in Idelson-Shein, "Meditations on a Monkey-Face," 53–58.

87. Zfatman, "Iggrot be-yidish," 234 (fol. 46r), 242 (fol. 51r–v).

88. Zfatman, "Iggrot be-yidish," 244 (fol. 52r–v).

89. Zfatman, "Iggrot be-yidish," 244, 246 (fols. 52v–53r). Quotation on p. 246 (fol. 53r).

90. Kauders, "What Power for Which Jews?" 558–60.

91. Biale, *Power and Powerlessness*, 7.

92. Lembke, "Ritter außer Gefecht," 81–82.

93. Starck, *Un beau livre d'histoires*, 723 (fol. 176v)–725 (fol. 177r).

94. Lembke, "Raging Rabbi," 208.

95. Zfatman, "Iggrot be-yidish," 243 (fol. 17r).

96. Akrish, *Ma'asiyot ve-sippurim*, fol. 7v. Cf. Yidls, *Gelilot erez Yisra'el*, 88.

97. Zfatman, "Iggrot be-yidish," 246 (fol. 53r–v). In the printed version, the king merely responds: "Dear child, do as you wish"; Zfatman, "Iggrot be-yidish," 247 (fol. 19v).

98. Zfatman, "Iggrot be-yidish," 228, 230 (fol. 42r). Quote on p. 230.

99. Shmeruk, *Illustrations in Yiddish Books*, 42–54.

100. For this common definition of the male Yiddish audience, see Introduction, note 38.

101. Resnick, *Marks of Distinction*, 145–49; Horowitz, "Dangerous Encounter." The effeminate qualities ascribed to Jewish men were also linked to menstruation as a malady that allegedly affected them; Chapter 1, 26.

102. Horowitz, *Reckless Rites*, 209.

103. Cuffel, *Gendering Disgust*, 190.

104. Idelson-Shein, "'What Have I to Do with Wild Animals?'" Cf. the discussion of men being raped in Rabbi Jacob Emden's writing on pp. 63–64. See also Idelson-Shein, *Difference of a Different Kind*, chap. 1.

105. *Ma'aseh Yehudit*, Ms. Opp. 714, fols. 63v–83r. The intertextual links between the tale of Judith and the narrative of David and Goliath are discussed by Zsengellér, "Judith as Female David." Another woman who takes revenge on Amalek appears in a sixteenth-century illuminated Yiddish manuscript; Wolfthal, *Picturing Yiddish*, 150.

106. Zfatman, "Iggrot be-yidish," 242 (fol. 51r-v), 243 (fol. 17r-v). Women are portrayed with similar passivity in *Kol Mevaser*: they are present but less active than their male counterparts. Here, we learn that the palace of King Aaron and his wife is in a city known as *Dam efro'aḥ* (chick's blood). The violent allusion conveyed by this city's name reinforces the Red Jews' aggressive nature, but the queen is only mentioned as an anonymous extra; Akrish, *Ma'asiyot ve-sippurim*, fol. 7v.

107. Bikard, "Šeder Nošim." Chava Weissler posits a negative correlation between the elite standing of a Jewish author and his assessment of women; Weissler, *Voices of the Matriarchs*, 16.

108. Ms. Opp. 714, fol. 27v; Rivkind, "Historical Allegory," 21.

109. See Federica Francesconi for early modern Italy; Francesconi, "Jewish Women in Early Modern Italy." See also Francesconi, *Invisible Enlighteners*. For Christian perspectives, see Chapter 1, 40–41.

110. Carlebach and Kaplan, "Jewish Women in Early Modern Central Europe," 143–44. Cf. Yiddish guides to women's religious obligations from this time that prescribe stricter teachings than their forerunners; Romer-Segal, "Yiddish Works," 47.

111. On misogyny in Jewish medical sources, considered against the backdrop of European discourse, see Idelson-Shein, "Of Wombs and Words." Idelson-Shein, "Monstrous Mame," and Idelson-Shein, "Meditations on a Monkey-Face" study the portrayal of powerful women as monstrous aberrations in Yiddish literature. As expressed through possession by a dybbuk, see Dauber, *In the Demon's Bedroom*, 202–8, with reference to Chajes, *Between Worlds*.

112. Frakes, *Emergence of Early Yiddish Literature*, 118.

113. Ms. Opp. 714, fol. 18r; Starck, *Un beau livre d'histoires*, 739 (fol. 180v).

114. On theoretical background, see the Introduction.

115. Neis, *Sense of Sight*, 213–16. Other pertinent passages include: JT Kiddushin 1:7, 61a, Leviticus Rabbah 20:1 (ed. Margaliot, 2:443–44), BT Sanhedrin 93b, BT Berakhot 63b.

116. Pastoureau, *Red*, 69–73. On red dye, see Greenfield, *A Perfect Red*; Chenciner, *Madder Red*; Padilla and Anderson, *A Red Like No Other*.

117. Jacquesson, "Mots de la couleur," 70.

118. On Jewish-Christian debates over the interpretation of this verse, see Posnanski, *Schiloh*.

119. Joseph, *Gründlicher beweiß*, fol. 21v.

120. Augusti, *Geheimnisse der Jüden*, 27–29.

121. Berliner, *Aus dem inneren Leben*, 36–37. Another oft-cited explanation for restrictions on Jews wearing colorful garments is that such clothing prompted envy among non-Jews; Makover, *Ha-levush ha-yehudi*, 187. For early modern sumptuary laws, see, e.g., Fram, "Sumptuary Laws."

122. Litt, *Jüdische Gemeindestatuten*, 265–66.

123. Moses Isserles on *Shulḥan arukh*, *Yoreh de'ah*, § 178. I thank Gadi Sagiv for this reference.

124. Lauffer, *Farbensymbolik*, 21–22; Peachey, *Dyeing*, 16–18.

125. Quote follows the translation in Lewis, *Jews of Islam*, 135–36. In 1452, for example, the city of Frankfurt legislated that Jewish residents of both genders must wear black overgarments; Hottenroth, *Deutsche Volkstrachten*, 1:130; Hottenroth, *Altfrankfurter Trachten*, 341–42; Andernacht, *Regesten*, 1:981. This requirement was nullified in 1549; Andernacht, *Regesten*, 2:811.

126. Akrish, *Ma'asiyot ve-sippurim*, fol. 6v.

127. Akrish, *Ma'asiyot ve-sippurim*, fol. 8r.

128. On the Rechabite clan (Jer. 35), see Nikolsky, "History of the Rechabites"; Nikolsky, "Rechabites in Ma'aseh Alexandros." On the legendary Sons of Moses, see Ginzberg, *Legends of the Jews*, 2:1088–90; Lazar, "Aseret ha-shvatim"; Lazar, *Ḥidot*, 13–16, 74–77; Rubin, *Between Bible and Qur'an*, 26–30, 46–48, 50–52. Cf. Noy and Ben-Amos, *Folktales of the Jews*, 455–56.

129. Adler, *Benjamin of Tudela*, 48.

130. Benjamin of Tudela, *Masa'ot Binyamin*, fol. 64r–v.

131. Epstein, "Eldad ha-Dani," 55 (Hebrew pagination); Adler, *Jewish Travellers*, 14.

132. The Red Jews are denoted *bnei moshi'im*, e.g., in *Ma'aseh Akdamut*, Ms. Opp. 714, fol. 26r; Rivkind, "Historical Allegory," 19; David, *Hebrew Chronicle*, 27n19.

133. Akrish, *Ma'asiyot ve-sippurim*, fol. 8v. According to an Ashkenazic tradition, the liturgical poem *Shir ha-Yiḥud li-Vnei Mosheh* was composed by the Sons of Moses beyond the Sambatyon; see Voß, *Disputed Messiahs*, 242–43n100. The song appears in several medieval and early modern manuscripts and printings from Germany and northern Italy. In his edition of this poem, Abraham Habermann erroneously classifies it as a seventeenth-century Sephardic composition; Habermann, *Shirei ha-yiḥud*, 131–50.

134. See Chapter 1, 26. On the alleged lack of musicality among Jews, see HaKohen, *Music Libel*.

135. Starck, *Un beau livre d'histoires*, 225 (fol. 56v), no. 102. On Jewish attitudes toward black skin, see Melamed, *Image of the Black*; Goldenberg, *Curse of Ham*; Goldenberg, *Black and Slave*. For Jewish acceptance of white as a color of beauty and attempts to "whiten" themselves, see Melamed, *Image of the Black*, 33; Schorsch, *Jews and Blacks*, 185–87; Idelson-Shein, *Difference of a Different Kind*, 125–26. See also another tale in the *Mayse Bukh* below.

136. Melamed, *Image of the Black*, 33–36; Schorsch, *Jews and Blacks*, 184; Cuffel, *Gendering Disgust*, 188–91.

137. Cited according to a manuscript in the Bodleian Library, Oxford, Ms. Opp. 757 (IMHM F 20981), in Rosenthal, *Sefer Yosef ha-mekaneh*, 95n1. English translation follows Melamed, *Image of the Black*, 37; cf. also 35–37, and Cuffel, *Gendering Disgust*, 191.

138. לימות המשיח נהיה כולנו ניכרים לטובה. See the facsimile edition of the printed edition Altdorf 1644; Talmage, *Sefer Hanizzahon*, §239. The Christian accusation references Isaiah 61:9: "Their offspring shall be known among the nations, their descendants in the midst of the peoples. All who see them shall recognize that they are a stock the Lord has blessed."

139. Joseph b. Nathan Official, *Sefer Yosef ha-mekaneh* (The book of Joseph the Zealot); Rosenthal, *Sefer Yosef ha-mekaneh*, 95; cited also in Melamed, *Image of the Black*, 34; Cuffel, *Gendering Disgust*, 191.

140. Idelson-Shein, "Othering from the Outside," 214–15. Other examples in Cuffel, *Gendering Disgust*, 187–96; Resnick, *Marks of Distinction*, 292–93; Idelson-Shein, *Difference of a Different Kind*, 149.

141. Berger, *Nizzahon Vetus*, 159 (Hebrew), 224 (English), no. 238. This text has received much scholarly treatment, e.g., in Marcus, "Jewish-Christian Symbiosis," 500; Melamed, *Image of the Black*, 37–38; Schorsch, *Jews and Blacks*, 179–80; Cuffel, *Gendering Disgust*, 191–92; Resnick, *Marks of Distinction*, 291–300. This source is indebted to a very similar passage that appears in the abovementioned work by Joseph Official; Rosenthal, *Sefer Yosef ha-mekaneh*, 95. Cf. also the dialogue between a Jew and a Christian about the Messiah, composed by Sebastian Münster and published in Latin and Hebrew in 1539; Münster, *Messias Christianorum et Judaeorum*, fol. A5v.

142. Jacquart and Thomasset, *Sexuality and Medicine*, 73–74; Cuffel, *Gendering Disgust*, 168 with note 68, 192, 194–95. By contrast, Kimḥi attributes the description of Esau as *admoni* in Genesis 25:25 to the reality that newborns tend to have red coloration.

143. Ms. Rawl. Or. 37, fol. 3r; Meerson and Schäfer, *Toledot Yeshu*, 1:168.

144. Bin Gorion, *Born Judas*, 2:250, no. 115.

145. יפה פנים לבן ואדום; Jacob b. Mordecai of Fulda, *Shoshanat Ya'acov*, fol. 8v, cf. fol. 4v. For similar examples of eighteenth- and nineteenth-century human taxonomies in Hebrew, see Idelson-Shein, *Difference of a Different Kind*, 125–26. On European views, see Introduction, 4.

146. Neis, *Sense of Sight*, 202–3.

147. Documented for modern Yiddish, with English quotation in Oișteanu, *Inventing the Jew*, 63; according to Schwarzfeld, "Evreii În Literatura Lor Populară," 36. Oișteanu understands this saying somewhat differently, meaning that a Red Jew can only be championed by one of his kin.

148. Starck, *Un beau livre d'histoires*, no. 102.

149. E.g. Starck, nos. 20 (BT Shabbat 127b), 157, 198, 223, 247 (*Midrash aseret ha-dibrot*, commandment 7,1); Jellinek, *Bet ha-Midrasch*, 1:79–80). Story no. 198 stems from *Meshalim shel Shlomo ha-melekh*; Jellinek, *Bet ha-Midrasch*, 4:150–51. For no. 157, cf. also Riedel, *Brantspigel*, 36.

150. Starck, *Un beau livre d'histoires*, no. 23 (BT Berakhot 5b). See also Starck, *Un beau livre d'histoires*, no. 67 (BT Bava Meẓia 84a).

151. Faierstein, *Ze'enah u-Re'enah*, 216. Cf. Rashi's commentary on Genesis 28:10.

152. Starck, *Un beau livre d'histoires*, no. 133 (BT Berakhot 20a). Cf. also no. 134.

153. Maimonides, *Guide for the Perplexed* 3:45, cited in Bland, *Artless Jew*, 94. Similarly, Israelite kings were required to be well-groomed, keeping their hair and beards neatly trimmed and wearing appropriate attire; Maimonides, *Mishneh torah*, vol. 14, "Laws of Kings," 2:5.

154. שמעו עמים כולם, המשתוממים על החומר והגולם ואינם בוחנים אם יש צורה ונפש בעולם. ראיתי כי אתם תמהים לנפש האדם פרא ואי אתם יודעים בו את הנפש והצורה, שהוא בעל מוסר ותורה והעולה על רוחכם שאין לו חכמה ומוסר, מפני שאינו מלובש כאדון ושר? ובאמת החושב כך מהשכל חסר כ"א [אם כי=] המוסר עם בגדים היפים אין בני מוסר כקופים, המלובשים פעמים בבגדי רקמה - הכי להם החכמה? ואם הפרדים מכוסים בבגדים ופעמוני זהב על צואריהם—הכי משפט הדעת להם? Horowitz, *Amudei beit Yehudah*, fol. 3v. I owe this reference to Iris Idelson-Shein.

155. Bland, *Artless Jew*, 76–78, 81; further examples on pp. 84–88, 149–52. See also Bland, "Medieval Jewish Aesthetics."

156. Resnick, *Marks of Distinction*, 296–300; Idelson-Shein, "Meditations on a Monkey-Face," 38–39; Idelson-Shein, "Othering from the Outside," 211; Bland, *Artless Jew*, 94, 149–51.

157. Berger, *Nizzahon Vetus*, 159 (Hebrew), 224 (English), no. 238.

158. Starck, *Un beau livre d'histoires*, nos. 134, 248. Kirchhan, *Simḥat ha-nefesh*, fol. 49v. Different versions of this story appear in rabbinic literature; see, e.g., Genesis Rabbah 73:10 (ed. Theodor/Albeck 853–55); Numbers Rabbah 9:34 (ed. Mirkin 9:212–13). For non-Jewish literature, see also Melamed, *Image of the Black*, 39, 75.

159. גאט האט דען בן אדם בישאפֿן מיט הולי לעבֿר. און פֿון אויסן ווינציג האט ער אים בישאפֿן דיא לעבֿר פֿון דיא אויגן דז ער זאל דר מיט זעהן. ער האט בישאפֿן דיא אויג בראן דז ער זאל קענין דיא איוגן צו מאבֿלין וועז ער שלאפֿט. און דז ער זאל ניט לוגן ביזה גשילט. וויא (ישעיה הנביא) האט גיזאגט (עוצם עיניו מראות ברע) דז איז טייטש ער שליסט צו זיינע אויגן פֿון צו זעהן אן ביז. Quoted in Baumgarten, "Representation of the Body," 66 (Yiddish), 68 (English). This English translation is my own and differs from Baumgarten's rendering. This passage references Isa. 33:15 and the Tosafist Moses b. Jacob of Coucy.

160. Hergershausen, *Liblikhe tefile*, fol. b2v.

161. I reference the Hebrew-English edition of the first Hebrew printing; Cohen, *Orchot Tzaddikim*, 4–5. Here I cite the Hebrew version because, elsewhere in his volume, Aaron incorporates direct quotations from a Hebrew edition. On *Orḥot Ẓaddikim*, see Berenbaum and Skolnik, "Orḥot Ẓaddikim."

162. Hergershausen, *Liblikhe tefile*, fol. b2v. Cf. Cohen, *Orchot Tzaddikim*, 16–19.

163. See, e.g., Bland, *Artless Jew*, 150. Cf. Sammern, "Red, White and Black," 122.

164. Cordovero, *Pardes Rimonim*, 4:35–38. On the color of *gevurah*, see also pp. 44–47. Cf. Scholem, "Farben und ihre Symbolik," 28–30. Cordovero further discusses the *sefirot* as "vessels, instruments used by the Craftsman . . . to do his work" in treatise 4 on "Substance and Vessels"; Cordovero, *Pardes Rimonim*, 1:146.

165. On this second-century sage's association with light symbolism, see Hasan-Rokem, "Rabbi Me'ir, the Illuminated"; Hasan-Rokem, "Rabbi Me'ir, May His Lamp Shine." On manuscripts that refer to Meir Shatz as Nehorai, see Landshut, *Columnae cultus*, 162; Ha-Cohen Fishman, "Akdamut," 11. On the association of these two rabbis, see also Chapter 4.

166. Carlebach, "Jews, Christians, and the Endtime," 331–33; Voß, *Disputed Messiahs*, 88. For an additional source, see Edrehi, *Historical Account of the Ten Tribes*, 21–22. See also Chapter 2, 53.

167. Neis, *Sense of Sight*, 203.

168. The practices associated with "visual piety" are detailed in Belting, *Likeness and Presence*; Frank, *Memory of the Eyes*.

169. For Yuval's thesis on remembrance as a form of active messianism, see *Two Nations in Your Womb*, 135–59. On God's bloodstained garment as a catalyst for summoning divine vengeance, see pp. 95–99, 135–36. Yehuda Liebes has shown that, according to a midrashic motif, God ensures perpetual remembrance of suffering by weaving Jewish martyrs into his porphyry; Liebes, "Helen's Porphyry." See also Scholem, "Farben und ihre Symbolik," 15. On the Rhenish fast days, see Zimmer, "Gezerot 1096."

170. Hoffman, "Akdamut," 171–73.

171. Interestingly, *Akdamut Milin* was apparently not recited in Worms, the hometown of its author; Raspe, "Vom Rhein nach Galiläa," 447–48; Voß, "Entangled Stories," 34–35.

172. See Wetzlar's Yiddish *Libes Briv* (Love letter) with an English translation by Faierstein, *Libes Briv*, 64–64, 69 (Yiddish), 111–13, 117 (English). *Shir ha-Yiḥud* was said daily in

many communities that followed the German-Polish rite until the mid-sixteenth century when, following a debate over its placement in the liturgy, diverse local practices emerged: this poem was then restricted to Sabbaths and festivals or, in some cases, solely to Yom Kippur. See Berliner, *Einheitsgesang*, 14–16; Elbogen, *Jewish Liturgy*, 72; Davidson, *Thesaurus*, 3:485, no. 1676.

173. Abraham Yagel, *Be'er sheva*, chap. 22; Bodleian Library, Oxford, Ms. Reggio 11 (IMHF F 22120), fol. 75r, cited in Neubauer, "Collections," 39. Neubauer erroneously cites the title of a different work by Yagel: *Beit Ya'ar ha-Levanon*. Cf. Neubauer, "Where Are the Ten Tribes?" 411. See also Yuspa Shammes, *Mayse nissim*, fol. 31r: "A story of *Akdamut* that is recited on Shavuot has been printed." On this megillah, "welche man in Deutschland am Pfingsten recitire," see Steinschneider, *Geschichtsliteratur*, 80, no. 91a. The copy that Yagel refers to was owned by Gershon b. Abraham of Porto. The records of the Mantuan censor report that the Port (Katz) family owned several copies of *Megiles Reb Meyer* (specifically, the Cremona imprint); Romer-Segal, "Sifrut yidish," 788n25. In his biography of Yagel, David Ruderman dates contact between Yagel and Gershon's family to circa 1576; Ruderman, *Kabbalah, Magic and Science*, 13.

174. The relationship between the liturgical recitation of *Ma'aseh Akdamut* and local fast days was first discussed by Lucia Raspe; Raspe, "Vom Rhein nach Galiläa," 440–41; Raspe, *Jüdische Hagiographie*, 196n226.

175. Turniansky, "Events in Frankfurt," 126. On second Purims, see also Yerushalmi, *Zakhor*, 46–48. On the role of Yiddish in domestic liturgy, see Baumgarten, *Introduction*, chap. 9.

176. Kattan Gribetz, "Hanged and Crucified," 176–79; Carlebach, *Anti-Christian Element*, 9.

CHAPTER 4

1. For the deep connection between translation and cultural exchange, see Burke and Hsia, *Cultural Translation*. Peter Burke stresses that mixing languages became more common in the early modern period as a result of migrations, including expulsions of Jews; Burke, *Languages and Communities*, 112. David Ruderman has defined Jewish mobility as a salient feature of the early modern era; Ruderman, *Early Modern Jewry*, chap. 1. For literary impact, see these studies in particular: Zfatman, *The Jewish Tale in the Middle Ages*; Raspe, *Jüdische Hagiographie*; Cohen, "From Solomon Bar Samson to Solomon Ibn Verga"; Raspe, "Portable Homeland"; Raspe, "Minhag and Migration."

2. On early modern Yiddish book production, see Baumgarten, *Introduction*, chap. 3; Baumgarten, *Peuple des livres*; Berger, *Producing Redemption in Amsterdam*. On Hebrew printing, see Habermann, *Hebrew Printers and Books*; Heller, *Sixteenth-Century Hebrew Book*.

3. Bibliographic data in Chapter 3, note 26.

4. On the manuscript and the editio princeps, see Chapter 2, notes 21 and 23. *Mayse dos da hayst Megiles Reb Meyer* (Amsterdam, 1660); cf. Zfatman, *Bibliography*, 44–45, no. 23; Rivkind, "Megilat R. Me'ir Shaẓ," 508; Vinograd, *Thesaurus*, no. 267; Friedberg, *Bet Eked Sepharim*, no. מ2927; Gutschow, *Inventory*, no. 40. The title page, which Rivkind quotes in part, mentions a certain Judah Leib, presumably from Amsterdam, who reprinted the Cremona edition several times; additional printings, now lost, may have been produced. *Ayn shen vunderlikh mayse . . . fun ayn glik rod* (Fürth, 1694); Bodleian Library, Oxford, Opp. 8° 1103

(10); cf. Zfatman, *Bibliography*, 66–67, no. 48; Rivkind, "Historical Allegory," 9, no. 1; Vinograd, *Thesaurus*, no. 39; Friedberg, *Bet Eked Sepharim*, no. מ2927; Cowley, *Catalogue of the Hebrew Printed Books*, 419, no. 5; Steinschneider, *Catalogus librorum Hebraeorum*, no. 6306.3. *Ayn sheyn mayse dos iz di geshikhtnis fun Rebe Meyer. Un fun den rotn yudlayn. Un fun den shvartsn minkh* (Amsterdam, 1704); Bodleian Library, Oxford, Opp. 8° 1112; cf. Zfatman, *Bibliography*, 86, no. 72; Rivkind, "Historical Allegory," 9, no. 2; Vinograd, *Thesaurus*, no. 770; Friedberg, *Bet Eked Sepharim*, no. מ2927; Cowley, *Catalogue of the Hebrew Printed Books*, 419, no. 6; Steinschneider, *Catalogus librorum Hebraeorum*, no. 6306.4; Gutschow, *Inventory*, no. 152. *Di geshikhtnis fun Rebe Meyer Shats un fun den rotn yudlayn un fun den shvartsen minkh* [Amsterdam, 1805]; JTS, New York, RARE YIDD PJ 5129 A2 M4 M4; cf. Zfatman, *Bibliography*, 166–67, no. 174; Rivkind, "Historical Allegory," 9, no. 3; Vinograd, *Thesaurus*, no. 2833; Friedberg, *Bet Eked Sepharim*, no. מ279; Steinschneider, *Catalogus librorum Hebraeorum*, no. 6306.4; Steinschneider, *Geschichtsliteratur*, 34–35, §22b; Seeligmann, *Catalog*, no. 495. *Ayn sheyne mayse fun Rebe Meyer der Akdomes gemakht hot vos man zingt um shvues voz gekumen iz unter dem Sambatyen. Un fun der rotn yudlin un fun dem shvarts minkh* [Lviv, 1805], fols. 4–8, included in a modest collection that includes three stories whose protagonists are heroes named Rabbi Meir. The copy in the JTS collection that Rivkind consulted, and is (still) listed in the library's card catalogue, seems to have been lost; cf. Zfatman, *Bibliography*, 166, no. 173; Rivkind, "Historical Allegory," 9–10, no. 4. Vinograd, *Thesaurus*, no. 388 and s.v. Megilat R. Me'ir erroneously identify a book about Me'ir b. Yehiel ha-Kadosh of Broda by this same title—printed in Cracow 1631/32 (Bodleian Library, Oxford, Opp. 4° 1406)—as another edition of *Ma'aseh Akdamut*. Cf. Steinschneider, *Catalogus librorum Hebraeorum*, no. 6310.

5. R 0082,I; R 0082,II. The voluminous materials from Reckendorf are preserved in the holdings of the Geniza Project in Veitshöchheim (near Würzburg). I am indebted to Elisabeth Singer Brehm of the Geniza Project for introducing me to these documents, and I extend special thanks to her and Erika Timm for their invaluable contributions to the identification of these fragments. For a detailed treatment of these fragments, see Voß, "Little Red Jews."

6. R 0082,II. An indication that this book was printed in Amsterdam is the production by Asher Anshel b. Eliezer, who was active there circa 1700. Cf., e.g., the similar typeface of his *Avkat Rahel* (1696/97), *Shirei Yehudah* (1697), *Shevet Yehudah* (1700), and *Mayse Bukh* (1701). In *Mayse Nissim* (1696), even the page area size and the number of lines per page are identical.

7. R 0082,I. The appearance of Gothic lettering was unusual except in the vicinity of Frankfurt am Main, where it was commonly used; thus, this element points to the origin of this fragment. With the exception of minor orthographic differences, the wording in this story is identical to the Fürth edition. Alternatively, this volume may have been printed in Frankfurt an der Oder, where a combination of Amsterdam letters and Gothic characters has been documented. Indeed, an undated edition of the Yiddish *Ma'aseh morenu rav Me'ir shali'ah zibbur* from Frankfurt an der Oder is listed in Salomon, *Catalogus*, 27. Cf. a quote of this entry in Steinschneider, "Jüdisch-Deutsche Literatur," 9, no. 21: 381, no. 164. However, this entry does not appear in his later catalogue; Steinschneider, *Catalogus librorum Hebraeorum*, no. 6306.4.

8. Yassif, "Early Versions," 214; Raspe, "Vom Rhein nach Galiläa," 437–38. In general, being linked to a piyyut would grant a story greater status; Raspe, *Jüdische Hagiographie*, 192, 195. See Chapter 3, 119.

9. Ms. Opp. 714, fol. 22r; Fürth 1694, fol. iv; Rivkind, "Historical Allegory," 11–12.
10. Ms. Opp. 714, fol. 21v; Fürth 1694, fol. iv; Rivkind, "Historical Allegory," 11–12.
11. Zfatman, "Iggrot be-yidish," 230 (fol. 43v).
12. See Zfatman, "Iggrot be-yidish," 226. The content of these two texts is nearly identical except for minor details.
13. Ms. Opp. 714, fol. 21v; Fürth 1694, fol. iv; Rivkind, "Historical Allegory," 11–12.
14. Ms. Opp. 714, fol. 26v; Fürth 1694, fol. 4r; Rivkind, "Historical Allegory," 21–22. Cf. Amsterdam 1704, fol. 3v; Amsterdam n.d., fol. 2r.
15. Rotman, "A Lamb and a Wolf," 513–15. On the relationship between orality and print, see Raspe, "Black Death in Jewish Sources."
16. Shlomo Berger stresses the transnational nature of the early modern Yiddish book market; Berger, "Yiddish Book Production in Amsterdam"; Berger, *Producing Redemption in Amsterdam*, 13, 211, 213; Berger, "Early Modern Yiddish," 284. See also Berger, "Diasporic Third Space"; Bar-Levav, "Amsterdam"; Baumgarten, *Peuple des livres*, 395–428.
17. Ms. Opp. 714, fol. 22r; Fürth 1694, fol. iv; Rivkind, "Historical Allegory," 11–12.
18. Such contextualizing features are also absent from Amsterdam n.d.
19. See Aptroot, "Western Yiddish Yontev-Bletlekh," 62n47. Reference to the Etz Haim Library, Amsterdam, 20B67[1], 20B67[19] (both "Red Jews"), and 20B67[10] ("Green Jews"), listed as nos. 477, 479, and 495 in Gutschow, *Inventory*; published in microfiche format by Gutschow, *Yiddish Publications from the Netherlands*.
20. See Chapter 1, 41–42.
21. Here I quote the Warsaw 1883 edition; *Me'ora'ot Zvi*, 43. On this work, see Meir, "Sefer Ḥalomei Qets Pela'ot"; Meir, "Me'ora'ot Tsvi."
22. In addition to the 1805 printing listed above, the modern Yiddish editions of *Ma'aseh Akdamut* known from Lviv are: *Ma'aseh gvurat ha-shem* (Lviv, 1839), JTS, New York, RBR YIDD. BM 530 M293 1839; Rivkind, "Historical Allegory," 10, no. 5; Vinograd, *Thesaurus*, no. 637; Friedberg, *Bet Eked Sepharim*, no. אֹ166. The 1839 edition, which seems to be based on a lost Hebrew print, was reprinted in the 1850s; *Sefer ma'aseh gvurat ha-shem*, NLI, Jerusalem, SO=23V14384; Vinograd, *Thesaurus*, no. 991.
23. For the lost print from 1805 Lviv, see Rivkind, "Historical Allegory," 10; Zfatman, *Bibliography*, 166, no. 173.
24. Bächtold-Stäubli, *Handwörterbuch*, 7:739.
25. *Sefer ma'aseh gvurot ha-shem* (Lviv, [1916]), YIVO, New York, 3/15637; NLI, Jerusalem, R 4=51 A 693; *Bibliography of the Hebrew Book*, no. 148875. Mendele Moykher Seforim, who wrote in both Hebrew and Yiddish, provides another example; e.g., the Hebrew version of his *The Brief Travels of Benjamin the Third* discussed in Chapter 5. See also the story *Ha-Avot ve-ha-Banim*; Mendele Moykher Sforim, *Kol kitvei*, 28.
26. Ms. Reggio 11, fol. 75r, cited in Neubauer, "Collections," 39.
27. See Chapter 1, 30.
28. Burke, *Languages and Communities*, chap. 5.
29. Rotman, "A Lamb and a Wolf," 514; Rotman, "Sexuality and Communal Space," 188–90.
30. On the preservation of Ashkenazic legends in Italy, see Raspe, "When King Dagobert Came to Halle." For the significance of local space in the creation of Jewish oikotypes of well-known folktales, see Bamberger, "King-Maker," 143–45. On the universal and local qualities of folktales, see Noy and Ben-Amos, *Folktales of the Jews*, xx–xxi.
31. E.g., IFA 462.

32. Peter Burke has observed that whatever is lost in translation points to cultural difference; Burke, "Cultures of Translation," 38. The bibliography on the inherent challenge of translation and its connection to cultural differences is vast. See, e.g., Apter, *Against World Literature*; Budick and Iser, *Translatability of Cultures*; Fabbri, "The Untranslatability of Faith." On the limits of transferring narratives interculturally, see Schneider, "Erzählungen als kulturelle Konstruktionen."

33. Yassif, "Early Versions," 215, confirms that the Hebrew translation of *Ma'aseh Akdamut* from 1630 has not been influential in literary history.

34. Edited by Yassif, "Early Versions," 217–26.

35. See Kohen's introduction to this tale; Yassif, "Early Versions," 218.

36. Yassif, "Early Versions," 218.

37. For an introduction to the Italian period in the history of Yiddish literature, see Shmeruk, "Prosa narrativa in Yiddish"; Shmeruk, "Yiddish Printing in Italy"; Turniansky and Timm, *Yiddish in Italia*.

38. Yassif, "Early Versions," 223, with 1 Sam. 17:44.

39. Yassif, "Early Versions," 225.

40. Ms. Opp. 714, fol. 32r–v; Rivkind, "Historical Allegory," 29, 31.

41. Yassif, "Early Versions," 222.

42. Yassif, "Early Versions," 218.

43. Yassif, "Early Versions," 222–23.

44. John Rylands Library, Manchester, Ms. Gaster 130, exempla no. 58. This manuscript is lost, but a copy is included in Ms. Gaster 962, vol. 1, fols. 132r–135r, no. 58. English abstract in Gaster, *Exempla of the Rabbis*, no. 369. In contrast to other tales, Gaster does not provide an annotated Hebrew edition of this source.

45. Printed in Ginzberg, *Halakhah ve-aggadah*, 229–32, no. 4; Bin Gorion, *Mi-mekor Yisra'el*, 2:13–15; also accessible online: http://folkmasa.org/b/mi_sipurp.php?mishtane=150. English translation: Bin Gorion, *Mimekor Yisrael*, 1:335–37, no. 172. Ginzberg erroneously dates this volume to 1775; in contrast, Brumer, *Catalog of Rabbinic Manuscripts*, no. 1791.

46. "ננס חגר וגבן"; Ginzberg, *Halakhah ve-aggadah*, 231.

47. Ginzberg, *Halakhah ve-aggadah*, 232 with n22.

48. IFA 462. On this and other related stories, see Chapter 5.

49. Rotman, *Dragons, Demons, and Wondrous Realms*, 239–341. Moti Benmelech has argued that the image of the Red Jews, which arrived in Italy with Ashkenazic immigrants, may have informed the belligerence attributed to the Ten Tribes in fifteenth- and sixteenth-century Italian Jewish thought; Benmelech, "Beyond the Sambatyon," 504–9; condensed English version of this article: Benmelech, "Back to the Future," 202–6.

50. On this rabbinic hero and the cult of his grave, see Boyarin, "Patron Saint of the Incongruous." For two stories about Meir Ba'al ha-Nes as a helper, see Noy and Ben-Amos, *Folktales of the Jews*, 71–86, nos. 11, 12.

51. IFA 286; on this story, see Chapter 5, 141. Such a variant is also attested by Ernst Daniel Goldschmidt as an oral tradition in 1971; Goldschmidt, "Akdamut Millin."

52. John Rylands Library, Manchester, Ms. Gaster 66 (IMHM F 15978). English abstract in Gaster, *Exempla of the Rabbis*, no. 340.

53. British Library, London, Ms. Or. 10385 (Ms. Gaster 1060), fols. 36r–38r; available online: https://www.nli.org.il/en/manuscripts/NNL_ALEPH000124688/NLI#$FL65542259. English abstract in Gaster, *Exempla of the Rabbis*, no. 445.

54. Gaster, *Exempla of the Rabbis*, 179.

55. Many folktales in the IFA depict "a miraculous rescue of a Jewish community from persecution by a king or a ruler" and, in some, the savior is a representative from the land of the Ten Tribes; see Baharav, *One Generation to Another*, 206–7; Stein, "Failed Marriage"; Noy and Ben-Amos, *Folktales of the Jews*, 466. I have identified the following five pertinent adaptations: IFA 943, 4311, 10103, 11289, 11292. Additional related tales from Morocco, Iraq, and Iran about Muslims' respect for the mighty Sons of Moses are: IFA 3602, edited in Kagan, "Ten Tribes," 151–52; IFA 11248, edited in Ben-Hayyim, *Grandpa Shelomo Tells*, 32–36, no. 7; IFA 13947; IFA 5616; IFA 5728, edited in Baharav, *One Generation to Another*, no. 36. An English translation of IFA 3602 is provided by Noy, *Moroccan Jewish Folktales*, 33, no. 2.

56. IFA 4311, related by Shalom ben Shalom in 1962. For an edition, see Baharav, *One Generation to Another*, 48–53, no. 15.

57. IFA 943, 11289, and 11292; printed and discussed in Stein, "Failed Union"; Stein, "Failed Marriage." An English translation of IFA 943 appears in Harel-Hoshen and Avner, *Beyond the Sambatyon*, 70.

58. IFA 10103, published in Noy, *Golden Feather*, 149–53, no. 18; Shenhar, *Ha-sippur ha-amami*, 68–80. An English translation titled "The Miracle of Tu b'Shevat" appears in Noy and Ben-Amos, *Folktales of the Jews*, 446–49, no. 50, quote on p. 447.

59. Clark, *Vanities of the Eye*, 21–22, 24. Cf. Jütte, *Geschichte der Sinne*, 101. For a brief discussion of the religious implications of blindness, see Paulson, *Enlightenment*, 7–9.

60. IFA 4311; Baharav, *One Generation to Another*, 51.

61. Noy and Ben-Amos, *Folktales of the Jews*, 449.

62. Noy and Ben-Amos, *Folktales of the Jews*, 449.

63. IFA 11289 and 11292. See Stein, "Failed Union"; Stein, "Failed Marriage."

CHAPTER 5

1. One Danite beyond the Sambatyon is described as black-haired in *Di royte yudlekh fun yener zayt Sambatyen*, 13. A story by Y. L. Peretz features both redheaded and blond Red Jews; Neugroschel, *Great Works*, 66.

2. See Chapter 4.

3. Lviv 1839, fol. 2r; Lviv 1916, fol. 4r.

4. IFA 462. On the parallel tale from 1785 Ravenna, see Chapter 4, 132–33.

5. *Sefer Akdamut* (Warsaw, 1902), 41–42, NLI, Jerusalem, 2 = 65 A 1614. Cf. Rivkind, "Megilat R. Me'ir Shaẓ," 508.

6. E.g., several versions in the NLI: *Akdamut*; *Akdamut milin*; *Me-ever le-nahar Sambatyon*. Cf. Hoffman, "Akdamut," 169n18.

7. On divorce before departure, see also IFA 462.

8. IFA 286 (*Shirat Akdamut*, recorded 1958), published in Hebrew and English (the last three lines are missing) by Shalva Weil in Harel-Hoshen and Avner, *Beyond the Sambatyon*, 29, 6; IFA 2208 (*Akdamut*, recorded 1960).

9. Despite having recorded approximately one hundred tales from memory for IFA, Tsoref is not a wholly reliable informant. Dov Noy has noted that some of his recordings are literary adaptations of written sources; therefore, they are not included in the annual IFA publication *A Tale for Each Month*. Indeed, Tsoref mentions an incident in the custom book by Judah Loew Kirchheim (ca. 1625, available in a modern edition) of a certain cantor in Worms whom God immediately swept up to heaven at the conclusion of singing the *Ak-*

*damut*. Whereas Kirchheim attributes his death to having intoned this song with such a beautiful voice and great fervor, Tsoref says that no one in that city was worthy of singing the *Akdamut* after Meir Shatz. Henceforth, *Akdamut* was no longer recited in Worms; IFA 286; cf. Peles, *Minhagot Warmaisa*, 258n8. On the challenges of working with narratives recorded by the IFA, see Noy and Ben-Amos, *Folktales of the Jews*, xxv–xxvi.

10. IFA 286.

11. Note that the Lviv editions of *Ma'aseh Akdamut*, which are essentially reprints of Old Yiddish editions from Amsterdam, retain "*rote yudn*."

12. *Eyn sheyne und vinderlikhe geshikhte fun di royte yudilekh* (Lviv, 1902), NLI, Jerusalem, RO=2003A5634; *Di royte yudlekh fun yener zayt Sambatyen* (Warsaw, 1913), 2–9, Widner Library, Harvard University, Y 10503.172. An English translation from another chapbook (Vilnius, 1912) appears in Ausubel, *Treasury of Jewish Folkore*, 526–29. These accounts all erroneously attribute this travelogue to Aron—rather than Gershon—ha-Levi. The Yiddish printings of *Gelilot Erez Yisra'el* from eastern Europe, which followed the editio princeps from Lublin 1635 and other editions from western Europe, are, e.g., Grodno 1796, Vilnius 1854, Vilnius 1856. The Hebrew translations, titled *Iggeret ha-Kodesh* (A letter of the holy), include Grodno 1795 and Warsaw 1874.

13. Shamir, *Mayse fun di royte yudlekh* (Warsaw, 1902; Vilnius, 1907; Vilnius, 1910); Shamir, *Mayse fun aseyres hashvotim in Sambatyen* (Vilnius, 1910).

14. On Shomer, see Dauber, "Shomer"; Miron, *Traveler Disguised*, s.v. "Shaykevitsh, N. M."

15. Mendele Moykher Sforim, *Ale verk*, 3–118. English translation: Mendele Moykher Sforim, *Tales of Mendele the Book Peddler*, 299–389. On Mendele as an author, see Miron, *Traveler Disguised*.

16. Mendele Moykher Sforim, *Tales of Mendele the Book Peddler*, 308.

17. Mendele Moykher Sforim, *Tales of Mendele the Book Peddler*, 333. On Mendele's complex relationship to Old Yiddish, see Bartal, "Garbayim, shot u-dli."

18. Mendele Moykher Sforim, *Tales of Mendele the Book Peddler*, 313.

19. Mendele, "Notes for My Literary Biography," quoted according to the English translation in Dawidowicz, *Golden Tradition*, 275.

20. This critique is a frequent trope in the literature of the Haskalah; Werses, "Aggadot al aseret ha-shevatim," 44. For the midrashic tradition that part of the Ten Tribes was exiled to the mountains of darkness, which also made it into the medieval Hebrew Alexander legend, see Voß, "Entangled Stories," 10–11 with n35.

21. Mendele Moykher Sforim, *Tales of Mendele the Book Peddler*, 359–61.

22. Mendele Moykher Sforim, *Tales of Mendele the Book Peddler*, 361.

23. Mendele Moykher Sforim, *Tales of Mendele the Book Peddler*, 333.

24. Mendele Moykher Sforim, *Tales of Mendele the Book Peddler*, 316. For Sendrel's broken Ukrainian, see Mendele Moykher Sforim, *Tales of Mendele the Book Peddler*, 334, 370. Neither character speaks Russian; Mendele Moykher Sforim, *Tales of Mendele the Book Peddler*, 381. On Mendele's use of various Jewish and non-Jewish languages and their political significance, see Bartal, "Garbayim, shot u-dli."

25. The changing political interpretations of Benjamin's travels have received significant scholarly attention: Miron and Norich, "Politics of Benjamin III"; Frieden, *Classic Yiddish Fiction*, 79–85; Ezrahi, *Booking Passage*, 52–67. For a broader discussion of the complexity of Zionist nationalism in Mendele's oeuvre, see Banbaji, *Mendele and the National Narrative*; Banbaji, "Mendele the Book-Peddler."

26. Mendele Moykher Sforim, *Kol kitvei*, 55–77.

27. Mendele Moykher Sforim, *Ale verk*, 4; Mendele Moykher Sforim, *Tales of Mendele the Book Peddler*, 302. On this idiom, see Harshav, *Polyphony of Jewish Culture*, 218.

28. Mendele Moykher Sforim, *Kol kitvei*, 77. This epilogue also appears in Mendele Moykher Sforim, *Tales of Mendele the Book Peddler*, 390–91.

29. First published in *Lu'aḥ aḥi'asaf* 10 (1903): 145–57, and included in Mendele Moykher Sforim, *Kol kitvei*, 469–74. These texts are discussed in detail in Werses, "Midreshei parodya." On their place in Mendele's critique, see Werses, "Aggadot al aseret ha-shevatim," 50–52; Bartal, "Ha-yehudim ha-admonim." I thank Israel Bartal for providing me with a draft of his forthcoming study. On the kabbalistic yeshivot in Jerusalem at the turn of the nineteenth century and their search for the Lost Tribes, against which Mendele polemicizes, see Meir, *Kabbalistic Circles*, 96–134; Meir, "Imagined Decline of Kabbalah."

30. Epstein, "Eldad ha-Dani"; Neubauer, "Collections"; Neubauer, "Where Are the Ten Tribes?"

31. His journey is detailed in a footnote; Mendele Moykher Sforim, *Kol kitvei*, 471n13.

32. Ezrahi, *Booking Passage*, 52.

33. Cf. Dauber, *Sholem Aleichem*, 147–49; Ezrahi, *Booking Passage*, 52.

34. The Yiddish version of *Di Royte Yudlekh* appears in Sholem Aleichem, *Ale verk*, 7–69. For an English translation, see Neugroschel, *Radiant Days, Haunted Nights*, 307–36; quote on p. 307. The original Yiddish text of "Lunatics" is included in Sholem Aleichem, *Ale verk*, 68–134. For an English translation, see Sholem Aleichem, *Land of Their Own*, 98–124.

35. Sholem Aleichem, *Land of Their Own*, 100.

36. Neugroschel, *Radiant Days, Haunted Nights*, chaps. 1–3.

37. Neugroschel, *Radiant Days, Haunted Nights*, 317; Sholem Aleichem, *Land of Their Own*, 107.

38. Cf. Bartal, "Ha-yehudim ha-admonim."

39. Sholem Aleichem, *Land of Their Own*, 98.

40. Neugroschel, *Radiant Days, Haunted Nights*, 314.

41. Sholem Aleichem, *Land of Their Own*, 99.

42. Sholem Aleichem, *Land of Their Own*, 102.

43. Sholem Aleichem, *Land of Their Own*, 115, 119.

44. Neugroschel, *Radiant Days, Haunted Nights*, 316.

45. All quotes: Neugroschel, *Radiant Days, Haunted Nights*, 318.

46. Neugroschel, *Radiant Days, Haunted Nights*, 319.

47. Neugroschel, *Radiant Days, Haunted Nights*, 322.

48. Sholem Aleichem, *Ale verk*, 45–67. Cf. Werses, "Aggadot al aseret ha-shevatim," 56. Since the addendum was published posthumously, it is not in the Warsaw edition of Sholem Aleichem's works, vol. 13 (1913), which only includes the first part of this story. Neugroschel, *Radiant Days, Haunted Nights*; translates the entire text.

49. Neugroschel, *Radiant Days, Haunted Nights*, 329–30.

50. On Sholem Aleichem's initial support for the revolution, followed by deep disappointment, and his parallel interest then disillusionment with American life and culture, see Dauber, *Sholem Aleichem*, 150–67, 182–94.

51. Sholem Aleichem, *Nayeste verk*, 183–202. On this story, see Werses, "Aggadot al aseret ha-shevatim," 57.

52. Sholem Aleichem, *Nayeste verk*, 193.

53. Sholem Aleichem, *Nayeste verk*, 197.

54. Sholem Aleichem, *Nayeste verk*, 202.
55. Sholem Aleichem, *Nayeste verk*, 157–82.
56. Sholem Aleichem, *Nayeste verk*, 160–63.
57. Sholem Aleichem, *Nayeste verk*, 173.
58. Sholem Aleichem, *Nayeste verk*, 174–75.
59. Prager, "Yiddish Matters."
60. For the Yiddish version, see Peretz, *Ale verk*, 14–72. An English translation is included in Neugroschel, *Great Works*, 60–104. In contrast to most other modern Yiddish works, Peretz uses the phrase *"royte yidn"* (Red Jews), rather than "little Red Jews."
61. Neugroschel, *Great Works*, 65.
62. Neugroschel, *Great Works*, 79–80.
63. Neugroschel, *Great Works*, 81.
64. Neugroschel, *Great Works*, 82.
65. Cf. Garrett, *Journeys Beyond the Pale*, 63–64.
66. Neugroschel, *Great Works*, 95.
67. Neugroschel, *Great Works*, 104, cf. 85–87.
68. Koller, *Marc Chagall*, 94–104; Harshav, *Polyphony of Jewish Culture*, chap. 8.
69. *The Jew in Bright Red* has previously been analyzed by several scholars. My interpretation of this painting draws on Harshav, "Role of Language in Modern Art"; Harshav, *Lost Jewish World*, 121–22; Harshav, *Polyphony of Jewish Culture*, 231; Rajner, "Chagall's Jew in Bright Red"; Koller, *Marc Chagall*, chap. 7.
70. Harshav, *Polyphony of Jewish Culture*, 220–21; Harshav, *Lost Jewish World*, 121. On the origins of the Wandering Jew in medieval Christian thought, see Chapter 1, 26.
71. Koller, *Marc Chagall*, 140.
72. In Yiddish, *tsumakhn (mit) an oyg* (to close an eye) can mean "to die"; Koller, *Marc Chagall*, 147.
73. Koller cites the Red Jews legend in modern Yiddish literature as a source for Chagall's painting; Koller, *Marc Chagall*, 144–47.
74. These details of Chagall's biography are included in Harshav, *Polyphony of Jewish Culture*, 210, 222. On Chagall's admiration for Sholem Aleichem, see also Rajner, "Chagall's Jew in Bright Red," 67–68.
75. Koller, *Marc Chagall*, 147–48.
76. Rajner, "Chagall's Jew in Bright Red," 64.
77. On *The War*, see Rajner, "Chagall's Jew in Bright Red," 63–64; Koller, *Marc Chagall*, 139.
78. Harshav, "Role of Language in Modern Art," 74; Harshav, *Lost Jewish World*, 121; Harshav, *Polyphony of Jewish Culture*, 231.
79. Harshav, *Lost Jewish World*, 121–22; Rajner, "Chagall's Jew in Bright Red," 66–68. See also Harshav, "Role of Language in Modern Art," 73–74; Koller, *Marc Chagall*, 143–44.
80. See, e.g., Gray, *About Face*, 108.
81. For additional examples from other European literatures, see Junkerjürgen, *Haarfarben*, 50–51; Lorenz, "Imaginierte Körperfarben," 190; Livak, *Jewish Persona*, 89–90; Oişteanu, *Inventing the Jew*, 40, 63–64; MacDonald, "'Red-Headed Animal.'" Junkerjürgen, *Haarfarben*, 49, claims that Jewish characters in nineteenth-century German literature are depicted with red hair more frequently than dark hair; however, his evidence is questionable.
82. Roth, *Radetzky March*, 167–68.
83. Rubinstein, *Members of the Tribe*, 13.

84. Popkin, "Jewish Indian Theory." On Jewish literature about the discovery of America and the search for the Lost Tribes among its native inhabitants, see also Melamed, "Discovery of America."

85. On the construct of the "Red Indian," see Neuber, "The 'Red Indian's Body'"; Kerner, "'The Invisible Body,'" 191–213; Shoemaker, "How Indians Got to Be Red." Abraham Farissol, for instance, described American Indians as having a black complexion with a reddish hue; Melamed, *Image of the Black*, 209.

86. On the role of skin color in discussions of whether the Lost Tribes were living in the Americas, see Melamed, *Image of the Black*, 209–12; Schorsch, *Jews and Blacks*, 186–87.

87. See Menasseh ben Israel, *Hope of Israel*.

88. Rubinstein, *Members of the Tribe*, 191n49.

89. Prilutski, *Yidishe folkslider*, 16. On Almi's biography and his interest in Polish Jewish folklore, see Gottesman, *Defining the Yiddish Nation*, 8–11.

90. This musical appears in the annotated bibliography of the Lawrence Marwick Collection of Copyrighted Yiddish Plays at the Library of Congress, Washington, DC, no. 10 (D 94731). It had apparently been lost before Lawrence Marwick, who headed the Hebraic Section of the Library of Congress until his death in 1981, catalogued these plays. Although he did not see this work himself, Marwick included it because of its appearance on a list in the U.S. Copyright Office. I thank Marion Aptroot for this reference.

91. On Almi's piece, see Rubinstein, *Members of the Tribe*, 14–16. All quotes according to Rubinstein.

92. Dubnow, *Buch des Lebens*, 1:279. I thank Richard Cohen for this reference. On the Odessa literary circle, see Dubnov-Erlich, *Life and Work of S. M. Dubnov*, 90–96.

93. On this society, see Zipperstein, *Elusive Prophet*, 21–66; Simon, *Ahad ha-am*, 76–94. For a collection of documents concerning the founding of *Bnei Mosheh*, its goals and activities, see Ahad ha-Am, *Kol kitvei*, 437–50.

94. On Ahad ha-Am's attitude toward Yiddish, see Zipperstein, *Elusive Prophet*, 222–24.

95. See §1 of the statutes of *Bnei Mosheh*; Ahad ha-Am, *Kol kitvei*, 439.

96. Bartal, "Ingathering of Traditions," 85–86.

97. Cf. Werses, "Aggadot al aseret ha-shevatim," 45–47.

98. On recurrent themes in Imber's Yiddish poetry, see Kabakoff, "Naphtali Herz Imber as a Yiddish Poet." See also, in greater detail on Imber's work, Kabakoff, *Naftali Herz Imber*.

99. *The Hebrew Puck* 2, no. 3 (1895): 45.

100. Imber, *Barkai ha-shlishi*, 12–17. This is the last volume in Imber's *Barkai* trilogy of Hebrew poetry. The Hebrew version of this poem in the anthology of Imber's poetry edited by Dov Sadan only includes its first four stanzas; Sadan, *Kol shirei Naftali Herz Imber*, 178.

101. Imber, *Barkai ha-shlishi*, 18–21. The Hebrew version is also included in Sadan, *Kol shirei Naftali Herz Imber*, 179–80.

102. Imber, *Barkai ha-shlishi*, 46–47.

103. Parfitt, *Lost Tribes of Israel*, 157.

104. Imber, *Barkai (he-ḥadash)*, 116–19. An abridged version appears in Sadan, *Kol shirei Naftali Herz Imber*, 219–20. A brief discussion of this poem appears in Werses, "Aggadot al aseret ha-shevatim," 45–46.

105. Imber, *Barkai (he-ḥadash)*, 117. Cf. Chapter 2, 63, on motifs from Jer. 31:8 and Jacob's limp in the Old Yiddish tale of the Red Jews.

106. Imber, *Barkai (he-ḥadash)*, 119.

107. This poem is included in Imber's first *Barkai* collection; Imber, *Barkai*, 69–72; Sadan, *Kol shirei Naftali Herz Imber*, 221–23.

108. Imber, *Barkai*, 71. Reference is to Deut. 32:30. Cf. Chapter 2, 63, Chapter 3, 91, 95, and Chapter 4, 135–37.

109. See Parfitt, *Road to Redemption*, 24–30.

110. "The Red Jews," reprinted in Kabakoff, *Master of Hope*, 131–33.

111. The article written in Yiddish is: Imber, "*Di royte idelekh*," n.p. Both articles are discussed in Nahshon, "Ha-yehudim ha-admonim"; Nahshon, "Metaphor of the Yemenite Jews."

112. Parfitt, *Road to Redemption*, 30, 52–53.

113. Kabakoff, *Master of Hope*, 131–32.

114. "The Red Jews," reprinted in Kabakoff, *Master of Hope*, 132. Cf. Imber, "*Di royte idelekh*," n.p.

115. Kabakoff, *Master of Hope*, 132. Cf. Imber, "*Di royte idelekh*," n.p.: "The entire tribe has red or ginger hair."

116. Imber, "*Di royte idelekh*," n.p.

117. Quoted in Parfitt, *Road to Redemption*, 24.

118. Kabakoff, *Master of Hope*, 132.

119. See Parfitt, *Road to Redemption*, 159–60. One early modern example is a German pamphlet from 1596 that identifies one leader of the Red Jews as a king from Japan (Joponia) whose legion is armed in a Japanese style; Gow, *Red Jews*, 282–83.

120. Kabakoff, *Master of Hope*, 132.

121. Imber, "*Di royte idelekh*," n.p.

122. Imber, "*Di royte idelekh*," n.p.

123. Imber, "*Di royte idelekh*," n.p.

124. Bartal, "Ingathering of Traditions," 78.

125. This poem is discussed in Novershtern, *Lure of Twilight*, 167–80.

126. Reinharz and Shavit, *Glorious, Accursed Europe*, 149–50.

127. *Le-se'udat aniyim* (To a feast of the poor), in Greenberg, *Collected Works*, 4:100. See also Wolf-Monzon, "Uri Zvi Greenberg," 42.

128. Greenberg, *Collected Yiddish Works*, 517–18.

129. *Ikh un mayn bruder fun Portugal* (Me and my brother from Portugal), reprint in *Di Goldene Keyt* 93 (1977): 60–61.

130. *Im Re'uveni u-Molkho be-ḥazer ha-mattarah bi-Yerushalayim* (With Re'uveni and Molkho in the court of the guard in Jerusalem), in Greenberg, *Streets of the River*, 323–26. Greenberg's "red song" is also discussed in Lipsker, *Red Poem Blue Poem*. On Reuveni and Molkho, see Chapter 1, 43–44.

131. Arnon, *Bibliyografiyah*, no. 2012.

132. *Shirat ashkavah le-Dov ha-Shiloni* (Requiem for Dov the Shilonite), in Greenberg, *Collected Works*, 9:158–64. I thank Gadi Sagiv for this reference.

133. See the online gallery of Tagger's paintings: https://www.tagger-siona.co.il/wp-content/uploads/2019/11/9.jpg.

134. Greenberg, *Collected Works*, 9:162–64.

135. אותיות בשמים: דמדמיות; Greenberg, *Collected Works*, 9:162. ושירו אדום כי בא מין הדם; Greenberg, *Collected Works*, 9:163.

136. Cf. the metaphorical meanings of the color red in Greenberg's poetry, namely blood, death, evil, and hope for redemption via the Hebrew wordplay דמדומים (twilight);

Dabi-Guri, "Ha-erekh ha-metaforali," 83–87. The land of the Red Jews is also depicted as a hopeful signpost in *Beit ha-ballahot* (The house of terror; 1958); Greenberg, *Collected Works*, 10:141–42, st. 5. I thank Avidov Lipsker for this reference.

137. Perlow, "Royte yidelekh." I thank Tamar Lewinsky for this reference. On Yiddish literary activity in DP camps in postwar Germany, see Lewinsky, *Displaced Poets*.

138. אן אפגעריסענער שבט פון גאנצן פאלק ישראל, פארווארפן איבערן סמבטיון, הינטער די הרי־חושך; Perlow, "Royte yidelekh."

139. מטן גרעסטן מסירת-נפש און העלדישקייט וואס עס איז זעלטן צו זען בײ אונדז ציוויליזירטע און קולטורעלע מענטשן; Perlow, "Royte yidelekh."

140. On the concept of muscular Jewishness, see Berkowitz, *Zionist Culture and West European Jewry*; Boyarin, *Unheroic Conduct*, 271–312; Presner, *Muscular Judaism*; Wildmann, "Jewish Gymnasts"; Wildmann, *Der veränderbare Körper*; Dekel, *Universal Jew*; Mayer, "From Zero to Hero."

141. See, in particular, Wildmann, *Der veränderbare Körper*.

EPILOGUE

1. See von Bernuth, *How the Wise Men Got to Chelm*, 27; on Trunk's oeuvre, see p. 24. The Red Jews are also mentioned in the Yiddish poem "Undzer zeyde Yoyne" by Yankev Fridman, which is included in his book of poetry from 1960; Fridman, *Legend of Noah Green*, 12. Unfortunately, I was unable to access an article on the Red Jews in Mexico by the American Yiddish poet Jacob Glatstein, published 1951 in the New York Hebrew-language journal *Ha-Do'ar* (The post); Glatstein, "Ha-yehudim ha-adumim shel Meksiko."

2. See Chapter 5, 140.

3. Levin on YouTube: https://www.youtube.com/watch?v=GoqFQIocUOQ.

4. Levin, "Encountering the Hasidic Enclave"; Osgood, "Hasidic Chic."

5. Osgood, "Hasidic Chic."

6. Batchelor, *Chromophobia*, 74. Similarly, John Gage has noted that color often communicates racial and sexual phobias; Gage, *Color and Culture*, 10.

7. Bale, *Feeling Persecuted*, 82.

8. This custom is discussed in two halakhic codes: *Arba'ah turim, Oraḥ ḥayyim* 61 and *Shulḥan arukh, Oraḥ ḥayyim* 61:5. The former associates this practice with BT Berakhot 13b, where Rabbi Judah ha-Nasi is described covering his eyes while reciting *Shema* to increase his concentration. I thank Rachel Furst for these references.

9. See Nolden, *In Lieu of Memory*, 150–51.

# Bibliography

### MANUSCRIPTS

Bodleian Library, Oxford
    Ms. Opp. 714
    Ms. Opp. 757
    Ms. Rawl. Or. 37
    Ms. Reggio 11
British Library, London, Ms. Or. 10385 (Ms. Gaster 1060)
City archives of Münster, Acta criminalia, no. 282
Geniza Project, Veitshöchheim
    R 0082,I
    R 0082,II
Institute of Microfilmed Hebrew Manuscripts, Jerusalem
    F 15978
    F 20496
    F 20981
    F 22120
    F 22740
Israel Folktale Archives, Haifa
    286
    462
    943
    2208
    3602
    4311
    5616
    5728
    10085
    10103
    11248
    11289
    11292
    13947
John Rylands Library, Manchester
    Ms. Gaster 66
    Ms. Gaster 130
    Ms. Gaster 962

## PRINTED SOURCES

Aaron b. Samuel of Hergershausen. *Liblikhe tefile oder greftige artsnay far guf un neshome.* Frankfurt am Main, 1709.
Abravanel, Isaac. *Perush ha-torah le-rabeinu Yiẓḥak Abravanel.* Ed. Yehudah Shaviv. Jerusalem: Sefarim Ḥorev, 2007.
Abulafia, Anna Sapir. "Bodies in the Jewish-Christian Debate." In *Framing Medieval Bodies*, ed. Sarah Kay and Miri Rubin, 123–37. Manchester: Manchester University Press, 1994.
Adam, Michael. *Ḥamishah ḥumshei torah.* Konstanz: Paulus Fagius, 1544.
Aderet, Anat. "Itineraries in Yiddish to Eretz-Israel in the 17th and 18th Centuries" (Hebrew). PhD diss., Bar-Ilan University, 2006.
Adler, Elkan Nathan, ed. *The Itinerary of Benjamin of Tudela: Critical Text, Translation and Commentary.* 1907. Reprint, New York: P. Feldheim, 1966.
———, ed. *Jewish Travellers in the Middle Ages: 19 Firsthand Accounts.* 1930. Reprint, London: Routledge, 2014.
Aescoly, Aaron Z. *Jewish Messianic Movements: Sources and Documents on Messianism in Jewish History from the Bar-Kokhba Revolt Until Recent Times* (Hebrew). 2nd ed. Jerusalem: Bialik Institute, 1956.
———. *The Story of David Hareuveni: Copied from the Oxford Manuscript* (Hebrew). 2nd ed. Jerusalem: Bialik Institute, 1993.
Ahad ha-Am. *Kol kitvei.* Jerusalem: Jewish Publishing House, 1947.
Aichele, Klaus. *Das Antichristdrama des Mittelalters der Reformation und Gegenreformation.* Dordrecht: Springer, 1974.
*Akdamut: Targum Akdamut le-idish u-lilshon ha-kodesh.* Jerusalem: Agudat ha-mekhinim, [1985].
*Akdamut milin ve-targumo.* Jerusalem: Talmud Tora Pinsk Karlin, [1990?].
Akrish, Isaac b. Abraham. *Ma'asiyot ve-sippurim min malkei Yisra'el.* Amsterdam, n.d.
Albeck, Chanokh, ed. *Midrash Bereshit Rabbati.* Reprint. Jerusalem: Mekiẓe Nirdamim, 1967.
Albrecht von Scharfenberg. *Der jüngere Titurel.* Ed. Werner Wolf. Bern: A. Francke, 1952.
Alexander, Philip S. "The Talmudic Concept of Conjuring (Ahizat Einayim) and the Problem of the Definition of Magic (Kishuf)." In *Creation and Re-Creation in Jewish Thought*, ed. Rachel Elior and Peter Schäfer, 7–25. Tübingen: Mohr Siebeck, 2005.
Aminoff, Irit. *Esau, My Brother: Father of Edom and Rome.* Jerusalem: Reuven Mas, 2015.
Amishai-Maisels, Ziva. "The Demonization of the 'Other' in the Visual Arts." In *Demonizing the Other: Antisemitism, Racism, and Xenophobia*, ed. Robert S. Wistrich, 44–72. Amsterdam: Harwood Academic Publishers, 1999.
Andernacht, Dietrich. *Regesten zur Geschichte der Juden in der Reichsstadt Frankfurt am Main von 1401–1519.* 4 vols. Forschungen zur Geschichte der Juden. Abt. B. Quellen. Hanover: Hahnsche Buchhandlung, 1996.
Anderson, Andrew Runni. *Alexander's Gate, Gog and Magog, and the Inclosed Nations.* Monographs of the Mediaeval Academy of America 5. Cambridge, MA: Mediaeval Academy of America, 1932.
Anderson, George K. *The Legend of the Wandering Jew.* 3rd ed. Hanover, NH: University Press of New England, 1991.
Apter, Emily. *Against World Literature: On the Politics of Untranslatability.* London: Verso, 2013.
Aptroot, Marion. "Western Yiddish Yontev-Bletlekh: Facing Modernity with Humor." *Jewish Studies Quarterly* 15 (2008): 47–67.

Arnheim, Rudolf. *Visual Thinking*. Berkeley: University of California Press, 1969.
Arnon, Yohanan. *Uri Zvi Greenberg: Bibliyografiyah shel mif'alo ha-sifruti u-ma she nikhtav alav, 1912–1978*. Tel Aviv: Hoza'at Adi Mozes, 1980.
Ashkenazi, Jacob b. Isaac of Janow. *Sefer ha-magid*. 3 vols. Lublin, 1622.
Ashley, Kathleen M., and Véronique Plesch. "The Cultural Processes of 'Appropriation.'" *Journal of Medieval and Early Modern Studies* 32, no. 1 (2002): 1–15.
Assaf, S. "Mikhtavim be-idish mi-Yerushalayim ir ha-kadosh." *Zion* 7 (1943): 65–72.
Auffarth, Christoph, and Sonja Kehrt, eds. *Glaubensstreit und Gelächter: Reformation und Lachkultur im Mittelalter und in der Frühen Neuzeit*. Religionen in der pluralen Welt: Religionswissenschaftliche Studien 6. Berlin: LIT-Verlag, 2008.
Augusti, Friedrich Albrecht. *Geheimnisse der Jüden von dem Wunder-Fluß Sambathjon, wie auch von denen rothen Jüden, in einem Brief-Wechsel mit denen heutigen Jüden, zur Erläuterung 2 Reg. 17,6 abgehandelt*. Erfurt, 1748.
Augustine. *De civitate Dei*. Turnhout: Brepols, 2010.
Ausubel, Nathan, ed. *A Treasury of Jewish Folklore: Stories, Traditions, Legends, Humor, Wisdom and Folk Songs of the Jewish People*. 3rd ed. New York: Crown Publishers, 1948.
Avrahami, Yael. *The Senses of Scripture: Sensory Perception in the Hebrew Bible*. The Library of Hebrew Bible/Old Testament Studies 545. New York: T & T Clark, 2011.
*Ayn shen vunderlich mayse . . . fun ayn glik rod*. Fürth: Zvi Hirsch b. Joseph ha-Levi, 1694.
*Ayn sheyn mayse dos iz di geshikhtnis fun Rebe Meyer. Un fun den rotn yudlayn. Un fun den shvartsn minkh*. Amsterdam: Süsskind Alexander b. Kalonymus Weilen, 1704.
*Ayn sheyne mayse fun Rebe Meyer der Akdomes gemakht hot vos man zingt um shvues voz gekumen iz unter dem Sambatyen. Un fun der rotn yudlin un fun dem shvarts minkh*. [Lviv, 1805].
Baader, Benjamin Maria, Sharon Gillerman, and Paul Lerner, eds. "Introduction: German Jews, Gender, and History." In *Jewish Masculinities: German Jews, Gender, and History*, 1–22. Bloomington: Indiana University Press, 2012.
———, eds. *Jewish Masculinities: German Jews, Gender, and History*. Bloomington: Indiana University Press, 2012.
Bächtold-Stäubli, Hanns. *Handwörterbuch des deutschen Aberglaubens*. 10 vols. Berlin: De Gruyter, 1927.
Baharav, Zalman. *One Generation to Another: Seventy-One Folktales Collected in Israel* (Hebrew). Tel Aviv: Tarbut Vechinuch, 1967.
Bale, Anthony. *Feeling Persecuted: Christians, Jews and Images of Violence in the Middle Ages*. Chicago: University of Chicago Press, 2010.
Bamberger, Joseph. "The King-Maker: Jewish Adaptations of Christian Legends." *Jewish Studies Quarterly* 20, no. 2 (2013): 129–45.
Banbaji, Amir. *Mendele and the National Narrative* (Hebrew). Or Yehudah: Devir, 2009.
———. "Mendele the Book-Peddler and the Ideology of Negation of Exile." *Iyyunim betekumat Yisra'el* 17 (2007): 81–106.
Barbu, Daniel, and Yaacov Deutsch, eds. *Toledot Yeshu in Context: The Jewish "Life of Jesus" in Ancient, Medieval, and Modern History*. Texts and Studies in Ancient Judaism 82. Tübingen: Mohr Siebeck, 2020.
Barbu, Daniel, and Yann Dahhaoui. "The Secret Booklet from Germany: Circulation and Transmission of *Toledot Yeshu* at the Borders of the Empire." In *Toledot Yeshu in Context: The Jewish "Life of Jesus" in Ancient, Medieval, and Modern History*, ed. Daniel Barbu and

Yaacov Deutsch, 187–230. Texts and Studies in Ancient Judaism 82. Tübingen: Mohr Siebeck, 2020.
Bar-Levav, Avriel. "Amsterdam and the Inception of the Jewish Republic of Letters." In *The Dutch Intersection: The Jews and the Netherlands in Modern History*, ed. Yosef Kaplan, 227–37. Brill's Series in Jewish Studies 38. Leiden: Brill, 2008.
Barmash, Pamela. "At the Nexus of History and Memory: The Ten Lost Tribes." *AJS Review* 29, no. 2 (2005): 207–36.
Baron, Salo W. *A Social and Religious History of the Jews*. Rev. ed. Vol. 3. New York: Columbia University Press, 1957.
Bartal, Israel. "Garbayim, shot u-dli: Leshon ha-ketivah shel Mendele." *Ha-Ivrit* 59 (2011): 87–107.
———. "Ha-yehudim ha-admonim ve-nahar ha-Sambatyon be-kitvei Mendele Mokher Sefarim ve-Shalom Aleikhem: Bein utopiya le-distopiya." In *Sambatyon: The Mythical Border in Time and Space*, ed. Moti Benmelech and Daniel Stein-Kokin, forthcoming.
———. "The Ingathering of Traditions: Zionism's Anthology Projects." *Prooftexts* 17, no. 1 (1997): 77–93.
Baruchson, Shifra. *Books and Readers: The Reading Interests of Italian Jews at the Close of the Renaissance* (Hebrew). Ramat Gan: Bar-Ilan University Press, 1993.
Batchelor, David. *Chromophobia*. London: Reaktion, 2007.
Baum, Jakob M. *Reformation of the Senses: The Paradox of Religious Belief and Practice in Germany*. Studies in Sensory History. Champaign: University of Illinois Press, 2018.
Baum, Paull Franklin. "Judas's Red Hair." *Journal of English and Germanic Philology* 21, no. 3 (1922): 520–29.
Baumgarten, Elisheva. *Practicing Piety in Medieval Ashkenaz: Men, Women, and Everyday Religious Observance*. Philadelphia: University of Pennsylvania Press, 2014.
Baumgarten, Jean. *Introduction to Old Yiddish Literature*. Trans. Jerold C. Frakes. Oxford: Oxford University Press, 2005.
———. *Le peuple des livres: Les ouvrages populaires dans la société ashkénaze XVIe–XVIIIe siècle*. Paris: Albin Michel, 2010.
———. "The Representation of the Body in Some Old Yiddish Ethical Texts." *Zutot: Perspectives on Jewish Culture* 8, no. 1 (2011): 63–74.
Bebel, Heinrich. *Fazetien*. Trans. Manfred Fuhrmann. Konstanz: Edition Isele, 2005.
Beinfeld, Solon, and Harry Bochner. *Comprehensive Yiddish-English Dictionary Based on the Dictionnaire Yiddish-Français*. Bloomington: Indiana University Press, 2013.
Beit-Arié, Malachi. *Catalogue of the Hebrew Manuscripts in the Bodleian Library: Supplement of Addenda and Corrigenda to Vol. I (A. Neubauer's Catalogue)*. Oxford: Clarendon Press, 1994.
Bejczy, István Pieter. *La lettre du prêtre Jean: Une utopie médiévale*. Paris: Imago, 2001.
Belting, Hans. *Likeness and Presence: A History of the Image Before the Era of Art*. Chicago: University of Chicago Press, 1994.
Ben-Amos, Dan. "Toward a Definition of Folklore in Context." *Journal of American Folklore* 34 (1971): 3–15.
Benayahu, Meir. *Hebrew Printing at Cremona: Its History and Printing* (Hebrew). Jerusalem: Ben Zvi Institute, 1971.
Ben-Dor Benite, Zvi. *The Ten Lost Tribes: A World History*. Oxford: Oxford University Press, 2009.
Ben-Hayyim, Hayyim. *Grandpa Shelomo Tells: 32 Folktales Told by Shelomo Ben-Hayyim* (Hebrew). Gevat: Gevat, 1980.

Benjamin of Tudela. *Masa'ot Binyamin*. Amsterdam, 1691.
———. *Masa'ot Binyamin*. Frankfurt am Main, 1711.
Benmelech, Moti. "Back to the Future: The Ten Tribes and Messianic Hopes in Jewish Society During the Early Modern Age." In *Peoples of the Apocalypse: Eschatological Beliefs and Political Scenarios*, ed. Felicitas Schmieder, Wolfram Brandes, and Rebekka Voß, 193–209. Millennium-Studien zu Kultur und Geschichte des ersten Jahrtausends n. Chr. 63. Berlin: De Gruyter, 2016.
———. "Beyond the Sambatyon: The Ten Lost Tribes of Israel in Early Modern Jewish Eyes" (Hebrew). *Zion* 77, no. 4 (2012): 491–527.
———. "History, Politics, and Messianism: David Ha-Reuveni's Origin and Mission." *AJS Review* 35, no. 1 (2011): 35–60.
———. *Shlomo Molcho: The Life and Death of Messiah Ben Joseph* (Hebrew). Jerusalem: Ben Zvi Institute, 2017.
Bennewitz, Ingrid, and Andrea Schindler, eds. *Farbe im Mittelalter: Materialität—Medialität—Semantik*. 2 vols. Berlin: Akademie Verlag, 2011.
Berenbaum, Michael, and Fred Skolnik, eds. "Orḥot Ẓaddikim." In *Encyclopaedia Judaica*, 15:469–70. Detroit: Macmillan, 2007.
Berger, David. *The Jewish-Christian Debate in the High Middle Ages: A Critical Edition of the Nizzahon Vetus*. Philadelphia: Jewish Publication Society of America, 1979.
———. "Mission to the Jews and Jewish-Christian Contacts in the Polemical Literature of the High Middle Ages." *American Historical Review* 91 (1986): 576–91.
———. "Three Typological Themes in Early Jewish Messianism: Messiah Son of Joseph, Rabbinic Calculations, and the Figure of Armilus." *AJS Review* 10, no. 2 (1985): 141–64.
Berger, Peter L. *Redeeming Laughter: The Comic Dimension of Human Experience*. 2nd ed. Berlin: De Gruyter, 2014.
Berger, Shlomo. "Diasporic Reading of Seventeenth Century Yiddish Itineraries to Erez Yisrael" (Hebrew). In *Ut Videant et Contigant: Essays on Pilgrimage and Sacred Space in Honour of Ora Limor*, ed. Yitzhak Hen and Iris Shagrir, 285–96. Ra'anana: Open University Press, 2011.
———. "Early Modern Yiddish and the Emergence of the Anonymous Reader." *Jewish Studies Quarterly* 26, no. 3 (2019): 282–88.
———. "Functioning Within a Diasporic Third Space: The Case of Early Modern Yiddish." *Jewish Studies Quarterly* 15, no. 1 (2008): 68–86.
———. *Producing Redemption in Amsterdam: Early Modern Yiddish Books in Paratextual Perspective*. Leiden: Brill, 2013.
———. "Yiddish Book Production in Amsterdam, 1650–1800: Local and International Aspects." In *The Dutch Intersection: The Jews and the Netherlands in Modern History*, ed. Yosef Kaplan, 203–12. Leiden: Brill, 2008.
Berkowitz, Michael. *Zionist Culture and West European Jewry Before the First World War*. Cambridge: Cambridge University Press, 1993.
Berliner, Abraham. *Aus dem inneren Leben der deutschen Juden im Mittelalter*. Berlin: Julius Benzian, 1871.
———. *Der Einheitsgesang: Eine literar-historische Studie*. Berlin: Itzkowski, 1910.
Bernstein, Ignaz. *Jüdische Sprichwörter und Redensarten*. 1908. Reprint, Wiesbaden: Fourier Verlag, 1988.
Bernuth, Ruth von. "Das Jischev fun Nar-Husen: Jiddische Narrenliteratur und jüdische Narrenkultur." *Aschkenas: Zeitschrift für Kultur und Geschichte der Juden* 25, no. 1 (2015): 133–44.

———. *How the Wise Men Got to Chelm: The Life and Times of a Yiddish Folk Tradition*. New York: New York University Press, 2016.

———. "Zwischen Kreuzrittern und Sarazenen: Der jüdische Held in Elia Levitas Bovo d'Antona." In *Das Potenzial des Epos: Die Altfranzösische Chanson de Geste im europäischen Kontext*, ed. Susanne Friede and Dorothea Kullmann, 411–31. Heidelberg: Winter, 2012.

Bertius, Petrus. *Geographischer eyn oder zusammengezogener Tabeln: Fünff unterschiedliche Bücher: In deren I. die ganze Welt in gemein II. Europa. III. Africa. IV. Asia. V. America vorgebildet und beschrieben wirdt*. Frankfurt am Main: Heinrich Lorentzen, 1612.

Bhabha, Homi K. *The Location of Culture*. London: Routledge, 1994.

Biale, David. *Blood and Belief: The Circulation of a Symbol Between Jews and Christians*. Berkeley: University of California Press, 2007.

———. "Counter-History and Jewish Polemics Against Christianity: The *Sefer Toldot Yeshu* and the *Sefer Zerubavel*." *Jewish Social Studies* 6, no. 1 (1999): 130–45.

———. *Power and Powerlessness in Jewish History*. New York: Schocken Books, 1986.

*The Bibliography of the Hebrew Book, 1473–1960*. Jerusalem: Institute for Hebrew Bibliography. http://www.hebrew-bibliography.com/.

Bierbrauer, Johann Jacob. *Beschreibung Derer Berüchtigten Jüdischen Diebes, Mörder- und Rauber-Banden*. Kassel: Estienne, 1758.

Biernoff, Suzannah. *Sight and Embodiment in the Middle Ages: Ocular Desires*. London: Palgrave Macmillan, 2002.

Bikard, Arnaud. "The Old Yiddish Šeder Nošim and the Querelle des Femmes." In *Women, Men and Books: Issues of Gender in Yiddish Discourse*, ed. Gennady Estraikh and Mikhail Krutikov, 7–18. Studies in Yiddish 16. Oxford: Legenda, 2019.

Bildhauer, Bettina. "Blood, Jews and Monsters in Medieval Culture." In *The Monstrous Middle Ages*, ed. Bettina Bildhauer and Robert Mills, 75–96. Cardiff: University of Wales Press, 2003.

———. *Medieval Blood*. Cardiff: University of Wales Press, 2006.

Billig, Michael. *Laughter and Ridicule: Towards a Social Critique of Humour*. London: Sage Publications, 2005.

Bin Gorion, Micha Josef, ed. *Der Born Judas: Legenden, Märchen und Erzählungen*. 2 vols. Wiesbaden: Insel-Verlag, 1959.

———. *Mimekor Yisrael: Classical Jewish Folktales*. Ed. Emanuel Bin Gorion. Trans. I. M. Lask. 3 vols. Bloomington: Indiana University Press, 1976.

———. *Mi-mekor Yisra'el: Ma'asiyot ve-sippurei am*. 2nd ed. 6 vols. Tel Aviv: Bialik Institute/Dvir, 1952.

Bischoff, Erich. *Ein jüdisch-deutsches Leben Jesu*. Leipzig: Wilhelm Friedrich, 1895.

Bland, Kalman P. *The Artless Jew: Medieval and Modern Affirmations and Denials of the Visual*. Princeton, NJ: Princeton University Press, 2001.

———. "Medieval Jewish Aesthetics: Maimonides, Body, and Scripture in Profiat Duran." *Journal of the History of Ideas* 54, no. 4 (October 1993): 533–59.

Blech, Benjamin. "The 'Parah Adumah' and the Symbolism of Color." *Dialogue for Torah Issues and Ideas* 3 (2012): 79–92.

Blitz, Yekutiel b. Isaac. *Ḥamishah ḥumshei torah nevi'im u-ketuvim bilshon Ashkenaz*. Amsterdam: Uri Phoebus b. Aaron ha-Levi, 1678.

Bøe, Sverre. *Gog and Magog: Ezekiel 38–39 as Pre-Text for Revelation 19,17–21 and 20,7–10*. Tübingen: Mohr Siebeck, 2001.

Boer, Wietse de. *Religion and the Senses in Early Modern Europe*. Leiden: Brill, 2013.

Böttrich, Christfried, Thomas K. Kuhn, and Daniel Stein-Kokin, eds. *Die Greifswalder Lehrsynagoge Johann Friedrich Mayers: Ein Beispiel christlicher Rezeption des Judentums im 18. Jahrhundert*. Leipzig: Evangelische Verlagsanstalt, 2016.

Bousset, Wilhelm. *The Antichrist Legend: A Chapter in Jewish and Christian Folklore*. London: Hutchinson, 1896.

Boveland, Karin, ed. *Der Antichrist und die fünfzehn Zeichen vor dem Jüngsten Gericht*. 2 vols. Hamburg: Wittig, 1979.

Boyarin, Daniel. "The Eye in the Torah: Ocular Desire in Midrashic Hermeneutic." *Critical Inquiry* 16, no. 3 (1990): 532–50.

———. "Masada or Yavneh? Gender and the Arts of Jewish Resistance." In *Jews and Other Differences: The New Jewish Cultural Studies*, ed. Daniel Boyarin and Jonathan Boyarin, 306–29. Minneapolis: University of Minnesota Press, 1997.

———. "Patron Saint of the Incongruous: Rabbi Me'ir, the Talmud, and Menippean Satire." *Critical Inquiry* 35 (2009): 523–51.

———. *Unheroic Conduct: The Rise of Heterosexuality and the Invention of the Jewish Man*. Contraversions: Critical Studies in Jewish Literature, Culture, and Society. Berkeley: University of California Press, 1997.

Braude, Benjamin. "Myths and Realities of Turkish-Jewish Contacts." In *Turkish-Jewish Encounters: Studies on Turkish-Jewish Relations Through the Ages*, ed. Mehmet Tütüncü, 15–28. Turquoise Studies 5. Haarlem: SOTA, 2001.

Bredekamp, Horst, and Pablo Schneider, eds. *Visuelle Argumentationen: Die Mysterien der Repräsentation und die Berechenbarkeit der Welt*. Munich: Verlag Wilhelm Fink, 2005.

Bregman, Marc. "Aqedah: Midrash as Visualization." *Journal of Textual Reasoning* 2, no. 1 (2003).

———. "Seeing with the Sages: Midrash as Visualization in the Legends of the Aqedah." In *Agendas for the Study of Midrash in the Twenty-First Century*, ed. Marc Lee Raphael, 2:84–100. Williamsburg, VA: College of William and Mary, 1999.

Bregoli, Francesca, and David B. Ruderman, eds. *Connecting Histories: Jews and Their Others in Early Modern Europe*. Philadelphia: University of Pennsylvania Press, 2019.

Bremer, Ernst, and Klaus Ridder, eds. *Jean de Mandeville, Reisen: Reprint der Erstdrucke der deutschen Übersetzungen des Michael Velser (Augsburg, bei Anton Sorg, 1480) und des Otto von Diemeringen (Basel, bei Bernhard Richel, 1480/81)*. Deutsche Volksbücher in Faksimiledrucken 21. Hildesheim: Olms, 1991.

Brennan, Teresa, and Martin Jay. *Vision in Context: Historical and Contemporary Perspectives on Sight*. New York: Routledge, 1996.

Brenner, Athalya. *Colour Terms in the Old Testament*. Journal for the Study of the Old Testament. Supplement Series 21. Sheffield: Sheffield Academic Press, 1982.

Brenz, Johannes. *Türcken Büchlein: Wie sich Prediger vnd Leien halten sollen/ so der Türck das Deudsche Land vberfallen würde. Christliche vnd nottürfftige vnterrichtung*. Wittenberg, 1531.

Brévart, Francis B. "The German Volkskalender of the Fifteenth Century." *Speculum* 63, no. 2 (1988): 312–42.

Brinkmann, Bodo, and Stephan Kemperdick. *Deutsche Gemälde im Städel 1500–1550*. Kataloge der Gemälde im Städelschen Kunstinstitut Frankfurt am Main 5. Mainz: Verlag Philipp von Zabern, 2005.

Brook, Kevin Alan. *The Jews of Khazaria*. Reprint. Lanham, MD: Rowman & Littlefield, 2004.

Brumer, Judah. *Catalog of Rabbinic Manuscripts*. 9 vols. Hebrew Manuscript Catalogs from the Jewish Theological Seminary. Microfiche edition. Sunningdale: Thompson Henry, 2006.

Buber, Salomon, ed. *Jalkut Machiri: Sammlung halachischer und hagadischer Stellen aus Talmud und Midraschim zu den 150 Psalmen von R. Machir ben Abba Mari*. Berdyczew: J. Scheftel, 1899.

———, ed. *Midrash lekaḥ tov: Ha-mekhuneh Pesikta zutarta al ḥamishah ḥumshei torah*. Vilnius: Romm, 1884.

Büchner, Anton. *Judas Ischarioth in der deutschen Dichtung: Ein Versuch*. Freiburg i. Br.: E. Guenther, 1925.

Budick, Sanford, and Wolfgang Iser, eds. *The Translatability of Cultures: Figurations of the Space Between*. Stanford, CA: Stanford University Press, 1996.

Burger, Christoph P. "Endzeiterwartung im späten Mittelalter: Der Bildertext zum Antichrist und den fünfzehn Zeichen vor dem Jüngsten Gericht in der frühesten Druckausgabe." In *Der Antichrist und die fünfzehn Zeichen vor dem Jüngsten Gericht: Kommentarband zum Faksimile der ersten typographischen Ausgabe eines unbekannten Straßburger Druckers, um 1480*, ed. Karin Boveland, 18–78. Hamburg: Wittig, 1979.

Burke, Peter. "Cultures of Translation in Early Modern Europe." In *Cultural Translation in Early Modern Europe*, ed. Peter Burke and Ronni Po-Chia Hsia, 7–38. Cambridge: Cambridge University Press, 2007.

———. *Languages and Communities in Early Modern Europe*. Cambridge: Cambridge University Press, 2004.

———. *Popular Culture in Early Modern Europe*. 3rd ed. Farnham: Ashgate, 2009.

Burke, Peter, and Ronni Po-Chia Hsia, eds. *Cultural Translation in Early Modern Europe*. Cambridge: Cambridge University Press, 2007.

Busuttil-Cesar, Stephanie. *Red*. Paris: Assouline Publishing, 2000.

Bynum, Caroline Walker. *Wonderful Blood: Theology and Practice in Late Medieval Northern Germany and Beyond*. Philadelphia: University of Pennsylvania Press, 2007.

Carben, Victor von. *De vita et moribus Judaeorum*. Paris, 1511.

———. *Hier inne wirt gelesen wie Her Victor von Carben. Welicher eyn Rabi der Juden gewest ist zu Cristlichem glawbn komen: Weiter vindet man dar Jn. eyn Costliche disputatz eynes gelerten Cristen. vnd eyns gelerten Juden. dar inne alle Jrthumb der Juden durch yr aygen schrifft aufgelost werden*. [Cologne], 1508.

Carlebach, Elisheva. *The Anti-Christian Element in Early Modern Yiddish Culture*. Braun Lectures in the History of the Jews in Prussia 10. Ramat Gan: Bar-Ilan University Press, 2003.

———. "Jews, Christians, and the Endtime in Early Modern Germany." *Jewish History* 14 (2000): 331–44.

———. *Palaces of Time: Jewish Calendar and Culture in Early Modern Europe*. Cambridge, MA: Belknap Press of Harvard University Press, 2011.

Carlebach, Elisheva, and Debra Kaplan. "Jewish Women in Early Modern Central Europe, 1500–1800." In *Jewish Women's History from Antiquity to the Present*, ed. Federica Francesconi and Rebecca Lynn Winer, 143–61. Detroit: Wayne State University Press, 2021.

Carmassi, Patrizia. "Purpurismum in Martyrio: Die Farbe des Blutes in mittelalterlichen Handschriften." In *Farbe im Mittelalter: Materialität—Medialität—Semantik*, ed. Ingrid Bennewitz and Andrea Schindler, 1:251–73. Berlin: Akademie Verlag, 2011.

Carruthers, Mary J. *The Book of Memory: A Study of Memory in Medieval Culture*. 2nd ed. Cambridge Studies in Medieval Literature 70. Cambridge: Cambridge University Press, 2008.

———. *The Craft of Thought: Meditation, Rhetoric, and the Making of Images, 400–1200*. 2nd ed. Cambridge: Cambridge University Press, 2000.
Cassen, Flora. *Marking the Jews in Renaissance Italy: Politics, Religion, and the Power of Symbols*. Cambridge: Cambridge University Press, 2017.
Chajes, J. H. *Between Worlds: Dybbuks, Exorcists, and Early Modern Judaism*. Philadelphia: University of Pennsylvania Press, 2003.
———. "Entzauberung and Jewish Modernity: On 'Magic,' Enlightenment, and Faith." *Simon Dubnow Institute Yearbook* 6 (2007): 191–200.
———. "Kabbalah and the Diagrammatic Phase of the Scientific Revolution." In *Jewish Culture in Early Modern Europe: Essays in Honor of David B. Ruderman*, ed. Richard I. Cohen, Natalie B. Dohrmann, Adam Shear, and Elchanan Reiner, 109–23. Cincinnati, OH: Hebrew Union College Press, 2014.
———. "Kabbalistic Diagram as Epistemic Image" (Hebrew). *Pe'amim: Studies in Oriental Jewry* 150–52 (2018): 235–88.
———. "Magic, Mysticism, and Popular Belief in Jewish Culture (1500–1815)." In *The Early Modern World (1500–1815)*, ed. Jonathan Karp and Adam Sutcliffe, 475–90. The Cambridge History of Judaism 7. Cambridge: Cambridge University Press, 2017.
———. "Rabbis and Their (In)Famous Magic: Classical Foundations, Medieval and Early Modern Reverberations." In *Jewish Studies at the Crossroads of Anthropology and History: Authority, Diaspora, Tradition*, ed. Ra'anan Boustan, Oren Kosansky, and Marina Rustow, 58–79. Philadelphia: University of Pennsylvania Press, 2011.
———. "Re-Envisioning the Evil Eye: Magic, Optical Theory, and Modern Supernaturalism in Jewish Thought." *European Journal of Jewish Studies* 15 (2020): 1–30.
———. "'Too Holy to Print': Taboo Anxiety and the Publishing of Practical Hebrew Esoterica." *Jewish History* 26, no. 1–2 (2012): 247–62.
Chartier, Roger. *The Cultural Uses of Print in Early Modern France*. Princeton, NJ: Princeton University Press, 1987.
———. "Culture as Appropriation: Popular Cultural Uses in Early Modern France." In *Understanding Popular Culture: Europe from the Middle Ages to the Nineteenth Century*, ed. Steven L. Kaplan, 229–53. Berlin: Mouton, 1984.
Chenciner, Robert. *Madder Red: A History of Luxury and Trade*. Richmond: Routledge, 2000.
Chen-Morris, Raz. *Measuring Shadows: Kepler's Optics of Invisibility*. University Park: Pennsylvania State University Press, 2016.
Chen-Morris, Raz, and Ofer Gal. *Baroque Science*. Chicago: University of Chicago Press, 2013.
Chidester, David. *Word and Light: Seeing, Hearing, and Religious Discourse*. Urbana: University of Illinois Press, 1992.
Christian, William A. *Local Religion in Sixteenth-Century Spain*. Princeton, NJ: Princeton University Press, 1981.
Cirkic, Jasmina. "Rotwelsch in der deutschen Gegenwartssprache." PhD diss., Johann Gutenberg Universität Mainz, 2006.
Clark, Stuart. *Thinking with Demons: The Idea of Witchcraft in Early Modern Europe*. Oxford: Oxford University Press, 1999.
———. *Vanities of the Eye: Vision in Early Modern European Culture*. Oxford: Oxford University Press, 2007.
Classen, Albrecht, ed. *Laughter in the Middle Ages and Early Modern Times: Epistemology of a Fundamental Human Behavior, Its Meaning, and Consequences*. Fundamentals of Medieval and Early Modern Culture 5. Berlin: De Gruyter, 2010.

Classen, Constance, ed. *A Cultural History of the Senses*. 6 vols. London: Bloomsbury, 2014.
———. "The Senses." In *Encyclopedia of European Social History from 1350 to 2000*, ed. Peter N. Stearns, 4:355–64. Detroit: Charles Scribner's Sons, 2001.
Clemen, Otto. *Flugschriften aus den ersten Jahren der Reformation*. 4 vol. 1907–11. Reprint, Nieuwkoop: Graaf, 1967.
Cohen, Gerson D. "Esau as Symbol in Early Medieval Thought." In *Studies in the Variety of Rabbinic Cultures*, 243–70. Philadelphia: Jewish Publication Society, 1991.
Cohen, Jeremy. "Antichrist and His Jewish Connections" (Hebrew). In *From Sages to Savants: Studies Presented to Avraham Grossman*, ed. Yosef Kaplan, B. Z. Kedar, and Joseph Hacker. Jerusalem: Zalman Shazar, 2010.
———. *Christ Killers: The Jews and the Passion from the Bible to the Big Screen*. Oxford: Oxford University Press, 2007.
———. "From Solomon Bar Samson to Solomon Ibn Verga: Tales and Ideas of Jewish Martyrdom in *Shevet Yehudah*." In *Studies in Medieval Jewish Intellectual and Social History: Festschrift in Honor of Robert Chazan*, ed. David Engel et al., 279–97. Leiden: Brill, 2012.
Cohen, Richard I. *Jewish Icons: Art and Society in Modern Europe*. Berkeley: University of California Press, 1998.
———. "The 'Wandering Jew' from Medieval Legend to Modern Metaphor." In *The Art of Being Jewish in Modern Times*, ed. Barbara Kirshenblatt-Gimblett and Jonathan Karp, 147–75. Philadelphia: University of Pennsylvania Press, 2007.
Cohen, Seymour J., trans. *Orchot Tzaddikim: The Ways of the Righteous*. 2nd ed. New York: Feldheim Publishers, 1974.
Cohen Roman, Oren. "Chivalric Scenes in Medieval Yiddish Epic." In *Yiddish Knights*, ed. Marion Aptroot, 7–22. Amsterdam Yiddish Symposium 14. Amsterdam: Menasseh ben Israel Institute, 2020.
Cordovero, Moses ben Jacob. *Pardes Rimonim: Orchard of Pomegranates*. Trans. Elyakim Getz. 4 vols. Monfalcone: Providence University, 2007.
Cowley, Arthur E. *A Concise Catalogue of the Hebrew Printed Books in the Bodleian Library*. 1929. Reprint, Oxford: Clarendon, 1971.
Cuffel, Alexandra. *Gendering Disgust in Medieval Religious Polemic*. Notre Dame, IN: University of Notre Dame Press, 2007.
Curschmann, Michael. "Pictura laicorum litteratura? Überlegungen zum Verhältnis von Bild und volkssprachlicher Schriftlichkeit im Hoch- und Spätmittelalter bis zum Codex Manesse." In *Pragmatische Schriftlichkeit im Mittelalter: Erscheinungsformen und Entwicklungsstufen*, ed. Hagen Keller, Klaus Grubmüller, and Nikolaus Staubach, 211–29. Munich: Fink, 1992.
Dabi-Guri, Lilian. "Ha-erekh ha-metaforali shel ha-ẓeva'im be-shirat Uri Zvi Greenberg: Heerot le-zikat shirato le-mekorot kabbaliyim." In *Poetry and Mysticism: Collected Papers in Honor of the Poet Shin Shalom*, ed. Yoav Elstein and Chaim Shoham, 73–87. Ramat Gan: Bar-Ilan University Press, 1985.
Dan, Joseph. "An Early Hebrew Source of the Yiddish 'Aqdamoth' Story." *Hebrew University Studies in Literature* 1 (1973): 39–46.
———. *The Hebrew Story in the Middle Ages* (Hebrew). Jerusalem: Keter Publishing House, 1974.
———. "The History of 'The Story of the Akdamut' in Hebrew Literature" (Hebrew). *Criticism and Interpretation* 9/10 (1976): 197–213.

Dapper, Olfert. *Umbständliche und eigentliche Beschreibung von Africa: Und denen darzu gehörigen Königreichen und Landschaften, als Egypten, Barbarien, Libyen, Biledulgerid, dem Lande der Negros, Guinea, Ethiopien, Abyssina, und den Africanischen Insulen; zusamt deren verscheidenen Nahmen, Grentzen, Städten, Flüssen, Gewächsen, Thieren, Sitten, Trachten, Sprachen, Reichthum, Gottesdienst un Regierung*. Amsterdam: Jacob von Meurs, 1670.

Darnton, Robert. "Peasants Tell Tales: The Meaning of Mother Goose." In *The Great Cat Massacre and Other Episodes in French Cultural History*, 9–72. New York: Vintage Books, 1985.

Dauber, Jeremy. *In the Demon's Bedroom: Yiddish Literature and the Early Modern*. New Haven, CT: Yale University Press, 2010.

———. "Shomer." In *YIVO Encyclopedia of Jews in Eastern Europe*, 2010. http://www.yivoencyclopedia.org/article.aspx/Shomer.

———. *The Worlds of Sholem Aleichem: The Remarkable Life and Afterlife of the Man Who Created Tevye*. Jewish Encounters Series. New York: Schocken Books, 2013.

David, Avraham, ed. *A Hebrew Chronicle from Prague, c. 1615*. Judaic Studies Series. Tuscaloosa: University of Alabama Press, 1993.

Davidson, Israel. *Thesaurus of Mediaeval Hebrew Poetry*. 1924–33. Reprint. 4 vols. [New York]: Ktav Publishing House, 1970.

Davies, Surekha. *Renaissance Ethnography and the Invention of the Human: New Worlds, Maps and Monsters*. Cambridge Social and Cultural Histories 24. Cambridge: Cambridge University Press, 2016.

Dawidowicz, Lucy S. *The Golden Tradition: Jewish Life and Thought in Eastern Europe*. New York: Holt, Rinehart, and Winston, 1996.

Dekel, Mikhal. *The Universal Jew: Masculinity, Modernity, and the Zionist Moment*. Evanston, IL: Northwestern University Press, 2010.

Della Porta, Giambattista. *Die Physiognomie des Menschen*. Ed. Theodor Lessing and Will Rink. Der Körper als Ausdruck, Bd. 1. Dresden: Madaus, 1930.

Denery, Dallas G. *Seeing and Being Seen in the Later Medieval World: Optics, Theology and Religious Life*. Cambridge Studies in Medieval Life and Thought, 4th ser., 63. Cambridge: Cambridge University Press, 2009.

Deutsch, Yaacov. "Jewish Anti-Christian Invectives and Christian Awareness: An Unstudied Form of Interaction in the Early Modern Period." *Leo Baeck Institute Year Book* 55 (2010): 41–61.

———. "The Second Life of the Life of Jesus: Christian Reception of Toledot Yeshu." In *Toledot Yeshu ("The Life Story of Jesus") Revisited: A Princeton Conference*, ed. Peter Schäfer, Michael Meerson, and Yaacov Deutsch, 283–95. Tübingen: Mohr Siebeck, 2011.

———. "Von der Iuden Ceremonien: Representations of Jews in Sixteenth-Century Germany." In *Jews, Judaism, and the Reformation in Sixteenth-Century Germany*, ed. Stephen G. Burnett and Dean Phillip Bell, 335–56. Studies in Central European Histories 37. Leiden: Brill, 2006.

Deutscher, Guy. *Through the Language Glass: Why the World Looks Different in Other Languages*. New York: Metropolitan Books, 2010.

Dieckmann, Bernhard. *Judas als Sündenbock: Eine verhängnisvolle Geschichte von Angst und Vergeltung*. Munich: Kösel, 1991.

Diemeringen, Otto von. *Reisebeschreibung/Der Antichrist und die fünfzehn Zeichen vor dem Jüngsten Gericht*. Ed. Klaus Ridder. Codices illuminati Medii Aevi 24. Munich: Lengenfelder, 1992.

Diemling, Maria. "Anthonius Margaritha and His 'Der Gantz Jüdisch Glaub.'" In *Jews, Judaism, and the Reformation in Sixteenth-Century Germany*, ed. Stephen G. Burnett and Dean Phillip Bell, 303–34. Studies in Central European Histories 37. Leiden: Brill, 2006.

Diemling, Maria, and Giuseppe Veltri, eds. *The Jewish Body: Corporeality, Society, and Identity in the Renaissance and Early Modern Period*. Studies in Jewish History and Culture 17. Leiden: Brill, 2009.

*Di geshikhtnis fun Rebe Meyer Shats un fun den rotn yudlayn un fun den shvartsen minkh*. [Amsterdam, 1805].

*Di royte yudlekh fun yener zayt Sambatyen*. Warsaw, 1913.

Dreeßen, Wulf-Otto. "Goliaths Schwestern und Brüder." In *Röllwagenbüchlein: Festschrift für Walter Röll zum 65. Geburtstag*, ed. Jürgen Jaehrling, Uwe Meves, and Erika Timm, 369–89. Tübingen: Niemeyer, 2002.

———. "Wigalois—Widuwilt: Wandlungen des Artusromans im Jiddischen." In *Westjiddisch. Le Yiddish occidental: Mündlichkeit und Schriftlichkeit. Actes du Colloque de Mulhouse*, ed. Wolfgang Starck, 84–98. Sprachlandschaft 2. Aarau: Sauerländer, 1994.

———. "Zur Rezeption deutscher epischer Literatur im Altjiddischen: Das Beispiel 'Wigalois'—'Artushof.'" In *Deutsche Literatur des späten Mittelalters: Hamburger Kolloquium 1973*, ed. Wolfgang Harms and Leslie Peter Johnson, 116–28. Berlin: E. Schmidt, 1975.

Drucker, Moses. *Sefer tela'ot Mosheh*. Halle, 1711.

Dubnov-Erlich, Sophie. *The Life and Work of S. M. Dubnov: Diaspora Nationalism and Jewish History*. Bloomington: Indiana University Press, 1991.

Dubnow, Simon. *Buch des Lebens: Erinnerungen und Gedanken. Materialien zur Geschichte meiner Zeit*. Ed. Verena Dorn. 3 vols. Göttingen: Vandenhoeck & Ruprecht, 2005.

Duggan, Lawrence G. "Reflections on 'Was Art Really the "Book of the Illiterate"?'" In *Reading Images and Texts: Medieval Images and Texts as Forms of Communication*, ed. Marielle Hagemann and Marco Mostert, 109–19. Turnhout: Brepols, 2005.

———. "Was Art Really the 'Book of the Illiterate'?" In *Reading Images and Texts: Medieval Images and Texts as Forms of Communication*, ed. Marielle Hagemann and Marco Mostert, 63–107. Turnhout: Brepols, 2005.

Durand, Dana Bennett. *The Vienna-Klosterneuburg Map Corpus of the Fifteenth Century: A Study in the Transition from Medieval to Modern Science*. Leiden: Brill, 1952.

Duzer, Chet van. "Hic sunt dracones: The Geography and Cartography of Monsters." In *The Ashgate Research Companion to Monsters and the Monstrous*, ed. Asa Simon Mittman and Peter J. Dendle, 387–435. Farnham: Ashgate, 2012.

Dyrness, William A. *Reformed Theology and Visual Culture: The Protestant Imagination from Calvin to Edwards*. Cambridge: Cambridge University Press, 2004.

Ecker, Hans-Peter. *Die Legende: Kulturanthropologische Annäherung an eine literarische Gattung*. Germanistische Abhandlungen 76. Stuttgart: Metzler, 1993.

Edelman, Charles. "Which Is the Jew That Shakespeare Knew? Shylock on the Elizabethan Stage." In *The Cambridge Shakespeare Library: Shakespeare's Times, Texts, and Stages*, ed. Catherine M. S. Alexander, 1:444–51. Cambridge: Cambridge University Press, 2003.

Edrehi, Moses. *An Historical Account of the Ten Tribes Settled Beyond the River Sambatyon, in the East; with Many Other Curious Matters Relating to the State of the Israelites in Various Parts of the World*. Philadelphia, 1853.

Efferhen, Heinrich. *Christliche Predigten auß dem XXXVIII. und XXXIX. Capitel Ezechiels: Von Gog vnnd Magog/ oder den Türcken*. Strasbourg: Theodosius Rihel, 1571.

Eidelberg, Shlomo. *R. Juspa, Shammash of Warmaisa (Worms): Jewish Life in Seventeenth Century Worms*. Jerusalem: Magnes Press, 1991.

Eilberg-Schwartz, Howard, ed. *People of the Body: Jews and Judaism from an Embodied Perspective*. Albany: State University of New York Press, 1992.

Eisenstein, Elizabeth. *The Printing Revolution in Early Modern Europe*. 2nd ed. Cambridge: Cambridge University Press, 2005.

Elbogen, Ismar. *Jewish Liturgy: A Comprehensive History*. Trans. Raymond P. Scheindlin. Philadelphia: Jewish Publication Society, 1993.

Ellingson, Ter. *The Myth of the Noble Savage*. Berkeley: University of California Press, 2001.

Emmerson, Richard Kenneth. *Antichrist in the Middle Ages: A Study of Medieval Apocalypticism, Art, and Literature*. Seattle: University of Washington Press, 1981.

Epstein, Abraham. "Eldad ha-Dani: Seine Berichte über die zehn Stämme und deren Ritus in verschiedenen Versionen nach Handschriften und alten Drucken mit Einleitung und Anmerkungen nebst einem Excurse über die Falascha und deren Gebräuche." In *Kitvei Avraham Epstein*, 2nd ed., ed. Abraham M. Habermann, 1:1–211 (Hebrew pagination). Jerusalem: Mosad Harav Kook, 1965.

Epstein, Marc Michael. "Another Flight into Egypt: Confluence, Coincidence and the Cross-Cultural Dialectics of Messianism and Iconographic Appropriation in Medieval Jewish and Christian Culture." In *Imagining the Self, Imagining the Other: Visual Representation and Jewish-Christian Dynamics in the Middle Ages and Early Modern Period*, ed. Eva Frojmovic, 33–52. Leiden: Brill, 2002.

———. "Bestial Bodies on the Jewish Margins: Race, Ethnicity, and Otherness in Medieval Manuscripts Illuminated for Jews." In *Monsters and Monstrosity in Jewish History: From the Middle Ages to Modernity*, ed. Iris Idelson-Shein and Christian Wiese, 69–85. London: Bloomsbury, 2019.

———. *Dreams of Subversion in Medieval Jewish Art and Literature*. University Park: Pennsylvania State University Press, 1997.

Erythropel, David Rupert. *Weckglock/ darinnen die schlaffende Teutschen wider die wachende Türcken auffgewecket werden*. Frankfurt am Main: Johann Spies, 1595.

Ettmüller, Ludwig, ed. *Die beiden ältesten deutschen Jahrbücher der Stadt Zürich*. Zurich: Zürcher und Furrer, 1844.

Euling, Karl, ed. *Chronik des Johan Oldecop*. Bibliothek des Literarischen Vereins in Stuttgart 90. Tübingen, 1891.

*Eyn sheyne und vinderlikhe gshikhte fun di royte yudilekh*. Lviv, 1902.

Ezrahi, Sidra DeKoven. *Booking Passage: Exile and Homecoming in the Modern Jewish Imagination*. Berkeley: University of California Press, 2000.

Fabbri, Paolo. "The Untranslatability of Faith." In *Translation Studies: Critical Concepts in Linguistics*, ed. Mona Baker, 1:184–97. London: Routledge, 2009.

Fabre-Vassas, Claudine. *The Singular Beast: Jews, Christians, the Pig*. New York: Columbia University Press, 1997.

Faierstein, Morris M., ed. *The Libes Briv of Isaac Wetzlar*. Atlanta: Scholars Press, 1996.

———. *Ze'enah u-Re'enah: A Critical Translation into English*. Studia Judaica 96. Berlin: De Gruyter, 2017.

Falk, Felix, and L. Fuks, eds. *Das Schemuelbuch des Mosche Esrim Wearba: Ein biblisches Epos aus dem 15. Jahrhundert*. 2 vols. Publications of the Bibliotheca Rosenthaliana. Assen: Van Gorcum, 1961.

Farissol, Abraham. *Iggeret orḥot olam*. Venice, 1586.

Fine, Steven. "Menorahs in Color: Polychromy in Jewish Visual Culture of Roman Antiquity." *Images* 6 (2013): 3–25.

Fischart, Johann. *Geschichtsklitterung (Gargantua): Text der Ausg. letzter Hand von 1590 mit einem Glossar*. Ed. Ute Nyssen. Darmstadt: Wissenschaftliche Buchgesellschaft, 1977.

Flügge, Marina. "Vom Anfang und vom Ende der Welt: Die mittelalterlichen Glasmalereien und die Zeit ihrer Entstehung." In *Die Chorfenster der St. Marienkirche in Frankfurt (Oder)*, ed. Detlef Karg, 75–118. Worms: Wernersche Verlagsgesellschaft, 2008.

Flusser, David. "The Four Empires in the Fourth Sibyl and in the Book of Daniel." *Israel Oriental Studies* 2 (1972): 148–75.

———, ed. *Sefer Yosippon*. 2 vols. Jerusalem: Bialik Institute, 1978–80.

Fontes, Manuel da Costa. *The Art of Subversion in Inquisitorial Spain: Rojas and Delicado*. West Lafayette, IN: Purdue University Press, 2005.

Foucault, Michel. *Discipline and Punish: The Birth of the Prison*. New York: Random House, 1977.

Fraenkel-Goldschmidt, Chava, ed. *The Historical Writings of Joseph of Rosheim: Leader of Jewry in Early Modern Germany*. Leiden: Brill, 2006.

Frakes, Jerold C., ed. *Early Yiddish Epic*. Judaic Traditions in Literature, Music and Art. Syracuse, NY: Syracuse University Press, 2014.

———, ed. *Early Yiddish Texts, 1100–1750*. Oxford: Oxford University Press, 2004.

———. *The Emergence of Early Yiddish Literature: Cultural Translation in Ashkenaz*. German Jewish Cultures. Bloomington: Indiana University Press, 2017.

Fram, Edward. "Some Preliminary Observations on the First Published Translation of Rashi's Commentary on the Pentateuch in Yiddish (Cremona, 1560)." *Hebrew Union College Annual* 86 (2016): 305–42.

———. "Sumptuary Laws in the Jewish Community of Cracow at the End of the Sixteenth and Beginning of the Seventeenth Century" (Hebrew). *Gal-Ed: On the History and Culture of Polish Jewry* 18 (2002): 11–23.

Francesconi, Federica. *Invisible Enlighteners: The Jewish Merchants of Modena, from the Renaissance to the Enlightenment*. Philadelphia: University of Pennsylvania Press, 2021.

———. "Jewish Women in Early Modern Italy." In *Jewish Women's History from Antiquity to the Present*, ed. Federica Francesconi and Rebecca Lynn Winer, 122–42. Detroit: Wayne State University Press, 2021.

Frank, Georgia. *The Memory of the Eyes: Pilgrims to Living Saints in Christian Late Antiquity*. Berkeley: University of California Press, 2000.

Freedberg, David. *The Power of Images: Studies in the History and Theory of Response*. Chicago: University of Chicago Press, 1989.

Frey, Winfried. "Die Juden im Frankfurter Passionsspiel." In *Gott in Frankfurt? Theologische Spuren in einer Metropole*, ed. Matthias Benad, 34–42. Frankfurt am Main: Athenäum, 1987.

———. "Passionsspiel und geistliche Malerei als Instrumente der Judenhetze in Frankfurt am Main um 1500." *Jahrbuch des Instituts für deutsche Geschichte* 13 (1984): 15–57.

Fridman, Yankev. *The Legend of Noah Green (Die legende Noyekh Grin)*. New York: World Jewish Culture Congress, 1960.

Friedberg, Chaim Bernhard. *Bet Eked Sepharim: Bibliographical Lexicon of the Whole Hebrew and Jewish-German Literature, Inclusive of the Arabic, Greek, Italian, Persian, Samaritan,*

*Spanish-Portuguese and Tartarian Works, Printed in the Years 1475–1900 with Hebrew Letters* (Hebrew). 2nd ed. 4 vols. Tel Aviv: Bar Juda, 1951.
Frieden, Ken. *Classic Yiddish Fiction: Abramovitsh, Sholem Aleichem, and Peretz.* Albany: State University New York Press, 1995.
Friedman, John. *The Monstrous Races in Medieval Art and Thought.* Cambridge, MA: Harvard University Press, 1981.
Friedrich, Markus. "Das Hör-Reich und das Sehe-Reich: Zur Bewertung des Sehens bei Luther und im frühneuzeitlichen Protestantismus." In *Evidentia: Reichweiten visueller Wahrnehmung in der Frühen Neuzeit*, ed. Gabriele Wimböck, Karin Leonhard, and Markus Friedrich, 451–79. Münster: LIT Verlag, 2007.
Frojmovic, Eva, ed. *Imagining the Self, Imagining the Other: Visual Representation and Jewish-Christian Dynamics in the Middle Ages and Early Modern Period.* Leiden: Brill, 2002.
*Fun tsvay maysim vunderbarlikh di do geshehen zayn in tsayten daz do gelebt hot man Moreinu Harov Rebbe Yitskhok Lurie.* Prague, ca. 1665.
Funkenstein, Saul. "History, Counterhistory, and Narrative." In *Probing the Limits of Representation: Nazism and the "Final Solution,"* ed. Saul Friedländer, 66–81. Cambridge, MA: Harvard University Press, 1992.
Füssel, Marian. "Die Kunst der Schwachen: Zum Begriff der 'Aneignung' in der Geschichtswissenschaft." *Sozial.Geschichte: Zeitschrift für historische Analyse des 20. und 21. Jahrhunderts*, n.s., 21, no. 3 (2006): 7–28.
———. "Zwischen Schlachtenlärm und Siegesklang: Zur akustischen Repräsentation von militärischer Gewalt im Siebenjährigen Krieg (1756–1763)." In *Krieg und Frieden im 18. Jahrhundert: Kulturgeschichtliche Studien*, ed. Stefanie Stockhorst, 149–66. Hanover: Wehrhahn, 2015.
Gage, John. *Color and Culture: Practice and Meaning from Antiquity to Abstraction.* Boston: Little, Brown, 1993.
———. *Colour and Meaning: Arts, Science and Symbolism.* London: Thames & Hudson, 1999.
———. *Colour in Art.* New York: Thames & Hudson, 2006.
Galina, Moses b. Elijahu. *Sefer ḥokhmat ha-yad im ḥokhmat ha-parzuf.* Frankfurt an der Oder, 1775.
Galinsky, Adam D., et al. "The Reappropriation of Stigmatizing Labels: Implications for Social Identity." *Research on Managing Groups and Teams* 5 (2003): 221–56.
———. "The Reappropriation of Stigmatizing Labels: The Reciprocal Relationship Between Power and Self-Labeling." *Psychological Science* 24 (2013): 2020–29.
Garrett, Leah V. *Journeys Beyond the Pale: Yiddish Travel Writing in the Modern World.* Madison: University of Wisconsin Press, 2003.
Gaster, Moses. *The Exempla of the Rabbis: Being a Collection of Exempla, Apologues and Tales Culled from Hebrew Manuscripts and Rare Hebrew Books.* 1924. Reprint, New York: Ktav Publishing House, 1968.
———, ed. *Ma'aseh Book: Book of Jewish Tales and Legends. Translated from the Judeo-German.* 2 vols. Schiff Library of Jewish Classics. Philadelphia: Jewish Publication Society, 1934.
Geiger, Ludwig. "Vor hundert Jahren: Mitteilungen aus der Geschichte der Juden Berlins." *Zeitschrift für die Geschichte der Juden in Deutschland* 2 (1889): 185–233.
Geller, Ewa. "Yiddish 'Regimen sanitatis Salernitatum' from Early Modern Poland: A Humanistic Symbiosis of Latin Medicine and Jewish Thought." In *Jewish Medicine and Healthcare in Central Eastern Europe: Shared Identities, Entangled Histories*, ed. Marcin

Moskalewicz, Ute Caumanns, and Fritz Dross, 13–25. Cham: Springer International Publishing, 2019.

Geller, Jay. "'Der Volf' or the Jew as Out(side of the) Law." In *Monsters and Monstrosity in Jewish History: From the Middle Ages to Modernity*, ed. Iris Idelson-Shein and Christian Wiese, 251–64. London: Bloomsbury, 2019.

Gerson, Christian. *Der Jüden Thalmud Fürnembster innhalt/ vnd Widerlegung/ In Zwey Bücher verfasset. Im Ersten Wird die gantze Jüdische Religion/ vnd falsche Gottesdienste beschrieben. Im Andern Werden dieselbe/ beydes durch die schrifft des Alten Testaments/ vnd des Thalmuds selbst/ gründlich widerlegt vnd vmbgestossen.* Goslar: Johann Vogt, 1607.

Gesenius, Friedrich Heinrich Wilhelm. *Hebrew and Chaldee Lexicon to the Old Testament Scriptures.* Trans. Samuel Prideaux Tregelles. London: Samuel Bagster and Sons, 1846.

Giesecke, Michael. *Der Buchdruck in der frühen Neuzeit. Eine historische Fallstudie über die Durchsetzung neuer Informations- und Kommunikationstechnologien.* Frankfurt am Main: Suhrkamp, 2006.

Gilman, Sander L. "'Die Rasse ist nicht schön'—'Nein, wir Juden sind keine hübsche Rasse!' Der schöne und der hässliche Jude." In *"Der schejne Jid": Das Bild des "jüdischen Körpers" in Mythos und Ritual*, ed. Sander L. Gilman, Robert Jütte, and Gabriele Kohlbauer-Fritz, 57–74. Vienna: Picus-Verlag, 1998.

———. *The Jew's Body.* London: Routledge, 1991.

———. *The Visibility of the Jew in the Diaspora: Body Imagery and Its Cultural Context.* Syracuse, NY: Syracuse University Press, 1992.

Gilman, Sander L., Robert Jütte, and Gabriele Kohlbauer-Fritz, eds. *"Der schejne Jid": Das Bild des "jüdischen Körpers" in Mythos und Ritual.* Vienna: Picus-Verlag, 1998.

Gilomen, Hans-Jörg. "Spätmittelalterliche Siedlungssegregation und Ghettoisierung, insbesondere im Gebiet der heutigen Schweiz." In *Stadt- und Landmauern: Abgrenzungen—Ausgrenzungen in der Stadt und um die Stadt*, ed. Brigitt Sigel, 3:85–106. Zurich: vdf Hochschulverlag, 1999.

Ginzberg, Louis. *Al halakhah ve-aggadah: Meḥkar u-massah.* Tel Aviv: Devir, 1960.

———, ed. *The Legends of the Jews.* 2 vols. 1909–38. Reprint, Philadelphia: Jewish Publication Society, 2003.

Girtler, Roland. *Rotwelsch: Die alte Sprache der Gauner, Dirnen und Vagabunden.* 2nd ed. Vienna: Böhlau, 2010.

Glatstein, Jacob. "Ha-yehudim ha-adumim shel Meksiko." *Ha-Do'ar*, November 27, 1951.

Goldenberg, David M. *Black and Slave: The Origins and History of the Curse of Ham.* Berlin: De Gruyter, 2017.

———. *The Curse of Ham: Race and Slavery in Early Judaism, Christianity, and Islam.* Princeton, NJ: Princeton University Press, 2003.

Goldschmidt, Ernst Daniel. "Akdamut Millin." In *Encyclopaedia Judaica*, ed. Fred Skolnik, 1:55. Detroit: Macmillan, 2007.

Gottesman, Itzik Nakhmen. *Defining the Yiddish Nation: The Jewish Folklorists of Poland.* Detroit: Wayne State University Press, 2003.

Gotzmann, Andreas. "Respectability Tested: Male Ideals, Sexuality, and Honor in Early Modern Ashkenazi Society." In *Jewish Masculinities: German Jews, Gender, and History*, ed. Benjamin Maria Baader, Sharon Gillerman, and Paul Lerner, 23–49. Bloomington: Indiana University Press, 2012.

Gow, Andrew C. "Gog and Magog on 'Mappamundi' and Early Printed World Maps: Orientalizing Ethnography in the Apocalyptic Tradition." *Journal of Early Modern History* 2, no. 1 (1998): 61–88.

———. "The Jewish Antichrist in Medieval and Early Modern Germany." *Medieval Encounters: Jewish, Christian and Muslim Culture in Confluence and Dialogue* 2, no. 3 (1996): 249–85.

———. "Kartenrand, Gesellschaftsrand, Geschichtsrand: Die legendären iudei clausi/inclusi auf mittelalterlichen und frühneuzeitlichen Weltkarten." In *Fördern und Bewahren: Studien zur europäischen Kulturgeschichte der frühen Neuzeit*, ed. Helwig Schmidt-Glintzer, 137–55. Wiesbaden: Harrassowitz, 1996.

———. "Red Jews." In *Trade, Travel, and Exploration in the Middle Ages: An Encyclopedia*, ed. John Block Friedman and Kristen Mossler Figg, 518. London: Routledge, 2000.

———. *The Red Jews: Antisemitism in an Apocalyptic Age, 1200–1600*. Studies in Medieval and Reformation Thought 55. Leiden: Brill, 1995.

Gradwohl, Roland. *Die Farben im Alten Testament: Eine terminologische Studie*. Beihefte zur Zeitschrift für die alttestamentliche Wissenschaft 83. Berlin: Töpelmann, 1961.

Grafenberg, Wirnt von. *Wigalois: Text der Ausgabe von J. M. N. Kapteyn übersetzt, erläutert und mit einem Nachwort versehen*. Ed. Sabine Seelbach and Ulrich Seelbach. Berlin: De Gruyter, 2005.

Gray, Richard T. *About Face: German Physiognomic Thought from Lavater to Auschwitz*. Detroit: Wayne State University Press, 2004.

Greenberg, Uri Zvi. *Collected Works* (Hebrew). 21 vols. Jerusalem: Bialik Institute, 1990–2021.

———. *Collected Yiddish Works* (Hebrew). Vol. 2. Jerusalem: Magnes Press, 1979.

———. *Streets of the River* (Hebrew). Jerusalem: Schocken, 1951.

Greenblatt, Stephen. "Shakespeare and Shylock?" *New York Review of Books* 57, no. 14 (2010).

Greenfield, Amy Butler. *A Perfect Red: Empire, Espionage, and the Quest for the Color of Desire*. New York: Harper Perennial, 2005.

Grimm, Jacob, and Wilhelm Grimm. *Deutsches Wörterbuch*. 33 vols. 1854–1971. Reprint, Munich: Deutscher Taschenbuch Verlag, 1999.

Groebner, Valentin. "Complexio/Complexion: Categorizing Individual Natures (1250–1600)." In *The Moral Authority of Nature*, ed. Lorraine Daston and Fernando Vidal, 361–83. Chicago: University of Chicago Press, 2004.

———. "Haben Hautfarben eine Geschichte? Personenbeschreibungen und ihre Kategorien zwischen dem 13. und dem 16. Jahrhundert." *Zeitschrift für Historische Forschung* 30 (2003): 1–18.

Gross, Avraham. "The Expulsion and the Search for the Ten Tribes." *Judaism* 41, no. 2 (1992): 130–47.

———. "The Ten Tribes and the Kingdom of Prester John: Rumors and Investigations Before and After the Expulsion from Spain" (Hebrew). *Pe'amim: Studies in Oriental Jewry* 48 (1991): 5–41.

Grossman, Avraham. *The Early Sages of Ashkenaz: Their Lives, Leadership and Works (900–1096)* (Hebrew). 2nd rev. ed. Jerusalem: Magnes Press, 1988.

Großmann, Georg Ulrich, ed. *Spiegel der Seligkeit: Privates Bild und Frömmigkeit im Spätmittelalter: Ausstellung, Germanisches Nationalmuseum, Nürnberg, 31. Mai bis 8. Oktober 2000*. Nuremberg: Germanisches Nationalmuseum, 2000.

Gubar, Susan. *Judas: A Biography*. New York: W. W. Norton, 2009.
Gutschow, Mirjam. *Inventory of Yiddish Publications from the Netherlands c. 1650–c. 1950*. Leiden: Brill, 2007.
———, ed. *Yiddish Publications from the Netherlands*. Leiden: IDC Publishers, 2004.
Habermann, Abraham M. *Shirei ha-yiḥud ve-ha-kavod*. Jerusalem: Mosad Harav Kook, 1948.
———. *Studies in the History of Hebrew Printers and Books* (Hebrew). Jerusalem: Ruben Mas, 1978.
Habicht, Tanja-Isabel, and Björn Reich. "Die Farbe der Erinnerung." In *Farbe im Mittelalter: Materialität—Medialität—Semantik*, ed. Ingrid Bennewitz and Andrea Schindler, 2:537–49. Berlin: Akademie Verlag, 2011.
Ha-Cohen Fishman, Yehuda Leib. "'Ha-akdamut' u-meḥabro." *Ha-tor* 3, no. 25–26 (1923): 11–15.
Hahn, Hans-Peter. "Cultural Appropriation: Power, Transformation and Tradition." In *Travelling Goods, Travelling Moods: Varieties of Cultural Appropriation (1850–1950)*, ed. Christian Huck and Stefan Bauernschmidt, 15–35. Frankfurt am Main: Campus Verlag, 2012.
Hahn, Thomas. "The Difference the Middle Ages Makes: Color and Race Before the Modern World." *Journal of Medieval and Early Modern Studies* 31, no. 1 (2001): 1–37.
Ha-Kohen, Isaac b. Simson. *Ḥamishah ḥumshei torah ve-ha-tikkun sofrim im perush Rashi*. Prague, 1610.
HaKohen, Ruth. *The Music Libel Against the Jews*. New Haven, CT: Yale University Press, 2012.
Ha-Kohen, Tuvia. *Ma'aseh Toviyyah*. Venice, 1708.
Hamburger, Jeffrey F. "Seeing and Believing: The Suspicion of Sight and the Authentication of Vision in Late Medieval Art and Devotion." In *Imagination und Wirklichkeit: Zum Verhältnis von mentalen und realen Bildern in der Kunst der Frühen Neuzeit*, ed. Klaus Krüger and Alessandro Nova, 47–69. Mainz: Von Zabern, 2000.
Hamburger, Jeffrey F., and Anne-Marie Bouché, eds. *The Mind's Eye: Art and Theological Argument in the Middle Ages*. Princeton, NJ: Department of Art and Archaeology, Princeton University, 2006.
Hamilton, Bernard, and C. F. Beckingham, eds. *Prester John: The Mongols and the Ten Lost Tribes*. Aldershot: Variorum, 1996.
Hannover, Nathan. *Abyss of Despair (Yeven Metsulah): The Famous 17th Century Chronicle Depicting Life in Russia and Poland During the Chmielnicki Massacres of 1648–1649*. Trans. Abraham J. Mesch. New Brunswick, NJ: Transaction Publishers, 1983.
Harari, Yuval. "Ancient Israel and Early Judaism." In *Guide to the Study of Ancient Magic*, ed. David Frankfurter, 139–74. Leiden: Brill, 2019.
Haraway, Donna. "The Persistence of Vision." In *Writing on the Body: Female Embodiment and Feminist Theory*, ed. Katie Conboy, Nadia Medina, and Sarah Stanbury. New York: Columbia University Press, 1997.
Harel-Hoshen, Sarah, and Yossi Avner, eds. *Beyond the Sambatyon: The Myth of the Ten Lost Tribes* (Hebrew). Tel Aviv: Beth Hatefutsoth, 1991.
Harshav, Benjamin. *Marc Chagall and the Lost Jewish World: The Nature of Chagall's Art and Iconography*. New York: Rizzoli, 2006.
———. *The Polyphony of Jewish Culture*. Stanford, CA: Stanford University Press, 2007.
———. "The Role of Language in Modern Art: On Texts and Subtexts in Chagall's Paintings." *Modernism/Modernity* 1, no. 2 (1994): 51–87.

Hasan-Rokem, Galit. "Rabbi Me'ir, May His Lamp Shine: On the Name as a Sign" (Hebrew). In *Lights: Light in Literature, Thought and Art*, ed. Emily Bilski, Amitai Mendelsohn, and Avigdor Shinan, 120–27. Tel Aviv: Am Oved, 2005.

———. "Rabbi Me'ir, the Illuminated and the Illuminating: Interpreting Experience." In *Current Trends in the Study of Midrash*, ed. Carol Bakhos, 227–43. Leiden: Brill, 2006.

Hasan-Rokem, Galit, and Alan Dundes, eds. *The Wandering Jew: Essays in the Interpretation of a Christian Legend*. Bloomington: Indiana University Press, 1986.

Heller, Eva. *Wie Farben auf Gefühl und Verstand wirken: Farbpsychologie, Farbsymbolik, Lieblingsfarben, Farbgestaltung*. Munich: Droemer, 2000.

Heller, Marvin J. "Moses Ben Abraham Avinu and His Printing-Presses." In *Studies in the Making of the Early Hebrew Book*, ed. Marvin J. Heller. Leiden: Brill, 2008.

———. *The Sixteenth-Century Hebrew Book: An Abridged Thesaurus*. 2 vols. Leiden: Brill, 2004.

Henry, John. "The Fragmentation of Renaissance Occultism and the Decline of Magic." *History of Science* 46 (2008): 1–48.

Hill, Charles E. "Antichrist from the Tribe of Dan." *Journal of Theological Studies*, n.s., 46, no. 1 (1995): 99–117.

Höfert, Almut. *Den Feind beschreiben: "Türkengefahr" und europäisches Wissen über das Osmanische Reich 1450–1600*. Frankfurt am Main: Campus Verlag, 2003.

Hoffman, Jeffrey. "Akdamut: History, Folklore, and Meaning." *Jewish Quarterly Review* 99, no. 2 (2009): 161–83.

Horowitz, Elliott. "Circumcised Dogs from Matthew to Marlowe." *Prooftexts* 27, no. 3 (2007): 531–45.

———. "A 'Dangerous Encounter': Thomas Coryate and the Swaggering Jews of Venice." *Journal of Jewish Studies* 52, no. 2 (2001): 341–53.

———. "Odd Couples: The Eagle and the Hare, the Lion and the Unicorn." *Jewish Studies Quarterly* 11 (2004): 243–58.

———. *Reckless Rites: Purim and the Legacy of Jewish Violence*. Princeton, NJ: Princeton University Press, 2008.

———. "The Way We Were: Jewish Life in the Middle Ages." *Jewish History* 1, no. 1 (1986): 75–90.

Horowitz, Judah b. Mordechai Halevi. *Amudei beit Yehudah*. Amsterdam: Leib Zosmans, 1766.

Horrox, Rosemary, ed. *The Black Death*. Manchester: Manchester University Press, 1994.

Hottenroth, Friedrich. *Altfrankfurter Trachten: Von den ersten geschichtlichen Spuren an bis ins 19. Jahrhundert*. 3 vols. in 1 vol. Frankfurt am Main: Heinrich Keller, 1912.

———. *Deutsche Volkstrachten: Vom XVI. Jahrhundert bis zum XIX. Jahrhundert*. 2nd ed. Frankfurt am Main: Heinrich Keller, 1923.

Howes, David, and Constance Classen. *Ways of Sensing: Understanding the Senses in Society*. London: Routledge, 2014.

Huber, Wolfgang. "Das Endgericht-Fenster der St. Marienkirche in Frankfurt (Oder): Ein theologischer Dialog mit einem mittelalterlichen Kunstwerk." In *Das spätgotische Antichristfenster: Eine biblische Botschaft im Zusammenspiel von Glas, Farbe und Licht*, ed. Brigitte Rieger-Jähner, 7–11. Frankfurt an der Oder: Museum Junge Kunst, 2007.

Hutten, Ulrich von. *Die Geschicht und Bekenntnis des getauften Juden Johannes Pfefferkorn*. N.p., 1514/15.

Idel, Moshe. "Kabbalistic Prayer and Colors." In *Approaches to Judaism in Medieval Times*, ed. David R. Blumenthal, 3:17–27. Atlanta: Scholars Press, 1988.

———. "Kavvanah and Colors: A Forgotten Kabbalistic Responsum" (Hebrew). In *Tribute to Sara: Studies in Jewish Philosophy and Kabbala Presented to Professor Sara O. Heller-Wilensky*, ed. Devorah Dimant, Shalom Rosenberg, and Moshe Idel, 1–14. Jerusalem: Magnes Press, 1994.

———. "On Judaism, Jewish Mysticism and Magic." In *Envisioning Magic*, ed. Peter Schäfer and Hans G. Kippenberg, 195–214. Leiden: Brill, 1997.

———. "Visualization of Colors, I: David Ben Yehudah He-Ḥasid's Kabbalistic Diagram." *Ars Judaica* 11 (2015): 31–54.

———. "Visualization of Colors, II: Implications of David Ben Yehudah He-Ḥasid's Diagram for the History of Kabbalah." *Ars Judaica* 12 (2016): 39–51.

Idelson-Shein, Iris. *Difference of a Different Kind: Jewish Constructions of Race During the Long Eighteenth Century*. Jewish Culture and Contexts. Philadelphia: University of Pennsylvania Press, 2014.

———. "Kill the Hen That Crows Like a Cock: Animal Encounters in Old Yiddish." *Journal of Jewish Studies* 71, no. 2 (2020): 321–44.

———. "Meditations on a Monkey-Face: Monsters, Transgressed Boundaries and Contested Hierarchies in a Yiddish Eulenspiegel." *Jewish Quarterly Review* 108, no. 1 (2018): 28–59.

———. "The Monstrous Mame: Mapping the Margins of Maternity in Early Modern Jewish Discourse." *Jewish Social Studies* 20, no. 3 (2014): 37–71.

———. "Rabbis of the (Scientific) Revolution: Revealing the Hidden Corpus of Early Modern Translations Produced by Jewish Religious Thinkers." *American Historical Review* 126, no. 1 (2021): 54–82.

———. "Of Wombs and Words: Migrating Misogynies in Early Modern Medical Literature in Latin and Hebrew." *AJS Review*, 46, no. 2 (2022): 243–69.

———. "'What Have I to Do with Wild Animals?': Glikl Bas Leib and the Other Woman." *Eighteenth-Century Studies* 44, no. 1 (2010): 57–77.

Imber, Naphtali Herz. *Barkai ha-shlishi o go'el ha-dam*. New York: A. Ch. Rosenberg, 1904.

———. *Barkai (he-ḥadash): Shirei Ẓion*. Zlotczow, 1900.

———. *Sefer Barkai*. Jerusalem, 1886.

*In disem biechlin wirt erfunden von complexion der menschen: Zu erlernen leypliche vnd menschliche natur/ ir sitten/ geberden vnd neyglicheit zu erkennen vnd vrteylen*. Strasbourg: Johannes Knobloch, 1516.

Indagine, Johannes. *Die kunst der Chiromantzey, uß besehung der hend, Physiognomey, uß anblick des menschens, Natürlichen Astrologey noch dem lauff der Son[n]en*. Strasbourg: Schott, 1523.

Iser, Wolfgang. *The Act of Reading: A Theory of Aesthetic Response*. Baltimore: Johns Hopkins University Press, 1978.

Jacob b. Mordecai of Fulda. *Shoshanat Ya'acov: Be-ḥokhmat ha-yad ve-ha-parẓuf vi-she'ar ha-avirim*. Amsterdam, 1706.

Jacobs, Martin. *Reorienting the East: Jewish Travelers to the Medieval Muslim World*. Philadelphia: University of Pennsylvania Press, 2014.

Jacquart, Danielle, and Claude Thomasset. *Sexuality and Medicine in the Middle Ages*. Trans. Matthew Adamson. Cambridge: Polity Press, 1988.

Jacquesson, Francois. "Les mots de la couleur en hébreu ancien." In *Histoire et géographie de la couleur*, ed. P. Dollus, Francois Jacquesson, and Michel Pastoureau, 67–130. Paris: Le Léopard d'Or, 2013.

Jaeger, Achim. *Ein jüdischer Artusritter: Studien zum jüdisch-deutschen "Widuwilt" ("Artushof") und zum "Wigalois" des Wirnt von Gravenberc*. Conditio Judaica 32. Tübingen: Niemeyer, 2000.
Jauss, Hans Robert. *Toward an Aesthetic of Reception*. Minneapolis: University of Minnesota Press, 1982.
Jay, Martin. *Downcast Eyes: The Denigration of Vision in Twentieth-Century French Thought*. Berkeley: University of California Press, 1994.
Jellinek, Adolph. *Bet ha-Midrasch: Sammlung kleiner Midraschim und vermischter Abhandlungen aus der ältern jüdischen Literatur nach Handschriften u. Druckwerken*. 2nd ed. 6 vols. Jerusalem: Bamberger & Wahrmann, 1938.
Jenks, Gregory C. *The Origins and Early Development of the Antichrist Myth*. Berlin: De Gruyter, 1991.
Joffe, Judah A., and Mark Yudel, eds. *Great Dictionary of the Yiddish Language*. 4 vols. New York: Yiddish Dictionary Committee, 1961.
Johnson, Willis. "The Myth of Jewish Male Menstruation." *Journal of Medieval History* 24, no. 3 (1998): 273–95.
Jonas, Justus. *Das siebend Capitel Danielis von des Türcken Gotteslesterung vnd schrecklich morderey*. Wittenberg, 1929.
———. *Ein Sermon von der Historien Judae Jscharioth/ vnd des Judas Kusse*. Halle, 1543.
Jones, Adrian. *The Nature of the Book: Print and Knowledge in the Making*. Chicago: University of Chicago Press, 1998.
Jones, Ann Rosalind, and Peter Stallybrass. *Renaissance Clothing and the Materials of Memory*. Cambridge: Cambridge University Press, 2007.
Jones, William Jervis. *German Colour Terms: A Study in Their Historical Evolution from Earliest Times to the Present*. Amsterdam: John Benjamins Publishing Company, 2013.
———. *Historisches Lexikon deutscher Farbbezeichnungen*. 5 vols. Berlin: Akademie Verlag, 2013.
Jordan, William Chester. "The Medieval Background." In *Struggles in the Promised Land: Towards a History of Black-Jewish Relations in the United States*, ed. Jack Salzman and Cornel West, 53–64. Oxford: Oxford University Press, 1997.
Joseph, Paul. *Gründlicher beweiß/ auß dem alten Testament/ vnd zum theil auß dem Jüdischen Talmud/ Wie daß Christus Jesus der Jungfrau Marie Son/ sey der wahre verheissene Messias vnd Heyland der Welt/ vnd die ander Person inn der heiligen Dreyfaltigkeit*. Altdorf, 1612.
Junkerjürgen, Ralf. *Haarfarben: Eine Kulturgeschichte in Europa seit der Antike*. Köln: Böhlau, 2009.
Jütte, Daniel. "Interfaith Encounters Between Jews and Christians in the Early Modern Period and Beyond: Toward a Framework." *American Historical Review* 118, no. 2 (2013): 378–400.
Jütte, Robert. *Geschichte der Sinne: Von der Antike bis zum Cyberspace*. Munich: Beck, 2000.
———. *Leib und Leben im Judentum*. Berlin: Jüdischer Verlag, 2016.
Kabakoff, Jacob, ed. *Master of Hope: Selected Writings of Naphtali Herz Imber*. New York: Herzl Press, 1985.
———. *Naftali Herz Imber "Ba'al Ha-Tikva."* Lod: Habermann Institute for Literary Research, 1991.
———. "Naphtali Herz Imber as a Yiddish Poet." In *Identity and Ethos: A Festschrift for Sol Liptzin on the Occasion of His 85th Birthday*, ed. Mark H. Gelber, 49–67. New York: Peter Lang, 1986.

Kagan, Zipora. "The Ten Tribes in the Folktales of Jewish Ethnic Groups" (Hebrew). *Mahanayim* 93–94 (1964): 148–57.

Kahana, Maoz. *From the "Noda be-Yehudah" to the "Hatam Sofer": Halakhic Writing in a Changing World*. Jerusalem: Zalman Shazar, 2015.

———. "The Lost Sefer Meirav and the Vision of Scientific Religion: An Unknown Chapter in the World of R. Yehonatan Eybeshütz" (Hebrew). *Zion* 84, no. 2 (2019): 229–77.

Kaplan, Debra. *Beyond Expulsion: Jews, Christians and Reformation Strasbourg*. Stanford, CA: Stanford University Press, 2011.

Karg, Detlef, ed. *Die Chorfenster der St. Marienkirche in Frankfurt (Oder)*. Worms: Wernersche Verlagsgesellschaft, 2008.

Kattan Gribetz, Sarit. "Hanged and Crucified: The Book of Ester and Toledot Yeshu." In *Toledot Yeshu ("The Life Story of Jesus") Revisited: A Princeton Conference*, ed. Peter Schäfer, Michael Meerson, and Yaacov Deutsch, 159–80. Tübingen: Mohr Siebeck, 2011.

Katz, David S. "Shylock's Gender: Jewish Male Menstruation in Early Modern England." *Review of English Studies* 50, no. 200 (1999): 440–62.

Katz, Dovid. *Yiddish and Power*. Basingstoke: Palgrave Macmillan, 2015.

Kauders, Anthony. "What Power for Which Jews? (Post) Modern Reflections of the Idea of Power in Jewish Historiography." In *Modern Judaism and Historical Consciousness: Identities, Encounters, Perspectives*, ed. Andreas Gotzmann and Christian Wiese, 349–67. Leiden: Brill, 2007.

Kaufmann, Thomas. "Das Judentum in der frühreformatorischen Flugschriftenpublizistik." *Zeitschrift für Theologie und Kirche* 95 (1998): 429–61.

———. *Türckenbüchlein: Zur christlichen Wahrnehmung türkischer Religion in Spätmittelalter und Reformation*. Göttingen: Vandenhoeck & Ruprecht, 2008.

Kaufmann, Thomas DaCosta. *The Mastery of Nature: Aspects of Art, Science and Humanism in the Renaissance*. Princeton, NJ: Princeton University Press, 1993.

Keil, Martha. "'. . . und seinem Köcher Anglis': Kulturtransfer, Polemik und Humor in jüdischen Geschäftsurkunden des mittelalterlichen Österreich." In *Festschrift für Friedrich Battenberg*, ed. Markus J. Wenninger and Rotraud Ries, 1:101–15. Aschkenas: Zeitschrift für Geschichte und Kultur der Juden 26, 2016.

Keller, Adelbert von, ed. *Fastnachtspiele aus dem 15. Jahrhundert*. Vols. 1–2. 1853. Reprint, Darmstadt: Wissenschaftliche Buchgesellschaft, 1965.

Kelly, Joan. "Did Women Have a Renaissance?" In *Women, History and Theory: The Essays of Joan Kelly*. Chicago: University of Chicago Press, 1986.

Kemp, Martin. "Vision and Visualisation in the Illustration of Anatomy and Astronomy from Leonardo to Galileo." In *1543 and All That: Image and Word, Change and Continuity in the Proto-Scientific Revolution*, ed. Guy Freeland and Anthony Corones, 17–51. Dordrecht: Kluwer Academic Publishers, 2000.

Kerner, Alex. "'The Invisible Body': Physiology and Levels of Humanity in Sixteenth Century Europe Following the Encounter with the Natives of the New World." PhD diss., Tel Aviv University, 2011.

Kessler, Herbert L. *Seeing Medieval Art*. Peterborough, Ont.: Broadview Press, 2004.

———. "Shaded with Dust: Jewish Eyes on Christian Art." In *Judaism and Christian Art: Aesthetic Anxieties from the Catacombs to Colonialism*, ed. Herbert L. Kessler and David Nirenberg, 74–114. Philadelphia: University of Pennsylvania Press, 2013.

———. *Spiritual Seeing: Picturing God's Invisibility in Medieval Art*. Philadelphia: University of Pennsylvania Press, 2000.

Kim, Dorothy. "Reframing Race and Jewish/Christians Relations in the Middle Ages." *Transversal: Journal for Jewish Studies* 13, no. 1 (2015): 52–64.

Kirchhan, Elhanan Henle. *Simḥat ha-nefesh*. Frankfurt am Main, 1707.

Kirchhof, Hans Wilhelm. *Wendunmuth*. Ed. Hermann Oesterley. Stuttgart: Litterarischer Verein, 1869.

Klibansky, Raymond, Erwin Panofsky, and Fritz Saxl. *Saturn and Melancholy: Studies in the History of Natural Philosophy, Religion and Art*. London: Nelson, 1964.

Knaeble, Susanne. "Ironische Distanzierung im Fokus intertextuellen Erzählens: Der westjiddische Widuwilt als Rezeptionsgegenstand." In *Ironie, Polemik und Provokation*, ed. Cora Dietl, Christoph Schanze, and Friedrich Wolfzettel, 85–108. Schriften der internationalen Artusgesellschaft, Sektion Deutschland/Österreich 10. Berlin: De Gruyter, 2014.

Knefelkamp, Ulrich. "Der Priesterkönig Johannes und sein Reich: Legende oder Realität?" *Journal of Medieval History* 14, no. 4 (1988): 337–55.

Knefelkamp, Ulrich, and Frank Martin, eds. *Der Antichrist: Die Glasmalereien in der Marienkirche in Frankfurt (Oder)*. Leipzig: Edition Leipzig, 2008.

Kogman-Appel, Katrin. "The Audiences of the Late Medieval Haggadah." In *Patronage, Production and Transmission of Texts in Medieval and Early Modern Jewish Cultures*, ed. Esperanza Alfonso and Jonathan Decter, 99–143. Turnhout: Brepols, 2014.

———. *A Mahzor from Worms: Art and Religion in a Medieval Jewish Community*. Cambridge, MA: Harvard University Press, 2012.

Köhler, Hans-Joachim, ed. *Flugschriften des frühen 16. Jahrhunderts (1501–1530)*. Zug: IDC Publishers, 1978.

Köhler, Manfred. *Melanchthon und der Islam: Ein Beitrag zur Klärung des Verhältnisses zwischen Christentum und Fremdreligionen in der Reformationszeit*. Reprint, [1937]. Hamburg: Severus Verlag, 2013.

Koller, Sabine. *Marc Chagall: Grenzgänge zwischen Literatur und Malerei*. Vienna: Böhlau, 2012.

Költsch, Anke. "Die abenteuerliche Reise des Josua ben Abraham Eschel (Johann Friedrich Augusti)." In *Beiträge zur Geschichte der Juden Schwarzburgs*, ed. Bettina Bernighausen, 109–17. Dresden: Sandstein, 2006.

Koppitz, Alfred, ed. *Der Göttweiger Trojanerkrieg*. Deutsche Texte des Mittelalters 29. Berlin: Weidmann, 1926.

Kramer, Michael. *Eyn vnderredung vom glawben, durch Micheln kromer, Pfarherr zu Cunitz, vnd eynem Judischen Rabien, mit namen Jacob vonn Brucks, geschehen ynß Richters hauße do selbst zu Cunitz. Mitwoch nach Andree M.D.xxiij*. Erfurt, 1523.

Krüger, Klaus. "Die Lesbarkeit von Bildern: Bemerkungen zum bildungssoziologischen Kontext von kirchlichen Bildausstattungen im Mittelalter." In *Bild und Bildung: Ikonologische Interpretationen vormoderner Dokumente von Erziehung und Bildung*, ed. Christian Rittelmeyer and Erhard Wiersing, 105–33. Wiesbaden: Harrassowitz, 1991.

Kuhn, Adalbert, and Wilhelm Schwartz. *Norddeutsche Sagen, Märchen und Gebräuche aus Meklenburg, Pommern, der Mark, Sachsen, Thüringen, Braunschweig, Hannover, Oldenburg und Westfalen. Aus dem Munde des Volkes*. Hildesheim: Olms, 1983.

Kühn, Christoph. *Jüdische Delinquenten in der Frühen Neuzeit: Lebensumstände delinquenter Juden in Aschkenas und die Reaktionen der jüdischen Gemeinden sowie der christlichen Obrigkeit*. Potsdam: Universitätsverlag, 2008.

Landau, Leo. *Arthurian Legends or the Hebrew-German Rhymed Version of the Legend of King Arthur*. Teutonica: Arbeiten zur germanischen Philologie 21. Leipzig: Eduard Avenarius, 1912.

Landshut, Eli'ezer. *Amudei ha-avodah (Columnae cultus): Reshimat rashei ha-paytanim*. Berlin: G. Bernstein, 1857.
Langer, Gerhard Josef. *Esau: Bruder und Feind*. Göttingen: Vandenhoeck & Ruprecht, 2009.
Langmuir, Gavin I. *Toward a Definition of Antisemitism*. Berkeley: University of California Press, 1996.
Largier, Niklaus. "Die Applikation der Sinne: Mittelalterliche Ästhetik als Phänomenologie rhetorischer Effekte." In *Das fremde Schöne: Dimensionen des Ästhetischen in der Literatur des Mittelalters*, ed. Manuel Braun and Christopher Young, 43–60. Trends in Medieval Philology 12. Berlin: De Gruyter, 2007.
Lauffer, Otto. *Farbensymbolik im deutschen Volksbrauch*. Hamburg: Hanseatischer Gildenverlag, 1948.
Lazar, Simon Menahem. "Aseret ha-shvatim." *Ha-Shilo'aḥ* 9 (1912): 46–56, 205–21, 352–63, 431–47, 520–28; 10 (1912): 42–56, 156–64, 226–35.
———. *Ḥidot ha-hagadot ha-nifla'ot al davar aseret ha-shvatim u-pitronan*. Drohobycz: Hamizpe, 1908.
Leb Bresch. *Ḥamishah ḥumshei torah im keẓat perush Rashi ve-im ha-haftarot*. Cremona: Vincenzo Conti, 1560.
Leeuwen, Theo van. *The Language of Colour: An Introduction*. Abingdon: Routledge, 2011.
Lehmann, Beat. *ROT ist nicht "rot" ist nicht (rot): Eine Bilanz und Neuinterpretation der linguistischen Relativitätstheorie*. Tübingen: Narr, 1998.
Leipold, Aletta, and Hans-Joachim Solms. "Farbbezeichnungen im Mittelhochdeutschen und Frühneuhochdeutschen." *Sprachwissenschaft* 34, no. 3 (2009): 317–40.
Lembke, Astrid. "Aventiuren in Aschkenas: Jüdische Aneignungen nichtjüdischer Texte und Erzählstoffe im vormodernen Europa." *Aschkenas: Zeitschrift für Geschichte und Kultur der Juden* 25, no. 1 (2015): 1–10.
———. "Das unwillige Untier: Ehe, Gefolgschaft und Autonomie in den französischen und jiddischen Werwolferzählungen Maries de France (12. Jh.) und im Mayse-Bukh (1602)." *Germanisch-Romanische Monatsschrift* 68 (2018): 1–16.
———. "The Raging Rabbi: Aggression and Agency in an Early Modern Yiddish Werewolf Tale (Mayse-Bukh 1602)." In *Monsters and Monstrosity in Jewish History: From the Middle Ages to Modernity*, ed. Iris Idelson-Shein and Christian Wiese, 201–12. London: Bloomsbury, 2019.
———. "Ritter außer Gefecht: Konzepte passiver Bewährung im Wigalois und im Widuwilt." *Aschkenas: Zeitschrift für Geschichte und Kultur der Juden* 25, no. 1 (2015): 63–82.
Lenowitz, Harris. *Jewish Messiahs: From the Galilee to Crown Heights*. New York: Oxford University Press, 1998.
Levin, Michael. "Encountering the Hasidic Enclave." *Jewish Book Council Visiting Scribe* (blog), October 16, 2013. https://www.jewishbookcouncil.org/pb-daily/encountering-the-hasidic-enclave.
Levin, Sala. "The Biggest Jewish Genetic Myths of All Time." *Moment Magazine* (July/August 2012): 28–31.
Lewinsky, Tamar. *Displaced Poets: Jiddische Schriftsteller im Nachkriegsdeutschland, 1945–1951*. Jüdische Religion, Geschichte und Kultur 9. Göttingen: Vandenhoeck & Ruprecht, 2008.
Lewis, Bernard. *Cultures in Conflict: Christians, Muslims, and Jews in the Age of Discovery*. New York: Oxford University Press, 1996.

---. *The Jews of Islam*. Princeton, NJ: Princeton University Press, 2014.
Liberles, Robert. "Jews and Christians in Early Modern Germany." *Leo Baeck Institute Year Book* 55, no. 1 (2010): 39–40.
Liebes, Yehuda. "Helen's Porphyry and Kiddush Ha-Shem" (Hebrew). *Daat: A Journal of Jewish Philosophy and Kabbalah*, no. 57/59 (2006): 83–119.
---. "Physiognomy in Kabbalah" (Hebrew). *Pe'amim: Studies in Oriental Jewry* 104 (2005): 21–40.
Limor, Ora, and Israel Jacob Yuval. "Judas Iscariot: Revealer of the Hidden Truth." In *Toledot Yeshu ("The Life Story of Jesus") Revisited: A Princeton Conference*, ed. Peter Schäfer, Michael Meerson, and Yaacov Deutsch, 197–220. Tübingen: Mohr Siebeck, 2011.
Linares, Marina. *Alles Wissenswerte über Farben: Farbenlehre, Kunsttheorie, Farbenpsychologie, Kulturgeschichte, neue Medien*. Essen: Die Blaue Eule, 2005.
---. "Kunst und Kultur im Mittelalter: Farbschemata und Farbsymbole." In *Farbe im Mittelalter: Materialität—Medialität—Semantik*, ed. Ingrid Bennewitz and Andrea Schindler, 1:297–311. Berlin: Akademie Verlag, 2011.
Lindberg, David C. *Theories of Vision from Al-Kindi to Kepler*. Chicago: University of Chicago Press, 1976.
Linn, Irving. "Widwilt Son of Gawain." PhD diss., New York University, 1942.
Lipsker, Avidov. *Red Poem Blue Poem: Seven Essays on Uri Zvi Grinberg and Two Essays on Else Lasker-Schüler* (Hebrew). Ramat Gan: Bar-Ilan University Press, 2010.
Lipton, Sara. *Dark Mirror: The Medieval Origins of Anti-Semitic Iconography*. New York: Metropolitan Books, 2014.
---. "The Jew's Face: Vision, Knowledge, and Identity in Medieval Anti-Jewish Caricature." In *Late Medieval Jewish Identities: Iberia and Beyond*, ed. Carmen Caballero-Navas and Esperanza Alfonso, 259–87. New York: Palgrave Macmillan, 2010.
Litt, Stefan. "Juden und Waffen im 16. und 17. Jahrhundert: Anmerkungen zu einem Alltagsphänomen." *Aschkenas: Zeitschrift für Geschichte und Kultur der Juden* 13, no. 1 (2003): 83–92.
---. *Jüdische Gemeindestatuten aus dem aschkenasischen Kulturraum 1650–1850*. Göttingen: Vandenhoeck & Ruprecht, 2013.
Livak, Leonid. *The Jewish Persona in the European Imagination: A Case of Russian Literature*. Stanford Studies in Jewish History and Culture. Stanford, CA: Stanford University Press, 2010.
Lorenz, Dagmar C. G. "Imaginierte Körperfarben: Zur Konstruktion und Kritik rassistisch besetzter Farbsemantiken das Jüdische betreffend." In *Die Farben imaginierter Welten: Zur Kulturgeschichte ihrer Codierung in Literatur und Kunst vom Mittelalter bis zur Gegenwart*, ed. Monika Schausten, 183–98. Literatur Theorie Geschichte. Berlin: Akademie Verlag, 2012.
Luther, Martin. *D. Martin Luthers Werke: Kritische Gesamtausgabe (Weimarer Ausgabe)*. Cambridge: Proquest, 2006.
*Ma'aseh gvurat ha-shem*. Lviv, 1839.
Maccoby, Hyam. *Judas Iscariot and the Myth of Jewish Evil*. New York: The Free Press, 1992.
MacDonald, Tara. "'Red-Headed Animal': Race, Sexuality and Dickens's Uriah Heep." *Critical Survey* 17, no. 2 (2005): 48–62.
MacIntyre. "Tradition and Translation." In *Translation Studies*, ed. Mona Baker, 198–214. London: Routledge, 2009.

Maimonides, Moses. *The Code of Maimonides (Mishneh Torah)*. 14 vols. Yale Judaica Series. New Haven, CT: Yale University Press, 1949.

Makover, Menachem. *Ha-levush ha-yehudi be-Eiropa be-mahalakh ha-dorot*. Bnei Brak: Hamodia, 2012.

Mandel, Werner. "Das Bild der Juden im Antichristfenster der St. Marienkirche zu Frankfurt (Oder)." In *Das spätgotische Antichristfenster: Eine biblische Botschaft im Zusammenspiel von Glas, Farbe und Licht*, ed. Brigitte Rieger-Jähner, 32. Frankfurt an der Oder: Museum Junge Kunst, 2007.

Mangelsdorf, Frank, ed. *Der gläserne Schatz: Die Bilderbibel der St. Marienkirche in Frankfurt (Oder)*. 2nd ed., revised and enlarged. Berlin: Das Neue Berlin, 2007.

Mann, Vivian B. *Jewish Texts on the Visual Arts*. Cambridge: Cambridge University Press, 2000.

Marcus, Ivan G. "A Jewish-Christian Symbiosis: The Culture of Early Ashkenaz." In *Cultures of the Jews: A New History*, ed. David Biale, 449–516. New York: Schocken, 2002.

———. "Jews and Christians Imagining the Other in Medieval Europe." *Prooftexts* 15 (1995): 209–26.

———. *Rituals of Childhood: Jewish Acculturation in Medieval Europe*. New Haven, CT: Yale University Press, 1998.

Margaliot, Mordechai, ed. *Midrash ha-gadol: Al ḥamishah ḥumshei torah*, vol. 1: *Sefer bereshit*. Reprint (1947). Jerusalem: Mosad Harav Kook, 1966/67.

———, ed. *Midrash va-yikra rabbah*. Vol. 1. Jerusalem: Misrad ha-ḥinukh ve-ha-tarbut, 1953.

Margaritha, Antonius. *Der gantz Jüdisch glaub mit sampt ainer gründtlichen vnd warhafften anzaygunge/ Aller Satzungen/ Ceremonien/ Gebetten/ Haymliche vnd offentliche Gebreuch/ deren sich dye Juden halten/ durch das gantz Jar/ Mit schönen vnd gegründten Argumenten wyder jren Glauben*. Augsburg: Heinrich Steiner, 1530.

Margolin, Jean-Claude. "Sur quelques ouvrages de la bibliothèque de Postel annotés de sa main." In *Guillaume Postel 1581–1981: Actes du colloque international d'Avranches 5–9 septembre 1981*, 109–30. Paris: Editions Guy Trédaniel, 1985.

Massyngbaerde, Ford J. "The Physical Features of the Antichrist." *Journal of the Study of the Pseudepigrapha* 14 (1996): 24–41.

Matt, Daniel C., ed. *The Zohar: Pritzker Edition*. 12 vols. Stanford, CA: Stanford University Press, 2004.

Matteoni, Francesca. "Blood Beliefs in Early Modern Europe." PhD diss., University of Hertfordshire, 2009.

———. "The Jew, the Blood and the Body in Late Medieval and Early Modern Europe." *Folklore* 119, no. 2 (2008): 182–200.

Mayer, Tamar. "From Zero to Hero." In *Gender Ironies of Nationalism: Sexing the Nation*, ed. Tamar Mayer, 283–307. London: Taylor and Francis, 2012.

*Mayse dos da hayst Megiles Reb Meyer*. Amsterdam: Uri Fayvsh b. Aaron ha-Levi, 1660.

McGinn, Bernard. *Antichrist: Two Thousand Years of the Human Fascination with Evil*. New York: Columbia University Press, 2000.

Meerson, Michael. "Physiognomy and Somatomancy: The Ways That Never Crossed." In *Envisioning Judaism: Studies in Honor of Peter Schäfer on the Occasion of His Seventieth Birthday*, ed. Ra'anan S. Boustan et al., 1:563–85. Tübingen: Mohr Siebeck, 2013.

Meerson, Michael, and Peter Schäfer, eds. *Toledot Yeshu: The Life Story of Jesus*. 2 vols. Texts and Studies in Ancient Judaism 159. Tübingen: Mohr Siebeck, 2014.

*Me-ever le-nahar Sambatyon . . . : Akdamut mevu'arot le-talmidim.* Jerusalem: Sefarim ḥinukhiyim, n.d.

*Megiles Reb Meyer.* Cremona: Vincenzo Conti, [ca. 1560].

Meier, Christel. "The Colourful Middle Ages: Anthropological, Social and Literary Dimension of Colour Symbolism and Colour Hermeneutics." In *Tradition and Innovation in an Era of Change*, ed. Rudolf Suntrup and Jan R. Veenstra, 227–56. Frankfurt am Main: Lang, 2001.

Meier, Christel, and Rudolf Suntrup. *Handbuch der Farbenbedeutung im Mittelalter*, vol. 2: *Lexikon der allegorischen Farbendeutung*. Pictura et poesis 30. Cologne: Böhlau, 2011.

———. "Zum Lexikon der Farbenbedeutungen im Mittelalter. Einführung zu Gegenstand und Methoden sowie Probeartikel aus dem Farbenbereich 'Rot.'" *Frühmittelalterliche Studien* 21 (1987): 390–478.

Meier, Eugen A. *Verträumtes Basel: Fünftausend Häusernamen—ein unbekanntes Kapitel Basler Stadtgeschichte*. Basel: Springer, 1974.

Meinung, Sandra. "Die Restaurierung im 19. Jahrhundert." In *Das spätgotische Antichristfenster: Eine biblische Botschaft im Zusammenspiel von Glas, Farbe und Licht*, ed. Brigitte Rieger-Jähner, 55–61. Frankfurt an der Oder: Museum Junge Kunst, 2007.

Meir, Jonatan. "The Imagined Decline of Kabbalah: The Kabbalistic Yeshiva Sha'ar Ha-Shamayim and Kabbalah in Jerusalem in the Beginning of the Twentieth Century." In *Kabbalah and Modernity: Interpretations, Transformations, Adaptations*, ed. Boaz Huss, Marco Pasi, and Kocku von Stuckrad, 197–220. Aries Book Series 10. Leiden: Brill, 2010.

———. *Kabbalistic Circles in Jerusalem (1896–1948)*. Aries Book Series 22. Leiden: Brill, 2016.

———. "Me'ora'ot Tsvi and the Construction of Sabbatianism in the Nineteenth Century." In *Making History Jewish: The Dialectics of Jewish History in Eastern Europe and the Middle East. Studies in Honor of Professor Israel Bartal*, ed. Pawel Maciejko und Scott Ury, 30–51. Studia Judaeoslavica 12. Leiden: Brill, 2020.

———. "Sefer Ḥalomei Qets Pela'ot (Meora'ot Tzvi 1814) and the Image of Sabbatianism in the 18th and 19th Centuries" (Hebrew). *Jewish Thought: Journal of the Goldstein-Goren International Center for Jewish Thought* 1 (2019): 125–67.

Meitlis, Jacob. *Das Ma'assebuch, seine Entstehung und Quellengeschichte, zugleich ein Beitrag zur Einführung in die altjiddische Agada*. Berlin: Mass, 1933.

———. "Some Extant Folktales in Yiddish Mss." *Fabula* 12 (1971): 212–17.

Melamed, Abraham. "The Discovery of America in Jewish Literature of the Sixteenth and Seventeenth Centuries" (Hebrew). In *Following Columbus: America 1492–1992*, ed. Miriam Eliav-Feldon, 443–64. Jerusalem: Zalman Shazar, 1997.

———. *The Image of the Black in Jewish Culture: A History of the Other*. London: Routledge, 2003.

Mellinkoff, Ruth. *Antisemitic Hate Signs in Hebrew Illuminated Manuscripts from Medieval Germany*. Jerusalem: Center for Jewish Art, 1999.

———. "Judas's Red Hair and the Jews." *Journal of Jewish Art* 9 (1982): 31–46.

———. *Outcasts: Signs of Otherness in Northern European Art of the Late Middle Ages*. 2 vols. Berkeley: University of California Press, 1993.

Menache, Sophia. "Tartars, Jews, Saracens and the Jewish-Mongol 'Plot' of 1241." *History: The Journal of the Historical Association* 81 (1996): 319–42.

Menasseh ben Israel. *The Hope of Israel: The English Translation by Moses Wall, 1652*. Ed. Henry Méchoulan and Gérard Nahon. London: Littman Library of Jewish Civilization, 1987.

———. *Sefer mikveh Yisra'el*. Trans. Mordechai b. Moses Drucker. Amsterdam, 1691.
Mendele Moykher Sforim. *Ale verk fun Mendele Moykher Sforim*. Vol. 10. Warsaw: Farlag Mendele, 1911.
———. *Kol kitvei Mendele Mokher Sefarim*. 8th ed. Tel Aviv: Devir, 1958.
———. *Tales of Mendele the Book Peddler: Fishke the Lame and Benjamin the Third*. Ed. Ken Frieden and Dan Miron. New York: Schocken, 1996.
Metzger, Thérèse, and Mendel Metzger. *Jewish Life in the Middle Ages: Illuminated Hebrew Manuscripts of the Thirteenth to the Sixteenth Centuries*. London: Alpine Fine Arts Collection, 1985.
Michels, Evi. "Yiddish *Toledot Yeshu* Manuscripts from the Netherlands." In *Toledot Yeshu in Context: The Jewish "Life of Jesus" in Ancient, Medieval, and Modern History*, ed. Daniel Barbu and Yaacov Deutsch, 231–62. Texts and Studies in Ancient Judaism 82. Tübingen: Mohr Siebeck, 2020.
Milano, Attilio, and Federica Francesconi. "Cremona." In *Encyclopaedia Judaica*, ed. Michael Berenbaum and Fred Skolnik, 5:283–84. Detroit: Macmillan, 2007.
Miles, Margaret. *Image as Insight: Visual Understanding in Western Christianity and Secular Culture*. Reprint. Eugene, OR: Wipf & Stock Pub, 2006.
Miller, William Ian. *The Anatomy of Disgust*. Cambridge, MA: Harvard University Press, 1997.
Milner, A. D., and Melvyn A. Goodale. *The Visual Brain in Action*. Oxford: Oxford University Press, 2006.
Mirkin, Moses, ed. *Midrash Rabbah*. 11 vols. Tel-Aviv: Yavneh, 1957–67.
Miron, Dan. *A Traveler Disguised: The Rise of Modern Yiddish Fiction in the Nineteenth Century*. Judaic Traditions in Literature, Music, and Art. Syracuse, NY: Syracuse University Press, 1996.
Miron, Dan, and Anita Norich. "The Politics of Benjamin III: Intellectual Significance and Its Formal Correlatives in Sh. Y. Abramovitsh's 'Masoes Benyomin Hashlishi.'" In *The Field of Yiddish; Studies in Language, Folklore, and Literature*, ed. Marvin Herzog, 4:1–115. Philadelphia: Institute for the Study of Human Issues, 1980.
Mitchell, W. J. Thomas. *Iconology: Image, Text, Ideology*. Reprint. Chicago: University of Chicago Press, 2009.
Müller, David Heinrich von. *Die Recensionen und Versionen des Eldad had-Dânî: Nach den alten Drucken von Constantinopel, Mantua und Venedig und den Handschriften von London, Oxford, Parma, Rom, St. Petersburg und Wien*. Denkschriften der Kaiserlichen Akademie der Wissenschaften in Wien: Philosophisch-historische Classe 42, Abt. 1. Vienna: Tempsky, 1892.
Münster, Sebastian. *Messias Christianorum et Judaeorum*. Basel: Heinrich Peter, 1539.
Musper, H. Theodor. *Der Antichrist und die fünfzehn Zeichen*. 2 vols. Munich: Prestel, 1970.
Myers, David N., ed. *Notes: Overcoming Matter?* Special issue *Jewish Quarterly Review* 95, no. 3 (2005): 435–507.
Nahshon, Gad. "Ha-yehudim ha-admonim: Ha-tadmit shel yehudei Teiman be-eynav shel Naphtali Herz Imber 'ba'al Ha-tikvah.'" *Moznayim* 70, no. 3 (1996): 19–20.
———. "The Metaphor of the Yemenite Jews in the Eyes of Naphtali Herz Imber, Author of Hatikvah" (Hebrew). *Tema: Journal of Judeo-Yemenite Studies* 6 (1998): 95–100.
Neher, André. *Jewish Thought and the Scientific Revolution of the Sixteenth Century: David Gans (1541–1613) and His Times*. Oxford: Oxford University Press, 1986.

Neis, Rachel Rafael. *Sense of Sight in Rabbinic Culture: Jewish Ways of Seeing in Late Antiquity*. Cambridge: Cambridge University Press, 2013.

Neubauer, Adolf. *Catalogue of the Hebrew Manuscripts in the Bodleian Library*. Reprint (1886). Oxford: Clarendon Press, 1994.

———. "Collections on Matters Pertaining to the Ten Tribes and the Sons of Moses" (Hebrew). *Kobez al Yad* 4 (1888): 9–74.

———. "Where Are the Ten Tribes?" *Jewish Quarterly Review* 1 (1889): 14–28, 95–114, 185–201, 408–23.

Neuber, Wolfgang. "The 'Red Indian's Body': The Physiognomy of the Indigenous American Between Exoticism and Learned Culture in the Early Modern Period." In *Modelling the Individual: Biography and Portrait in the Renaissance*, ed. Karl Enenkel, Betsy de Jong-Crane, and Peter Liebregts, 93–107. Amsterdam: Rodopi, 1998.

Neugroschel, Joachim. *The Great Works of Jewish Phantasy and Occult*. New York: Overlook, 1987.

———, ed. *Radiant Days, Haunted Nights: Great Tales from the Treasury of Yiddish Folk Literature*. New York: Duckworth, 2005.

*Neüwe Zeittung/ Von dem grossen Heer der roten Juden/ so auß den Gebirgen/ Caspij genant/ in Asia herfür kommen*. [Nuremberg], 1562.

*Newe Zeittung: Von den Newen Juden/ so aus dem gebirge Caspir kommen sein/ mit Zweimalhunderttausent vnd Sieben vnd Sechtzig tausent Mannen/ in willens das gelobte Land widerumb einzunemen/ Vnd nennen sich von nachfolgenden Sechs geschlechten*. Cologne: Nikolaus Schreiber, 1574.

Niborski, Yitskhok, Bernard Vaisbrot, and Simon Neuberg. *Dictionnaire Yiddish-Français*. 2nd ed. Paris: Bibliothèque Medem, 2011.

Nigrinus, Georg. *Jüden Feind. Von den Edlen Früchten der Thalmudischen Jüden/ so jetziger zeit in Teutschelande wonen/ ein ernstel wol gegründte Schrifft* . . . [Strasbourg], 1570.

Nikolsky, Ronit. "The History of the Rechabites and the Jeremiah Literature." *Journal for the Study of the Pseudepigrapha* 13, no. 2 (2002): 185–207.

———. "The Rechabites in Ma'aseh Alexandros and in the Medieval Ben Sira." *Zutot* 4 (2004): 35–41.

Nirenberg, David. *Aesthetic Theology and Its Enemies: Judaism in Christian Painting, Poetry, and Politics*. Hanover, NH: Brandeis University Press, 2015.

Nolden, Thomas. *In Lieu of Memory: Contemporary Jewish Writing in France*. Syracuse, NY: Syracuse University Press, 2006.

Novershtern, Avraham. *The Lure of Twilight: Apocalypse and Messianism in Yiddish Literature* (Hebrew). Jerusalem: Magnes Press, 2003.

Noy, Dov, ed. *The Golden Feather: Twenty Folktales Narrated by Greek Jews* (Hebrew). Haifa: Ethnological Museum and Folklore Archives, 1976.

———, ed. *Moroccan Jewish Folktales*. New York: Herzl, 1966.

———. "Motif-Index of Talmudic-Midrashic Literature." PhD diss., University of Indiana, 1954.

Noy, Dov, and Dan Ben-Amos, eds. *Folktales of the Jews*. Vol. 1. Philadelphia: Jewish Publication Society, 2006.

Nussbaum, Martha C. *Upheavals of Thought: The Intelligence of Emotions*. Cambridge: Cambridge University Press, 2003.

Nutton, Vivian. "Humoralism." In *Companion Encyclopedia of the History of Medicine*, ed. W. F. Bynum and Roy Porter, 1:281–91. London: Routledge, 1993.

Oberman, H. A. "The Stubborn Jews: Timing the Escalation of Antisemitism in Late Medieval Europe." *Leo Baeck Institute Year Book* 34, no. 1 (1989): 11–25.

Offenberg, Sara. "A Jewish Knight in Shining Armor: Messianic Narrative and Imagination in Ashkenazic Illuminated Manuscripts." *University of Toronto Journal of Jewish Thought* 4 (2014): 1–14.

Ofrat, Gideon. *Back to the Sea* (Hebrew). Tel Aviv: Omanut Yisrael, 1990.

Oișteanu, Andrei. *Inventing the Jew: Antisemitic Stereotypes in Romanian and Other Central-East European Cultures*. Studies in Antisemitism. Lincoln: University of Nebraska Press, 2009.

Osborne, Roy. *Books on Colour, 1495–2015: History and Bibliography*. Raleigh, NC: Lulu Press, 2015.

Osgood, Kelsey. "Hasidic Chic: New Exhibit Explores the Sartorial Elements of Hasidic Culture." *Jewcy*, July 19, 2013. https://www.jewcy.com/arts-and-culture/hasidic-chic-new-exhibit-explores-the-sartorial-elements-of-hasidic-culture/.

Pach, Hilde. "Moushe's Choices: Was the Compositor of the Oldest Yiddish Newspaper a Creator or an Epigone?" *Studia Rosenthaliana* 40 (2007–8): 195–204.

Padilla, Carmella, and Barbara Anderson, eds. *A Red Like No Other: How Cochineal Colored the World*. New York: Skira Rizzoli, 2015.

Paivio, Allan. *Imagery and Verbal Processes*. New York: Holt, Rinehart, and Winston, 1971.

Parfitt, Tudor. *The Lost Tribes of Israel: The History of a Myth*. London: Weidenfeld & Nicolson, 2002.

———. *The Road to Redemption: The Jews of the Yemen, 1900–1950*. Leiden: Brill, 1996.

Pastoureau, Michel. "Ceci est mon sang: Le christianisme médiéval et la couleur rouge." In *Le pressoir mystique: Actes du colloque de recloses, 27 mai 1989*, ed. Danièle Alexandre-Bidon, 43–56. Paris: Les éditions du cerf, 1990.

———. *Couleurs, images, symboles: Études d'histoire et d'anthropologie*. Paris: Le Léopard d'or, 1989.

———. *Figures et couleurs: Études sur la symbolique et la sensibilité médiévales*. Paris: Le Léopard d'or, 1986.

———. *Red: The History of a Color*. Princeton, NJ: Princeton University Press, 2017.

Paucker, Arnold. "Yiddish Versions of Early German Prose Novels." *Journal of Jewish Studies* 10, no. 3–4 (1959): 151–67.

Paulson, William R. *Enlightenment, Romanticism, and the Blind in France*. Princeton, NJ: Princeton University Press, 1987.

Peachey, Stewart, ed. *Dyeing: Clothes of the Common People in Elizabethan and Early Stuart England*. Bristol: Stuart Press, 2013.

Peles, Israel, ed. *R. Juda Löw Kirchheim: The Customs of Worms Jewry* (Hebrew). Jerusalem: Machon Yerushalayim, 1987.

Peretz, Y. L. *Ale verk*. Vol. 5. New York: CYCO, 1947.

Perlow, Isaac. "Royte yidelekh." *Undzer Veg* 17, no. 80 (1947): 10.

Perry, Micha. *Eldad's Travels: A Journey from the Lost Tribes to the Present*. Routledge Focus. London: Routledge, 2019.

———. "The Imaginary War Between Prester John and Eldad the Danite and Its Real Implications." *Viator: Medieval and Renaissance Studies* 41, no. 1 (2010): 1–23.

Perry, Micha, and Rebekka Voß. "Approaching Shared Heroes: Cultural Transfer and Transnational Jewish History." *Jewish History* 30 (2016): 1–13.

Petrovskii-Shtern, Iokhanan. *Anti-Imperial Choice: The Making of the Ukrainian Jew*. New Haven, CT: Yale University Press, 2009.

Petzold, Andreas. "The Iconography of Color." In *The Routledge Companion to Medieval Iconography*, ed. Colum Hourihane, 437–52. London: Routledge, 2017.

Pfeifer, Wolfgang. *Etymologisches Wörterbuch des Deutschen*. 3 vols. Berlin: Akademie Verlag, 1989.

Pfister, Kurt. *Das puch von dem Entkrist*. Leipzig: Insel-Verlag, 1925.

Phillips, Bríd. *Shakespeare and Emotional Expression: Finding Feeling Through Colour*. London: Routledge, 2022.

*Phisionomi vnd Chiromanci: Eyn news Complexion buechlein/ der menschen geburt/ sitten/ geberden vnd neygligkeyten/ auß der Phisionomie/ Chiromanci/ den siben Planeten/ zwölff Zeichen/ vnd den XXXvj. Bildern deß Himels/*... Strasbourg: Cammerlander, 1540.

Pleij, Herman. *Colors Demonic and Divine: Shades of Meaning in the Middle Ages and After*. New York: Columbia University Press, 2004.

Pollak, Michael. "The Revelation of a Jewish Presence in Seventeenth-Century China: Its Impact on Western Messianic Thought." In *The Jews of China*, ed. Jonathan Goldstein, 1:50–70. Armonk, NY: Sharpe, 1999.

Pomata, Gianna. "Menstruating Men: Similarity and Difference of the Sexes in Early Modern Medicine." In *Generation and Degeneration: Tropes of Reproduction in Literature and History from Antiquity Through Early Modern Europe*, ed. Valeria Finucci and Kevin Brownlee, 109–52. Durham, NC: Duke University Press, 2001.

———. "Observation Rising: Birth of an Epistemic Genre, 1500–1650." In *Histories of Scientific Observation*, ed. Lorraine Daston and Elizabeth Lunbeck, 45–80. Chicago: University of Chicago Press, 2011.

Popkin, Richard H. "The Rise and Fall of the Jewish Indian Theory." In *Menasseh Ben Israel and His World*, ed. Yosef Kaplan, Henry Mechoulan, and Richard H. Popkin, 63–82. Leiden: Brill, 1989.

Popović, Mladen. "4Q186. 4QZodiacal Physiognomy: A Full Edition." In *The Mermaid and the Partridge: Essays from the Copenhagen Conference [June 2009] on Revising Texts from Cave Four*, ed. George J. Brooke and J. Högenhaven, 221–58. Leiden: Brill, 2011.

———. *Reading the Human Body: Physiognomics and Astrology in the Dead Sea Scrolls and Hellenistic-Early Roman Period Judaism*. Studies on the Texts of the Desert of Judah 67. Leiden: Brill, 2007.

Porte, Wilhelm. *Judas Ischarioth in der bildenden Kunst*. Berlin: Draeger, 1883.

Porter, Martin. *Windows of the Soul: Physiognomy in European Culture, 1470–1780*. Oxford Historical Monographs. Oxford: Clarendon Press, 2005.

Posnanski, Adolf. *Schiloh: Ein Beitrag zur Geschichte der Messiaslehre*, vol. 1: *Die Auslegung von Genesis 49,10 im Altertume bis zu Ende des Mittelalters*. Leipzig: J. C. Hinrichs, 1904.

Posselt, Alfred H. *Geschichte des chazarisch-jüdischen Staates*. Vienna: Verlag des Vereins zur Förderung und Pflege des Reformjudentums, 1982.

Prager, Leonard. "Yiddish Matters: Sholem-Aleykhem's 'Alemen Glaykh.'" *Mendele Review: Yiddish Literature and Language* 3, no. 9 (blog), May 22, 1999. http://yiddish.haifa.ac.il/tmr/tmr03/tmr03009.txt.

Presner, Todd. *Muscular Judaism: The Jewish Body and the Politics of Regeneration*. London: Routledge, 2007.

Prilutski, Noah. *Yidishe folkslider*. Vol. 1. Warsaw: Bikher far ale, 1911.

Przybilski, Martin. *Kulturtransfer zwischen Juden und Christen in der deutschen Literatur des Mittelalters*. Berlin: De Gruyter, 2010.

Pulliam, Heather. "Color." *Studies in Iconography* 33 (2012): 3–14.

Raba, Joel. *Between Remembrance and Denial: The Fate of the Jews in the Wars of the Polish Commonwealth During the Mid-Seventeenth Century as Shown in Contemporary Writings and Historical Research*. Boulder, CO: East European Monographs, 1995.

Ragotzky, Hedda. "Fastnacht und Endzeit: Zur Funktion der Antichrist-Figur im Nürnberger Fastnachtspiel des 15. Jahrhunderts." *Zeitschrift für deutsche Philologie* 121, no. 1 (2002): 54–71.

Rajner, Mirjam. "Chagall's Jew in Bright Red." *Ars Judaica* 4 (2008): 61–80.

Ramos, Manuel João. *Essays in Christian Mythology: The Metamorphosis of Prester John*. Lanham, MD: University Press of America, 2006.

Raspe, Lucia. "The Black Death in Jewish Sources: A Second Look at Mayse Nissim." *Jewish Quarterly Review* 94 (2004): 471–89.

———. *Jüdische Hagiographie im mittelalterlichen Aschkenas*. Tübingen: Mohr Siebeck, 2006.

———. "Minhag and Migration: Yiddish Custom Books from Sixteenth-Century Italy." In *Regional Identities and Cultures of Medieval Jews*, ed. Javier Castano, Talya Fishman, and Ephraim Kanarfogel, 241–59. London: Littman Library of Jewish Civilization, 2018.

———. "On Men and Women Reading Yiddish: Between Manuscript and Print." *Jewish Studies Quarterly* 26, no. 3 (2019): 199–202.

———. "Portable Homeland: The German-Jewish Diaspora in Italy and Its Impact on Ashkenazic Book Culture, 1400–1600." In *Early Modern Ethnic and Religious Communities in Exile*, ed. Yosef Kaplan, 26–43. Newcastle upon Tyne: Cambridge Scholars Publishing, 2017.

———. "Vom Rhein nach Galiläa: Rabbi Meir Schatz von Worms als Held hagiographischer Überlieferung." *Aschkenas: Zeitschrift für Geschichte und Kultur der Juden* 17, no. 2 (2007): 431–55.

———. "When King Dagobert Came to Halle: Place and Displacement in Medieval Jewish Legend." *Jewish Studies Quarterly* 20 (2013): 146–58.

Ravid, Benjamin. "From Yellow to Red: On the Distinguishing Head-Covering of the Jews of Venice." *Jewish History* 6, no. 1–2 (1992): 179–210.

Recio, Belinda. *The Essence of Red*. Salt Lake City, UT: Gibbs Smith, 1996.

Reed, Stephen K. *Cognition: Theories and Applications*. 9th ed. Belmont, CA: Wadsworth Cengage Learning, 2013.

Reich, Rosalie. *Tales of Alexander the Macedonian: A Medieval Hebrew Manuscript. Text and Translation with a Literary and Historical Commentary*. New York: Ktav Publishing House, 1972.

Reiner, Elchanan. "The Ashkenazi Elite at the Beginning of the Modern Era: Manuscript Versus Printed Book." *Polin: Studies in Polish Jewry* 10 (1997): 85–98.

———. "On the Roots of the Urban Jewish Community in Poland in the Early Modern Period" (Hebrew). *Gal-Ed: On the History and Culture of Polish Jewry* 20 (2006): 13–37.

Reinharz, Jehuda, and Yaacov Shavit. *Glorious, Accursed Europe*. Waltham, MA: Brandeis University Press, 2010.

Reißer, Ulrich. *Physiognomik und Ausdruckstheorie der Renaissance: Der Einfluss charakterologischer Lehren auf Kunst und Kunsttheorie des 15. und 16. Jahrhunderts*. Munich: Scaneg, 1997.

Renaut de Bâgé. *Le Bel Inconnu (Li Biaus Descouneüs; The Fair Unknown)*. Ed. Karen L. Fresco. 1992. Reprint, London: Routledge, 2020.

Resnick, Irven M. *Marks of Distinction: Christian Perceptions of Jews in the High Middle Ages*. Washington, DC: Catholic University of America Press, 2012.

———. "Medieval Roots of the Myth of Jewish Male Menses." *Harvard Theological Review* 93, no. 3 (2000): 241–63.

Ridder, Klaus. "Emotion und Reflexion in erzählender Literatur des Mittelalters." In *Codierungen von Emotionen im Mittelalter/Emotions and Sensibilities in the Middle Ages*, ed. C. Stephen Jaeger and Ingrid Kasten, 203–21. Berlin: De Gruyter, 2003.

Riedel, Sigrid. *Moses Henochs Altschul-Jeruschalmi "Brantspigel": Transkribiert und ediert nach der Erstausgabe Krakau 1596*. Frankfurt am Main: Peter Lang, 1993.

Rieger-Jähner, Brigitte, ed. *Das spätgotische Antichristfenster: Eine biblische Botschaft im Zusammenspiel von Glas, Farbe und Licht*. Frankfurt an der Oder: Museum Junge Kunst, 2007.

Ritzmann, Iris. "Judenmord als Folge des 'Schwarzen Todes': Ein medizinhistorischer Mythos?" *Medizin, Geschichte und Gesellschaft* 17 (1998): 101–30.

Rivkind, Isaac. "The Historical Allegory of Rabbi Meir Shatz" (Yiddish). *Studies in Philology* 3 (1929): 1–42.

———. "Megilat R. Me'ir Shaẓ (He'arot le-Ma'aseh Akdamut)." *Ha-do'ar* 9, no. 30 (1930): 507–9.

Rivlin, Robert, and Karen Gravelle. *Deciphering the Senses: The Expanding World of Human Perception*. New York: Simon and Schuster, 1985.

Röcke, Werner, and Hans Rudolf Velten, eds. *Lachgemeinschaften: Kulturelle Inszenierungen und soziale Wirkungen von Gelächter im Mittelalter und in der Neuzeit*. Berlin: De Gruyter, 2005.

Rogers, Francis M. *The Quest for Eastern Christians Travels and Rumor in the Age of Discovery*. Minneapolis: University of Minnesota Press, 1962.

Rohrbacher, Stefan, and Michael Schmidt. *Judenbilder: Kulturgeschichte antijüdischer Mythen und antisemitischer Vorurteile*. Reinbek bei Hamburg: Rowohlt, 1991.

Röhrich, Lutz. *Folktales and Reality*. Bloomington: Indiana University Press, 1991.

Romer-Segal, Agnes. "Sifrut yidish ve-kahal koreiha ba-me'ah ha-17: Yeẓirot be-yidish be-reshimot ha-'zikuk' mi-Mantova, 1595." *Kirjath Sepher* 53, no. 4 (1978): 779–90.

———. "Yiddish Works on Women's Commandments in the Sixteenth Century." In *Studies in Yiddish Literature and Folklore*, ed. Chava Turniansky, 37–59. Jerusalem: Hebrew University, 1986.

Rosen, Tova. "Kazahrs, Mongols, and the Pains of the Time of Messiah." In *Between History and Literature*, ed. Michal Oron, 42–59. Tel Aviv: Dionon, 1983.

Rosenberg, Warren. *Legacy of Rage: Jewish Masculinity, Violence, and Culture*. Amherst: University of Massachusetts Press, 2001.

Rosenfeld, Hans-Friedrich. "And. \*roda, ahd. \*matara, mlat. gaisto, gaisdo, ahd. retza, frühmhd. risza, rizza, 'Färberröte, Krapp, Rubia tinctorum L.' und Verwandtes." In *Festschrift für Gerhard Cordes zum 65. Geburtstag*, ed. Friedhelm Debus and Joachim Hartig, 2:257–298. Neumünster: Karl Wachholtz Verlag, 1976.

Rosenthal, Judah. *Sefer Yosef ha-mekaneh*. Jerusalem: Mekiẓe Nirdamim, 1970.

Rosenwein, Barbara H. "Feudal War and Monastic Peace: Cluniac Liturgy as Ritual Aggression." *Viator: Medieval and Renaissance Studies* 2 (1972): 129–57.

Rosenzweig, Claudia. *Bovo d'Antona by Elye Bokher: A Yiddish Romance. A Critical Edition with Commentary*. Leiden: Brill, 2016.

———. "The History of Jesus' Life in a Eighteenth-Century Yiddish Manuscript (NLI Heb. 8° 5622)." In *Toledot Yeshu in Context: The Jewish "Life of Jesus" in Ancient, Medieval, and Modern History*, ed. Daniel Barbu and Yaacov Deutsch, 263–316. Texts and Studies in Ancient Judaism 82. Tübingen: Mohr Siebeck, 2020.

———. "When Jesus Spoke Yiddish: Some Remarks on a Yiddish Manuscript of the 'Toledot Yeshu' (MS. Günzburg 1739)." *PaRDeS: Zeitschrift der Vereinigung für Jüdische Studien* 21 (2015): 199–214.

Roth, Cecil. *Die Haggadah von Sarajevo*. 2nd ed. Leipzig: Seemann-Verlag, 1967.

Roth, Ernst, and Leo Prijs. *Die Handschriften der Stadt- und Universitätsbibliothek Frankfurt am Main*. Vol. 1. Verzeichnis der orientalischen Handschriften in Deutschland 6. Stuttgart: Steiner, 1982.

Roth, Joseph. *Radetzky March*. Trans. Geoffrey Dunlop. New York: Viking Press, 1933.

Rothkrug, Lionel. "Peasant and Jew: Fears of Pollution and German Collective Perceptions." *Historical Reflections/Réflexions Historiques* 10, no. 1 (1983): 59–77.

Rotman, David. *Dragons, Demons, and Wondrous Realms: The Marvelous in Medieval Hebrew Narrative* (Hebrew). Modi'in: Dvir, 2016.

———. "A Lamb and a Wolf, an Author and Fiction: Hebrew Adaptations of Aesopian Fables from the Middle Ages to Early Modern Era" (Hebrew). In *Studies in Honor of Prof. Eli Yassif*, ed. Tova Rosen, Nili Arye-Sapir, Tsafi Sebba-Elran, and David Rotman, 495–537. TE'UDA: The Chaim Rosenberg School of Jewish Studies Research 28, 2018.

———. "Sexuality and Communal Space in Stories About the Marriage of Men and She-Demons." In *Monsters and Monstrosity in Jewish History: From the Middle Ages to Modernity*, ed. Iris Idelson-Shein and Christian Wiese, 187–200. London: Bloomsbury, 2019.

Rubin, Miri. "Opfer und Erlösung in der christlichen Ikonographie." In *Blut: Kunst, Macht, Politik, Pathologie. Katalog der Ausstellung Frankfurtam Main*, ed. James M. Bradburne, 89–99. Munich: Prestel, 2001.

Rubin, Uri. *Between Bible and Qur'an: The Children of Israel and Islamic Self-Image*. Princeton, NJ: Darwin Press, 1999.

Rubinstein, Rachel. *Members of the Tribe: Native America in the Jewish Imagination*. Detroit: Wayne State University Press, 2010.

Rublack, Ulinka. *The Crimes of Women in Early Modern Germany*. Oxford: Clarendon Press, 2001.

Ruderman, David B. *Early Modern Jewry: A New Cultural History*. Princeton, NJ: Princeton University Press, 2010.

———. *Jewish Thought and Scientific Discovery in Early Modern Europe*. Detroit: Wayne State University Press, 2001.

———. *Kabbalah, Magic and Science: The Cultural Universe of a Sixteenth-Century Jewish Physician*. Cambridge, MA: Harvard University Press, 1988.

———. *The World of a Renaissance Jew: The Life and Thought of Abraham ben Mordecai Farissol*. Cincinnati: Hebrew Union College Press, 1981.

Rudolph, Conrad. "La resistenza all'arte nell'Occidentale." In *Arti e storia nell Medioevo*, ed. Enrico Castelnuovo and Giuseppe Sergi, 3:49–84. Turin: Einaudi, 2004.

———. *The "Things of Greater Importance": Bernard of Clairvaux's Apologia and the Medieval Attitude Toward Art*. Philadelphia: University of Pennsylvania Press, 1990.

Sadan, Dov. *Kol shirei Naftali Herz Imber*. Tel Aviv: Morchechai Newman, [1950].
Sadowski, Dirk. "Hebräischer Buchdruck in Halle und Jeßnitz in der ersten Hälfte des 18. Jahrhunderts: Die Proselyten-Drucker Moses ben Avraham Avinu und Israel bar Avraham." In *Mission ohne Konversion? Studien zu Arbeit und Umfeld des Institutum Judaicum et Muhammedicum in Halle*, ed. Brigitte Klosterberg and Grit Schorch, 135–53. Hallesche Forschungen 51. Halle: Verlag der Franckeschen Stiftungen, 2019.
Saenger, Paul. *Space Between Words: The Origins of Silent Reading*. Stanford, CA: Stanford University Press, 2001.
Sagiv, Gadi. "Dazzling Blue: Color Symbolism, Kabbalistic Myth, and the Evil Eye in Judaism." *Numen* 64 (2017): 183–208.
———. "Deep Blue: Notes on the Jewish Snail Fight." *Contemporary Jewry* 35 (2015): 285–313.
———. *Jewish Blues: A History of a Color in Judaism*. Philadelphia: University of Pennsylvania Press, 2023.
Said, Edward. *Orientalism*. 1978. Reprint, London: Penguin, 2003.
Salamon, Avrohom Yaacov, ed. *Akdamus Millin: With a New Translation and Commentary Anthologized from the Traditional Rabbinic Literature*. 2nd ed. Brooklyn, NY: Mesorah Publications, 1993.
Salomon, Isaak Seeligmann Berend. *Catalogus der seit vielen Jahren berühmten vollständigen hebreischen Bibliothek des ehemaligen Prager Ober-Rabbiners weiland Herrn David Oppenheimers*. Hamburg: Johann Michael Brauer, 1782.
Sammern, Romana. "Red, White and Black: Colors of Beauty, Tints of Health and Cosmetic Materials in Early Modern English Art Writing." In *Early Modern Color Worlds*, ed. Tawrin Baker, Sven Dupré, Sachiko Kusukawa, and Karin Leonhard, 109–39. Leiden: Brill, 2016.
Schäfer, Peter. "Agobard's and Amulo's Toledot Yeshu." In *Toledot Yeshu ("The Life Story of Jesus") Revisited: A Princeton Conference*, ed. Peter Schäfer, Michael Meerson, and Yaacov Deutsch, 27–48. Tübingen: Mohr Siebeck, 2011.
———. *Mirror of His Beauty: Feminine Images of God from the Bible to the Early Kabbalah*. Princeton, NJ: Princeton University Press, 2002.
Schäfer, Peter, Michael Meerson, and Yaacov Deutsch, eds. *Toledot Yeshu ("The Life Story of Jesus") Revisited: A Princeton Conference*. Tübingen: Mohr Siebeck, 2011.
Schawelka, Karl. *Farbe: Warum wir sie sehen, wie wir sie sehen*. Weimar: Verlag der Bauhaus-Universität, 2007.
Scheiber, Alexander, and Louis Tardy. "L'echo de la premiere manifestation de David Reubeni dans les brochures de colportage allemande de l'epoque." *Revue des Etudes Juives* 32 (1973): 595–601.
Schipper, Jeremy. *Disability and Isaiah's Suffering Servant*. Oxford: Oxford University Press, 2011.
Schlie, Heike. "Erscheinung und Bildvorstellung im spätmittelalterlichen Kulturtransfer: Die Rezeption der Imago pietatis als Selbstoffenbarung Christi in Rom." In *Das Bild der Erscheinung: Die Gregorsmesse im Mittelalter*, ed. Andreas Gormans and Thomas Lentes, 59–121. Berlin: Reimer, 2007.
Schmidt, Peter. "Kleben statt malen: Handschriftenillustration im Augustiner-Chorfrauenstift Inzigkofen." In *Studien und Texte zur literarischen und materiellen Kultur der Frauenklöster im späten Mittelalter*, ed. Falk Eisermann, Eva Schlotheuber, and Volker Honemann, 243–83. Leiden: Brill, 2004.

Schmieder, Felicitas. "Christians, Jews, Muslims and Mongols: Fitting a Foreign People into the Western Christian Apocalyptic Scenario." *Medieval Encounters: Jewish, Christian and Muslim Culture in Confluence and Dialogue* 12, no. 2 (2006): 274–95.

Schneider, Ingo. "Erzählungen als kulturelle Konstruktionen: Über Bedingungen des Fremdverstehens und Grenzen des Erzählens zwischen den Kulturen." In *Erzählen zwischen den Kulturen*, ed. Sabine Wienker-Piepho and Klaus Roth, 21–32. Münchner Beiträge zur interkulturellen Kommunikation 17. Münster: Waxmann, 2004.

Schneider, Jane. "Peacocks and Penguins: The Political Economy of European Cloth and Colors." *American Ethnologist* 5 (1978): 413–47.

Scholem, Gershom. "Ein Fragment zur Physiognomik und Chiromantik aus der Tradition der spätantiken jüdischen Esoterik." In *Liber Amicorum: Studies in Honour of Prof. Dr. C. J. Bleeker*, 175–93. Leiden: Brill, 1969.

———. "Farben und ihre Symbolik in der jüdischen Überlieferung und Mystik." In *The Realm of Color/Die Welt der Farben (Vorträge gehalten auf der Eranos-Tagung in Ascona, vom 23. bis 31. August 1972)*, ed. Adolf Portmann, 41:1–49. Eranos-Jahrbuch. Leiden: Brill, 1974.

———. *Sabbatai Sevi: The Mystical Messiah, 1626–1676*. Princeton, NJ: Princeton University Press, 2016.

Sholem Aleichem. *Ale verk fun Sholem Aleichem*. Vol. 5. New York: Forverts, 1944.

———. *Di nayeste verk*. Warsaw: Tsentral, 1915.

———. *Why Do the Jews Need a Land of Their Own?* Trans. Joseph Leftwich and Mordecai S. Chertoff. New York: Herzl Press Publication, 1984.

Schorsch, Ismar. "A Meditation on Maoz Zur." *Judaism: A Quarterly Journal of Jewish Life and Thought* 37, no. 4 (1988): 459–64.

Schorsch, Jonathan. *Jews and Blacks in the Early Modern World*. Cambridge: Cambridge University Press, 2004.

Schreckenberg, Heinz. *Die christlichen Adversus-Judaeos-Texte und ihr literarisches und historisches Umfeld (11.–13. Jh.): Mit einer Ikonographie des Judenthemas bis zum 4. Laterankonzil*. 3rd enlarged ed. Vol. 2. Frankfurt am Main: Peter Lang, 1997.

———. *Die Juden in der mittelalterlichen Kunst Europas*. Göttingen: Vandenhoeck & Ruprecht, 1996.

Schreiner, Stefan. "Isaiah 53 in the Sefer Hizzuk Emunah ('Faith Strengthened') of Rabbi Isaac b. Abraham of Troki." In *The Suffering Servant: Isaiah 53 in Jewish and Christian Sources*, ed. Peter Stuhlmacher and Bernd Janowski, 418–61. Grand Rapids, MI: Eerdmans, 2004.

Schudt, Johann Jacob. *Jüdische Merckwürdigkeiten: Vorstellende was sich curieuses und denckwürdiges in den neuern Zeiten bey einigen Jahrhunderten mit denen in alle IV. Theile der Welt, sonderlich durch Teutschland, zerstreuten Juden zugetragen: sammt einer vollständigen Franckfurter Juden-Chronick, darinnen der zu Franckfurt am Mayn wohnenden Juden, von einigen Jahr-Hunderten, biss auff unsere Zeiten, merckwürdigste Begebenheiten enthalten: Benebst einigen, zur Erläuterung beygefügten Kupffern und Figuren*. 3 vols. Frankfurt-Leipzig: S. T. Hocker, 1714.

Schwarz (Nigri), Peter (Petrus). *Stern Meschiah*. Esslingen, 1477.

Schwarzfeld, Moses. "Evreii în literatura lor populară: Studiu etnico-psichologic." In *Anuar pentru israeliți: Cu un supliment calendaristic pe anii 5658 și 5659 (1897–1899)*, ed. Moses Schwarzfeld, 1–37. Bucharest: Universală, 1898.

Schwoebel, Robert. *The Shadow of the Crescent: The Renaissance Image of the Turk (1453–1517)*. New York: St. Martin's Press, 1967.
Scott, James C. *Domination and the Arts of Resistance: Hidden Transcripts*. New Haven, CT: Yale University Press, 1990.
Scribner, Robert W. *Religion and Culture in Germany (1400–1800)*. Ed. Lyndal Roper. Leiden: Brill, 2001.
———. "Ways of Seeing in the Age of Dürer." In *Dürer and His Culture*, ed. Dagmar Eichberger and Charles Zika, 93–117. Cambridge: Cambridge University Press, 1998.
Seeligmann, Sigmund. *Catalog der reichhaltigen Sammlung Hebräischer u. Jüdischer Bücher, Handschriften, Portraits etc. nachgelassen von N. H. van Biema in Amsterdam*. Amsterdam: Joachimsthal, 1904.
*Sefer Akdamut*. Warsaw, 1902.
*Sefer Eldad ha-Dani*. [Dessau, 1700?].
*Sefer Eldad ha-Dani*. Jessnitz, 1723.
*Sefer ma'aseh gvurat ha-shem*. 1839. Reprint, Lviv, [1850s].
*Sefer ma'aseh gvurot ha-shem*. Lviv, [1916].
*Sefer magishei minḥah*. 3 vols. Amsterdam: Moshe Frankfurt, 1725.
*Sefer me'ora'ot Ẓvi: Sippur ḥalumot kez ha-pela'ot*. Warsaw: Nathan Shriftgisser, 1885.
Sela, Shulamit. "The Genealogy of Sefo Ben Elifaz: The Importance of a Genizah Fragment for Jossipon's History." In *Genizah Research After Ninety Years: The Case of Judeo-Arabic. Papers Read at the Third Congress of the Society for Judeo-Arabic Studies*, ed. Joshua Blau and Stefan C. Reif, 138–43. Cambridge: Cambridge University Press, 1992.
Sewell, John. "The Son Rebelled and So the Father Made Man Alone: Ridicule and Boundary Maintenance in the Nizzahon Vetus." In *Laughter in the Middle Ages and Early Modern Times: Epistemology of a Fundamental Human Behavior, Its Meaning, and Consequences*, ed. Albrecht Classen, 295–324. Fundamentals of Medieval and Early Modern Culture 5. Berlin: De Gruyter, 2010.
Shachar, Isaiah. *The Judensau: A Medieval Anti-Jewish Motif and Its History*. London: Warburg Institute, 1974.
Shamir. *Mayse fun di royte yudlekh*. Warsaw, 1902; Vilnius, 1907; Vilnius, 1910.
Shamir. *Mayse fun aseyres hashvotim in Sambatyen*. Vilnius, 1910.
Shandler, Jeffrey. *Adventures in Yiddishland: Postvernacular Language and Culture*. Berkeley: University of California Press, 2005.
———. *Yiddish: Biography of a Language*. Oxford: Oxford University Press, 2020.
Shenhar, Aliza. *Ha-sippur ha-amami shel edot Yisra'el*. Tel Aviv: Tcherikover, 1982.
Shmeruk, Chone. "Gli inizi della prosa narrativa in Yiddish e il suo centro in Italia" (Hebrew). In *Scritti in memoria di Leone Carpi: Saggi sull'Ebraismo Italiano*, ed. Daniel Carpi, Attilio Milano, and Alexander Rofé, 119–40. Jerusalem: Fondazione Sally Mayer, 1967.
———. *The Illustrations in Yiddish Books of the Sixteenth and Seventeenth Centuries: The Texts, the Pictures and Their Audience* (Hebrew). Jerusalem: Akademon Press, 1986.
———. *Yiddish Literature: Aspects of Its History* (Hebrew). Tel-Aviv: Porter Institute for Poetics and Semiotics, 1978.
———. "Yiddish Printing in Italy" (Hebrew). *Italia: Studi e ricerche sulla cultura e sulla letteratura degli ebrei d'Italia* 3, no. 1–2 (1982): 112–75.
Shmeruk, Chone, and Israel Bartal. "Tela'ot Mosche: The First Geographical Description of Eretz Israel in Yiddish" (Hebrew). *Cathedra* 40 (1986): 121–37.

Shoemaker, Nancy. "How Indians Got to Be Red." *American Historical Review* 102, no. 3 (1997): 625–44.

Shoham-Steiner, Ephraim. "The Clash over Synagogue Decorations in Medieval Cologne." *Jewish History* 31 (2017): 1–36.

———. *On the Margins of a Minority: Leprosy, Madness, and Disability Among the Jews of Medieval Europe*. Trans. Chaim Waltzman. Detroit: Wayne State University Press, 2014.

Shyovitz, David I. *A Remembrance of His Wonders: Nature and the Supernatural in Medieval Ashkenaz*. Philadelphia: University of Pennsylvania Press, 2017.

Sigal-Klagsbald, Laurence, and Richard I. Cohen, eds. *Le juif errant: Un témoin du temps*. Paris: Musée d'art et d'histoire du Judaïsme, 2001.

Silber, Michael K. "From Tolerated Aliens to Citizen-Soldiers: Jewish Military Service in the Era of Joseph II." In *Constructing Nationalities in East Central Europe*, ed. Pieter M. Judson and Marsha L. Rozenblit, 19–36. Austrian and Habsburg Studies 6. New York: Berghahn Books, 2004.

Silva, Romano, and Enrico Castelnuovo, eds. *Il colore nel Medioevo: Arte, simbolo, tecnica*. Lucca: Istituto storico lucchese, 1996.

Simon, Leon. *Ahad Ha-am, Asher Ginzberg: A Biography*. Philadelphia: Jewish Publication Society of America, 1960.

Simonsohn, Shlomo. "Sefarim ve-sifriyot shel yehudei Mantova, 1595." *Kirjath Sepher* 37, no. 1 (1961): 103–22.

Smith, A. Mark. *From Sight to Light: The Passage from Ancient to Modern Optics*. Chicago: University of Chicago Press, 2014.

Smith, Katherine Allan. "Saints in Shining Armor: Martial Asceticism and Masculine Models of Sanctity, ca. 1050–1250." *Speculum* 83, no. 3 (2008): 572–602.

Smith, Pamela H. "Art, Science, and Visual Culture in Early Modern Europe." *Isis* 97, no. 1 (2006): 83–100.

Spivak, Gayatri C. "Can the Subaltern Speak? Speculations on Widow Sacrifice." *Wedge* 7/8 (1985): 120–30.

Sponsler, Claire. "In Transit: Theorizing Cultural Appropriation in Medieval Europe." *Journal of Medieval and Early Modern Studies* 32, no. 1 (2002): 17–39.

Staffelsteiner, Paul. *Ein seltzam vnd wunderbarlichs Gespraech/ Von zweyen Juedischen Rabinen gehalten/ Welches ein Ehrlicher Mann ohn alle geferd bekommen/ wie der Bericht hernach erfolgen wirdt*. 1572.

Stanislawski, Michael. "A Preliminary Study of a Yiddish 'Life of Jesus' (Toledot Yeshu): JTS Ms. 2211." In *Toledot Yeshu ("The Life Story of Jesus") Revisited: A Princeton Conference*, ed. Peter Schäfer, Michael Meerson, and Yaacov Deutsch, 79–87. Tübingen: Mohr Siebeck, 2011.

———. "Toward the Popular Religion of Ashkenazic Jews: Yiddish-Hebrew Texts on Sex and Circumcisions." In *Mediating Modernity: Challenges and Trends in the Jewish Encounter with the Modern World. Essays in Honor of Michael A. Meyer*, ed. Michael Brenner and Lauren B. Strauss, 93–106. Detroit: Wayne State University Press, 2008.

———. "The Yiddish Shevet Yehudah: A Study in the 'Ashkenization' of a Spanish-Jewish Classic." In *Jewish History and Jewish Memory: Essays in Honor of Yosef Hayim Yerushalmi*, ed. Elisheva Carlebach, John M. Efron, and David N. Myers, 134–49. Tauber Institute for the Study of European Jewry Series 29. Hanover, NH: Brandeis University Press, 1998.

Starck, Astrid. *Un beau livre d'histoires: Eyn shön Mayse bukh. Facsimilé de l'editio princeps de Bâle (1602)*. Basel: Schwabe, 2004.

Starck-Adler, Astrid. "Mayse-Bukh and Metamorphosis." *Bulletin du Centre de Recherche Français à Jérusalem* 8 (2001): 156–72.

Steger, Hugo. *David, rex et propheta: König David als vorbildliche Verkörperung des Herrschers und Dichters im Mittelalter, nach Bilddarstellungen des achten bis zwölften Jahrhunderts.* Nuremberg: H. Carl, 1961.

Stein, Dina. "The Failed Marriage with the Ten Lost Tribes." *AJS Perspectives* (Fall 2014). http://perspectives.ajsnet.org/the-peoples-issue/the-failed-marriage-with-the-ten-lost-tribes/.

———. "The Failed Union Between a Yemenite and the Savior from the Ten Lost Tribes: Folk Narratives and Early Traditions Reconsidered" (Hebrew). *Pe'amim: Studies in Oriental Jewry* 144 (2015): 81–121.

Stein-Kokin, Daniel. "Toward the Source of the Sambatyon: Shabbat Discourse and the Origins of the Sabbatical River Legend." *AJS Review* 37, no. 1 (2013): 1–28.

Steinschneider, Moritz. *Catalogus librorum Hebraeorum in Bibliotheca Bodleiana.* Berlin: Friedlaender, 1852.

———. *Die Geschichtsliteratur der Juden in Druckwerken und Handschriften.* 1905. Reprint, New York: Arno Press, 1980.

———. "Jüdisch-Deutsche Literatur, nach einem handschriftlichen Katalog der Oppenheim'schen Bibliothek (in Oxford), mit Zusätzen und Berichtigungen." *Serapeum: Zeitschrift für Bibliothekswissenschaft, Handschriftenkunde und ältere Litteratur* 9, nos. 20–21 (1848): 313–36, 344–52, 363–68, 375–84; 25, no. 5 (1864): 65–79.

Stolberg, Michael. "A Woman Down to Her Bones: The Anatomy of Sexual Difference in the Sixteenth and Early Seventeenth Centuries." *Isis* 94, no. 2 (2003): 274–99.

Stow, Kenneth R. *Alienated Minority: The Jews of Medieval Latin Europe.* Cambridge, MA: Harvard University Press, 1996.

———. *Jewish Dogs: An Image and Its Interpreters.* Stanford, CA: Stanford University Press, 2006.

———. "Medieval Jews on Christianity." *Rivista di storia del Cristianesimo* 4, no. 1 (2007): 73–100.

Strack, Hermann L. *Jüdisches Wörterbuch, mit besonderer Berücksichtigung der gegenwärtig in Polen üblichen Ausdrücke.* Leipzig: Hinrichs, 1916.

Strickland, Debra H. "Monsters, Demons, and Jews in the Painting of Hieronymus Bosch." In *Monsters and Monstrosity in Jewish History: From the Middle Ages to Modernity*, ed. Iris Idelson-Shein and Christian Wiese, 42–68. London: Bloomsbury, 2019.

———. *Saracens, Demons, and Jews: Making Monsters in Medieval Art.* Princeton, NJ: Princeton University Press, 2003.

Suckale, Robert. "Über den Anteil christlicher Maler an der Ausmalung hebräischer Handschriften der Gotik in Bayern." In *Geschichte und Kultur der Juden in Bayern: Aufsätze*, ed. Manfred Treml and Wolfgang Weigand, 123–34. Munich: Saur, 1988.

Suntrup, Rudolf. "Farbe—Färber—Farbsymbolik: 3. Farbsymbolik." In *Lexikon des Mittelalters*, 4:289–91. Munich: Metzler, 1989.

———. "Liturgische Farbenbedeutung im Mittelalter und in der frühen Neuzeit." In *Symbole des Alltags, Alltag der Symbole: Festschrift für Harry Kühnel zum 65. Geburtstag*, ed. Gertrud Blaschitz et al., 445–67. Graz: Akademische Druck- und Verlagsanstalt, 1992.

Tachau, Katherine H. *Vision and Certitude in the Age of Ockham: Optics, Epistemology and the Foundations of Semantics, 1250–1345.* Leiden: Brill, 1988.

Talmage, Frank, ed. *Sefer Hanizzahon: Yom-Tov Lipmann Mülhausen* (Hebrew). Kuntresim: Texts and Studies 59–60. Jerusalem: Dinur Center, 1984.

Tammen, Silke. "Rot sehen—Blut berühren: Blutige Seiten und Passionsmemoria in einem spätmittelalterlichen Andachtsbüchlein (Brit. Libr., Ms. Egerton 1821)." In *Die Farben imaginierter Welten: Zur Kulturgeschichte ihrer Codierung in Literatur und Kunst vom Mittelalter bis zur Gegenwart*, ed. Monika Schausten, 1:303–22. Berlin: Akademie Verlag, 2012.

Taussig, Michael Thomas. *What Color Is the Sacred?* Chicago: University of Chicago Press, 2009.

Teller, Adam. "Jewish Literary Responses to the Events of 1648–1649 and the Creation of a Polish-Jewish Consciousness." In *Culture Front: Representing Jews in Eastern Europe*, ed. Benjamin Nathans and Gabriella Safran, 17–45. Philadelphia: University of Pennsylvania Press, 2008.

———. "Kill or Be Killed? Realities and Representations of Violence in Seventeenth Century Ukraine." *Early Modern Workshop: Resources in Jewish History* 10: *Jews and Violence in the Early Modern Period* (2013): 1–56. https://fordham.bepress.com/emw/emw2013/emw2013/2/.

———. "'To Take Arms Against a Sea of Troubles': Violent Responses by Jews During the 1648 Chmielnicki Uprising and Their Historical Significance" (Hebrew). In *Am ve-Olam: A Tribute to Israel Bartal*, ed. Jonatan Meir, Gershon D. Hundert, and Dmitry Shumsky, 303–13. Jerusalem: Zalman Shazar, 2019.

Teplitsky, Joshua. *Prince of the Press: How One Collector Built History's Most Enduring and Remarkable Jewish Library*. New Haven, CT: Yale University Press, 2019.

Teter, Magda. *Jews and Heretics in Catholic Poland: A Beleaguered Church in the Post-Reformation Era*. Cambridge: Cambridge University Press, 2006.

Theodor, Julius, and Chanokh Albeck, eds. *Bereschit Rabba mit kritischem Apparat und Kommentar* (Hebrew). 3 vols. Jerusalem: Wahrmann Books, 1965.

Thiers, Jean-Baptiste. *Histoire des perruques: Où l'on fait voir leur origine, leur usage, leur forme, l'abus & l'irrégularité de celles des ecclésiastiques*. Paris, 1690.

Thompson, Stith. *Motif-Index of Folk-Literature: A Classification of Narrative Elements in Folktales, Ballads, Myths, Fables, Mediaeval Romances, Exempla, Fabliaux, Jest-Books and Local Legends*. 3rd ed. 6 vols. Bloomington: Indiana University Press, 1975.

Timm, Erika. "Abraham ibn Ezra und das Maiśebuch." In *Leket: Yiddish Studies Today*, ed. Marion Aptroot, Efrat Gal-Ed, Roland Gruschka, and Simon Neuberg, 281–308. Yiddish: Editions and Research 1. Düsseldorf: Düsseldorf University Press, 2012.

———. *Paris un Wiene: Ein jiddischer Stanzenroman des 16. Jahrhunderts von (oder aus dem Umkreis von) Elia Levita*. Tübingen: Niemeyer, 1996.

———. "Wie Elia Levita sein Bovobuch für den Druck überarbeitete: Ein Kapitel aus der italo-jiddischen Literatur der Renaissancezeit." *Germanisch-Romanische Monatsschrift* 72 (1991): 61–81.

Toepfer, Regina. "Das Leiden Christi in Farbe: Zur Funktion der Bühnenanweisungen des 'Donaueschinger Passionsspiels.'" In *Farbe im Mittelalter: Materialität—Medialität—Semantik*, ed. Ingrid Bennewitz and Andrea Schindler, 2:767–80. Berlin: Akademie Verlag, 2011.

———. "Frühneuzeitliche Wende auf der Frankfurter Bühne? Das 'Frankfurter Passionsspiel' und Paul Rebhuns 'Susanna' zwischen Theater und Kult." *Zeitensprünge* 14 (2010): 137–61.

Töppen, Wolfgang. "Das Bildprogramm." In *Das spätgotische Antichristfenster: Eine biblische Botschaft im Zusammenspiel von Glas, Farbe und Licht*, ed. Brigitte Rieger-Jähner, 25. Frankfurt an der Oder: Museum Junge Kunst, 2007.

———. "39 Scheiben des Antichristfensters mit 37 Erklärungen des jeweiligen Inhalts." In *Das spätgotische Antichristfenster: Eine biblische Botschaft im Zusammenspiel von Glas, Farbe und Licht*, ed. Brigitte Rieger-Jähner, 33–45. Frankfurt an der Oder: Museum Junge Kunst, 2007.

Touber, Anthonius H., ed. *Das Donaueschinger Passionspiel: Nach der Handschrift mit Einleitung und Kommentar*. Stuttgart: Reclam, 1985.

Trachtenberg, Joshua. *The Devil and the Jews: The Medieval Conception of the Jew and Its Relation to Modern Antisemitism*. 2nd ed. Philadelphia: Jewish Publication Society of America, 1983.

———. *Jewish Magic and Superstition: A Study in Folk Religion*. 1939. Reprint, Philadelphia: University of Pennsylvania Press, 2004.

Trivellato, Francesca. *The Familiarity of Strangers: The Sephardic Diaspora, Livorno, and Cross-Cultural Trade in the Early Modern Period*. New Haven, CT: Yale University Press, 2009.

Turniansky, Chava. "The Events in Frankfurt am Main (1612–1616) in Megillas Vints and in an Unknown Yiddish 'Historical' Song." In *Schöpferische Momente des europäischen Judentums in der frühen Neuzeit*, ed. Michael Graetz, 121–37. Heidelberg: Winter, 2000.

———. *Language, Education and Knowledge Among East European Jews* (Hebrew). Polin: The Jews of Eastern Europe: History and Culture 7. Ra'anana: Open University of Israel, 1994.

———. "Yiddish and the Transmission of Knowledge in Europe." *Jewish Quarterly Review* 15 (2008): 5–18.

Turniansky, Chava, and Erika Timm, eds. *Yiddish in Italia: Manuscripts and Printed Books*. Milan: Associazione Italiana degli Amici dell'Università di Gerusalemme, 2003.

Ullendorf, Edward, and Charles F. Beckingham, eds. *The Hebrew Letters of Prester John*. Oxford: Oxford University Press, 1982.

Uther, Hans-Jörg. *The Types of International Folktales: A Classification and Bibliography; Based on the System of Antti Aarne and Stith Thompson*. 3 vols. Helsinki: Suomalainen Tiedeakatemia, 2004.

Veltri, Giuseppe. *Magie und Halakha: Ansätze zu einem empirischen Wissenschaftsbegriff im spätantiken und frühmittelalterlichen Judentum*. Tübingen: Mohr Siebeck, 1997.

*Verzeychnuß Vnd kurtzer auszug/ auß etlicher Hochgelehrter (auch vieler anderer Gottseliger Menner vnd erfarner der Hebreyschen sprach) beschreibungen/ von den erschrecklichen Gottslesterungen/ wider vnsern Herrn Christum/ die Jungkfraw Maria/ wider alle Christen vnd weltliche Oberkeyt/ So von den Juden teglich geuebt wirdt*. N.p., [ca. 1560].

Vinograd, Yeshayahu. *Thesaurus of the Hebrew Book* (Hebrew). 2 vols. Jerusalem: Institute for Computerized Bibliography, 1995.

*Von ainer grosse meng vnnd gewalt der Juden die lange zeyt mit vnwonhafftigen Wüsten beschlossen vnd verborgen gewesen/ Yetzunder auß gebrochen vnd an tag kommen seyn/ Dreyssig tag reyß von Jherusalem sich nydergeschlagen/ Was sy fürgenommen haben findt man nachlaut dises Sendbrieffs zum tayl glaubliche Vnderricht*. [Augsburg]: [Steiner], 1523.

Voß, Rebekka. *Disputed Messiahs: Jewish and Christian Messianism in the Ashkenazic World During the Reformation*. Trans. John R. Crutchfield. Detroit: Wayne State University Press, 2021.

———. "Entangled Stories: The Red Jews in Premodern Yiddish and German Apocalyptic Lore." *AJS Review* 36, no. 1 (2012): 1–41.

———. "Eschatological Avengers or Messianic Saviors? Violence and Physical Strength in the Vernacular Legend of the Red Jews." *Early Modern Workshop: Resources in Jewish History* 10: *Jews and Violence in the Early Modern Period* (2013). http://fordham.bepress.com/emw/emw2013/emw2013/4/.

———. "'Jüdische Irrlehre' oder exegetisches Experiment? Die Restitution Israels im 16. Jahrhundert." *Frühneuzeit-Info* (2011): 5–22.

———. "Little Red Jews: A Yiddish Variant of the Ten Lost Tribes." In *Worlds of Old Yiddish Literature*, ed. Diana Matut and Simon Neuberg. Studies in Yiddish. Oxford: Legenda, forthcoming.

———. "Messias der Vergeltung: Gewaltvorstellungen im jüdischen Messianismus und ihre christliche Wahrnehmung." In *Gewalterfahrung und Prophetie*, ed. Peter Burschel and Christoph Marx, 381–413. Cologne: Böhlau, 2013.

———. "Propter seditionis Hebraicae: Judenfeindliche Apokalyptik und ihre Auswirkungen auf den jüdischen Messianismus." In *Antichrist: Konstruktionen von Feindbildern*, ed. Wolfram Brandes and Felicitas Schmieder, 197–217. Berlin: Akademie Verlag, 2010.

———. "The Sense of Sight and Visual Trickery in Toldot Yeshu and Ma'ase Akdamut." *Early Modern Workshop: Resources in Jewish History* 16: *Senses and Perceptions* (2019), forthcoming. https://research.library.fordham.edu/emw/emw2019/emw2019/.

Vulpius, Christian August. "Der Wunder-Fluß Sambathjon und die rothen Juden." In *Curiositäten der physisch-literarsich-artistischen-historischen Vor- und Mitwelt zur angenehmen Unterhaltung für gebildete Leser*, 4:527–35. Weimar: Landes-Industrie-Comptoirs, 1815.

Wackernagel, Wilhelm. "Die Farben- und Blumensprache des Mittelalters." In *Kleinere Schriften*, vol. 1: *Abhandlungen zur deutschen Althertums- und Kunstgeschichte*, 143–240. Leipzig: Hirzel, 1872.

Wagner, Bettina, ed. *Die "Epistola presbiteri Johannis" lateinisch und deutsch: Überlieferung, Textgeschichte, Rezeption und Übertragungen im Mittelalter. Mit bisher unedierten Texten*. Tübingen: Max Niemeyer, 2000.

Wahrman, Dror. *The Making of the Modern Self: Identity and Culture in Early Modern England*. New Haven, CT: Yale University Press, 2004.

Wander, Karl Friedrich Wilhelm. *Deutsches Sprichwörter-Lexikon: Ein Hausschatz für das Deutsche Volk*. Vol. 3. Leipzig: Brockhaus, 1873.

Wanzeck, Christiane. *Zur Etymologie lexikalisierter Farbwortverbindungen: Untersuchungen anhand der Farben Rot, Gelb, Grün und Blau*. Amsterdam: Rodopi, 2003.

Wartofsky, Marx W. "Pictures, Representations, and the Understanding." In *Logic and Art: Essays in Honor of Nelson Goodman*, ed. Richard Rudner and Israel Scheffler, 150–62. Indianapolis: Bobbs-Merrill, 1972.

———. "Picturing and Representing." In *Perception and Pictorial Representation*, ed. Dennis F. Fisher and Calvin F. Nodine, 272–83. New York: Praeger, 1979.

Weber, Annette. "Das Antichristfenster der Marienkirche in Frankfurt (Oder) im kulturhistorischen Kontext." In *Der Antichrist: Die Glasmalereien in der Marienkirche in Frankfurt (Oder)*, ed. Ulrich Knefelkamp and Frank Martin, 80–101. Leipzig: Edition Leipzig, 2008.

———. "The Hanged Judas of Freiburg Cathedral: Sources and Interpretations." In *Imagining the Self, Imagining the Other: Visual Representation and Jewish-Christian Dynamics in the Middle Ages and Early Modern Period*, ed. Eva Frojmovic, 165–88. Leiden: Brill, 2002.

Weinreich, Max. *History of the Yiddish Language*. 2 vols. New Haven, CT: Yale University Press, 2008.

———. "Internal Bilingualism in Ashkenaz." In *Voices from the Yiddish: Essays, Memoirs, Diaries*, ed. Irving Howe and Eliezer Greenberg, 279–88. Ann Arbor: University of Michigan Press, 1972.

Weinreich, Uriel. *Modern English-Yiddish, Yiddish-English Dictionary*. New York: YIVO Institute for Jewish Research, 2012.

Weissler, Chava. "For Women and for Men Who Are Like Women: The Construction of Gender in Yiddish Devotional Literature." *Journal of Feminist Studies in Religion* 5, no. 2 (1989): 7–24.

———. *Voices of the Matriarchs: Listening to the Prayers of Early Modern Jewish Women*. Boston: Beacon Press, 1998.

Wenzel, Edith. "Zur Judenproblematik bei Hans Folz." *Zeitschrift für deutsche Philologie* 101 (1982): 79–104.

Wenzel, Horst. *Hören und Sehen, Schrift und Bild: Kultur und Gedächtnis im Mittelalter*. Munich: Beck, 1995.

———. *Spiegelungen zur Kultur der Visualität im Mittelalter*. Berlin: Schmidt, 2009.

Werses, Shmuel. "Ha-aggadot al aseret ha-shevatim ve-ha-Sambatyon u-darkei kelitatan be-sifruteinu ha-ḥadashah." *Jerusalem Studies in Jewish Folklore* 9 (1986): 38–66.

———. "Midreshei parodya shel Mendele Mokher Sefarim." In *Sefer Dov Sadan: Kovez meḥkarim*, ed. Shmuel Werses, Nathan Rotenstreich, and Chone Shmeruk, 146–64. Tel Aviv: Hakibbutz Hameuchad, 1977.

Westerhoff-Sebald, Ingrid. "Der moralisierte Judas: Mittelalterliche Legende, Typologie, Allegorie im Bild." PhD diss., University of Zurich, 1996.

White, Hayden. "The Forms of Wildness: Archaeology of an Idea." In *The Wild Man Within: An Image in Western Thought from the Renaissance to Romanticism*, ed. Edward Dudley and Maximilian E. Novak, 3–38. Pittsburgh: University of Pittsburgh Press, 1972.

Wierzbicka, Anna. "The Meaning of Color Terms: Cromatology and Culture." *Cognitive Linguistics* 1, no. 1 (1990): 99–150.

Wiesner, Merry. *Women and Gender in Early Modern Europe*. 3$^{rd}$ ed. Cambridge: Cambridge University Press, 2008.

Wildmann, Daniel. *Der veränderbare Körper: Jüdische Turner, Männlichkeit und das Wiedergewinnen von Geschichte in Deutschland um 1900*. Schriftenreihe Wissenschaftlicher Abhandlungen des Leo Baeck Instituts 73. Tübingen: Mohr Siebeck, 2009.

———. "Jewish Gymnasts and Their Corporeal Utopias in Imperial Germany." In *Emancipation Through Muscles: Jews and Sports in Europe*, 27–43. Lincoln: University of Nebraska Press, 2006.

Wilke, Carsten L. "From Deicide to Diaspora: The Construction of Jewish World History in Johann Jacob Schudt's Latin Writings." *Frankfurter Judaistische Beiträge* 40 (2015): 141–65.

Wistinetzki, Jehuda, and Jakob Freimann, eds. *Das Buch der Frommen nach der Rezension in Cod. de Rossi No. 1133* (Hebrew). 1924. Reprint, Jerusalem: Wahrmann Verlag, 1969.

Wistrich, Robert S. "The Devil, the Jews and Hatred of the 'Other.'" In *Demonizing the Other: Antisemitism, Racism, and Xenophobia*, ed. Robert S. Wistrich, 1–15. Jerusalem: Harwood Academic Publishers, 2011.

Witzenhausen, Joseph b. Alexander Josel. *Torah nevi'im u-ketuvim milshon ha-kodesh ne'etakim u-vilshon Ashkenaz nikhtavim*. Amsterdam: Emanuel b. Josef Athias, 1686.

Wolf-Monzon, Tamar. "Uri Zvi Greenberg and the Pioneers of the Third Aliyah: A Case of Reception." *Prooftexts* 29 (2009): 31–62.
Wolfson, Elliot R. *Through a Speculum That Shines: Vision and Imagination in Medieval Jewish Mysticism.* Princeton, NJ: Princeton University Press, 1994.
Wolfthal, Diane. *Picturing Yiddish: Gender, Identity, and Memory in the Illustrated Yiddish Books of Renaissance Italy.* Leiden: Brill, 2004.
———. "Remembering Amalek and Nebuchadnezzar: Biblical Warfare and Symbolic Violence in Two Images in Italian Renaissance Yiddish Book of Customs." In *Artful Armies, Beautiful Battles: Art and Warfare in Early Modern Europe*, ed. Pia Cuneo, 181–211. Leiden: Brill, 2002.
Wunder, Heide. *He Is the Sun, She Is the Moon: Women in Early Modern Germany.* Trans. Thomas J. Dunlap. Cambridge, MA: Harvard University Press, 1998.
Yaari, Abraham. *Meḥkerei sefer: Prakim be-toldot ha-sefer ha-ivri.* Jerusalem: Mosad Harav Kook, 1957.
Yaniv, Shlomo. "'Ha-ḥevra ha-utopit' me-ever le-Sambatyon." *Karmelit* 21/22 (1977): 277–91.
———. "Ha-moshi'a me-ereẓ aseret ha-shvatim." *Alei-Siach* 7/8 (1980): 125–31.
Yassif, Eli. "The Body Never Lies: The Body in Medieval Jewish Folk Narratives." In *People of the Body: Jews and Judaism from an Embodied Perspective*, ed. Howard Eilberg-Schwartz, 203–21. Albany: State University of New York Press, 1992.
———, ed. *The Book of Memory, That Is, the Chronicles of Jerahme'el* (Hebrew). Tel Aviv: Chaim Rosenberg School of Jewish Studies, 2001.
———. *The Hebrew Folktale: History, Genre, Meaning.* Bloomington: Indiana University Press, 1999.
———. "Local Identity: Spatial Consciousness and Social Tensions in Hebrew Legends from Medieval Ashkenaz." In *Jüdische Kultur in den SchUM-Städten: Literatur—Musik—Theater*, ed Karl E. Grözinger, 39–54. Wiesbaden: Harrassowitz, 2014.
———. "Rashi Legends and Medieval Popular Culture." In *Rashi, 1040–1990; hommage à Ephraïm E. Urbach. Congrès européen des Etudes juives [IV, 1990]*, ed. Gabrielle Sed-Rajna, 483–92. Paris: Cerf, 1993.
———. "'Toledot Yeshu': Folk-Narrative as Polemics and Self Criticism." In *"Toledot Yeshu" ("The Life Story of Jesus") Revisited: A Princeton Conference*, ed. Peter Schäfer, Michael Meerson, and Yaacov Deutsch, 101–35. Tübingen: Mohr Siebeck, 2011.
———. "Two Early Versions of the Aqdamoth Story" (Hebrew). *Criticism and Interpretation* 9/10 (1976): 214–26.
Yates, Frances A. *The Art of Memory.* London: Routledge, 1966.
Yehoyesh. *Torah nevi'im u-ketuvim im tirgum yidish fun Yehoyesh.* 4th ed. New York: Yehoash Farlag Gezelshaft, 1953.
Yerushalmi, Yosef Hayim. *Zakhor: Jewish History and Jewish Memory.* Seattle: University of Washington Press, 1982.
Yidls, Gershon ben Eliezer Segal. *Gelilot ereẓ Yisra'el: Im tirgum le-ivrit ba-shem iggeret ha-kodesh.* Ed. Yitzhak Ben Zvi. Mekorot Ereẓ Yisra'el 5. Jerusalem: Mosad Harav Kook, 1953.
*Yoẓerot.* Prague, 1605.
Yuspa Shammes. *Sefer mayse nissim.* Amsterdam, 1696.
Yuval, Israel Jacob. "Jewish Messianic Expectations Towards 1240 and Christian Reactions." In *Toward the Millennium: Messianic Expectations from the Bible to Waco*, ed. Peter Schäfer and Mark R. Cohen, 105–21. Leiden: Brill, 1998.

———. "'They Tell Lies: You Ate the Man': Jewish Reactions to Ritual Murder Accusations." In *Religious Violence Between Christians and Jews: Medieval Roots, Modern Perspectives*, ed. Anna Sapir Abulafia, 86–106. Basingstoke: Palgrave, 2002.

———. *Two Nations in Your Womb: Perceptions of Jews and Christians in Late Antiquity and the Middle Ages*. Trans. Jonathan Chipman. Berkeley: University of California Press, 2006.

Zabolotnaya, Natasha Esther. "Cosmology and Color Symbolism in R. Eleazar of Worms." *Kabbalah: Journal for the Study of Jewish Mystical Texts* 12 (2004): 45–80.

Zarncke, Friedrich, ed. *Der Priester Johannes*. 2 vols. 1876–79. Reprint, Hildesheim: Olms, 1980.

Zeman, Sonja. "Ut pictura poesis? The Poetics of Verbal Imagery." In *Expressive Minds and Artistic Creations: Studies in Cognitive Poetics*, ed. Szilvia Csábi, 233–54. Oxford: Oxford University Press, 2018.

Zemon Davis, Natalie. "From 'Popular Religion' to Religious Cultures." In *Reformation Europe: A Guide to Research*, ed. Steven Ozment, 321–41. St. Louis: Center for Reformation Research, 1982.

Zfatman, Sara. "Iggrot be-yidish mi-sof ha-me'ah ha-16 be-inyan aseret ha-shevatim." *Kobez al Yad* NF 10 (1982): 217–52.

———. *The Jewish Tale in the Middle Ages: Between Ashkenaz and Sepharad* (Hebrew). Jerusalem: Magnes Press, 1993.

———. *The Marriage of a Mortal Man and a She-Demon: The Transformations of a Motif in the Folk Narrative of Ashkenazi Jewry in the Sixteenth–Nineteenth Centuries* (Hebrew). Yiddish: Texts and Studies. Jerusalem: Akademon Press, 1987.

———. "Yiddish Narrative Prose from Its Beginnings to 'Shivei ha-Besht' (1504–1814)" (Hebrew). PhD diss., Hebrew University of Jerusalem, 1983.

———. *Yiddish Narrative Prose from Its Beginnings to "Shivei ha-Besht" (1504–1814): An Annotated Bibliography* (Hebrew). Research Projects of the Institute of Jewish Studies Monograph Series 6. Jerusalem: Hebrew University, 1985.

Ziegler, Joseph. *On the Use of the "New Sciences" (Medicine, Alchemy, Astrology, and Physiognomy) for Religious Purposes c. 1300*. Berlin: Max-Planck-Institut für Wissenschaftsgeschichte, 2005.

———. "Physiognomy, Science, and Proto-Racism, 1200–1500." In *The Origins of Racism in the West*, ed. Miriam Eliav-Feldon, 181–99. Cambridge: Cambridge University Press, 2009.

———. "Text and Context: On the Rise of Physiognomic Thought in the Later Middle Ages." In *De Sion Exibit Lex et Verbum Domini de Hierusalem: Essays on Medieval Law, Liturgy and Literature in Honour of Amnon Lindner*, ed. Yitzhak Hen, 159–82. Cultural Encounters in Late Antiquity and the Middle Ages 1. Turnhout: Brepols, 2001.

Ziegler, Philip. *The Black Death*. London: Collins, 1969.

Zimmer, Eric. "Gezerot 1096 be-sifrei ha-minhagim bi-yemei ha-beinayim u-va-et ha-ḥadashah: Yeẓirah ve-hitpashtut shel tiksei ha-avelut." In *Yehudim mul ha-ẓelav: Gezerot 1096 ba-historiyah u-va-historiografiyah*, ed. Yom-Tov Assis, 157–70. Jerusalem: Magnes Press, 2000.

Zipperstein, Steven J. *Elusive Prophet: Ahad Ha'am and the Origins of Zionism*. Berkeley: University of California Press, 1993.

Zsengellér, József. "Judith as Female David." In *Religion and Female Body in Ancient Judaism and Its Environments*, ed. Géza G. Xeravitz, 186–210. Deuterocanonical and Cognate Literature Studies 28. Berlin: De Gruyter, 2015.

Zunz, Leopold. *Literaturgeschichte der synagogalen Poesie.* 1865. Reprint, Hildesheim: Olms, 1966.

*Zwo warhaffte wunder seltzame neuwe Zeitung. Die Erste: Wie hundert mal tausend/ vnd sechs vnd neuntzig tausent Juden/ nemlich das Geschlecht Roboam/ Gad/ Asar/ Jsaac/ Sabulon/ vnd Manasses vom Berg Caspin/ dem Tuercken in das Landt gefallen/ vnd viel feste Staett vnnd Schloesser eingenommen haben/ auß Venedig/ Rom/ Constantinopel/ im Julio vnd Augusto deß 96. Jars warhafftig geschrieben*... Lindau: Hans Ludwig Brem, 1596.

*Zwo warhafftige newe Zeittung.* Vienna: Leonhart Nossinger, 1596.

# Index

Abraham (biblical figure), 145, 154
Abraham b. Elijah, 113
Abraham ibn Ezra, 81–82
Abramovich, Sholem Yankev. *See* Mendele Moykher Sforim
Abravanel, Isaac, 58
*admoni. See* ruddy
Africa, 42, 46–47, 90. *See also* Ethiopia
*Aggadot ha–Admonim*, 145
*agunah*, 107, 140
Ahad ha-Am, 157–158
*Akdamut Milin*, 21, 56, 60, 67, 118–119, 123, 130, 139, 143, 150
Akrish, Isaac, 86, 89, 96
*Alemen Glaykh*, 150
Alexander the Great, 23–25, 35–36, 41–44; Alexander Romance, 23, 221
Almi, A., 156–157
Amazons, 41, 195
America, 2, 42, 149, 152, 159; Native Americans, 6, 139, 155–157
Amsterdam, 75, 86–87, 121–123, 125–126, 156
Anshel Moses. *See* Wallich, Christoph
Antichrist, 1, 17, 21–23, 25, 29, 33–35, 40–41, 52, 67, 71–78, 96; play, 34–35, 193; window, 24, 35, 38, 40, 71. *See also* tau cross
*Antichrist and the Fifteen Signs of the Final Judgement*, 34
apocalypse, 17, 21–23, 31, 34, 39, 42–49, 77–79, 84, 163–164, 196
Arabia, 6, 87, 160; Judeo-Arabic, 18, 126, 135. *See also* Yemen
Arthurian romance, 24, 64–65
Asia, 23–25, 36, 42, 46–47, 90, 140
Assyrians, 1, 22
Attias, Moshe, 136–137
Augusti, Friedrich Albrecht, 52–55, 75, 85, 92, 109

Austria, 42, 155
*avodah zarah. See* idolatry

*ba'al ḥalomot. See* dream, dream interpreter
*ba'al shemot. See* divine names, master of
Babylonia, 44
baptism, 71, 194
beauty, 3–5, 31, 66–67, 111–115, 118, 156; Jewish, 111–114
Benedictine, 36
Benjamin of Tudela, 46, 57, 111, 142–143
Bernard of Clairvaux, 15
Bertius, Petrus, 87
Bertram of Minden, 29
Bible, 14, 23–24, 45, 48–49, 66, 109, 199, 202; Bible commentary, 66, 76, 81
black, 3–4, 23, 27, 30, 110, 113; dress, 109–111, 147; hair, 26, 112, 139, 147, 154, 156; Jews, 46, 48, 148; skin 46, 90, 112, 115–116. *See also* magic, black; monk, black
blind, blindness, 1, 15, 53–54, 62, 65, 71, 78, 90, 136–137, 153; color–blindness, 14
block–book, 7, 22, 34
blood, 3–4, 14, 28–33, 37, 76–79, 113, 117, 159, 164
*Bnei Mosheh. See* Moses, Sons of
*Bnei Mosheh* (secret society), 157–158
*Bnei Moshi'im. See* savior, Sons of Saviors
*Bnei Rekhav. See* Rechabites
*Book of Complexions*, 127
*Bovo d'Antona*, 97
Brenz, Johannes, 48
*The Brief Travels of Benjamin the Third*, 142–146
Brooklyn, 140, 168, 171
Buenos Aires, 167

Cain (biblical figure), 29, 67
Canaan. *See* Israel, land of

cannibalism, 28, 36
Carben, Victor von, 53, 93
Caspian Mountains. *See* Caucasus
Caspian Sea, 36, 47
Catholic, 54, 75–76
Caucasus, 30, 36, 41–44, 47, 87
Chabor Desert, 43, 87
Chagall, Marc, 18, 152–155
Chazars, 6, 155
Chelm, fools of, 167
children, 10, 28, 65, 72, 82, 86, 89, 91–92, 98, 103–105, 109–110, 113, 116, 134–135, 140, 168, 201–202
Chmielnicki uprising, 101
Cocles, Bartolomeo della Rocca, 27
color symbolism, 2–6, 13–15, 26, 37, 47, 54, 57, 67, 79, 117, 155, 169
*complexio* (humoral theory), 4, 26, 58
complexion. *See* skin
*Concerning a Great Multitude and Host of Jews*, 36, 40, 43
Constantinople, 42, 44
Conti, Vincenzo, 76
convert, 22, 28, 50, 53–56, 85–86, 109–110, 131, 134–135, 140, 198
Cordovero, Moses, 12, 117

Dan, tribe of, 23, 71, 136
Daniel, Book of, 30, 35
David (biblical figure), 5, 45, 65–67, 76, 97–98, 114, 118, 127, 130–132
deception, 3, 15–16, 27, 31, 37, 53–54, 71, 75, 100–101
demon, 24–25, 41, 54, 61–62, 69–73
devil, 22, 27–28, 39, 60, 70, 77, 68–69, 188
*Di Royte Yidelekh* (play by Almi), 156
*Di Royte Yudlekh* (novel by Sholem Aleichem). See *The Little Red Jews*
divine names, 69–70, 73–74, 91–91, 98, 135, 139, 205; master of, 59, 176
dog, 30, 36; Jews as dogs, 100
Dominican, 37, 47
Doré, Gustave, 155
DPs, 164–165
*Dray khupes*, 151–52
dream, 54, 59, 150–151, 200; dream interpreter, 59
dress, 29, 110, 115. *See also* black, dress; red, dress; white, dress
Drucker, Moses, 86–89

Dubnow, Simon, 157
dwarf, 64, 132, 152, 201

Ebstorf World Map, 36
Edom, 32–33, 65–66, 76–77, 114, 119, 128, 159–160. *See also* Esau
Egypt, 43, 46, 72, 77 105, 120, 135, 149. *See also* Exodus
Eldad ha-Dani, 23, 57, 63, 90, 111, 142–145
Elijah (biblical prophet), 29
Elye Bokher, 97
emotion, 4, 13, 27, 36–39, 49, 80, 82, 117, 186–187, 193
emperor: Holy Roman, 35, 43–44, 124–125; Byzantine, 88
Ephraim, tribe of, 63
Esau, 5, 32–33, 45, 58, 66–67, 76, 98, 113; Mount Esau, 77, 176
Esther (biblical figure), 91, 108, 119; Esther, Scroll of, 119–120
Ethiopia, 46
ethnography, 6–7, 17, 29, 42, 45–48, 53, 90, 146–147
Exodus, 46, 105, 120
Eybeschütz, Jonathan, 113
eye, 12, 14–16, 21, 26, 38, 58–62, 65–66, 78, 81, 90, 92, 116–118, 136–137, 153–154, 169–170, 181; evil eye, 68, 140; eye play, 58, 140; mind's eye, 12, 38, 59–60, 68, 117, 130, 153
Ezekiel, Book of, 71

Farissol, Abraham, 87–88, 142, 224
fire, 3, 14, 27, 40, 61, 72, 74, 76, 99, 155
Fischart, Johann, 41, 47, 88
Folz, Hans, 71
fox, 30
Frankfurt am Main, 37–39, 49, 53, 75, 87, 96, 119, 123
Frankfurt an der Oder, 21, 34, 52
Freytag, Gustav, 155
Fürth, 75, 110, 124–125

Galina, Moses b. Elijah, 58
Gaon of Vilna, 113
*Gelilot Ereẓ Yisra'el*, 89, 141
Ginzberg, Asher. *See* Ahad ha-Am
Glikl of Hameln, 106
Gog and Magog, 23–24, 30, 36, 40–41, 43, 47–48, 176
Goliath, 64–67, 76–77, 130, 132
Greenberg, Uri Zvi, 158, 162–166

hair, 4, 28, 41, 75. *See also* black, hair; red, hair
ha-Kohen, Tuvia, 57
Hannover, Natan Notte, 101
Ḥasidei Ashkenaz, 70
Hasidism 140, 156, 158, 168
Haskalah, 122, 144, 147–148, 152, 154, 166
hat, Jewish, 21, 25, 36, 41, 47
hearing, 111, 130. *See also* sound
Hebrew, 2, 9–11, 17–18, 23, 27, 31, 56, 94, 99, 102, 105, 108, 122, 127–130, 138–139, 147–148, 158–159, 162, 166, 171
*Histoire des perruques*, 28
Holbein the Elder, Hans, 37–38
Holocaust, 164–167, 171
Holy Land. *See* Israel, land of
Horowitz, Judah, 115
Hottenroth, Friedrich, 155
humoral theory, 4, 14, 26–27, 45, 58, 194

iconoclasm, 14, 17, 42, 49
idolatry, 54, 70, 110
*Iggeret Orḥot Olam*, 87–88
illusion, 31, 37, 49, 53–54, 58, 68–71, 78
illustration, 2, 11, 19, 28, 36, 45, 55, 188–198, 203
Imber, Naphtali Herz, 19, 158–163, 166
India, 87, 207
Isaac b. Moses of Vienna, 15
Islam, 135. *See also* Muslim
Israel (people), 16, 22, 32, 53, 55, 59–60, 63, 65–66, 71, 77–78, 85–86, 92, 94–96, 106, 109, 111, 131, 137, 145, 159–160, 164; Israelites 40, 46, 64, 77, 87, 105, 112, 115, 132, 134–135; land of, 36, 43, 46, 72, 86, 89–90, 93, 125–126, 132, 134, 137, 143, 145, 148–149, 154, 159–160, 163, 165, 170–171; Northern Kingdom of, 22, 87. *See also* Jacob
Isserles, Moses, 110
Italy, 18, 70, 122, 125–126, 129, 132, 139, 213, 219
*iudei clausi*, 35, 48

Jacob (biblical figure), 32, 58, 66, 76, 78, 98, 160
Jacob b. Mordecai of Fulda, 58
Jacobus de Voragine, 40, 193
Japan, 159–162, 225
Jeremiah, Book of, 63, 160
Jerusalem, 43, 46, 71, 74, 79, 93, 109, 132, 136, 139–140, 145, 163, 222
Jesus, 5, 21, 23, 26, 29, 37–39, 45, 49, 72–76, 81, 109, 194; second coming of, 33, 67

Jew, *in Bright Red*, 18, 152–154; Blue, 41; effeminate, 106, 212, 165; Green, 153–154, 215; muscular (*Muskeljude*), 138, 162, 165–166; *in Red*, 153–154
Jonas, Justus, 29–30, 33–35, 43, 48–50
Joseph (biblical figure), 76, 163
Joseph, Paul, 109
Joshua b. Abraham Herschel. *See* Augusti, Friedrich Albrecht
Judas Iscariot, 5, 29, 37–39, 67, 73–74, 150, 197
Judensau (Jew's sow), 29, 191
Judith, Book of, 106, 212

Kabbalah, 12, 14, 69, 117, 131, 145, 203
Kaufmann, Isidor, 155
*kefizat ha-derekh*, 60, 134, 137
Kepler, Johannes, 12, 68
Kimḥi, David, 66, 76, 106, 112, 214
Kirchhof, Hans Wilhelm, 27
Kishinev pogroms, 146, 149, 159
*Kitser masoes Binyomin hashlishi*. *See The Brief Travels of Benjamin the Third*
knight, 38, 64–65, 97, 103, 110–111
Kohen, Israel b. Abraham, 129–131
*Kol Mevaser*, 86, 88–91, 94, 96, 104, 110–111, 133, 212

Ladino, 18, 126, 136
last judgement, 21, 34–35
Last Supper, 29, 38–39
Latin, 2–3, 23, 26–27, 30–31, 35–36, 57, 127, 183, 191
*Legenda Aurea*. *See* Jacobus de Voragine
*Lekaḥ Tov*, 76
Levin, Michael, 168, 171
Levites. *See* Moses, Sons of
*Liber physionomiae*. *See* Scotus, Michael
*Liblikhe Tefile*, 117
limp, 60, 77–78, 96, 133, 160, 177, 206
*The Little Red Jews* (novel by Sholem Aleichem), 146–149
*Lunatics*, 146–148
Luria, Isaac, 123
Luther, Martin, 43, 45–46, 48–50
Luzzatto, Simone, 97
Lviv, 53, 121–122, 125–126, 139, 141, 162

*Ma'aseh Akdamut*, 6–7, 17–18, 56–84, 89–95, 98, 102, 104, 107, 117, 120–143, 150, 160, 168–171. *See also Megiles Reb Meyer*

*Ma'aseh Toviyyah*, 57
Maccabees, 159
magic, 14–15, 40, 54, 64, 68–75, 81, 91, 98–99, 104, 130–32, 140, 200, 202, 204; black, 40, 70–71, 173; magical contest, 15, 59–62, 66, 73–74, 80, 130–31, 140, 169; magician, 40, 59–78, 130–32, 139–140, 202
Maimonides, 115–116
Manasseh, tribe of, 63
Mandeville, John, 41, 191
*mappa mundi*, 7, 36, 47. See also Ebsdorf Word Map; *Nova Cosmigraphia*
Margaritha, Antonius, 53, 56
Mary, 118
maskilim. See Haskalah
Maurus Hrabanus, 32
*Mayse Bukh*, 81–82, 99, 108, 112, 115–116, 125
*Mayse Nissim*, 99
*Me'ora'ot Zvi*, 125
*Megiles Reb Meyer*, 56, 76, 119–120, 123
Meir Ba'al ha-Nes, 133–134
Meir of Rothenburg, 15
Meir Shatz of Worms, 7, 17, 56, 59–60, 82, 93, 107, 118–119, 123–124, 132–134, 137–141
Melanchthon, Philipp, 48–50
Melito of Sardis, 32
Menasseh ben Israel, 156
Mendele Moykher Sforim, 18, 142–146, 151–158, 166
menstruation, Jewish male, 26, 212
*Meshugga'im*. See *Lunatics*
Messiah, 1, 17, 22–23, 26, 29, 34–35, 42, 52–55, 71–72, 78, 92–95, 109, 112, 119–120, 143, 148–152, 156–157, 161–163; Messiah's donkey, 29
Midrash, 23, 76, 115, 215; *Midrash ha-Gadol*, 32; *Midrash Rabbah*, 66, 76; *Midrash va-Yera*, 145–146. See also *Lekah Tov*
Molkho, Solomon, 44, 163
Mongols, 6, 25, 196
monk, black, 59–63, 64, 69–76, 78, 80–82, 95, 98, 123–125, 131–132, 139–140
Mordechai (biblical figure), 108
Moses (biblical figure), 29, 77, 87, 134, 148, 158; Sons of, 23, 111, 126, 131, 135–136, 140–141, 147, 160, 209, 213, 220
Moses Ashkenazi of Candia, 86
mountains of darkness, 143, 144, 146, 164, 171, 221

music, 111, 114, 116, 156
Muslim, 4, 43, 90, 134, 137, 196. See also Islam

New Testament, 43, 71–73, 75
New York, 149, 159, 167. See also Brooklyn
Nigrinus, Georg, 33, 40
Nordau, Max, 165
*Nova Cosmigraphia*, 36, 47

Odessa, 157
Okuń, Edward, 155
*Orhot Zaddikim*, 117
Ottoman Empire, 42–45, 86–89, 125, 136. See also Turks

Palestine, 2, 19, 118, 139, 148, 158–162, 165–166. See also Israel, land of
pamphlet, 30–31, 34–36, 43–46, 79, 145, 151
panopticon, 54, 62
*Pardes Rimonim*, 117
Passion play, 37–39, 49
Peretz, Y. L., 18, 142, 151–152, 223
Perlow, Isaac, 164–165
Pfefferkorn, Johannes, 28
physiognomy, 4–6, 25–27, 47, 57, 66, 114
*piku'ah nefesh*, 93, 130–132, 140
piyyut, 32, 56, 119, 123, 130–132, 139–141
plague, 39–40, 99
Poland, 86, 101, 122, 125, 131, 134, 139–141, 156, 162
polemic, 7, 13, 17, 26, 29, 40, 53–54, 62, 71–81, 97, 101, 113, 153, 186, 188–189
pope, 43, 81
Porta, Giambattista della, 27
Prague, 53, 89, 112, 117, 122
prayer, 14–15, 69, 77, 95–97, 119, 150, 156, 169–170; prayer books, 15, 56–57
Prester John, 46, 88–95, 98, 102–103, 107, 110–111, 124, 145
Prilutski, Noah, 156
Protestant, 49–50, 54, 75–76, 79, 195
Pseudo-Methodius, 23
Purim, 119–120, 125; Purim play, 91, 101, 108

rabbinic literature, 12, 14, 67, 76, 94, 108, 115, 120, 156. See also Midrash; Talmud
Rabinovitch, Solomon. See Sholem Aleichem
race, 36, 85, 154, 157, 162
Rashi, 4, 12, 23, 32, 66, 112, 141

Ravnitzky, Yehoshua, 157
Rechabites, 111
red: beard, 1, 5, 9, 18, 24–29, 34, 38, 58, 106, 153, 155, 161, 164, 168, 188, 190–191, 198; dress, 9, 21, 41, 51, 55, 76, 110–111, 202; hair, 1, 5, 9, 13, 16, 18–19, 24–30, 32, 37–38, 42, 48, 50, 57–58, 72, 90, 106, 112, 139, 147, 151–157, 161, 164, 168, 190–191, 206; little Red Jew, 6, 60–83, 89–92, 98–107, 118–119; Red Sea, 43–50, 86–88
redemption, 32, 52, 62, 71, 77, 79, 82, 93–95, 105, 151, 154, 158–159, 162
redness, 2–6, 9, 17, 22–33, 46–50, 58, 65–67, 84, 113–114, 127–129, 155, 158, 163, 168–170. *See also* ruddy
Reformation, 17, 24, 33, 41–42, 48–49, 54, 75
Reuveni, David, 43–46, 163
Revelation, Book of, 23, 30, 40, 71
revenge, 22–23, 30, 80–82, 97, 100–101, 159, 212
Roth, Joseph, 155
Rotwelsch, 31
Rozier, Gilles, 171
Rubin, Reuven, 155, 164
ruddy, 1, 4–5, 18, 24, 26–27, 32, 34, 37, 42, 46, 55, 65–66, 76, 114, 118, 121, 127, 130, 138, 161, 164
Russia, 5, 125–126, 144–146, 149–154, 159, 162
Rüst, Hans, 47

Sabbath, 53, 88, 92–95, 104, 107, 111, 118, 130, 132, 135, 149, 216
*Safed letter*, 89–95, 98, 102–106, 123–124, 134–135
Sambatyon, 7, 9, 18, 22, 34–36, 40, 46–48, 50–59, 63, 79, 85–95, 104–114, 118, 121, 125–150, 160–167, 207, 213
Samuel, Book of, 64–66, 118, 132–133
satan. *See* devil
Saul (biblical figure), 65–66, 132
savior, 18, 35, 63, 71, 82, 120, 132–137, 220; messianic saviors, 71, 77; Sons of Saviors, 77, 111. *See also* Messiah
Schudt, Johann Jacob, 96
Schwab, Dietrich, 29
Scotus, Michael, 27
*Sefer ha–Middot*. *See Orḥot Ẓaddikim*
*Sefer ha–Niẓẓaḥon* (ca. 1400), 112
*Sefer Ḥokhmat ha–Parẓuf*. *See Sefer Toldot Adam*
*Sefer Niẓẓaḥon Yashan*, 26, 33, 113, 116, 206

*Sefer Shevet Musar*, 116
*Sefer Tela'ot Mosheh*, 86
*Sefer Toldot Adam*, 58
*Sefer Viku'aḥ Teshuvah la–Minim*, 112
senses, 12, 15, 36–38, 68, 116–117, 169. *See also* hearing; vision
Sephardic, 18, 58, 126, 131, 136, 156, 161
Shakespeare, William, 28, 187
Shavuot, 7, 60, 67, 118–119
Shaykevitsh, Nokhem Meyer. *See* Shomer
*Shema Yisra'el*, 69, 169
Sheps, Elijah Haim. *See* Almi, A.
*Shirat ha–Yam*. *See* Song of the Sea
*Shir ha–Yiḥud*, 119. *Shir ha–Yiḥud li-Vnei Mosheh*, 213
Shlonsky, Dov, 164
*Shmuel–Bukh*, 64, 86
Shoah. *See* Holocaust
Sholem Aleichem, 18, 142, 146–154, 157, 166, 171
Shomer, 142
*Shoshanat Ya'acov*, 58, 114
sight. *See* vision
*Simḥat ha–Nefesh*, 116
skin color, 4–5, 26–27, 224. *See also* black, skin; ruddy; white, skin
Song of the Sea, 77
sorcerer; sorcery. *See* magic; magician
sound, 39, 69, 111
St. Mary's Church, 21, 52–53, 55
Suleiman the Magnificent, 43–44, 96

Tagger, Sionah, 164
Talmud, 23, 53, 75, 97, 108, 112, 115, 133–134, 144
tau cross, 34, 71
*Toldot Yeshu*, 72–75, 78, 81, 113, 120, 206
Trunk, Yekhiel Yeshaye, 167
tsar, 144, 149, 159
*Tsene Rene*, 76, 115
Tsoref, Efraim, 141, 220–221
Turks, 35, 41–45, 47–50, 90. *See also* Ottoman Empire

ugliness, 4, 67, 112–113, 115, 203; Jewish, 26, 38, 90, 111, 113, 116
United States. *See* America

vengeance. *See* revenge
*Viduvilt*, 64–65, 97, 103
Vilnius, 141

violence, 3, 13, 31, 39, 49, 80–81, 97–99, 149, 191
vision, 2, 5, 12–16, 54, 58–59, 62–63, 67–68, 100, 116, 120, 130, 136, 158, 160; crisis of 68, 15–17, 42, 54 68
Vulpius, Christian August, 85

Wallich, Christoph, 53
Walsperger, Andreas, 36
Wandering Jew, 2, 18–19, 26, 138, 151–157, 166
Warsaw, 141, 156–157, 208
werewolf, 99–100, 104–108
Wetzlar, Isaac, 119
wheel of fortune, 69–72, 123
white, 3–5, 28, 164; dress, 164; skin, 58, 66, 90, 112–114, 116, 153–156, 213

*Wigalois*, 64–65
World War I, 154, 157
World War II, 167
Worms, 29, 98–99, 107, 141

Yagel, Abraham, 119, 126
yellow, 126, 135–137, 160–162
Yemen, 126, 135–137, 160–162
*Yeven Mezulah*, 101
Yidls, Gershon b. Eliezer Segal, 89
Yochanan (Talmudic rabbi), 115–118
Yom Tov Lipmann Mühlhausen, 112
Yuzpa Shammes, 98–99

Zion, 77, 176; Zionism, 19, 144–149, 152, 157–166

# Acknowledgments

Throughout this project, a *longue durée* study in every sense, many friends and colleagues have supported me with their expertise and advice and inspired me in numerous ways. A million heartfelt thanks go to Iris Idelson-Shein, who carefully read and reread drafts of the manuscript. As my most critical reader, her insightful comments helped me shape my thoughts. I am indebted to Richard Cohen, Alexandra Cuffel, Katrin Kogman-Appel, Claudia Rosenzweig, Dudu Rotman, David Ruderman, Evelyn Runge, Gadi Sagiv, and Regina Toepfer for their salient remarks on the different chapters. I am especially grateful to the readers who reviewed the book for Penn Press for their thoughtful engagement with my work. My research also benefited from many other suggestions from Marion Aptroot, Israel Bartal, Dan Ben-Amos, Ruth von Bernuth, Rahel Blum, Yossi Chajes, Joseph Dan z"l, Jeremy Dauber, Ken Frieden, Rachel Furst, Sander Gilman, Andrew Gow, Elisabeth Hollender, Robert Jütte, Rella Kushelevsky, Astrid Lembke, Avidov Lipsker, Jonathan Meir, Simon Neuberg, Elchanan Reiner, Yael Sela, Kenneth Stow, Wolfgang Treue, Chava Turniansky, Shmuel Werses z"l, Eli Yassif, Israel Yuval, Sara Zfatman, and Nimrod Zinger. I thank all of them as well as the participants in the colloquia, workshops, and conferences at which I have discussed the Red Jews.

Over the years, several grants and fellowships have generously supported my research on the Red Jews: a Dr. Meyer-Struckmann Postdoctoral Scholarship from the German Academic Scholarship Foundation, a Harry Starr Fellowship in Judaica at Harvard University, a Dina Abramowicz Emerging Scholar Fellowship at YIVO, New York, a research grant from the Heinrich Hertz-Foundation, and, most recently, an ARCHES Award. Much of the writing of this book was carried out while I was a visiting scholar at the Oxford Centre for Hebrew and Jewish Studies, the Herbert D. Katz Center for Advanced Judaic Studies at the University of Pennsylvania in Philadelphia, and Tel Aviv University, and as a Young Academy summer guest at the Wissenschaftskolleg zu Berlin. I am deeply grateful for the warm reception and intellectual stimulation that these institutions offered me.

Thanks also to the helpful and friendly staff of the libraries and archives whose collections I consulted, especially César Merchán-Hamann of the Bodleian Library in Oxford and Idit Pintel-Ginsberg of the Israel Folktale Archives at the University of Haifa, as well as the staff at the British Library, the Geniza Project Veitshöchheim, the Harvard Library, the Jewish Theological Seminary Library, the John Rylands Library at the University of Manchester, the National Library of Israel in Jerusalem, the New York Public Library, and the YIVO Institute for Jewish Research in New York.

Sue Oren and Rebecca Wolpe, who also translated the Appendix, have done an admirable job with English-language editing. My student assistant Alena Rabenau has been of great help in the final stages of preparing the manuscript for print. I wish to thank the editorial staff at Penn Press, especially former senior humanities editor Jerome Singerman and editor in chief Walter Biggins, for bringing this book to press. I owe a great debt to David Ruderman, former editor of the Jewish Culture and Contexts series, who first encouraged publication with Penn Press. Shaul Magid, Francesca Trivellato, and Steven Weitzman continued to support this project. Generous financial support from Beth Shalom Aleichem in Tel Aviv enabled me to include the illustrations of the Red Jews in color.

My husband, Robert, has patiently accepted my frequent travels in the footsteps of the Red Jews to England, Israel, and the United States. His encouragement, love, and sense of humor are a constant source of inspiration. Only occasionally would he remind me to "just finish this book!" I finally did, and I dedicate it to him, with great love.